PEOPLE, MARKETS, GOODS:
ECONOMIES AND SOCIETIES IN HISTORY

Volume 5

Population, Welfare and Economic Change in Britain 1290–1834

PEOPLE, MARKETS, GOODS:
ECONOMIES AND SOCIETIES IN HISTORY

ISSN: 2051–7467

Series editors
Barry Doyle – University of Huddersfield
Nigel Goose – University of Hertfordshire
Steve Hindle – The Huntington Library
Jane Humphries – University of Oxford
Kevin O'Rourke – University of Oxford

The interactions of economy and society, people and goods, transactions and actions are at the root of most human behaviours. Economic and social historians are participants in the same conversation about how markets have developed historically and how they have been constituted by economic actors and agencies in various social, institutional and geographical contexts. New debates now underpin much research in economic and social, cultural, demographic, urban and political history. Their themes have enduring resonance – financial stability and instability, the costs of health and welfare, the implications of poverty and riches, flows of trade and the centrality of communications. This new paperback series aims to attract historians interested in economics and economists with an interest in history by publishing high quality, cutting edge academic research in the broad field of economic and social history from the late medieval/early modern period to the present day. It encourages the interaction of qualitative and quantitative methods through both excellent monographs and collections offering path-breaking overviews of key research concerns. Taking as its benchmark international relevance and excellence it is open to scholars and subjects of any geographical areas from the case study to the multi-nation comparison.

PREVIOUSLY PUBLISHED TITLES IN THE SERIES ARE
LISTED AT THE END OF THE VOLUME

Population, Welfare and Economic Change in Britain 1290–1834

Edited by

Chris Briggs, P. M. Kitson and S. J. Thompson

THE BOYDELL PRESS

First published 2014
The Boydell Press, Woodbridge

ISBN 978 1 84383 955 2

The Boydell Press is an imprint of Boydell & Brewer Ltd
PO Box 9, Woodbridge, Suffolk IP12 3DF, UK
and of Boydell & Brewer Inc.
668 Mt Hope Avenue, Rochester, NY 14620-2731, USA
website: www.boydellandbrewer.com

A catalogue record for this book is available
from the British Library

The publisher has no responsibility for the continued existence or accuracy of URLs for
external or third-party internet websites referred to in this book, and does not guarantee
that any content on such websites is, or will remain, accurate or appropriate.

This publication is printed on acid-free paper

Typeset by BBR, Sheffield

Contents

Figures

Tables

Contributors

Lorraine Barry is a specialist in GIS (Geographical Information Systems) based in the School of Geography, Archaeology and Palaeoecology at The Queen's University of Belfast.

Jeremy Boulton is Professor of Urban History at Newcastle University. He has published widely on many aspects of the capital's economy, society and demography between 1550 and 1825, and is currently working on welfare and demography in Georgian Westminster. Since 2004 he has been leading the Pauper Lives project (http://research.ncl.ac.uk/pauperlives), which is based on reconstructing the lives of those who inhabited the large parish workhouse of St Martin-in-the-Fields in London's West End (1725–1824).

Chris Briggs is Lecturer in Medieval British Economic and Social History, University of Cambridge; a Fellow of Selwyn College; and a member of the Cambridge Group for the History of Population and Social Structure. He is the author of *Credit and village society in fourteenth-century England* (2009).

Bruce M. S. Campbell is a Fellow of the British Academy and Professor emeritus of Medieval Economic History at The Queen's University of Belfast. His research focuses on the interactions between climate, disease and society during the thirteenth and fourteenth centuries. He is the author of *English seigniorial agriculture, 1250–1450* (2000), (with Ken Bartley) *England on the eve of the Black Death: an atlas of lay lordship, land, and wealth, 1300–49* (2006), and three collections of essays.

Tracy K. Dennison is Professor of Social Science History at the California Institute of Technology. Her research focuses on institutions and economic development in eastern Europe, especially imperial Russia. She has published a number of articles on this subject, as well as a book, *The institutional framework of Russian serfdom* (Cambridge, 2011).

Nigel Goose has recently retired from his post as Professor of Social and Economic History at the University of Hertfordshire. He has published extensively in the fields of English urban, economic and social, and population history between the fourteenth and twentieth centuries. Recent books include *A history of Doughty's Hospital, Norwich, 1687–2009* (University of Hertfordshire Press, 2010) and *Children and child labour in industrial England: diversity and agency, 1750–1914*, co-edited with Katrina Honeyman (Ashgate, 2013).

Richard Hoyle is Professor of Rural History at the University of Reading and editor of *Agricultural History Review*. He has published extensively on the economic history of the sixteenth and seventeenth centuries and on the popular politics of the period, notably the Pilgrimage of Grace and petitioning. His monograph on *Tenure in Tawney's century* is nearing completion.

P. M. Kitson was successively a research student (1999–2004) and a Research Associate (2004–13) at the Cambridge Group for the History of Population and Social Structure. He now works at the National Audit Office in London.

Julie Marfany is Lecturer in Modern Economic and Social History at Durham University. Her research interests are in poverty, poor relief, population and the origins of industrialisation. Her publications include: *Land, proto-industry and population in Catalonia, c.1680–1829. An alternative transition to capitalism?* (Ashgate, 2012). She is currently engaged in a new research project examining poverty and poor relief in rural southern Europe in comparative perspective.

Rebecca Oakes is a Lecturer at the University of Winchester. She is an historian of late medieval England, specialising in the demographic, economic and social impacts of plague. Her work focuses on the experiences of scholars at the medieval colleges of the Universities of Cambridge and Oxford. The chapter in this volume comes out of research undertaken during her British Academy Postdoctoral Fellowship at the Cambridge Group for the History of Population and Social Structure.

Sheilagh Ogilvie is Professor of Economic History at the University of Cambridge. Her research explores European economic development from the eleventh to the nineteenth century. Her publications include *State corporatism and proto-industry: the Württemberg Black Forest, 1580–1797* (1997), *A bitter living: women, markets, and social capital in early modern Germany* (2003), and *Institutions and European trade: merchant guilds, 1000–1800* (2011), as well as articles on serfdom, communities, guilds, women, demography, proto-industry, trade, finance, and consumption.

S. J. (Stephen) Thompson was formerly J. H. Plumb Fellow and Director of Studies in History at Christ's College, Cambridge (2011–13) and Junior Research Fellow in History at St John's College, Cambridge (2009–11). He completed his Ph.D. in Economic History at the Cambridge Group for the History of Population and Social Structure in 2010. He has published articles in the *Historical Journal* and the *Economic History Review*. He now works in financial regulation supervising wholesale capital markets.

Samantha Williams is a Senior Lecturer in the Institute of Continuing Education at the University of Cambridge, Official Fellow of Girton College, and an Affiliated Researcher at the Cambridge Group for the History of Population and Social Structure. She is author of *Poverty, gender and life-cycle under the English poor law, c.1760–1834* (Boydell & Brewer, 2011) and co-editor (with Alysa Levene and Thomas Nutt) of *Illegitimacy in Britain 1700–1920* (Palgrave Macmillan, 2005).

Sir E. A. (Tony) Wrigley, FBA is the author of *Continuity, chance and change* (1988); *Poverty, progress, and population* (2004); and *Energy and the English industrial revolution* (2010). His research interests focus on the industrial revolution viewed as the product of progressive changes taking place in England over the three centuries between the reigns of Elizabeth and Victoria.

Margaret Yates was Director of the Centre for Economic History at the University of Reading and Senior Lecturer in Medieval History. Her publications include *Town and countryside in western Berkshire 1327–1600* (2007). She acted as joint editor and contributor to the second edition of *An historical atlas of Berkshire* (2012), and has recently published articles in *Economic History Review* and *Continuity and Change*.

Acknowledgements

The chapters in this book developed out of papers presented at Fitzwilliam College, Cambridge in September 2011 as part of a conference on 'Population, economy and welfare, c.1200–2000', organized by the editors. This meeting was held to celebrate the scholarly achievements of Richard Smith, following his retirement as Professor of Historical Geography and Demography in the Department of Geography, University of Cambridge, at the end of 2010. We would particularly like to thank Richard, who was also Director of the Cambridge Group for the History of Population and Social Structure from 1994 to 2012, for his intellectual generosity, encouragement and support. The editors are also grateful to everyone who took part in the 2011 meeting, especially those whose conference papers we were unable to include in this book. We also thank the following for providing financial support: the Managers of the George Macaulay Trevelyan and Ellen McArthur Funds, Faculty of History, University of Cambridge; the Centre for History and Economics, Cambridge and Harvard; and the Economic History Society.

The Editors
1 April 2014

Abbreviations

ADB	Arxiu Diocesà de Barcelona
AHG	Arxiu Històric de Girona
BLARS	Bedfordshire and Luton Archives and Records Service
BRO	Berkshire Record Office
CAMPOP	Cambridge Group for the History of Population and Social Structure
CJ	*Commons Journal*
COWAC	City of Westminster Archives Centre
GDP	Gross Domestic Product
NCA	Oxford, New College Archives
ODNB	*Oxford Dictionary of National Biography*
OED	*Oxford English Dictionary*
PP	*Parliamentary Papers*
RGADA	Rossisskii Gosudarstvennyi Arkhiv Drevnikh Aktov (Russian State Archive of Old Documents)
RGIA	Rossisskii Gosudarstvennyi Istoricheskii Arkhiv (Russian State Historical Archive)
TNA	London, The National Archives
VCH	Victoria County History
WCA	Winchester College Archive

Abbreviations

Introduction

CHRIS BRIGGS, P. M. KITSON AND S. J. THOMPSON

This is a book about the character, causes and consequences of population change between the late thirteenth century and the early nineteenth century. Its focus is England, but this case is set in context through chapters which compare English material with evidence from Scotland, Wales, various parts of southern and northern Continental Europe, and Russia.

Overall, these five centuries were a period of demographic growth in England and Great Britain. Bruce Campbell's estimates presented below suggest that the population of Great Britain almost doubled between 1290 and 1801, rising from approximately 5.8 million to around 10.8 million, while that of England rose from 4.75 million to 8.6 million (Table 2.1). Between those two dates, it is possible to identify two separate phases of long-term population change. The first is a 400-year 'long demographic cycle', usually described as broadly Malthusian in character and lasting from c.1300 to c.1700, during which the population level declined from its medieval peak, rose strongly in the sixteenth century, and began to plateau once more by the later seventeenth century.[1] The second phase is an eighteenth- and early-nineteenth-century era of much more rapid population growth. Commenting on this phase of growth in his chapter below, Tony Wrigley notes that between 1731 and 1821 the population increased from 5.41 million to 11.46 million, or by a striking 112 per cent.

These different phases of England's demographic history form the essential background to the studies that follow. Yet the primary concern of this volume is not the charting of aggregate population trends, or

---

[1] R. M. Smith, 'Plagues and peoples: the long demographic cycle, 1250–1670', in *The peopling of Britain: the shaping of a human landscape*, ed. P. Slack and R. Ward (Oxford, 2002), pp. 177–210.

even the detailed statistical investigation of the demographic processes underlying those trends, a style of analysis that at times causes historical demography to appear to be, as Campbell notes, a 'technical and highly specialised subject'. Instead, the principal objective of the book is to present new research and arguments which shed light on the historical contexts of demographic decisions broadly defined: decisions about marriage, migration, household formation, retirement, child-bearing, work and saving. In this Introduction, we provide an overview of the chapters which follow, and also tease out a fundamental conceptual question that is present throughout the book as a whole. Drawing on the title of Sheilagh Ogilvie's chapter, one might say that our theme is the oscillation between choices and constraints in shaping demographic and economic behaviour in the past. In other words, to what extent did demographic decisions and outcomes reflect the free choice of individual agents in response to changing economic opportunities and imperatives, as opposed to the constraints that humanly devised social, legal and political structures impose in any given society, and that themselves are also subject to alteration over time? Of these structures, or institutions, those which provided for the welfare of the poor are among the most important in the present context. It is therefore natural and appropriate that 'welfare' should form the third component of this book's title, along with 'population' and 'economic change'.

✳✳✳

In the book's first chapter, Tony Wrigley revisits John Hajnal's seminal 1965 essay on 'European marriage patterns'.[2] Wrigley shows how profoundly Hajnal's insights about the distinctive characteristics of marriage and household formation in western Europe have informed larger discussions within economic and demographic history in the last fifty years, discussions to which Wrigley himself has of course made a highly influential contribution. As is well known, within the period covered by this book, and from at least the later middle ages, western Europe – or more precisely the North Sea basin region, including England – was unusual in a wider European and global context for displaying such features as a relatively high proportion of women and men never marrying, the propensity of many young persons to spend time between their teens

2   J. Hajnal, 'European marriage patterns in perspective', in *Population in history. Essays in historical demography*, ed. D. V. Glass and D. E. C. Eversley (London, 1965), pp. 101–43.

and marriage as servants in the households of persons other than their parents, and the strong tendency for couples to establish new households at marriage.[3] Wrigley's model of population growth and living standards, summarised in Figure 1.1, relates to the 'organic economy' that prevailed in the period covered by this book, in which the most basic constraint on production was that imposed by the finite supply of land.[4] In this model, population growth was bound to cease at the point when fertility and mortality became equal. Wrigley's key observation here, however, is that the fertility-driven 'low pressure' demographic regime prevailing in England and the North Sea basin region allowed population growth to be halted at a higher standard of living than would otherwise have been the case.

In terms of this book's central concern with the influence of choices and constraints upon behaviour, Wrigley's chapter represents the strongest statement in favour of the importance of economic opportunities – choices – in shaping demographic outcomes. For Wrigley, as for T. R. Malthus, the key relationship is (as Wrigley puts it here) 'the interplay between production and population'. In particular, nuptiality, and thus fertility, were closely related to changes in real income. 'In other parts of the world', Wrigley writes, 'the timing of marriage for women was, so to speak, determined by biology. In north-west Europe it was heavily influenced by economic circumstances.' If there was a constraint that prevented exponential economic and demographic growth within the organic economy, it was a physical constraint arising from the finite supply of land. It was not primarily a constraint arising from institutional or human weaknesses. In the English case, crucially, this physical constraint was mediated by millions of individual demographic choices to produce a precociously advanced economy.

Bruce Campbell (writing with Lorraine Barry), like Wrigley, reflects on the nature of long-term population change. However, Campbell's primary concern is less with the trends and dynamics of population, and more with its shifting geographical distribution over time. Campbell describes

3   For a controversial recent thesis about the origins and effects of these and related characteristics of north-west Europe, see T. De Moor and J. L. van Zanden, 'Girl power: the European marriage pattern and labour markets in the North Sea region in the late medieval and early modern period', *Economic History Review* 63 (2010), 1–33.
4   For further discussion, see E. A. Wrigley, 'The transition to an advanced organic economy: half a millennium of English agriculture', *Economic History Review* 59 (2006), 435–80.

how the mapping of population densities, which was an important feature of pioneering work in English historical demography undertaken by geographers in the 1960s, fell out of favour as scholars in the field turned increasingly to microstudies of fertility and mortality. The key contribution of Campbell's chapter is to bring mapping back to centre stage in the historical study of population, through a demonstration of the capacity of GIS (Geographic Information Systems) to permit the presentation, comparison and interpretation of data in novel ways. Campbell's ingenious combination of a cluster of sources provides the basis for a new map (Figure 2.2) of the distribution of English, Welsh and Scottish population in 1290, at its medieval maximum. This map is then compared with Richard Lawton's equivalent map for 1801, based on the census (Figure 2.3). The contrasts and similarities are most revealing.

Like that of Wrigley, Campbell's chapter also offers insights into the balance of choices and constraints underpinning particular demographic decisions and outcomes. In reflecting upon the contrasts that emerge from a comparison of the geographical distributions of population in 1290 and 1801, Campbell suggests that at the earlier date institutional factors appear to have been the decisive influence upon relative regional population densities, whereas economic forces, resources and opportunities seem to have been of greatest significance in this respect at the latter date. In proposing that manorial lordship, rules about personal status (freedom and serfdom), and tenurial structures exercised a significant hold over medieval marriage patterns, freedom of movement and household formation, Campbell allows the medieval institutional framework a strong constraining role over individual demographic and economic decisions.

As Campbell observes, the description and interpretation of population totals, trends and distributions at the national and regional scale is a very different kind of exercise from the microstudy of unusually well-documented local populations and social groups. Yet both approaches are essential to a fuller understanding of past population change. Furthermore, owing to the nature of the surviving source materials, detailed reconstructions of small-scale populations are likely to remain especially prominent among demographic studies of the English middle ages, even though doubts will always remain about the typicality of the populations investigated. Such studies are perhaps epitomised by the work on mortality rates and adult life expectancy levels between the later fourteenth and early sixteenth centuries carried out by John Hatcher and

Barbara Harvey in relation to the communities of Benedictine monks at Canterbury, Westminster and Durham. The excellent records kept by these communities provide evidence of falling fifteenth-century life expectancies and high volatility in annual death rates among the monastic populations, which can be associated with an unfavourable and worsening disease environment.[5] The wider implication of this evidence is, of course, that high mortality across all social groups, rather than the behaviour of nuptiality and fertility, must play the greater role in explaining the marked failure of the English population to display significant growth in the fifteenth and early sixteenth centuries.[6]

Rebecca Oakes's chapter represents a microstudy based on the records relating to two exceptionally well-documented late medieval populations: the scholars of Winchester College and New College, Oxford. The scholars belonged to exclusively male, urban populations who lived together in close proximity, and thus shared key characteristics with the Benedictine monks studied by Harvey and Hatcher. Indeed, the central question of Oakes's study is one originally posed in the studies of monastic populations: to what extent did the place of origin of new entrants to the community affect their subsequent life chances in an urban environment where the level of exposure to disease was comparatively high? The detailed evidence on the place of origin of scholars entering Winchester College allows Oakes to conclude that while boys from a rural background may have been slightly more likely to die while at Winchester than those with urban origins, this effect became more muted as we observe the scholars once they had passed from Winchester to New College. Although Oakes's results on new entrants to Winchester College relate only to adolescents, they are nonetheless suggestive of the 'urban penalty' suffered by rural immigrants in this period.

If Oakes's chapter demonstrates the value of the focused microstudy based on exceptional data, Julie Marfany's chapter is the first of several in the book to adopt a much broader canvas and seek to advance understanding through comparison over space and time. Her aim is to question just how different England in particular and northern Europe in general were from France, Spain and other southern parts of the Continent.

---

5 See the works cited in n.3, p. 80 below.
6 For a recent discussion of these studies, see R. M. Smith, 'Measuring adult mortality in an age of plague: England, 1349–1540', in *Town and countryside in the age of the Black Death: essays in honour of John Hatcher*, ed. M. Bailey and S. Rigby (Turnhout, 2012), pp. 43–85.

Marfany's starting point is similar to Wrigley's in that she recognises the basic contrasts in family forms and other key demographic features that distinguished northern from southern Europe. For example, the tendency to form nuclear households, high levels of migration, and the relative weakness of kinship ties were all, she notes, features encountered more frequently in the north than the south.

However, Marfany's primary interest lies in the welfare systems of the two regions, and in questioning the extent to which these differed as greatly as is commonly believed. Proponents of the idea of a marked north–south divide within Europe would, Marfany notes, highlight contrasts in welfare regimes that are closely related to family forms. That is, they would see welfare provision in northern Europe as relatively generous, in terms of the share of the national income spent on the poor, and as efficacious within rural as well as urban areas. By contrast, this common view would see poor relief in southern Europe as being relatively haphazard in general, less generous than in the north, and more likely to be confined to urban centres. Even such a broad view would of course allow that within each larger European region there were significant variations. Most notably, the English poor law was clearly unique within seventeenth- and eighteenth-century Europe. This was a social security system established by a series of national statutes, which from 1572 onwards required all parishes in England and Wales to relieve their own poor through a parochial property tax. This system increasingly involved the provision of outdoor relief, in the form of regular (pensions) and casual payments in cash or kind to the poor in their own homes.

While not denying that the publicly funded welfare system of the English poor law was unparalleled within Europe, Marfany nonetheless argues that historians may have underestimated the extent and efficacy of poor relief in southern Europe, or at least that they may not yet have gathered enough evidence to reach a final judgement. Marfany also usefully reminds us that systems of welfare in general, and the English poor law in particular, constituted institutions with the capacity to shape demographic behaviour and outcomes. Marfany mentions several possible beneficial demographic consequences of a strong system of outdoor poor relief in the countryside, such as the reduction of infant and child mortality rates, and the lessening of the impulse towards migration to towns in search of relief in periods of agrarian crisis.[7]

---

7 Here Marfany draws particularly heavily on R. M. Smith, 'Social security as a

Marfany reflects on the relative generosity of welfare systems in the societies she examines, concluding that although under the English poor law provision was more generous than elsewhere, especially in the countryside, the reasons for this remain unclear. In her chapter, Samantha Williams looks more closely at the complex debate surrounding the generosity of the English poor law during its 'crisis', that is, the era at the end of the eighteenth century when the costs of relief were mounting rapidly. Williams's chapter, like Oakes's, exemplifies the virtues of a microstudy based on a painstaking methodology that can only be undertaken for a small number of locations owing to the large quantity of research labour involved, and the need for particular combinations of exceptionally complete and detailed records. Through her case study of the communities of Campton and Shefford (Bedfordshire), Williams asks whether the elderly poor were 'squeezed' in the later eighteenth and early nineteenth centuries, in the sense of losing out as recipients of relief at the expense of other groups, such as pauperised male-headed households. She concludes that there was no decline in the numbers of elderly relieved or in the generosity of the care they received; if anything, the reverse was the case.

Williams explores the operation of the poor law on the ground in a rural and small market town context. Jeremy Boulton meanwhile undertakes the same exercise in the rather different setting of the large metropolitan parish of St Martin-in-the-Fields. In Campton and Shefford, the vast majority of welfare payments in both cash and kind were made in the form of outdoor relief, while indoor relief in the Campton and Shefford workhouses appears to have played only a minor role. In St Martin-in-the-Fields, by contrast, the opening of a workhouse in 1724 and the imposition of the 'workhouse test', whereby the receipt of relief was made conditional upon entering the workhouse, led to a drastic curtailment of outdoor relief. Although reduced, however, such relief did not disappear entirely. Some paupers continued to receive what amounted to pensions, even if they were classified as extraordinary payments. Like Marfany and Williams, Boulton engages with the debate about the generosity of the poor law, his main point being that average levels of expenditure are hard to gauge in parishes that offered both indoor and outdoor relief, and displayed a constantly shifting balance between the two.

developmental institution? The relative efficacy of poor relief provisions under the English old poor law', in *History, historians and development policy: a necessary dialogue*, ed. C. A. Bayly, V. Rao, S. Szreter and M. Woolcock (Manchester, 2011), pp. 75–102.

Like Marfany, Boulton also reflects on the likely demographic responses to the institutional structures provided by the poor law. In particular, he speculates on the fate of those elderly recipients of outdoor relief who were unwilling to enter the workhouse of St Martin-in-the-Fields, and therefore found themselves suddenly deprived of a former source of income. The outmigration of such persons from the capital in search of other means of support strikes Boulton as a likely outcome, and one deserving of further investigation.

In Stephen Thompson's contribution, the focus moves much more explicitly to the connections between the institutions of the English poor law, and demographic change. As noted above in relation to Marfany's chapter, revisionist work on early modern England's precocious welfare system has stressed its advantages, highlighting its potential for alleviating demographic problems, and promoting economic growth.[8] Yet the English poor law's relationship to demographic behaviour has not always been seen in such a positive light.

Thompson revisits Malthus's view, expressed in his first *Essay on the principle of population* of 1798, that welfare transfer payments to the able-bodied poor tended to stimulate marriage and thereby 'increase population without increasing the food for its support'. Thompson does not seek to determine whether 'Malthus was right' in claiming that the labouring poor at the close of the eighteenth century displayed, as Thompson puts it, a 'susceptibility to improvident marriages and fertility-driven welfare-dependency'. Instead, he presents a variety of new evidence relating to corporations of the poor – bodies set up by parliamentary statute which often united several parishes with the aim of establishing workhouses as a replacement for outdoor relief – that, when seen in the round, demonstrates the heterogeneous institutional character of the poor law's structures, and their complex and shifting relationship to underlying demographic patterns.

In terms of this book's central concern with the determinants of demographic outcomes, Thompson comes closest to Wrigley in his reluctance to assign undue weight to the causal influence of institutional factors. Demographic and economic processes, Thompson tentatively concludes, were in the period under consideration occurring 'upstream'

---

8   See also P. M. Solar, 'Poor relief and English economic development before the Industrial Revolution', *Economic History Review* 48 (1995), 1–22; M. Kelly and C. Ó Gráda, 'The poor law of old England: institutional innovation and demographic regimes', *Journal of Interdisciplinary History* 41 (2011), 339–66.

of England's institutional welfare arrangements. Telling evidence to this effect emerges from analysis of poor rate expenditure and demographic measures in Suffolk. Population growth between 1781 and 1821 was faster on average in eastern Suffolk, an area characterised by numerous poor law corporations, than it was in the hundreds of western Suffolk, which remained largely unincorporated. This finding runs contrary to Malthusian expectations, since average per capita poor relief was higher in the slower growing, unincorporated hundreds – where outdoor relief remained the norm – than in the faster growing, incorporated hundreds which embraced the workhouse. The comparatively vibrant labour markets of the county's eastern portion represent one likely alternative explanation for its relatively strong population growth. In this instance, economic choice and opportunity appear to have been of greater significance than institutional constraints in shaping demographic outcomes.

The chapter by Nigel Goose and Margaret Yates, like that of Marfany, is a reminder that the formal and state-sponsored system of the poor law represented just one part of the picture of early modern welfare, even within England. Private philanthropy also remained very important and, from the middle ages onwards, one example of this was the endowed almshouse which provided accommodation for small numbers of the elderly poor. Goose and Yates combine a microstudy of the Raymond almshouses, founded in late-seventeenth-century Newbury (Berkshire), with an attempt to reconstruct what they call the 'historical geography' of almshouse provision in England and Wales over the long run.

Of course, in quantitative terms, almshouses were a relatively minor sector of welfare provision. The figures presented here suggest that no more than perhaps 3 per cent of those aged sixty or over were accommodated in almshouses at any time from the early sixteenth to the late nineteenth century (Table 8.1). Yet almshouse provision varied very widely indeed in terms of its geographical provision, in ways that are not yet fully understood. Berkshire seems to have been especially fortunate in possessing a significant number of prominent merchants and tradesmen, such as Philip Jemmett, founder of the Raymond almshouses, who were keen both to provide for the local poor and to commemorate themselves and their families through the endowment of almshouses.

As already noted above, several chapters touch on the relationship between institutions on the one hand, and demographic and economic decision-making on the other. Tracy Dennison's chapter, and Sheilagh Ogilvie's which follows it, go further and put this relationship centre stage.

Furthermore, in referring to 'institutions' and their effects, both Dennison and Ogilvie make it much clearer than the other contributors that they wish to engage explicitly with a wider body of literature in economics (the 'New Institutional Economics'), development studies and economic history which insists that 'institutions matter' for economic growth. This literature takes much of its inspiration from the work of Nobel Laureate Douglass C. North. Although it is characterised by a good deal of debate about the meaning of the term 'institution', within this broad approach North's classic definition of institutions as 'the rules of the game in a society or ... the humanly devised constraints that shape human inter-action' still remains influential.[9] As noted above, the English poor law can certainly be treated as a formal institution in the sense intended by North.

Dennison's concern is not with the poor law but with another insti-tution which had the potential to exert an influence on pre-industrial demographic and economic outcomes, namely serfdom. As Campbell's chapter shows, because of its rules relating to marriage and mobility, serfdom was almost certainly among the institutional features of late-thirteenth-century England whose influence underpins the local variations displayed by his 1290 map of population distribution.[10] Dennison's contribution provides further food for thought in relation to Campbell's argument. Her central point is that although a collection of characteristic structures that we can call an institution and to which we can give a label (in this case 'serfdom') was often present in more than one society, such institutions rarely if ever exerted their effects in the same way in all such societies. Thus institutions that were superficially similar in two different settings can have very different effects, depending on the larger institu-tional framework in which the particular institution was embedded, and on the specificities of that institution's operation on the ground.

9   D. C. North, *Institutions, institutional change and economic performance* (Cambridge, 1990), p. 3. For recent works of European economic history which show the influence of the institutional approach, see K. G. Persson, *An economic history of Europe. Knowledge, institutions and growth, 600 to the present* (Cambridge, 2010), and J. L. van Zanden, *The long road to the industrial revolution: the European economy in a global perspective, 1000–1800* (Leiden, 2009).

10   For English serfdom as an institution, see C. Briggs, 'English serfdom, c.1200–c.1350: towards an institutionalist analysis', in *Schiavitu e servaggio nell'economia europea. Secc. XI–XVIII/Slavery and serfdom in the European economy from the 11th to the 18th centuries. XLV settimana di studi della Fondazione istituto internazionale di storia economica F. Datini, Prato 14–18 April 2013*, ed. S. Cavaciocchi (Florence, 2014), pp. 13–32.

Dennison develops this point through a comparison of serfdom in medieval England and eighteenth-century Russia. By exploring serfdom's relationship with three other key components of rural society in these two societies – the manor or estate, the community, and the state legal system – Dennison is able to suggest key contrasts in the operation of serfdom in these two very different geographical and temporal settings. Her conclusion is that medieval English serfdom was situated within a larger institutional framework much less inimical to future economic progress than was the case in pre-emancipation Russia.

Like Dennison, Ogilvie is concerned with the human environment and the constraints it imposed on economic and demographic behaviour. In exploring the influence of such constraints on a pan-European scale and across the entirety of the medieval and early modern periods, Ogilvie selects essentially the same three key structures investigated by Dennison: the manorial system, peasant communities, and legal regimes. All of these structures limited individual agency and actions in a wide range of different spheres, including those with indirect demographic consequences, such as marriage and migration. Ogilvie demonstrates just how pervasive such constraints were across pre-industrial Europe as a whole. For example, community, landlord and state all took a hand at various times and in various places in producing laws and customs whose effect was to restrict freedom of marriage. A crucial issue obviously concerns the effectiveness with which this bewildering array of laws and customs was enforced, and the nature and severity of the penalties imposed. Ogilvie argues that an appeal to the widespread evidence of evasion and intermittent enforcement of manorial, community and state rules and laws misses the point, since even if a rule was only enforced sometimes, or had only the potential of being enforced, it could still exert an influence on behaviour and decisions. If Wrigley's chapter represents the book's strongest statement in support of economic choices as the primary influence upon demographic outcomes, Ogilvie's chapter, by contrast, provides its most forthright assessment of the extent to which those outcomes were shaped by constraining human forces.

Given that one purpose of this volume is to explore the traits that distinguished England from other pre-industrial European societies, it is no surprise that it contains numerous references to Alan Macfarlane's *The origins of English individualism* (1978), a book which made claims about the exceptional absence of traditional or peasant society from England since the medieval period that are still generating debate nearly forty years after their publication.[11] Richard Hoyle takes Macfarlane as the starting point for his arguments concerning the implications of the individual-istic nature of property ownership that prevailed among merchants and tradesmen before the nineteenth century. In approaching this topic, Hoyle combines the two methods exemplified in the present volume, inter-spersing a microstudy based on the autobiography of Lancaster grocer William Stout (1665–1752) with a wider set of comparative reflections.

Hoyle argues that prior to the comparatively late emergence of the 'firm', in the sense of a partnership or joint-stock operation, most businesses were run by individuals – usually males – trading on their own and without the formal involvement of other family members. The legal procedures that followed the death or bankruptcy of the individual tradesman were designed to effect the efficient winding-up of his business. There was no mechanism to ensure that the business could or would be carried on by the tradesman's widow or offspring, and indeed there was no assumption that this would occur. A man's son might choose to take up the same trade as his father, but any business started by the son would be a distinct legal entity, and its success or failure would depend largely upon his own personal attributes. Thus Hoyle returns us once again to the theme of choices and constraints. As Hoyle puts it, there were 'fundamental structures within English law' that reduced the scope for the emergence of multigenerational business enterprises that were not dependent on the fortunes of a single individual, and thus acted as a potentially significant economic constraint. Equally, in this system of individualistic property ownership, demographic shocks could trigger economic consequences. In particular, episodes of high mortality, and the termination of numerous individual businesses that followed, had the potential to result in reduced economic activity and increased unemployment that would persist until new enterprises could be established.

***

Our title *Population, welfare and economic change* lays claim to a broad historical territory. Not surprisingly, therefore, each of the individual chapters in this volume presents further findings and arguments, not summarised here, which touch on a plethora of debates within the social, economic and demographic history of Britain before the early nineteenth

11   A. Macfarlane, *The origins of English individualism. The family, property and social transition* (Oxford, 1978).

century. Yet with regard to the book's central concern with the historical contexts for individual decisions about such issues as courtship, marriage, child-bearing, retirement, and saving, a clear conclusion emerges. This is that such demographic decision-making in the past cannot be viewed as a straightforward or fluid process in which individuals or groups responded in an unconstrained fashion to changing economic indicators and opportunities. Of course, as Wrigley reminds us below in his overview of the demographic regime of north-west Europe, such economic imperatives in the shape of changing real incomes were fundamental to the process of marriage and household formation. Yet equally, the remainder of the chapters provide numerous examples of institutions acting to constrain, if not of course entirely to eliminate, individual choice. Among these, the English poor law, an institution with no real equivalent elsewhere in Europe, and possessing the potential to influence demographic outcomes in a wide variety of respects, stands out as particularly worthy of attention.

There is much in the relationship between demography and institutions that we have been unable to explore. For instance, in this book we have tended to focus solely on evidence that reveals institutions producing demographic effects, but not *vice versa*. There are obvious disadvantages in viewing causation as working in one direction only in this way. Thompson's chapter shows up this danger especially clearly, since one of its purposes is to demonstrate how some important aspects of the institutional evolution of the poor law represented a response to burgeoning demographic growth, especially in London and other urban areas. One must also bear in mind the larger point that the parochial welfare system itself may be viewed at least in part as an institutional solution to England's distinctive demographic regime, which tended to leave many of the elderly, in particular, vulnerable and without support.[12] Similarly, not enough is said in this book about the long-term evolution of the various English institutions possessing the potential to shape demographic outcomes. Bruce Campbell's chapter goes the furthest in this regard, suggesting that institutional influences on the geographical distribution of population lessened between the thirteenth and the nineteenth centuries. Yet as Campbell himself notes, this is merely a hypothesis – one of many raised for the first time in this book – which awaits systematic testing in the future.

12 P. Laslett, 'Family, kinship and collectivity as systems of support in pre-industrial Europe: a consideration of the "nuclear-hardship" hypothesis', *Continuity and Change* 3 (1988), 153–75.

European Marriage Patterns and their Implications: John Hajnal's Essay and Historical Demography during the Last Half-Century

E. A. WRIGLEY

Hajnal's essay was published in 1965. The opening sentences ran as follows:

> The marriage pattern of most of Europe as it existed for at least two centuries up to 1940 was, so far as we can tell, unique or almost unique in the world. There is no known example of a population of non-European civilization which has had a similar pattern.[1]

Hajnal then gave statistical substance to his assertion by demonstrating the scale and consistency of the contrast in marriage patterns between the countries of western and northern Europe on the one hand and those in eastern Europe in 1900, a date by which the spread of census taking provided reliable statistics showing the proportion of men and women single in the age groups 20–24, 25–29, and 45–49. Table 1.1 shows that the contrast was stark. Indeed the table may understate the contrast. In each grouping there were marginal cases (Spain in the western group and Greece in the eastern group, for instance) so that the starkness of the contrast between the core area in each group is greater than the table suggests.

Hajnal then made use of data for a range of countries in Asia and Africa to show that in extra-European countries at dates chiefly in the

---

1   J. Hajnal, 'European marriage patterns in perspective', in *Population in history. Essays in historical demography*, ed. D. V. Glass and D. E. C. Eversley (London, 1965), pp. 101–43 (p. 101).

Table 1.1. Percentages single in three age groups: western and eastern
Europe in 1900

	Men		Women	
	Western Europe	Eastern Europe	Western Europe	Eastern Europe
20–4	88	65	72	27
25–9	53	27	42	8
45–9	13	5	16	3

Source: J. Hajnal, 'European marriage patterns in perspective', in *Population in history.
Essays in historical demography*, ed. D. V. Glass and D. E. C. Eversley (London, 1965),
pp. 101–43 (tab. 1, p. 101).
Note: The listed percentages are simple averages with no weighting for population size. A
more sophisticated exercise which took population size into account, however, would not
change the scale of the contrast.

first half of the twentieth century, marriage patterns were very similar to
those in eastern Europe. In particular, only roughly a quarter of women
were still single in the age group 20–24, and in the 45–49 age group the
comparable figure was only 2 or 3 per cent.[2]

The bulk of the subsequent text of the essay was concerned with the
question of when the 'western' pattern emerged. Hajnal considered in
turn evidence relating to the eighteenth century, the middle ages, and
the ancient world before turning to non-statistical evidence. He came
to the tentative conclusion that, in medieval times, marriage patterns
in western Europe did not differ greatly from those elsewhere and that
it was probably in the sixteenth century that change took place, initially
among elite groups and only later in the general population. Hajnal was
very careful to emphasise the fragility and uncertainty of the evidence
available to him. In a sense, the chief message he delivered was that it was
both desirable and probably feasible to settle conclusively many questions
which he was obliged to leave open. As he put it:

> The question about the origins of the specifically European marriage
> pattern ought to be answered by historians well versed in Europe's
> economic and social history back into the Middle Ages, as well as experi-
> enced in handling such statistical material as can be reconstructed for

2   Subsequent research has shown that although the sharp contrast between the two areas
is valid as a generalisation there are many local exceptions to it.

periods earlier than the eighteenth century. A demographer accustomed only to deal with modern data cannot go very far.[3]

Despite the disclaimer in the last sentence of this quotation, there followed a truly remarkable critical survey of the existing secondary literature relevant to this issue in English, French, German, Dutch, Italian, Hungarian, Danish and Icelandic. In the course of the survey and in a concluding section, Hajnal was able to throw light on many topics related to the marriage patterns he surveyed, such as sex-differential migration, polygamy (both simultaneous and 'successive'), age difference at marriage, sex-selective infanticide, the effects of differing mortality patterns, etc.

In the concluding section of his essay, Hajnal also turned to the wider significance of the marriage patterns which he had described. He began by drawing attention to the fact that he was describing a feature of west European society whose importance had been stressed by Malthus, especially in the later editions of the famous *Essay* in which the significance of the 'preventive check' was given greater prominence. He drew attention to the likelihood that the west European marriage pattern would result in lower levels both of fertility and mortality than in other marriage regimes, and went on to discuss such points as the apparent paradox that household size in 'western' and 'eastern' marriage systems might be similar even though in the former it was very rare for there to be more than one married couple in a household whereas elsewhere this was much more common. He ended by noting modestly that 'some at least of the data presented have probably been mis-interpreted';[4] by asserting that there were good prospects of 'obtaining substantial further information on the origins and spread of the European marriage pattern';[5] and by summarising what he considered his work had demonstrated:

It has been shown (1) that the distinctively European pattern can be traced back with fair confidence as far as the seventeenth century in the general population; (2) that its origins lie somewhere about the sixteenth century in several of the special upper class groups available for study and in none of these groups was the pattern European before the sixteenth century; (3) the little fragmentary evidence which exists

3 Ibid., p. 106.
4 Ibid., p. 134.
5 Ibid., p. 135.

for the Middle Ages suggests a non-European pattern, as do scraps of information for the ancient world.[6]

Hajnal's essay was both an admirable statement of current knowledge and a powerful stimulant to new work on the topics he surveyed. Such work has been greatly assisted by the development of new methods for securing accurate information about the demography of societies before the era of state censuses and vital registration systems, notably by using techniques such as family reconstitution and inverse projection to make more effective use of the information in parish registers in the early modern period. This research has largely confirmed Hajnal's exposition of the key features of the west European marriage system except in one respect. He was uncertain about the timing of the establishment of the north-west European marriage system but doubted its presence in the sixteenth century except among certain elite groups. Family reconstitution studies have shown that it was well established in England by the end of the sixteenth century. It is unlikely that it was then a recent development. There is suggestive evidence that it was normal in England in earlier centuries.[7]

In the remainder of this essay I shall attempt to place Hajnal's work in the context of the research carried out in recent decades on economic history and historical demography, or, to express the point more simply, on production and population in the past. First, however, it is convenient to say something about the way in which he extended his initial survey and especially his use of the new findings on household composition which became available in the two decades following the publication of 'European marriage patterns in perspective'.

Household formation systems

In 1983, eighteen years after the appearance of his essay on the European marriage patterns, Hajnal published a further essay in which he took into account the large volume of research on marriage, household structure, and family systems which had been published in the interim.[8] He returned

6   Ibid., p. 134.
7   R. M. Smith, 'Hypothèses sur la nuptialité en Angleterre aux XIIIe–XIVe siècles', *Annales. Économies, Sociétés, Civilisations* 38 (1983), 107–36.
8   J. Hajnal, 'Two kinds of pre-industrial household formation system', in *Family forms in historic Europe*, ed. R. Wall, J. Robin and P. Laslett (Cambridge, 1983), pp. 65–104.

to a topic on which he had touched in his earlier essay, seeking to show that the household formation systems in north-west Europe were as distinctive as its marriage patterns and that the two were intimately connected, that they functioned as a single system. The flood of new information enabled him to treat this topic much more decisively than had earlier been possible. And he returned also to the apparent paradox concerning the size of households in north-west Europe compared with areas with early and universal marriage. Convention in north-west Europe meant that it was very rare for there to be more than one married couple in the same household, whereas in what Hajnal termed 'joint household systems', which were the norm elsewhere, it was common for a couple on marriage to join an existing household. Households containing two or more married couples were therefore frequently encountered in the rest of the world. It might seem natural to expect that, on average, households would be larger where the joint household system existed than in north-west Europe. The mass of empirical material available to him in the early 1980s suggested that mean household size was virtually identical in both household systems, averaging roughly five in both cases.

It is important to note when describing the 'western' pattern that, in this second essay, Hajnal restricted his attention to a smaller area than in the first essay in which he had drawn the oft-quoted imaginary line from Leningrad to Trieste, dividing 'western' from 'eastern' Europe. He focused on north-west Europe rather than the whole of western Europe, an area he defined as consisting of Scandinavia (excluding Finland but including Iceland), the British Isles, the Low Countries, the German-speaking area of Europe, and northern France; effectively, the countries surrounding the North Sea basin.[9]

In explaining the apparent paradox, he pointed to a structural feature of societies in north-west Europe that was unknown elsewhere. A notably high percentage of young men and women in the North Sea basin countries spent much of the period between their early teens and marriage in service, living in the households not of their parents but of a master who was not usually a relative. Servants, like apprentices, almost invariably

---

9 It was becoming apparent that Mediterranean Europe formed a third area where the marriage and family systems differed from the 'western' and 'eastern' areas. The chapters by Christiane Klapisch on medieval Tuscany ('Household and family in Tuscany in 1427'), and by Jacques Dupâquier and Louis Jadin on eighteenth-century Corsica ('Structure of household and family in Corsica, 1769–71') in *Household and family in past time*, ed. P. Laslett and R. Wall (Cambridge, 1972), reflect this point.

remained single during their period of service. Characteristically, a servant stayed with a given master for a period of a year. The servant received food and lodging and a cash payment frequently given as a lump sum at the end of the year.[10] In the paradigm case, at the termination of each period of service, a servant would either seek a further year of service at a local annual hiring fair, or, if he or she had found a future partner and if they had between them secured the necessary resources, they would join the adult world by marrying and setting up a new household. In many parishes in the immediate aftermath of the hiring fair there was a striking surge of marriages as young men and women exchanged service for matrimony.[11] Spending years in service was as normal for girls as for boys. By hiring servants in this way, households could adjust their domestic labour force to match their need for additional hands. Male servants (servants in husbandry) provided much of the agricultural labour force as a whole. Female servants paralleled this role in dairying and with poultry. The average number of servants in a household in early modern north-west Europe was similar to the number of relatives living in joint households elsewhere in the world. This fact resolved the apparent paradox concerning average household size in the two systems.[12]

The key feature of the joint household system, which kept their average size at the same level as in north-west Europe, was what Hajnal termed its 'splitting rule'. On marriage, the newly married couple joined an existing household and therefore the husband, though married, was not a household head, but at a later date the husband, either by succeeding to the headship of the household he had joined or by leaving it and setting up and heading a new household, would combine the two roles of husband and head. In a comparison of Danish parishes in 1801, exemplifying the north-west European case, and fifteenth-century Pisa where the joint family system was normal, Hajnal concluded that: 'The mean age at entry to headship in the Pisan population was probably of the same order

10   A. Kussmaul, *Servants in husbandry in early modern England* (Cambridge, 1981), pp. 35–9.

11   Ibid., pp. 97–9.

12   It is perhaps unfortunate and a source of confusion that the word 'servant', with its Victorian connotations, is used both for young men and women living and working in farming households in rural areas in early modern Europe, and also for urban domestic staff in later times whose terms of service were very different. Farm servants were frequently drawn from the same sections of rural society as the heads of the households in which they served.

of magnitude as in the Danish population, i.e. in the region of 30 years of age.'[13] Since the ratio of total population to household heads determines mean household size, the later in life that men became household heads, the larger the average household. It was perfectly possible, therefore, for a society with a north-west European marriage system in which marriage was unusually late to have a larger average household size than a joint family community where 'splitting' occurred at a sufficiently young age.

Hajnal was concerned primarily to integrate the flood of new information about household structure with his earlier analysis of marriage patterns but he touched on wider issues, such as the ways in which the distinctive features of society in north-west Europe were conducive to higher standards of living and to facilitating economic growth. To these issues I now turn.

The implications of the west European marriage system for living standards

Perhaps the most striking single feature of the social system of early modern north-west Europe was the substantial proportion of adult women who survived beyond the age of child-bearing without marrying (Table 1.1). In other parts of the world, once a woman had become sexually mature she very soon became a wife. The timing of marriage for women was, so to speak, determined by biology.[14] In north-west Europe it was heavily influenced by economic circumstances. If a couple wished to marry they were first obliged to secure sufficient resources to enable them to set up a new household. For many men and women this meant a long wait and for some the opportunity never arose. Women contracted a first marriage in their mid-twenties rather than in their later teens as elsewhere and, in general, between a tenth and a fifth ended their child-bearing period without ever having married. The implications of this unusual state of affairs can be explored by making a series of assumptions which may at best do no more than illustrate the possibilities involved, yet they are suggestive and may encourage further work to narrow present uncertainties.

13 Hajnal, 'Two kinds of pre-industrial household formation system', p. 87.
14 There are, of course, plenty of exceptions to this generalisation, and Eastern Europe was far from a monolithic block in this regard. There were significant variations in female age at marriage in several countries. This was true, for example, in Russia: T. Dennison, *The institutional framework of Russian serfdom* (Cambridge, 2011), pp. 71–6.

Consider first what might be termed the workforce implications. Single women in north-west Europe participated in the labour force much as men did. Married women did so far less commonly. This did not mean that they played no part in productive activities. In many occupations it was, in effect, the household rather than the individual that was active in production and married women contributed substantially to household output, sharing tasks with their husbands. This was true, for example, of many forms of textile production. Nevertheless their individual contributions were not as great as those of single women. The demands of pregnancy and childcare took up many waking hours and reduced both work opportunity and work capacity during the period of child-bearing and beyond. Moreover, they were far less free than single women to undertake work which involved absence from the home for most of the working day. As an illustration of the possibilities open to north-west Europe but not in other areas of the world, consider the following highly artificial comparison. In the first community 15 per cent of women remain single throughout life and those who marry do so at age twenty-five. In the second community all women marry and do so at age twenty. Assume further that the output of a single woman in the labour force is on average 75 per cent of that of a man, while that of a married woman is 25 per cent of that of a man. Taking the age distribution of men and women in level 8 of model North in the tables constructed by Coale and Demeny (expectation of life at birth: 37.5 years for women, 34.5 years for men),[15] and assuming that the population growth rate is zero, these assumptions result in a significant difference in productive potential between the two populations.[16] Women in the north-west European case produce 37.5 per cent more than women living elsewhere, while for the labour force as a whole (men and women combined) the difference is 9.5 per cent (male output is, of course, the same in the two cases).

Needless to say, this calculation begs more questions than it answers. While it is reasonable to suppose that the output of single women was less than that of men, if only for reasons of physical strength in circumstances where much of the mechanical energy used in production came from human muscle, it is much more difficult to achieve a realistic assessment of the contribution of married women to output. This is in part because

15 A. J. Coale and P. Demeny, *Regional model life tables and stable populations* (Princeton, 1966), p. 227.
16 I assume that working life began at age fifteen and ended at sixty-five.

of the 'market economy' problem. It is in principle possible to take into account a married woman's part in the textile output of a cloth-making household since the product enters the market and is there valued. To take a trivial example, it is less easy to evaluate an activity like shelling peas since shelled peas, unlike peas in the pod, did not pass through the market. Unlike, say, the threshing of grain, therefore, pea shelling was not evaluated by a market mechanism (though, once the shelling of peas became a factory activity, the situation changed). A similar point might be made for major activities such as the preparation and serving of food in the home though, in this case, restaurant meals might provide a 'market' comparison. Whether the 25 per cent assumption embodied in the calculation reported in the last paragraph is defensible is, therefore, partly determined by how non-market activities are regarded. However, it is a simple matter to embody an alternative assumption in a parallel calculation using the same method of estimation but a different approach to estimating the contribution of married women to 'production'.

A second important difference between the marriage regimes of the type found in early modern north-west Europe and those in the rest of the world arises from their characteristically different mortality levels. For simplicity, the contrast between the two is again calculated on the assumption that in both cases the population is stable and stationary. Different assumptions within the range of growth rates found in pre-industrial populations would not greatly alter the picture since high rates of growth were never sustained over long periods, except sometimes in lands of new settlement. Even a rate of growth of 0.5 per cent per annum means that numbers rise by two-thirds in a century. Over a 500-year period, the same rate of growth would cause the population to increase twelve times. For most of human history, therefore, it is safe to assume that growth rates were close to zero. Universal and early marriage tends to result in relatively high fertility. Where marriage is late and a significant fraction of the population never marries, fertility is normally substantially lower.[17]

---

17 It does not necessarily follow, of course, that early and universal marriage will invariably result in high fertility. Prolonged breastfeeding of babies, during which the likelihood of a new pregnancy is much reduced, conventions about abstention from intercourse while breastfeeding continued, and a variety of other customs and practices could substantially reduce marital fertility rates. In some communities infanticide was widely practised, thus reducing effective fertility. In some Asian contexts, such practices may have given rise to a production/population balance as benign as that produced by a north-west European marriage system. For example, in the Japanese village of Nakahara in the

Since population growth rates are close to zero over any substantial period of time, mortality must roughly equal fertility. High fertility must be paralleled by comparably high mortality.[18] This in turn means that infant and child mortality rates are significantly lower in one context than in the other. Crude death rates in England in the seventeenth century, a period of slight population growth, averaged 27 per thousand.[19] Outside the North Sea basin area they were on average significantly higher, perhaps 10 per thousand higher in stationary populations, though varying considerably. In model North tables level 8 (expectation of life at birth for the sexes combined thirty-six years; crude death rate 28 per thousand), about 62 per cent of each birth cohort will survive to age fifteen. At level 5 (expectation of life at birth twenty-eight years and a crude death rate of 35 per thousand), the comparable percentage of children surviving to age fifteen is 52 per cent.[20]

The difference between the two regimes may well be understated by the preceding calculation which is deliberately conservative. Using less conservative assumptions, the difference in survivorship might well be two-thirds compared with one-half. If age fifteen is taken to be the point in the life cycle at which children begin to make a substantial net contribution to production where previously in economic terms they were a burden to be sustained, the comparative advantage of a North Sea basin marriage pattern is clear. A higher proportion of the 'investment' in children was productive where mortality in infancy and childhood was at a lower level. In both regimes the intrinsic growth rate is zero and numbers in successive generations are the same, but the cost of achieving this both in demographic and in economic terms is substantially different, suggesting an advantage in countries round the North Sea basin compared with other areas.

In considering the implications of a regime in which fertility and

late eighteenth century, a variety of customs and practices existed which ensured that demographic growth was avoided in spite of early and universal marriage. T. C. Smith, *Nakahara: family farming and population in a Japanese village, 1717–1830* (Stanford, 1977).

18   This issue is discussed at greater length in E. A. Wrigley, 'No death without birth: the implications of English mortality in the early modern period', in *Problems and methods in the history of medicine*, ed. R. Porter and A. Wear (London, 1987), pp. 133–50.

19   E. A. Wrigley, R. S. Davies, J. E. Oeppen and R. S. Schofield, *English population history from family reconstitution, 1580–1837* (Cambridge, 1997), tab. A9.1, pp. 614–15.

20   These figures are approximate: I have avoided, for example, making allowance for the different sex ratios at birth.

mortality were both relatively low, it is important to note that relatively small differences in average output per head and therefore in individual purchasing power may have significant implications for the aggregate structure of demand and therefore both for the structure and the growth prospects of an economy. The differing income elasticities of demand for basic necessities and for what the classical economists sometimes referred to as 'comforts' ensure this. To illustrate the point, though once again oversimplifying drastically, suppose one family's income consists of a hundred units and that eighty of these units are spent on food, housing, fuel, and clothing, leaving twenty units remaining for 'comforts'. A neighbouring family enjoys an income of 120 units and spends ninety of these on necessities, which, however, leaves thirty units for 'comforts'. A country which consisted of families of the second sort would therefore experience a demand for manufactures and services 50 per cent greater than in a country inhabited by families of the first sort, even though average incomes were only 20 per cent higher. A 'low-pressure' demographic system such as characterised the North Sea basin countries, with modest levels of fertility and mortality, is better placed to encourage growth in secondary and tertiary activities than a 'high-pressure' system where fertility and mortality are both high and living standards suffer in consequence.

The evidence from English inventories in the seventeenth and eighteenth centuries suggests that the range of goods commonly found in households increased appreciably. Crockery, cutlery, cooking utensils, fire-irons, curtains, window glass, clocks, mirrors and many similar products became normal items of household equipment in a rising proportion of inventories.[21] Goods such as these were manufactured in larger quantities to match the rise in demand which in turn changed the balance between different occupations. The proportion of the labour force engaged in agriculture declined substantially with offsetting rises in secondary and tertiary employment.[22] An increased purchase of a range of goods of this

21   M. Overton, J. Whittle, D. Dean and A. Hann, *Production and consumption in English households, 1600–1750* (London, 2004), esp. chap. 5. Inventory evidence provided the basis for a particularly illuminating description of the acquisition of new household goods by different groups within the coalmining and industrial parish of Whickham in Durham: D. Levine and K. Wrightson, *The making of an industrial society: Whickham 1560–1765* (Oxford, 1991), pp. 231–41.
22   In Elizabethan England roughly three-quarters of the male labour force worked in agriculture; by c.1800 this proportion had fallen to little more than one-third. E. A. Wrigley, 'The transition to an advanced organic economy: half a millennium of English

type reflects a change in the structure of aggregate demand, which in turn suggests that a growing proportion of the population were able routinely to purchase the 'comforts' of life.[23]

The sensitivity of marriage trends to economic circumstances

The fact that in north-west Europe an unusually high proportion of women of child-bearing age remained single, and the relatively modest level of mortality associated with the area's low fertility may both have been conducive to the establishment and preservation of improved living standards. A third feature of the North Sea basin marriage pattern, however, was probably of greater importance in this respect. This lay in its responsiveness to changing economic circumstances, which in turn made fertility trends sensitive to the prevailing economic trends. Figure 1.1 illustrates the difference between the north-west European situation and that found in societies in which the timing and extent of marriage was very little affected by economic circumstances. It is intended to direct attention to a problem which limited growth in all organic economies.

For reasons familiar to the classical economists, it was physically impossible in organic economies to engender exponential growth. The very process of growth ensured that beyond a certain point expansion must become more and more difficult. The problem may be summarised as follows. Land, no less than labour and capital, was essential to virtually all forms of material production, but the supply of land was limited.[24] Since in general the best land was settled first, increasing the supply of food and industrial raw materials necessarily meant taking into cultivation poorer quality land, or using existing land more intensively, or both. Advances in agricultural techniques might postpone the inevitable but it could only be a postponement. This implied that the return to each additional unit of labour and capital must eventually fall, causing growth to decelerate and eventually cease. And this was not a problem due at

---

agriculture', *Economic History Review* 59 (2006), 435–80 (pp. 453–4). Current research at CAMPOP should enable more accurate estimates to be made in the near future.

23   There is an excellent review of this range of issues in R. S. Schofield, 'Family structure, demographic behaviour, and economic growth', in *Famine, disease and the social order in early modern society*, ed. J. Walter and R. Schofield (Cambridge, 1989), pp. 279–304.

24   This issue and others related to it are more fully explored in E. A. Wrigley, *Energy and the English industrial revolution* (Cambridge, 2010).

Figure 1.1. Demographic regimes and standards of living

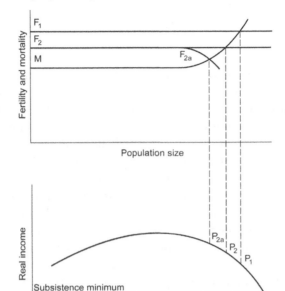

bottom to institutional weaknesses, constitutional defects, an inappropriate legal framework, or any other human frailties or social conventions. It sprang from physical and biological facts. As Ricardo remarked at the end of a passage in which he set out the argument fully:

> Whilst the land yields abundantly, wages may temporarily rise, and the producers may consume more than their accustomed proportion; but the stimulus which will thus be given to population, will speedily reduce the labourers to their usual consumption. But when poor lands are taken into cultivation, or when more capital and labour are expended on the old land, with a less return of produce, the effect must be permanent. A greater proportion of that part of the produce which remains to be divided, after paying rent, between the owners of stock and the labourers will be apportioned to the latter. Each man may, and probably will, have a less absolute quantity; but as more labourers are employed in proportion to the whole produce retained by the farmer, the value of a greater proportion of the whole produce will be absorbed

by wages, and consequently the value of a smaller proportion will be devoted to profits. *This will necessarily be rendered permanent by the laws of nature, which have limited the productive powers of the land* [my italics].[25]

Although growth had to cease in all organic economies, however, it need not always halt at the same point. Populations were not necessarily pushed to the edge of an imaginary Malthusian precipice. Figure 1.1 shows three possibilities in each of which population growth is halted because fertility and mortality are equal. In each case, the standard of living associated with the population total is indicated by the vertical line drawn from the point of intersection of fertility and mortality to the curve representing income level. The least favourable situation is that brought about by a high and invariant fertility as shown by F_1. Since population growth must cease, mortality rises gradually to equal fertility but the resulting population total is large and, due to pressure on the limited supply of land, living standards are depressed. Because the fertility level in effect determines the mortality level, a lower fertility level, such as that shown in F_2, brings some relief since population growth ceases at a lower level with beneficial implications for living standards. If, as in F_{2a}, fertility, rather than being invariant at a given level, is also sensitive to deteriorating economic circumstances, there is a further gain in living standards since population growth ceases at a point closer to the optimum than is possible where mortality alone changes as numbers rise.

Whether the existence of the north-west European marriage system did routinely tend to prevent populations from being pushed closer to the Malthusian precipice than in other marriage regimes needs further comparative study before any large generalisations can be justified. Figure 1.2, however, shows that nuptiality trends in early modern England closely paralleled the secular fluctuations in the real wage. Both the crude first marriage rate and female age at marriage moved in sympathy with the real wage index (the plot of marriage is inverted because a rise in the real wage is expected to be associated with a fall in marriage age and *vice versa*). A caveat, however, is needed. The real wage index is based on male wages only and in effect assumes that the number of days worked each year does not vary. Moreover, it covers only a fraction of the whole workforce.

25   D. Ricardo, *On the principles of political economy and taxation* [1817] in *The works and correspondence of David Ricardo*, ed. P. Sraffa with the collaboration of M. H. Dobb, 11 vols (Cambridge, 1951–73), vol. 1, pp. 125–6.

Figure 1.2. Crude first marriage rates, female age at marriage, and real wage trends in England from the mid sixteenth to the mid nineteenth century

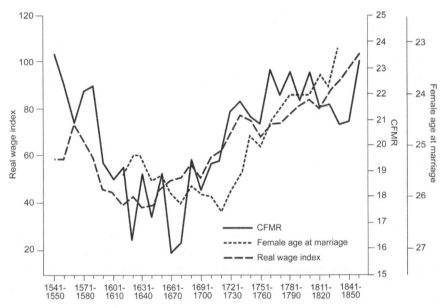

Sources: CFMR and real wage index: E. A. Wrigley, 'British population during the "long" eighteenth century, 1680–1840', in *The Cambridge economic history of modern Britain, 1: Industrialisation, 1700–1860*, ed. R. Floud and P. Johnson (Cambridge, 2004), pp. 57–95 (fig. 3.7, p. 78). Age at marriage: E. A. Wrigley, R. S. Davies, J. E. Oeppen and R. S. Schofield, *English population history from family reconstitution, 1580–1837* (Cambridge, 1997), tab. 5.3, p. 134.
Notes: The CFMR was calculated by relating first marriages to a weighted average of the population in the four five-year age groups 15–34 in which most marriages took place. Further details may be found in the sources quoted above. The female age at marriage was calculated from bachelor/spinster marriages.

Ideally, household rather than individual earnings would be a better guide and should take into account, for example, the likelihood that both the average length of the working day and the number of days worked each year varied over time. Nevertheless, Figure 1.2 provides persuasive, if not conclusive, evidence that levels of nuptiality were strongly affected by prevailing trends in real income, and in a fashion that would secure a higher standard of living than would otherwise have been possible. It is simple to demonstrate, furthermore, that the wide swings in nuptiality were matched by parallel changes in fertility. In the half-century 1631–80, when marriage was late and many men and women remained single, the gross reproduction rate in England averaged 1.94; in the half-century 1781–1830, a period of early and more nearly universal marriage, it averaged 2.65, an increase of 37 per cent.[26]

Since a reduction in living standards caused a parallel decline in nuptiality and thus indirectly in fertility, a society of the north-west European type was in less danger of having the bulk of its population reduced to bare subsistence than a society where nuptiality was not responsive to the same signal. The necessity of acquiring the means to establish a new household before marrying provided a mechanism which strengthened the likelihood that population growth would cease before living standards were drastically reduced; the F_{2a} situation is much preferable to that associated with F_1.

The difference between the standards of living associated with F_1 and F_{2a} in Figure 1.1 may not appear dramatic at first sight, but it is in this context that the arithmetic illustration of the possible implications of the income elasticity of demand for different products is significant.[27] Where fertility levels were high and were not sensitive to economic circumstances it was likely that most families would have no choice but to devote the bulk of their income to the purchase of necessities and therefore that they would have little to spend on anything other than food, clothing, fuel, and housing.[28] Arresting population growth at an earlier stage meant higher real incomes and a significantly different aggregate demand structure.

Nuptiality change with the advent of the industrial revolution

One final aspect of the 'model' that Hajnal was describing deserves attention. In his second article, when explaining how average household size was little different in north-west Europe from areas where the joint household system prevailed, he described the nature of service in early modern north-west Europe. Young men and women in the countryside spent several years in farm service in their teens and early twenties, during which

26 Wrigley et al., English population history, tab. A9.1, pp. 614–15.
27 See above, p. 25.
28 In a 'traditional' peasant economy in which market sales and purchases were only of minor importance, a comparable result could arise, as, for example, by the excessive subdivision of holdings.

Figure 1.3. Real wage change and population growth rates in England

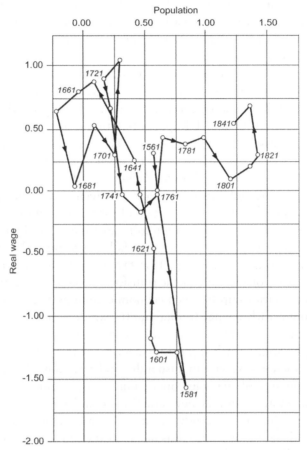

Source: E. A. Wrigley, 'Coping with rapid population growth: how England fared in the century preceding the Great Exhibition of 1851', in *Structures and transformations in modern British history*, ed. D. Feldman and J. Lawrence (Cambridge, 2011), pp. 24–53 (fig. 1.1, p. 27).

they attempted to accumulate sufficient savings to enable them to marry. As servants they were expected to remain single. This was implicitly a system which was applicable only to a predominantly rural society (though in some measure the same result could be secured in towns through apprenticeship since apprentices were only free to marry when their period of service ended). Service in husbandry, however, became progressively less important

during the eighteenth century, partly because of changes in the organisation of agricultural production but chiefly because agriculture provided
employment for a steadily decreasing fraction of the young workforce. By
the beginning of the nineteenth century little more than a third of the male
labour force worked on the land.

It is instructive to compare the course of change in the eighteenth
century with what happened two centuries earlier. Figure 1.3 shows that
the sixteenth and early seventeenth centuries conformed to what might be
termed the Malthusian model. Rapid population growth was accompanied
by a severe depression in living standards. The population of England rose
by three-quarters in the ninety years between 1541 and 1631, from 2.83
million to 4.93 million.[29] Real wages declined markedly by 30–40 per cent
(Figure 1.2). In the eighteenth and early nineteenth centuries population
growth was much faster. Between 1731 and 1821, also a ninety-year period,
the population rose from 5.41 million to 11.46 million,[30] or by 112 per cent,
but real wages probably rose rather than falling precipitately, as was to be
expected in an organic economy. This fact is perhaps the most striking
single illustration of the scale of the transformation of the economy in the
interim. The relationship between economic circumstances and marriage
trends did not greatly change throughout the whole period (Figure 1.2) but,
since the relative importance of agriculture in the occupational structure of
the country changed markedly, it is evident that the recruitment of young
men and women into service in husbandry and related work was no longer
the main regulator of marriage opportunity for a majority of the young
labour force. How should the new situation be understood?

In England in the sixteenth century, agriculture was the dominant
employer and the urban sector was small. Although London was already
growing rapidly, the bulk of the increase in population occurred in rural
areas, depressing wage levels and restricting employment opportunities,
the kind of development which Malthus had supposed unavoidable. In the
eighteenth century *rates of natural increase* were much higher, and were
not greatly different in rural areas from the rest of the country, but *rates of
population growth* were radically different. Growth rates in rural areas were
relatively modest, in industrial and urban areas far higher. Or, to express the
same point differently, people living in rural areas were able to escape what
would otherwise have been the dire consequences of overrapid population

29   Wrigley *et al.*, *English population history*, tab. A9.1, pp. 614–15.
30   Ibid.

growth by migrating to urban and industrial centres. Overall, the supply of and the demand for labour remained roughly in balance and marriage opportunities were not reduced as they would have been in earlier times.[31] The fact that between 1750 and 1850 population growth rates in England were far higher than in neighbouring continental countries probably reflected a more rapid rise in employment opportunities than elsewhere, encouraging earlier and more universal marriage.[32] The mechanism by which population growth was kept in balance with economic opportunity may have changed but the outcome remained similar.

While the conventions governing marriage decisions in early modern England and north-west Europe may have helped to limit the severity of distress when production and population were not in balance, it is clear that they did not always prevent great suffering as the experience of England in the sixteenth century clearly demonstrates. Other areas round the North Sea basin were similarly troubled until a much later date. The fact that in most parts of Europe a very high proportion of the labour force worked on the land even at the beginning of the nineteenth century is indirect testimony to a structure of aggregate demand which left only limited opportunities for growth in the secondary and tertiary sectors of the economy. Equally, however, there were important exceptions to this picture of limited change.

The Netherlands and England diverge from other European countries

As a coda to this discussion of Hajnal's treatment of European marriage patterns and their concomitants, it is of interest to consider the histories of the Netherlands and England in the early modern period since they demonstrate both the scope for variation in organic economies and the nature of an escape route from its restrictions. The two countries

---

31 These issues are explored at greater length in E. A. Wrigley, 'Coping with rapid population growth: how England fared in the century preceding the Great Exhibition of 1851', in *Structures and transformations in modern British history*, ed. D. Feldman and J. Lawrence (Cambridge, 2011), pp. 24–53.

32 The population of England during this century increased by 183 per cent. The comparable percentages for other European countries were as follows: the Netherlands 63, France 48, Germany 108, Sweden 94, Italy 56, Spain 72. Wrigley, *Energy and the English industrial revolution*, tab. 6.1, p. 155.

illustrate the value of the existence of the west European marriage system in enhancing the possibility of raising living standards, while also showing why such progress was normally limited.

De Vries and van der Woude in their magisterial survey of Dutch economic history throughout the early modern period chose as its title *The first modern economy*. In the seventeenth century the Dutch republic was the envy of the rest of Europe. It possessed a vibrant economy and had secured a higher standard of living than any of its neighbours. It had ceased to depend principally upon agriculture; both its commerce and industry had grown rapidly and had achieved a marked sophistication. De Vries and van der Woude argued that the Netherlands displayed all the key characteristics of a market capitalist economy, describing how it flourished for more than a hundred years before reaching at best a plateau in the eighteenth century. They noted that the Dutch example made it clear that the creation of a capitalist economy was not in itself a guarantor of persistent growth.[33]

Well-informed contemporaries turned to the Dutch example in the hope of securing comparable advances. Adam Smith's assessment is of particular interest. His view parallels the conclusions of de Vries and van der Woude. He regarded the Netherlands as providing a clue to the probable future course of events in Britain, which appeared to be following the path trodden earlier by the Netherlands.[34] But this path suggested a very uncertain future. Smith was firm in asserting signs of the inevitable deceleration which was the penalty of rapid growth. In particular he stressed the very low level of interest rates in Holland, which he regarded as evidence that opportunities for profitable investment had been largely exhausted. As a result Dutch capital was increasingly invested abroad rather than at home.[35] And when stagnation supervened it was, in his view, an open question whether the relative prosperity that had been achieved could be preserved or whether the gains in living standards that

33   J. de Vries and A. van der Woude, *The first modern economy: success, failure and perseverance of the Dutch economy, 1500–1815* (Cambridge, 1997), pp. 711–22.

34   He wrote: 'In a country fully stocked in proportion to all the business it had to transact, as great a quantity of stock would be employed in every particular branch as the nature and extent of the trade would admit. The competition, therefore, would everywhere be as great, and consequently the ordinary profit as low as possible.' A. Smith, *An inquiry into the nature and causes of the wealth of nations*, ed. E. Cannan, 5th edn, 2 vols (1904; Chicago, 1976), vol. 1, p. 106. He went on to note, 'The province of Holland seems to be approaching near to this state.' (p. 108).

35   Ibid., vol. 1, pp. 102–3.

had taken place would evaporate. In regard to the general case, which by implication applied to the Netherlands and Britain no less than to other countries, he was inclined to pessimism:

> In a country which had acquired that full complement of riches which the nature of its soil and climate, and its situation with respect to other countries, allowed it to acquire; which could, therefore, advance no further, and which was not going backwards, both the wages of labour and the profits of stock would probably be very low. In a country fully peopled in proportion to what either its territory could maintain or its stock could employ, the competition for employment would necessarily be so great as to reduce the wages of labour to what was barely sufficient to keep up the number of labourers, and, the country being already fully peopled, the number could never be augmented.[36]

In their discussion of the interplay of production and population de Vries and van der Woude note that: 'In an economy dominated by Malthusian forces, economic expansion is necessarily limited, episodic, and stunted.'[37] In their view, the Netherlands remained subject to Malthusian forces until the mid sixteenth century but before the end of the century had moved into a different regime, overcoming the problem of inadequate food supply by international trade with the Baltic and redeploying labour from agriculture into secondary and tertiary activities with an accompanying increase in family purchasing power. In this novel situation, the population grew rapidly from a combination of natural increase and in-migration as long as the economy prospered, but the developing economic crisis from the 1660s onwards saw population growth cease. Nor, in contrast to most European countries, did it resume in the mid eighteenth century: the economy continued to stagnate. In seeking to explain the absence of population growth over a period that lasted for one-and-a-half centuries, they refer to the high average age at marriage and a 'rigorously nuclear family structure', which resulted in 'probably the smallest households in Europe'.[38] They describe an economy that for a period succeeded in advancing production ahead of population. When growth faltered, a sympathetic decline in nuptiality helped the country to maintain, though no longer to enhance, the standard of living of the population.

36 Ibid., vol. 1, p. 106.
37 De Vries and van der Woude, *The first modern economy*, p. 688.
38 Ibid., p. 689.

Table 1.2. Total populations and populations living in towns with 10,000 or more inhabitants (population in thousands)

The Netherlands and the British Isles

	1600	1650	1700	1750	1800
Total population	8,300	10,300	11,100	12,500	18,200
Urban population	649	1,150	1,506	1,881	3,121
Urban percentage	7.8	11.2	13.6	15.0	17.1

Other European countries

Total population	69,600	64,300	70,300	81,700	104,500
Urban population	5,274	5,046	5,958	7,052	9,057
Urban percentage	7.6	7.8	8.5	8.6	8.7

Source: J. de Vries, European urbanization 1500–1800 (Cambridge, MA, 1984), tab. 3.6, pp. 36–7 and app. 1.
Note: The other European countries were: Scandinavia, Belgium, Germany, France, Switzerland, Italy, Spain, Portugal, Austria–Czechoslovakia and Poland.

That the existence of the North Sea basin marriage system in the Netherlands may not only have proved beneficial at the end of the Dutch 'golden age' but may also have assisted the early stages of growth is suggested in van Zanden's recent writing. One of the features of Dutch society that helps to explain what he terms the 'little divergence', in which the Low Countries and England drew apart from other European countries, was 'girl power': in brief, the different status of women in marriage and more generally in the household and the labour market which was linked to the west European marriage system.[39]

Van Zanden illustrated the existence of the 'little divergence' with a graph showing that, whereas real wages in a range of European cities in the late middle ages were closely similar, from the sixteenth century onwards real wages in Amsterdam and London rose and they gradually drew clear of other cities where real wages in contrast tended to decline in the seventeenth and eighteenth centuries.[40] Table 1.2 uses a different data source to illustrate the same point. The countries of the 'little divergence'

39 J. L. van Zanden, The long road to the industrial revolution: the European economy in a global perspective, 1000–1800 (Leiden, 2009), pt 2.
40 Ibid., fig. 8, p. 97.

were marginally less urbanised than other parts of Europe in 1600 but by 1800 their urban percentage was twice as high as elsewhere. The table is no more than a summary concealing as much as it reveals. For example, in 1600 the Netherlands was already much more heavily urbanised than other parts of Europe with 24 per cent of its population in towns with 10,000 or more inhabitants, whereas England and Wales, and still more Scotland and Ireland, lagged well behind the Europe average. In the eighteenth century, in contrast, the Dutch urban percentage fell slightly at a time of hectic advance in the British Isles.[41] Yet perhaps the most striking single feature of European urbanisation in the early modern period is not what changed but what did not. If the Netherlands and the British Isles are excluded from the calculation, the level of urbanisation in the rest of Europe barely changed in the seventeenth and eighteenth centuries. Indeed a more refined calculation might well suggest decline rather than virtual stagnation since if every element in a growing population retains its same relative size the proportion of the total population to be found in the large units is bound to rise. For example, to retain the same *relative* size within a population which rises from, say, 1 million to 1.2 million, a town of 9,000 inhabitants initially will rise into the 10,000-plus category at some point.

Needless to say, there is a considerable margin for error both in the calculation of real wages and in the changes in urban percentages, but both point to a continent largely lacking in signs of substantial change in economic structure away from the fringes of the North Sea basin. In some countries, indeed, there was probably regression, as, for example, in Italy.[42] In much of Europe, in short, the world which Malthus sought to characterise, and whose demography and family structure were brought sharply into focus by Hajnal, displayed few signs of major change before the nineteenth century.

Adam Smith, as we have noted, though well aware of the recent progress in the Netherlands and Britain, did not view their future optimistically. In the Dutch case, his expectation of a cessation of growth proved justified though living standards remained on relatively high plateau. But England did not continue to follow the Dutch trajectory as he had expected. Growth accelerated rather than subsiding.

41 J. de Vries, *European urbanization 1500–1800* (Cambridge, MA, 1984), tab. 3.6, pp. 36–7 and app. 1.
42 P. Malanima, 'Measuring the Italian economy, 1300–1861', *Rivista di Storia Economica* 19 (2003), 265–95.

Britain enters a new world

To succeed in escaping the fate which the classical economists were unanimous in prophesying, it was essential that the country should move to a different productive base. The classical economists assumed that the product of the land was necessarily the basis of all production; that all economies must be organic economies. As long as this was true their forebodings were justified, but the key point was concealed because their fears were expressed in terms of the fixed supply of land. The proximate constraint was indeed the limited supply of land but the underlying problem was the fact that the land was almost the sole source of energy. All material production and all forms of transport necessarily involve expenditure of energy and in organic economies plant photosynthesis was the ultimate source of the great bulk both of heat and mechanical energy.[43] The continuation of economic growth in Britain at a rate which outstripped the population growth rate was only possible because a steadily increasing proportion of the energy consumed in the production process came from fossil fuel. It required, so to speak, not just one but two capitalist revolutions.

Adam Smith, by describing the potential inherent in the division of labour in a market economy, and by following Bernard Mandeville in extolling the wider benefits to the community as a whole of the pursuit of individual self-interest, had shown the improvement in productive efficiency achievable with a capitalist, market economy. The benefits to be obtained were, as Smith pointed out, closely related to the scale of capital invested.[44] But to break free from the constraints implied by dependence upon plant photosynthesis as the ultimate source of useful energy a different type of capitalism was needed. Coal represented a capital stock built up by plant photosynthesis over hundreds of millions of years whereas the energy captured by the annual round of plant photosynthesis in organic economies provided access only to a single year's supply. Coal, and later other fossil fuels, could therefore sustain continued expansion by supplying energy as needed. Without a source of this type, prolonged expansion of production was physically impossible. Energy consumption could expand to match production need rather than production being restricted to a limited supply of energy. Initially coal was used only to provide heat energy and

43   Wrigley, *Energy and the English industrial revolution.*
44   Smith, *Wealth of nations*, vol. 1, pp. 364–5.

the supply of mechanical energy remained dependent upon the application of human and animal muscle with limited support from wind and water power, but with the development of an effective steam engine, the supply of both forms of energy could be expanded at will.[45]

It is worth noting that there is a sense in which the Netherlands, in enlarging its sources of energy supply, partially anticipated what happened later in England. Industries such as brewing, brickmaking, salt boiling and dye manufacture require abundant heat energy. In providing the requisite heat for these industries in the Netherlands peat played the part which was later played by coal in England. Peat, like coal, represents a store of plant photosynthesis, a means of escape from dependence upon the product of an annual cycle of plant growth. The energy capital stored in peat is only a tiny fraction of that provided by coal, but in the mid seventeenth century the annual consumption of heat energy per head derived from peat in the Netherlands was approximately double the comparable English figure from coal.[46] A century later the situation was reversed. By the mid eighteenth century, coal already provided more than three-fifths of the total consumption of energy in England and Wales, and, with output rising twelvefold over the next hundred years, by the 1850s more than 90 per cent of energy consumption was derived from coal.[47] What happened in England was rapidly mirrored elsewhere. As a result, productive possibilities were transformed by the process which came to be termed the industrial revolution, and the model of the relationship between production and population which Malthus had originally proposed lost its relevance. It is one of the intriguing ironies of intellectual history that Malthus, who first proposed the model in a form which captured widespread attention, should have formulated it in the country and in the period when for the first time in human history it was ceasing to portray reality.

Marriage patterns lose their earlier relevance

It is mildly ironic that in his initial description of the extent of the contrast between marriage patterns in western Europe and those to be found in eastern Europe, Hajnal made use of census data from the early

45   These issues are discussed much more fully in Wrigley, *Energy and the English industrial revolution*.
46   Ibid., p. 221.
47   Ibid., tab. 4.2, p. 94.

twentieth century since, although the extent of the contrast between east and west was then still clear and marked, it had ceased to hold its earlier significance. It was once reasonable to assume that the average age at which women married, and the proportion of women who never married, would jointly determine the level of fertility in a population. Where the west European marriage patterns prevailed, the fertility level was likely to be substantially lower than in communities where women married young and very few remained unmarried throughout their lives. Given that both age at marriage and proportions never marrying were often sensitive to changing economic circumstances, countries in western Europe were arguably less likely to be pressed close to a Malthusian precipice than was the case elsewhere. But the tension between population growth and productive capacity, which had seemed universal and inescapable, continued only as long as the land was the source of almost all the raw materials entering material production and of the great bulk of the energy used in agriculture, manufacture, and transport.[48] This ceased to be true as the industrial revolution progressively transformed the situation.

The classical economists regarded it as clear beyond argument that if the incomes of the labouring poor improved this must tend to reduce mortality and, by facilitating earlier marriage, increase fertility. The resulting rise in the rate of population growth would increase the number of those seeking employment and drive down wages. Adam Smith summarised the issue bluntly:

> the demand for men, like that for any other commodity, necessarily regulates the production of men; quickens it when it goes too slowly, and stops it when it advances too fast. It is this demand which regulates and determines the state of propagation in all the different countries of the world.[49]

The industrial revolution made assertions such as this obsolete. Secular growth trends became exponential rather than asymptotic. Economic growth became capable of matching or exceeding population growth. The changing relationship between real wages and population growth

---

48   That the land was the source of raw materials is self-evidently true of all vegetable and animal raw materials, but it was true indirectly of minerals also since the smelting of ores depended on the heat generated from burning wood/charcoal.

49   Smith, *Wealth of nations*, vol. 1, p. 89. Malthus, incidentally, despite his reputation, came to hold a more nuanced view of the tension between production and population.

rates visible in Figure 1.3 exemplifies the disappearance of what had been a prevailing pattern. Since a rising population growth rate no longer signified a downward trend in real wages, young people were not obliged to postpone decisions to marry as had happened in the later sixteenth and early seventeenth centuries. For a time, population increased at a previously unprecedented rate. Soon, however, a further change undermined another assumption about the west European marriage pattern and caused population growth to decelerate. The close relationship between levels of nuptiality and trends in fertility weakened and ultimately disappeared as the control of fertility within marriage became widespread and effective. Late marriage and frequent celibacy remained characteristic of western Europe but no longer carried the same implications in distinguishing living standards and growth prospects which had once been the case.

Hajnal was conscious of the close relationship between the central topic of his 1965 essay and the writings of Malthus. He remarked that 'The main theme of this paper is not new. It is one of the main topics of Malthus' *Essay* and indeed implicit in its very structure'.[50] Malthus's model of the interplay between production and population was important not only in drawing attention to the necessary tension between the two in all organic economies but also in suggesting that, while population growth must cease and that therefore fertility and mortality must become equal, the necessary equality might be reached at different levels. The relative importance of the 'positive' and 'preventive' checks could give rise to a balance between fertility and mortality over a range of different equilibrium points. He became increasingly conscious that in many European populations the preventive check operated effectively because of conventions and pressures affecting marriage age and the prevalence of celibacy. He lacked, however, the accurate and comprehensive demographic data to quantify many of the most important variables in this context. Though the problem was far less serious, this remained true to a degree when Hajnal published his essay. He was obliged to stress the tentative nature of many of his findings. But the lucid and comprehensive manner in which Hajnal examined the whole range of questions which relate to the tension between production and population prior to the industrial revolution proved to be a powerful stimulus to further work. It is now almost half a century since his essay appeared but it is still the case that all research and scholarship in the field he surveyed remain greatly in his debt.

50   Hajnal, 'European marriage patterns in perspective', p. 130.

2

The Population Geography of Great Britain c.1290: a Provisional Reconstruction[1]

BRUCE M. S. CAMPBELL AND LORRAINE BARRY

A trio of publications made 1964 an auspicious year for historical population studies. Hollingsworth's innovative reconstruction of the demography of the British peerage over four centuries linked information on birth, marriage and death for a clearly defined and well-documented social group.[2] Lawton deployed census returns for Great Britain in 1801 to map the distribution of population across the entire island at the earliest date for which comprehensive and relatively reliable data are available.[3] And, in *Tenure and mobility*, Raftis made pioneering use of manorial court rolls to reconstitute the social and demographic experience of late-medieval customary tenants.[4] That same year, Wrigley and Laslett founded

1   This essay is dedicated with affection and respect to Richard Smith, who, since earliest postgraduate days at Cambridge, has been an unfailing source of inspiration and encouragement. The GIS component of the chapter was undertaken in conjunction with the project 'Historical patterns of development and underdevelopment: origins and persistence of the Great Divergence (HI-POD)' (Contract Number SSH7-CT-2008-225342), directed by Kevin O'Rourke and Stephen Broadberry, as part of the European Commission's 7th Framework Programme for Research. It also draws upon results from the project 'Reconstructing the national income of Britain and Holland, c.1270/1500 to 1850', led by Broadberry and funded by the Leverhulme Trust (Reference Number F/00215AR).

2   T. H. Hollingsworth, *The demography of the British peerage*, supplement to *Population Studies* 18 (2) (London, 1964).
3   R. W. Lawton, 'Historical geography: the industrial revolution', in *The British Isles: a systematic geography*, ed. J. Wreford Watson and J. B. Sissons (Edinburgh and London, 1964), pp. 221–44 (p. 228). His analysis also extended to Ireland using the first Irish census of 1821.
4   J. A. Raftis, *Tenure and mobility: studies in the social history of the medieval English village* (Toronto, 1964).

the Cambridge Group for the History of Population and Social Structure (CAMPOP), dedicated primarily to researching the demographic history of England.[5] Then in 1965, in *The world we have lost*, Laslett explored many of the themes that CAMPOP researchers would subsequently investigate and in 1966, reconstitution studies were launched in earnest with the appearance of Wrigley's path-breaking demographic analysis of Colyton (Devon) from 1541 to 1871.[6]

Scholarly priorities quickly shifted from description of population trends and patterns to analysis of demographic behaviour, with a corresponding change of focus from national populations to individual communities and social groups.[7] Medievalists responded with a spate of manorial case studies.[8] Thus, Razi's 1980 reconstruction of social and demographic trends on the manor of Halesowen (Worcestershire) from 1270 to 1400 explicitly attempted to achieve with court rolls the kind of analytical insights into individual life-cycle decisions and actions which early modernists were demonstrating could be obtained from parish registers.[9] Henceforth, aggregate studies, such as Wrigley and Schofield's *Population history of England*, would be painstakingly constructed from the bottom up based on detailed microstudies and individual reconstitutions.[10] The methodological rigour demanded by this approach meant that historical demography shed the popular appeal with which Laslett had endowed it and became a technical and highly specialised subject.

5 E. A. Wrigley, 'Small-scale but not parochial: the work of the Cambridge Group for the History of Population and Social Structure', *Family and Community History* 1 (1998), 27–36.

6 P. Laslett, *The world we have lost: England before the Industrial Revolution* (London and New York, 1965); E. A. Wrigley, 'Family limitation in pre-industrial England', *Economic History Review* 19 (1966), 82–109.

7 For example, R. T. Vann and D. Eversley, *Friends in life and death: the British and Irish Quakers in the demographic transition, 1650–1900* (Cambridge, 1992).

8 Z. Razi and R. M. Smith, 'The historiography of manorial court rolls', in *Medieval society and the manor court*, ed. Z. Razi and R. M. Smith (Oxford, 1996), pp. 1–35 (pp. 22–33).

9 Z. Razi, *Life, marriage and death in a medieval parish: economy, society and demography in Halesowen, 1270–1400* (Cambridge, 1980). See also L. R. Poos, Z. Razi and R. M. Smith, 'The population history of medieval English villages: a debate on the use of manor court records', in *Medieval society*, ed. Razi and Smith, pp. 298–368.

10 E. A. Wrigley and R. S. Schofield, *The population history of England, 1541–1871: a reconstruction* (London, 1981), and especially the sequel volume E. A. Wrigley, R. S. Davies, J. E. Oeppen and R. S. Schofield, *English population history from family reconstitution 1580–1837* (Cambridge, 1997).

The earlier enterprise to quantify and map the country's population at benchmark points in time, championed above all by Darby, fell out of favour.[11] In any case, its main tasks had largely been accomplished (or so it then seemed). The first British censuses had been mapped, albeit at the scale of English and Welsh registration districts and Scottish counties, by Lawton.[12] Between 1952 and 1967, five regional volumes had revealed the distribution of Domesday population at the level of individual hundreds which, when stitched together, yielded the single national distribution map unveiled in 1973 and much reproduced since.[13] Already in 1972, Sheail had mapped at a similar hundredal scale the national distributions of wealth and taxpayers in 1524/5, and in 1973, Glasscock followed with a corresponding map of lay wealth in 1334.[14] This allowed systematic comparison of the changing spatial distributions of people and wealth 1086–1334–1524/5, published in 1979 and achieved using largely manual methods of data manipulation and mapping.[15] Thereby were highlighted localities and regions of gain and loss and above or below average change.

11   Darby's interest in population mapping is evident in H. C. Darby (ed.), *An historical geography of England before AD 1800: fourteen studies* (Cambridge, 1936), and expressed most fully in its sequel, H. C. Darby (ed.), *A new historical geography of England* (Cambridge, 1973).

12   Lawton, 'Historical geography'.

13   H. C. Darby, *The Domesday geography of eastern England* (Cambridge, 1952); H. C. Darby and I. B. Terrett, *The Domesday geography of midland England* (Cambridge, 1954); H. C. Darby and E. M. J. Campbell, *The Domesday geography of south-east England* (Cambridge, 1962); H. C. Darby and I. S. Maxwell, *The Domesday geography of northern England* (Cambridge, 1962); H. C. Darby and R. W. Finn, *The Domesday geography of south-west England* (Cambridge, 1967). H. C. Darby, 'Domesday England', in *A new historical geography of England*, ed. Darby, pp. 39–74 (p. 46). The individual Domesday vills are mapped and listed in H. C. Darby and G. R. Versey, *Domesday gazetteer* (Cambridge, 1975). A final volume synthesises results for the whole of England: H. C. Darby, *Domesday England* (Cambridge, 1977). A preliminary county-level map of Domesday population had appeared in: H. C. Darby, 'The economic geography of England, AD 1000–1250', in *An historical geography of England before AD 1800*, ed. Darby, pp. 165–229 (p. 209).

14   J. Sheail, 'The distribution of taxable population and wealth in England during the early sixteenth century', *Transactions of the Institute of British Geographers* 55 (1972), 111–26; R. E. Glasscock, 'England *circa* 1334', in *A new historical geography of England*, ed. Darby, pp. 136–85 (p. 139). R. E. Glasscock (ed.), *The lay subsidy of 1334* (London, 1975), lists the tax contributions of each vill by county and hundred.

15   H. C. Darby, R. E. Glasscock, J. Sheail and G. R. Versey, 'The changing geographical distribution of wealth in England: 1086–1334–1525', *Journal of Historical Geography* 5 (1979), 247–62.

A county distribution of population using the 1377 poll tax returns had been produced by Pelham in 1936, and in 1973, Darby employed Rickman's county estimates to map successive changes in the distribution of population between 1600, 1700 and 1800.[16] Most of these distribution maps were included in the *New historical geography of England* (1973), which constituted the culmination of this distinctive historiographic tradition.[17]

Maps, however, were inconsequential to the new breed of historical demographers, who scarcely employed them other than to plot the individual parishes used in analysis. Moreover, when population distribution maps have been needed, it is mostly versions of those created by Darby and his disciples that have been reproduced. In a 1988 essay, for example, Smith included redrawings of Darby's 1973 Domesday population map, Pelham's 1936 poll tax population map, and Sheail's Tudor taxpayer map.[18] This is both a tribute to the quality of the work undertaken in the Darby era and a comment upon how moribund that brand of historical geography had by then become.

Having been out of academic favour for a generation, historical mapping is now experiencing a revival.[19] After all, maps are indispensable for identifying and locating extremes and anomalies, establishing the norms, placing detailed case studies in context, and promoting

16   R. A. Pelham, 'Fourteenth-century England', in *An historical geography of England before AD 1800*, ed. Darby, pp. 230–65 (p. 232); H. C. Darby, 'The age of the improver: 1600–1800', in *A new historical geography of England*, ed. Darby, pp. 302–88 (pp. 306–7). Rickman's pre-1801 county estimates are reassessed in E. A. Wrigley, 'Rickman revisited: the population growth rates of English counties in the early modern period', *Economic History Review* 62 (2009), 711–35.

17   R. A. Dodgshon and R. A. Butlin (eds), *An historical geography of England and Wales* (London, 1978) exemplifies the same approach but includes Wales.

18   R. M. Smith, 'Human resources', in *The countryside of medieval England*, ed. G. Astill and A. Grant (Oxford, 1988), pp. 188–212 (pp. 197, 199 (for which the correct source is Pelham, 'Fourteenth-century England', p. 232), 201).

19   Examples include: L. Kennedy, P. S. Ell, E. M. Crawford and L. A. Clarkson, *Mapping the Great Irish Famine: a survey of the famine decades* (Dublin, 1999); *A vision of Britain through time: a vision of Britain between 1801 and 2001, including maps, statistical trends and historical descriptions*, http://www.visionofbritain.org.uk (accessed 2 September 2014); B. M. S. Campbell and K. Bartley, *England on the eve of the Black Death: an atlas of lay lordship, land and wealth, 1300–49* (Manchester, 2006). CAMPOP is currently host to a major population mapping exercise: 'The population geography of England and Wales c.1379–1911': http://www.hpss.geog.cam.ac.uk/research/projects/occupations/englandwales1379-1911 (accessed 2 September 2014).

comparative thinking at a hierarchy of scales. Moreover, the advent of Geographical Information Science (GIS) has transformed the potential for organising, linking, manipulating and mapping historical data and thereby helped engender a renewed interest in spatial analysis as a historical tool.[20] At the same time, the realisation has grown that reconstitution, whether of parishes or manors, is by its nature a selective exercise and therefore complementary to, rather than a substitute for, reconstruction of population totals, trends and distributions.[21] In fact, its exacting data demands render it non-viable for entire periods, regions, or social and religious groups.[22] Instead, demographic attention has switched to specific well-recorded groups – tenants-in-chief, will-makers, Benedictine monks, and scholars at Winchester and New College Oxford – with all the issues of representativeness that such microstudies present.[23]

Meanwhile, emergence of historical national income analysis is placing renewed emphasis upon the size, geographical distribution, and social and occupational structures of populations.[24] The associated broadening of historical enquiry beyond England to embrace the whole of Great Britain also means that the exclusion of Wales and Scotland from the source-based population reconstructions made by Darby and his co-workers is a serious limitation.[25] Wrigley and Schofield's exclusive focus upon England is more inexplicable, given that between 1536 and 1543 Wales was formally united and annexed to England and Welsh parish registers exist in some

20 I. Gregory and P. Ell, *Historical GIS: technologies, methodologies and scholarship* (Cambridge, 2007).

21 For the dangers of too exclusive a reliance upon parish registers: R. B. Outhwaite, 'Age at marriage in England from the late seventeenth to the nineteenth century', *Transactions of the Royal Historical Society*, Fifth Series, 23 (1973), 55–70.

22 Poos, Razi and Smith, 'The population history of medieval English villages'.

23 R. M. Smith, 'Measuring adult mortality in an age of plague: England, 1349–1540', in *Town and countryside in the age of the Black Death: essays in honour of John Hatcher*, ed. M. Bailey and S. Rigby (Turnhout, 2012), pp. 43–85.

24 G. Clark, 'The long march of history: farm wages, population and economic growth, England 1209–1869', *Economic History Review* 60 (2007), 97–135, and S. N. Broadberry, B. M. S. Campbell, A. Klein, B. van Leeuwen and M. Overton, *British economic growth, 1270–1870* (Cambridge, 2014).

25 R. R. Davies, *The matter of Britain and the matter of England: an inaugural lecture delivered before the University of Oxford on 29 February 1996* (Oxford, 1996). Pan-British perspectives are offered by C. Dyer, *Making a living in the middle ages: the people of Britain 850–1520* (New Haven and London, 2002); S. H. Rigby (ed.), *A companion to Britain in the later middle ages* (Oxford, 2003); R. H. Britnell, *Britain and Ireland 1050–1530: economy and society* (Oxford, 2004).

numbers from the 1660s.[26] After 1543, England and Wales constituted a single national unit, extended by act of union to include Scotland from 1707. Moreover, in both cases *de facto* union had occurred earlier, with Edward I's conquest of Wales in 1282–84 and union of the crowns of Scotland and England in 1603. If the aim is to reconstruct and understand 'national' patterns and trends, this successively extended territory ought to be the basic unit of analysis. Herein lies the pioneering significance of Lawton's mapping of the population of the whole Great Britain for 1801.[27]

Five hundred years earlier, c.1290, a constellation of English, Welsh and Scottish sources provide a corresponding opportunity to reconstruct the population geography of the whole of Great Britain.[28] This chapter presents the results of such a reconstruction for the earliest date at which the exercise is possible. Its evidential base are the assessments for the ecclesiastical *Taxatio* of 1291 (the only medieval pan-British tax), receipts from the lay subsidy levied upon England in 1290 and then Wales in 1292/3 (the first subsidy to include both territories), and the pre-1286 Scottish sheriffdom tax assessments of lay and ecclesiastical estates.[29] Since none of these sources record population *per se*, fundamental to the exercise is the assumption that broad similarities existed between the distributions of taxable wealth, taxpayers and population. The approach employed has been to use these various tax assessments to disaggregate estimates of the total populations

26   The explanation given is that 'Welsh parish registers are in principle comparable to the English, but in practice they appear to have been more defectively kept, and proportionately far fewer begin at an early date': Wrigley and Schofield, *Population history*, p. 10. For extant Welsh registers see C. J. Williams and J. Watts-Williams, *Cofrestri Plwyf Cymru/Parish Registers of Wales*, 2nd edn (Aberystwyth, 2000).

27   Lawton, 'Historical geography'.

28   B. M. S. Campbell, 'Benchmarking medieval economic development: England, Wales, Scotland, and Ireland *circa* 1290', *Economic History Review* 61 (2008), 896–945.

29   J. H. Denton, 'The valuation of the ecclesiastical benefices of England and Wales in 1291–2', *Historical Research: The Bulletin of the Institute of Historical Research* 66 (1993), 231–50; S. Davnall, J. H. Denton, S. Griffiths, D. Ross and B. Taylor, 'The *Taxatio* database', *Bulletin of the John Rylands University Library of Manchester* 74 (1992), 89–108; *Taxatio ecclesiastica Angliae et Walliae auctoritate P. Nicholai IV, circa AD 1291: printed by command of His Majesty King George III in pursuance of an address of the House of Commons of Great Britain*, ed. T. Astle, S. Ayscough and J. Caley (London, 1802); S. Jenks, 'The lay subsidies and the state of the English economy (1275–1334)', *Vierteljahrschrift für Sozial- und Wirtschaftsgeschichte* 85 (1998), 1–39 (p. 31); K. Williams-Jones (ed.), *The Merioneth lay subsidy roll 1292–3* (Cardiff, 1976); A. Stevenson, 'Taxation in medieval Scotland', in *Atlas of Scottish history to 1707*, ed. P. G. B. McNeill and H. L. MacQueen (Edinburgh, 1996), pp. 298–308 (p. 299).

of England, Wales and Scotland to, respectively, their constituent counties, deaneries and sheriffdoms. A combination of methods is then used to disaggregate these county/deanery/sheriffdom subtotals to the level of individual vills or their equivalent. It is from these micro-estimates that a potential surface map of the population distribution of the whole of Great Britain has been generated, providing the basis for direct comparison with the equivalent population distribution revealed by the 1801 census.

The total population of Great Britain in 1290 and 1801

Establishing the size of the population c.1290 is the necessary first step in the reconstruction of its distribution. In the case of England, the Domesday Survey and first poll tax provide a secure basis for estimating the country's population at the benchmark years of 1086 and 1377 (Table 2.1). Between these two dates, counts of tenant numbers and the replacement rates of male tenants-in-chief chart the rise and fall of population and allow the derivation of further aggregate estimates at key points in time, including 1290 (Tables 2.1 and 2.2).[30] These, in turn, provide a basis for inferring the lesser populations of Wales and Scotland, on the principle that their populations remained in a relatively constant size ratio to that of England. In 1086, England supported an estimated population of 1.7 million. This makes generous allowances of 150,000 for townspeople (imperfectly recorded by the Domesday survey) and 50,000 for inhabitants of the four northernmost counties (unvisited by the Domesday commissioners) and, in accordance with Darby's upper-bound estimate, assumes a relatively large mean household size of five (ranging from a minimum of four for slaves to a maximum of eight for tenants-in-chief).[31] It also accommodates Sally Harvey's point that there is likely to have been significant underrecording of freemen as yet unattached to any lord or manor, by allowing a sliding scale of omissions from zero for tenants-in-chief to a generous 25 per cent for free tenants, with an overall omission rate of 10 per cent.[32]

Careful reworking of data on tenant numbers largely assembled by Hallam, implies that over the next 200 years the population grew almost

30   Broadberry *et al.*, *British economic growth*.
31   Darby, *Domesday England*, pp. 87–90, whose maximum estimate is 1.6 million and includes 120,000 for townspeople and 25,000 for the four northernmost counties.
32   S. Harvey, 'Domesday England', in *The agrarian history of England and Wales, II: 1042–1350*, ed. H. E. Hallam (Cambridge, 1988), pp. 45–136 (pp. 46–9).

Table 2.1. Estimated total populations of Great Britain in 1290 and 1801

Country:	A Population 1290	B Population 1801	C Increase 1290–1801 B ÷ A
England	4.75 m.	8.60 m.	× 1.8
Wales	0.30 m.	0.60 m.	× 2.0
Scotland	0.75 m.	1.60 m.	× 2.1
Great Britain	5.80 m.	10.80 m.	× 1.9

Sources: England 1290: S. N. Broadberry, B. M. S. Campbell, A. Klein, B. van Leeuwen and M. Overton, *British economic growth, 1270–1870* (Cambridge, 2014). Wales and Scotland 1290: B. M. S. Campbell, 'Benchmarking medieval economic development: England, Wales, Scotland, and Ireland *circa* 1290', *Economic History Review* 61 (2008), 896–945 (pp. 928–31). England and Wales 1801: E. A. Wrigley and R. S. Schofield, *The population history of England, 1541–1871: a reconstruction* (London, 1981), p. 577. Scotland 1801: B. R. Mitchell and P. Deane, *Abstract of British historical statistics* (Cambridge, 1962), p. 6.

threefold to approximately 4.75 million by 1290 (Table 2.1).[33] For the first 150 years growth averaged over 0.5 per cent per annum, an impressive rate over such an extended length of time for a pre-industrial population (Table 2.2).[34] Thereafter it slowed, until by the 1290s, numbers had virtually ceased to grow at all.[35] Significant losses from the serious dearth of 1293–95 and great famine of 1315–21 were subsequently made good so that by 1348 the population may have numbered around 4.8 million.[36] It was then dramatically reduced to 2.5 million in 1377 by the four great plague pandemics of 1348/9, 1360/1, 1369 and 1375.[37]

[33] H. E. Hallam, 'Population movements in England, 1086–1350', in *Agrarian history*, ed. Hallam, pp. 508–93 (pp. 536–93); Broadberry, Campbell and van Leeuwen, 'English medieval population'.

[34] English annual growth rates averaged 0.52 per cent from 1541 to 1661, slowed to 0.10 per cent from 1661 to 1741, and accelerated to 1.02 per cent from 1741 to 1861. Calculated from Wrigley and Schofield, *Population history*, pp. 208–9.

[35] The decline from fast to zero growth is especially apparent on the Bishop of Winchester's multi-manorial complex at Taunton, Somerset: J. Z. Titow, 'Some evidence of the thirteenth century population increase', *Economic History Review* 14 (1961), 218–24.

[36] Broadberry *et al.*, *British economic growth*. Recovery from the famine of 1315–21 was uneven: R. M. Smith, 'Demographic developments in rural England, 1300–48: a survey', in *Before the Black Death: studies in the 'crisis' of the early fourteenth century*, ed. B. M. S. Campbell (Manchester, 1991), pp. 25–77 (pp. 37–52).

[37] Broadberry *et al.*, *British economic growth*.

Table 2.2. Estimated population of England, 1086–1348

Date	Indexed tenant numbers	Population extrapolated from Domesday (m.)	Mean annual growth rate
1086	100	1.70	
			0.58%
1190	182	3.09	
			0.52%
1250	248	4.22	
			0.30%
1290	279	4.75	
			0.02%
1348	283	4.81	

Sources: For indexed tenant numbers and Domesday population, see text.

Previous estimates of late-medieval agricultural output have cast doubt on the capacity of domestic agriculture to feed a population in excess of 4.5 million.[38] These were premised on a maximum arable area of 4.25 million hectares (10.5 million acres), just short of the 4.33 million hectares seemingly under the plough at the start of the nineteenth century.[39] Reassessment of this key parameter nevertheless suggests that the arable area may have been underestimated, both in 1801 and 1290.[40] Thus, according to both Prince and Holderness, contemporary estimates suggest an arable acreage of around 4.5 million hectares in 1801, which then expanded to a securely documented 5.6 million hectares in 1836/71, when Victorian high farming was at fullest stretch under the stimulus of surging domestic demand for grain and other staple foodstuffs.[41] Although there are sound topographical, institutional, technological and economic reasons for supposing that significantly less land was under arable cultivation in 1290 than in the mid nineteenth century, it is not inconceivable that the tillage area could have been greater in 1290 than 1801, when much former medieval arable still remained under permanent pasture.[42]

38 B. M. S. Campbell, *English seigniorial agriculture, 1250–1450* (Cambridge, 2000), pp. 399–406.
39 M. Overton and B. M. S. Campbell, 'Production et productivité dans l'agriculture anglais, 1086–1871', *Histoire et Mesure*, 11 (1996), 255–97 (pp. 290–1).
40 Broadberry *et al.*, *British economic growth*.
41 H. C. Prince, 'The changing rural landscape, 1750–1850', and B. A. Holderness, 'Prices, productivity, and output', in *The agrarian history of England and Wales, VI: 1750–1850*, ed. G. E. Mingay (Cambridge, 1989), pp. 7–83 and 84–189 (pp. 31–2, 127); *Agricultural returns for Great Britain for 1871* (PP, 1871, LXIX).
42 Broadberry *et al.*, *British economic growth*.

In fact, on generous assumptions there may have been as much as 5.3 million hectares of tillage in 1290 (almost double that in 1086), which on known patterns of cropping, levels of yields, and kilocalorie conversion rates of raw grain to bread, pottage and ale could have supplied a population of 4.75 million with a daily diet of around 1,400 grain-based kilocalories.[43] Augmented with pastoral and horticultural products and fish, this was just sufficient to provide the average daily per capita intake of 2,000 kilocalories that Livi-Bacci considers to have been the minimum required to meet basic subsistence needs.[44] English mean per capita kilocalorie intake was little better in 1801, when wage earners' real incomes were again being squeezed hard. Nevertheless, agriculture was feeding almost twice as many mouths, the proportion of households dependent upon a bare-bones basket of consumables was much reduced, and the contents of the basket was more varied.[45]

For Wales in 1290 there is no good reason to change the estimate of 0.3 million (equivalent to one-sixteenth of the population of England) proposed by Williams-Jones and generally accepted by historians of the principality.[46] By 1801, Scotland's population was a little over two-and-a-half times that of Wales (Table 2.1), so if a similar ratio had prevailed in 1290, Scotland's population would have been approximately 0.75–0.80 million. Extrapolating northern English population densities to Scotland also suggests that 0.75 million is the most credible figure.[47] Adding these estimates for Wales and Scotland to that for England yields a total of 5.8 million for Great Britain as a whole in 1290. Over the next five centuries the population almost doubled to 10.8 million, increasing marginally faster in Wales and Scotland than more urbanised England (Table 2.1), where high urban mortality rates acted as a brake upon growth.[48]

43   For the arable area in 1086 see Campbell, *English seigniorial agriculture*, pp. 386–9; Broadberry *et al.*, *British economic growth*.

44   M. Livi-Bacci, *Population and nutrition: an essay on European demographic history*, trans. T. Croft-Murray with C. Ipsen (Cambridge, 1990), p. 27.

45   Broadberry *et al.*, *British economic growth*.

46   Williams-Jones (ed.), *Merioneth lay subsidy roll*, pp. xxxv–lix; Campbell, 'Benchmarking', pp. 927–8. Compare Wrigley and Schofield, *Population history*, p. 571.

47   Campbell, 'Benchmarking', p. 930.

48   E. A. Wrigley, 'A simple model of London's importance in changing English society and economy 1650–1750', *Past and Present* 37 (1967), 44–70 (pp. 45–9); R. M. Smith, 'Geographical aspects of population change in England 1500–1730', in *An historical geography of England and Wales*, ed. R. A. Dodgshon and R. A. Butlin, 2nd edn (London, 1990), pp. 151–79 (p. 172).

The populations of English counties, Welsh deaneries and Scottish sheriffdoms in 1290

These estimates of total population can be geographically disaggregated to the scale of the English county, Welsh deanery and Scottish sheriffdom using information provided by the English lay subsidy levied in 1290, Welsh ecclesiastical *Taxatio* assessments of 1291, and pre-1286 Scottish sheriffdom tax assessments of lay and ecclesiastical estates. In the case of England, the county tax receipts to the 1290 lay subsidy recorded in the Exchequer Pipe Roll of 1295, converted into numbers of taxpayers per county using the average tax paid per taxpayer per county as calculated from the vill-level returns to the lay subsidies of 1327 and 1332, provide one basis for estimating each county's share of the total population of 4.75 million (Table 2.3, Estimate A).[49] Numbers of poll tax payers per county in 1377 provide another (Table 2.3, Estimate B).[50] In both cases, values for the exempted county palatines of Cheshire and Durham have been interpolated from the contributions paid by their immediate neighbours.

For the thirty-six counties south of Cheshire and Durham, the county population estimates obtained by these two methods yield a correlation coefficient of +0.92. A weighted combination of the two (Table 2.3, Estimate C) makes allowance for the fact that the 1290 subsidy was a means-tested tax whereas the poll tax was imposed at a flat rate upon all adults, and consequently, but for the post-1290 differential impact of war with Scotland and four major plagues, would be a truer guide to the distribution of population. These are the county population estimates summarised in the final column of Table 2.3 and third column of Table 2.4. Estimated numbers of urban residents in towns with at least 2,000 inhabitants (Table 2.4, column five) are subtracted to yield an estimate of rural population per county (Table 2.4, column six). Note that, at this date, metropolitan Middlesex is the sole county to which this makes a significant difference. The mean rural population density of each county expressed per square kilometre is then given in the final column of Table 2.4.[51] England as a whole had a mean rural population density of 33 per

49 Campbell, 'Benchmarking', pp. 925–6.
50 Campbell, 'Benchmarking', pp. 925–6.
51 Population density has been variously expressed per square mile (Darby and his associates), per thousand acres (Lawton), and per hectare (Vision of Britain). Smith, 'Human resources', pp. 196–202, followed the example of the United Nations and calculated it per square kilometre.

Table 2.3. The derivation of English county population estimates c.1290

County	Tax received 1290 £	Tax per taxpayer 1327/32 £	Estimated taxpayers in 1290	Poll tax payers 1377	Estimated population in 1290 based on		
					(A) 1290 lay subsidies	(B) 1377 poll tax	(C) (A) × ⅓ + (B) × ⅓
Bedfordshire	1,727	2.25	768	20,339	63,968	69,785	65,907
Berkshire	2,287	3.11	735	22,723	61,282	77,965	66,843
Buckinghamshire	2,544	2.40	1,060	24,672	88,318	84,653	87,096
Cambridgeshire	3,483	2.12	1,643	29,252	136,888	100,367	124,715
Cheshire	ND	ND	ND	ND	52,720	56,733	54,058
Cornwall	522	1.25	418	34,474	34,791	117,598	62,393
Cumberland	1,782	2.46	724	12,519	60,354	42,954	54,554
Derbyshire	2,354	2.32	1,015	24,289	84,553	83,338	84,148
Devon	1,839	1.04	1,768	47,701	147,339	163,668	152,782
Dorset	1,854	1.58	1,173	34,241	97,767	117,485	104,340
Durham	ND	ND	ND	ND	73,719	46,098	64,512
Essex	4,371	2.18	2,005	50,917	167,069	174,702	169,613
Gloucestershire	4,019	2.21	1,818	45,314	151,522	155,478	152,841
Hampshire	2,407	2.14	1,125	39,126	93,730	134,246	107,235
Herefordshire	1,986	2.29	867	16,721	72,246	57,372	67,288
Hertfordshire	2,194	2.17	1,011	19,975	84,231	68,537	78,999
Huntingdonshire	1,353	1.71	792	14,169	65,952	48,615	60,173
Kent	7,475	3.82	1,957	59,451	163,060	203,983	176,701
Lancashire	1,166	1.60	729	23,880	60,747	81,935	67,809
Leicestershire	2,095	2.49	841	33,831	70,109	116,078	85,432
Lincolnshire	9,099	1.97	4,619	95,119	384,840	326,364	365,348
Middlesex & London	4,009	4.33	926	34,557	77,127	118,569	90,941

County	Tax received 1290 £	Tax per taxpayer 1327/32 £	Estimated taxpayers in 1290	Poll tax payers 1377	Estimated population in 1290 based on		
					(A) 1290 lay subsidies	(B) 1377 poll tax	(C) (A) × ⅓ + (B) × ⅓
Norfolk	9,783	1.68	5,823	97,817	485,203	335,622	435,343
Northamptonshire	3,865	2.22	1,741	41,702	145,069	143,084	144,407
Northumberland	3,365	1.90	1,771	16,809	147,561	57,674	117,599
Nottinghamshire	2,007	2.38	843	28,885	70,271	99,108	79,883
Oxfordshire	2,909	2.68	1,085	27,338	90,440	93,800	91,560
Rutland	532	1.88	283	5,994	23,572	20,566	22,570
Shropshire	1,988	1.45	1,371	26,828	114,236	92,050	106,841
Somerset	2,907	1.61	1,866	56,074	150,471	192,396	164,446
Staffordshire	1,343	1.98	678	22,489	56,515	77,162	63,397
Suffolk	6,075	2.25	2,700	62,562	224,974	214,658	221,535
Surrey	1,669	1.71	976	18,039	81,341	61,894	74,859
Sussex	3,129	2.12	1,476	36,195	122,980	124,189	123,383
Warwickshire	2,160	2.08	1,038	30,264	86,522	103,839	92,295
Westmorland	743	1.84	404	7,389	33,658	25,353	30,889
Wiltshire	4,454	2.33	1,912	45,825	159,293	157,231	158,606
Worcestershire	1,352	1.87	723	16,099	60,256	55,238	58,583
Yorkshire, E. Riding	2,769	2.00	1,385	42,458	115,369	145,678	125,472
Yorkshire, N. Riding	3,699	1.89	1,957	40,433	163,057	138,730	154,948
Yorkshire, W. Riding	3,031	1.99	1,523	48,149	126,921	165,205	139,683
ENGLAND	116,347	2.10	55,489	1,354,419	4,750,041	4,750,001	4,750,027

Sources: S. Jenks, 'The lay subsidies and the state of the English economy (1275–1334)', *Vierteljahrschrift für Sozial- und Wirtschaftsgeschichte* 85 (1998), 1–39 (p. 31); B. M. S. Campbell and K. Bartley, *England on the eve of the Black Death: an atlas of lay lordship, land and wealth, 1300–49* (Manchester, 2006), pp. 338–9; R. B. Dobson, *The Peasants' Revolt of 1381*, 2nd edn (Basingstoke and London, 1983), pp. 54–9.

Notes: Italicised figures are interpolations. The slight differences in the totals for England in the last three columns are the product of rounding the component county estimates to the nearest whole number.

Table 2.4. Estimated English county rural population densities c.1290

County (ranked by rural population density)	Area km²	Total population	Total population per km²	Total urban population	Total rural population	Rural population per km²
Norfolk	5,333	435,343	82	25,900	409,443	77
Huntingdonshire	958	60,173	63	2,800	57,373	60
Rutland	391	22,570	58	0	22,570	58
Northamptonshire	2,585	144,407	56	7,200	137,207	53
Suffolk	3,875	221,535	57	16,900	204,635	53
Bedfordshire	1,228	65,907	54	2,000	63,907	52
Cambridgeshire	2,258	124,715	55	10,400	114,315	51
Lincolnshire	6,910	365,348	53	30,500	334,848	48
Hertfordshire	1,616	78,999	49	2,000	76,999	48
London & Middlesex	767	90,941	119	55,000	35,941	47
Buckinghamshire	1,924	87,096	45	0	87,096	45
Wiltshire	3,440	158,606	46	7,700	150,906	44
Oxfordshire	1,917	91,560	48	11,800	79,760	42
Gloucestershire	3,240	152,841	47	21,600	131,241	41
Essex	3,981	169,613	43	9,500	160,113	40
Kent	4,048	176,701	44	14,800	161,901	40
Dorset	2,678	104,340	39	0	104,340	39
Somerset	4,227	164,446	39	5,000	159,446	38
Leicestershire	2,155	85,432	40	5,400	80,032	37
Surrey	1,963	74,859	38	5,000	69,859	36
Yorkshire, E. Riding	3,056	125,472	41	17,110	108,362	35

County (ranked by rural population density)	Area km²	Total population	Total population per km²	Total urban population	Total rural population	Rural population per km²
Nottinghamshire	2,155	79,883	37	6,900	72,983	34
Warwickshire	2,512	92,295	37	9,500	82,795	33
Berkshire	1,950	66,843	34	5,700	61,143	31
Sussex	3,784	123,383	33	5,250	118,133	31
Derbyshire	2,616	84,148	32	2,900	81,248	31
Worcestershire	1,826	58,583	32	3,700	54,883	30
Herefordshire	2,183	67,288	31	5,500	61,788	28
Shropshire	3,481	106,841	31	11,400	95,441	27
Yorkshire, N. Riding	5,579	154,948	28	14,900	140,048	25
Durham	2,572	64,512	25	2,600	61,912	24
Hampshire	4,170	107,235	26	10,300	96,935	23
Devon	6,768	152,782	23	9,600	143,182	21
Northumberland	5,252	117,599	22	9,900	107,699	21
Cheshire	2,481	54,058	22	3,300	50,758	20
Staffordshire	2,997	63,397	21	2,700	60,697	20
Yorkshire, W. Riding	7,345	139,683	19	12,190	127,493	17
Cornwall	3,600	62,393	17	0	62,393	17
Westmorland	2,049	30,889	15	0	30,889	15
Lancashire	4,996	67,809	14	0	67,809	14
Cumberland	3,963	54,554	14	2,100	52,454	13
ENGLAND	130,828	4,750,027	36	369,050	4,380,977	33

Sources: Total population per county from Table 2.3; urban population per county from Campbell, 'Benchmarking', pp. 908–9.
Notes: Urban population = all those living in towns with at least 2,000 inhabitants. Rural population = total population less urban population. *Italicised* figures are interpolations.

square kilometre at this temporal peak in its medieval population, ranging from a minimum of 13 per square kilometre in rainy and mountainous Cumberland to a maximum of 77 per square kilometre in highly congested Norfolk.[52]

The 1290 lay subsidy was extended to Wales in 1291 but the extant returns of 1292/3 are unfortunately too incomplete to allow estimation of the populations of counties and marcher lordships on a similar basis to England.[53] Instead, the valuations of ecclesiastical benefices and prebends and their aggregations into the forty-nine medieval Welsh deaneries, as given in the contemporary *Taxatio* with its comprehensive coverage of the entire principality and its four constituent dioceses of Bangor, Llandaff, St Asaph, and St Davids, provide a more secure basis for undertaking this exercise.[54] Given the tiny territories and uncertain boundaries of numbers of these deaneries and, for ecclesiastical reasons, the exceptional concentration of wealth in a few, such as Brecon, they have been aggregated into twelve geographically coherent groupings broadly comparable in scale to the smaller of the English counties (Table 2.5). Each deanery grouping's population is then assumed to have been proportionate to its share of Welsh ecclesiastical wealth and the population density of each computed accordingly, as given in the final column of Table 2.5. Note that as Cardiff alone among Welsh towns may have supported a population of 2,000, these are *de facto* rural population densities.[55] Unsurprisingly, average densities in mountainous Wales were less than half those in England, and in the most thinly peopled parts of mid and west Wales sank to around 7 per square kilometre. The south-western deaneries of Pembroke and Rhos alone supported densities in excess of the English average (Tables 2.4 and 2.5).

Taxatio assessments are also available for each of the twelve Scottish dioceses but, with the sole exception of the archdeaconry of Lothian, not at the subsidiary level of deanery.[56] More useful, because of their closer

---

52   B. M. S. Campbell, 'The agrarian problem in the early fourteenth century', *Past and Present* 188 (2005), 3–70. Norfolk's rural population density would rise to 86 per square kilometre if calculated on the 1290 and 1327/32 lay subsidies alone.

53   TNA, PRO E 179/242/48–60; Williams-Jones (ed.), *Merioneth lay subsidy roll*.

54   *Taxatio*, pp. 272–94; Davnall et al., '*Taxatio* database', pp. 106–7; J. Denton and B. Taylor, 'The 1291 valuation of the ecclesiastical benefices of Llandaff diocese', *Archaeologia Cambrensis* 147 (1998), 133–58.

55   Campbell, 'Benchmarking', p. 909.

56   Stevenson, 'Taxation', pp. 300–1.

Table 2.5. Estimated Welsh deanery populations and population densities c.1290

Dioceses	Arch-deaconries	Grouped deaneries (ranked by rural population density)	No. of benefices	Assessed value 1291	Area km²	Estimated population	Population per km²
St Davids	St Davids	Pembroke, Rhos	54	£666	799	34,699	43.42
St Davids & Llandaff	Brecon & Llandaff	Ewyas, Abergavenny, Lower Gwent, Newport, Usk	82	£665	1,345	38,093	28.31
Bangor & St Asaph	Merioneth & St Asaph	Dyffryn Clwyd, Englefield, Iall & Stratalwen, Maelor, Nandhendwe, Rhos & Rufoniog	60	£759	2,087	43,493	20.84
St Davids	Cardigan & St Davids	Cemais, Penbidiog	31	£249	692	14,247	20.58
Llandaff	Llandaff	Groneath & Kenfig, Llandaff	55	£523	1,620	[1]29,944	18.48
Bangor	Anglesey	Cantress, Dindaethwy, Taebolyon	15	£209	706	11,983	16.98
Bangor & St Asaph	Merioneth & St Asaph	Arwystli, Cadewain, Caereinion, Mechan, Mochnant & Welshpool, March & Cynllaith	42	£509	2,008	29,173	14.53
St Davids	Carmarthen	Carmarthen & Ystrad Tywi, Gower, Kidwelly	42	£351	1,906	20,088	10.54
Bangor	Bangor & Merioneth	Arfon, Arlechwedd, Lleyn, Merioneth	16	£233	1,432	13,355	9.33
St Davids	Brecon	Brecon, Builth, Elvel & Maelenith	59	£582	3,613	33,339	9.23
St Davids	Cardigan	Emlyn, Sub Aeron, Ultra Aeron	34	£307	2,484	17,613	7.09
Bangor & St Asaph	Merioneth & St Asaph	Arddudwy, Mawddwy & Cyfeiliog, Penllyn, Dinmael & Edeyrnion	23	£244	2,017	13,973	6.93
WALES			513	£5,237	20,710	300,000	14.49

Sources: Deaneries, numbers of benefices and valuations (spiritualities only) from S. Davnall, J. H. Denton, S. Griffiths, D. Ross and B. Taylor, 'The *Taxatio* database', *Bulletin of the John Rylands University Library of Manchester* 74 (1992), 89–108 (pp. 106–7). Deanery boundaries reconstructed from *Valor ecclesiasticus temp. Henr. VIII: Auctoritate regia institutus. Printed by command in pursuance of an address of the House of commons of Great Britain*, 6 vols (London, 1821), IV. Deanery areas derived using GIS. Welsh population from Table 2.1. Grouped deanery populations are proportionate to their respective shares of aggregate assessed wealth.

Note: [1] includes Cardiff, probably the only Welsh town with at least 2,000 inhabitants (Campbell, 'Benchmarking', p. 909).

Table 2.6. Estimated Scottish sheriffdom populations and population densities c.1290

Sheriffdom (ranked by rural population density)	Area km²	Pre-1286 tax assessment	Estimated total pop.	Total pop. per km²	Estimated urban pop.	Estimated rural pop.	Rural pop. per km²
Fife	1,416	£3,755	51,398	36.30		51,398	36.30
Roxburgh	1,911	£3,780	51,696	27.05		51,696	27.05
Edinburgh (Lothian)	1,803	£3,685	50,393	27.95	3,000	47,393	26.29
Lanark	2,194	£4,110	56,221	25.63		56,221	25.63
Stirling	1,201	£1,805	24,684	20.55		24,684	20.55
Peebles	897	£1,300	17,772	19.81		17,772	19.81
Forfar (Angus)	2,548	£3,790	51,830	20.34	2,500	49,330	19.36
Berwick	1,190	£2,220	30,368	25.52	7,500	22,868	19.22
Clackmannan with Kinross	365	£425	5,805	15.90		5,805	15.90
Ayr	2,865	£3,285	44,958	15.69		44,958	15.69
Kincardine (Mearns)	938	£1,045	14,273	15.22		14,273	15.22
Dunbarton	1,386	£1,515	20,724	14.95		20,724	14.95
Wigtown	1,340	£1,315	17,983	13.42		17,983	13.42
Perth	6,616	£6,360	87,040	13.16	3,500	83,540	12.63
Aberdeen	5,302	£4,605	63,030	11.89	5,000	58,030	10.94
Dumfries	5,319	£4,045	55,363	10.41		55,363	10.41
Banff	1,536	£1,045	14,283	9.30		14,283	9.30
Selkirk	676	£295	4,036	5.97		4,036	5.97
Argyll (Lorne & Kintyre)	12,177	£3,480	47,610	3.91		47,610	3.91
Cromarty, Inverness & Moray	23,974	£2,960	40,533	1.69		40,533	1.69
SCOTLAND	75,641	£54,820	750,000	9.92	21,500	728,500	9.63

Sources: Sheriffdoms, their valuations and boundaries from A. Stevenson, 'Taxation in medieval Scotland', in *Atlas of Scottish history to 1707*, ed. P. G. B. McNeill and H. L. MacQueen (Edinburgh, 1996), pp. 298–308 (p. 299). Sheriffdom areas derived using GIS. Scottish population from Table 2.1.
Notes: Sheriffdom populations are proportionate to their respective shares of aggregate assessed wealth. Urban population = all those living in towns with at least 2,000 inhabitants (listed in Campbell, 'Benchmarking', p. 910). Rural population = total population less urban population.

spatial coverage, are the assessments of lay and ecclesiastical estates recorded in 1366 but made during the reign of Alexander III (r.1249–86).[57] These are available for the country's twenty-one sheriffdoms (the Scottish counterpart of shires) and are used as the basis of the disaggregation of Scottish population given in Table 2.6, following the deanery-based method used for Wales. Note that the two smallest and very unequally assessed sheriffdoms of Clackmannan and Kinross have been combined to form a single unit. Estimated urban populations for the handful of towns with more than 2,000 inhabitants are then deducted to yield an initial estimate of each sheriffdom's rural population.[58]

Although Scotland was, on average, more thinly peopled than either England or Wales, population densities in the Border sheriffdom of Roxburgh and the lowland sheriffdoms of Lanark, Edinburgh and Stirling (Table 2.6) were on a par with those prevailing immediately south of the Border in Northumberland, Durham and the North Riding of Yorkshire (Table 2.4). Densities in Fife, consistently Scotland's wealthiest and most populous sheriffdom, compared favourably with those in the East Riding of Yorkshire, Leicestershire and Surrey (Tables 2.6 and 2.4). In stark contrast, on this method of reckoning, the harsh and mountainous northern and western highlands and islands, from Argyll to Cromarty, amounting to almost half the kingdom's area and served by a sixth of its parish churches, contained less than an eighth of the population – some 17,500–20,000 households – with an average density of fewer than 4 per square kilometre.[59]

Sharpening the focus: point-level mapping of the populations of England, Wales and Scotland in 1290

When historical population maps were plotted manually, employment of such relatively large administrative units as counties and deaneries offered obvious practical advantages. The advent of GIS has transformed this situation, since potential or surface maps can be generated from point-level

---

57 Stevenson, 'Taxation', p. 299.
58 Campbell, 'Benchmarking', pp. 910 and 913.
59 D. E. R. Watt, N. F. Shead, M. Ash, R. G. Cant, R. Oram and I. Fisher, 'Parish churches about 1300', in Atlas of Scottish history, ed. McNeill and MacQueen, pp. 347–62. In 1755, average densities from Argyll to Sutherland were mostly in the range 4–8 per square kilometre: calculated from http://www.ancestor.abel.co.uk/stats.html (accessed 28 July 2012).

information and the greater the density of points the more accurately contoured the surface generated from them.[60] Point-level generation of surface values also liberates the mapping of historical data from an anachronistic dependence upon nineteenth- and twentieth-century boundary information. Campbell and Bartley (2006) have demonstrated the utility of this technique with reference to the distributions of taxpayers and taxable wealth recorded for a combined total of 14,500 unique tax vills by the lay subsidies of 1327, 1332 and 1334 as well as for the looser spatial coverage of *Inquisitiones post mortem* from the period 1300–49.[61] It is this technique which is employed here to generate a potential map of the population of Great Britain in 1290.

In the case of England the individual county estimates of population in 1290 (Table 2.4) have been disaggregated to vill level using the relative numbers of taxpayers recorded per vill in 1327/32 or, in the case of those counties (Buckinghamshire, Derbyshire, Herefordshire, Middlesex, Northamptonshire, Northumberland, and the East Riding of Yorkshire) which lack such information, the tax assessment per vill in 1334.[62] This is on the assumption that intra-county distributions of taxpayers and wealth changed little between 1290 and 1327/32/34. In the case of Hertfordshire, it is possible to test this assumption since it alone retains a complete tax roll itemising taxpayers and tax paid at vill level for the entire county in 1290.[63] Unfortunately, corresponding information for the 1327/32 lay subsidies has not survived but comparison can be made with the vill-level returns to the 1334 lay subsidy.[64] The resultant correlation coefficients are reassuringly high (+0.88 for taxpayers per vill in 1290 against tax per vill in 1334 and +0.85 for tax per vill in 1290 against tax per vill in 1334) and

---

60   G. F. Bonham-Carter, *Geographic Information Systems for geoscientists: modelling with GIS* (Kidlington, 1994); E. Wattel and P. van Reenen, 'Visualisation of extrapolated social-geographical data', in *Structures and contingencies in computerized historical research*, ed. O. Boonstra, G. Collenteur and B. O. van Elderen (Hilversum, 1995), pp. 253–62; Campbell and Bartley, *Eve of the Black Death*, pp. 8–10; Gregory and Ell, *Historical GIS*, pp. 21–2.

61   Campbell and Bartley, *Eve of the Black Death*.

62   Numbers transcribed from the original subsidy rolls by R. E. Glasscock; database created by K. Bartley as part of the project 'The Geography of Seignorial Land-ownership and Use, 1270–1349', funded by the Leverhulme Trust. For analyses of these data see Campbell and Bartley, *Eve of the Black Death*, pp. 313–49.

63   TNA, PRO E 179/120/2. For Hertfordshire alone the intra-county distribution of population is therefore based upon recorded numbers of taxpayers per vill in 1290.

64   Glasscock (ed.), *Lay subsidy*, pp. 131–5.

confirm, as expected, a high degree of continuity in the local distributions of taxpayers and wealth over this forty- to fifty-year period.

In most cases it is a straightforward matter to allocate each county's estimated population in 1290 between its component tax vills in 1327/32/34 according to the numbers of taxpayers or amount of tax paid at the latter date. Kent is an exception, since its local tax units were lathes and not vills.[65] In its case, the creation of point-level data has entailed, first, disaggregating the county estimate of population by lathe and, second, then apportioning each lathe's population equally between its component vills. Cheshire and Durham present a different problem, since as autonomous palatinates they were exempt from the 1327/32/34 lay subsidies. Their interpolated populations have therefore been shared among the benefices recorded in the 1291 *Taxatio* in proportion to each benefice's valuation.[66] Since there were fewer benefices than tax vills in northern England this has resulted in a lower density of points than in other northern counties. The English total of 11,905 vill-level data points are an average of 4.78 kilometres apart. Experimentation showed that a domed kernel with a radius five times greater of 25 kilometres (i.e. 1,964 square kilometres) and average of 180 points per kernel yields the most continuous and smoothly contoured potential surface. With smaller radii, the surface breaks up and some individual vill values acquire undue prominence.[67]

Creating an equivalent set of data points for Wales and Scotland presents a different challenge since correspondingly comprehensive vill-level tax data do not survive. Extant returns to the Welsh lay subsidy of 1291 are too fragmentary to be useful and although 1291 benefice valuations do exist for Wales they are lacking for most of Scotland.[68] Rather than treat Wales differently from Scotland, a common solution has been applied to both, taking account of the fact that in their mountainous terrains population density undoubtedly declined with increasing altitude. This inverse relationship between rural population density and elevation is clearly evident in England (Figure 2.1), where mean densities below 300 feet (91 metres) were more than double those above 600 feet (183 metres) and permanent settlement effectively ceased above 1,000 feet (305 metres).

65 Glasscock (ed.), *Lay subsidy*, pp. 140–8.
66 *Taxatio*, pp. 258–60 and 314–16; Davnall *et al.*, '*Taxatio* database'.
67 Kernel density calculates the density of point features around each output raster cell.
68 Stevenson, 'Taxation', pp. 300–1.

Figure 2.1. The inverse relationship between population density and elevation in England in 1290

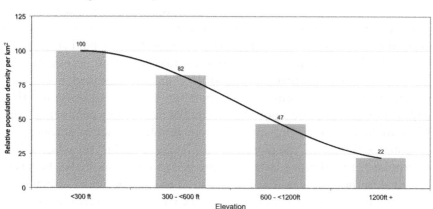

Source and method: Calculated from the national dataset of vill-level population estimates.

First, a regular grid of points at 1 kilometre intervals has been applied to both countries. Each grouped deanery or sheriffdom's population has then been distributed across these points according to their respective elevations in accordance with the linear relationship between population density and elevation established for England. A potential surface has then been interpolated from these elevation-weighted point values using a domed kernel with a radius of 12.5 kilometres and cell size of 1 kilometre. This is half the radius of the kernel applied to England, where the density of point values is significantly lower and less regularly distributed, and results in a more sharply focused surface. For kernels overlapping the Anglo-Welsh and Anglo-Scottish borders the values calculated are products of the irregular English vill-based distribution of points in combination with the regular 1 kilometre grids of Welsh and Scottish points.

Since a kernel radius of 25 kilometres works best for England and that of 12.5 kilometres works best for Wales and Scotland, the final potential surface map of the rural population density of all three countries (Figure 2.2) has been produced by splicing together these two sets of results to produce a single composite 'best-fit' map of the whole of Great Britain. Finally, to avoid artificially depressed values when kernels overlap the coast and consequently include zero values, point values on the landward side of the coast have been extrapolated to the seaward side,

Figure 2.2. The population of Great Britain in 1290 (point-based potential surface)

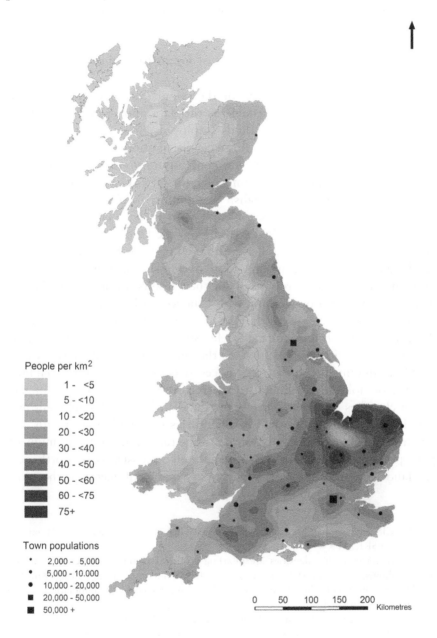

Source: See text.

surface values calculated and the result then clipped to fit the coastline.[69] The resultant density distribution is of the rural population only; towns and cities with populations of at least 2,000 are mapped separately.

The population geography of Great Britain in 1290

The completed distribution map of the population of Great Britain in 1290 (Figure 2.2) is only as reliable as the data upon which it is based, the assumptions made and methods employed. How much and in what ways the result deviates from the true distribution of population can never be known, since there are no contemporary censuses, vital registration statistics or poll taxes from which the latter can be reconstructed. The configuration of the English population is obviously the most securely documented and accords well with earlier and later distributions reconstructed at hundredal level from the Domesday survey (1086) and at county level from the first poll tax (1377).[70] For neither Wales nor Scotland are equivalent comparisons an option although there is scope for improving the historical robustness of their results. In the case of Wales, this can be achieved by working with benefice- rather than deanery-level valuations (as in the case of Cheshire and Durham) and cross-referencing them against the fragmentary 1291 lay-subsidy returns.[71] In the case of Scotland, and with the aid of GIS, the pre-1286 sheriffdom valuations could be combined with the 1291 diocesan assessments and the weighted result geographically anchored to the reconstructed distribution of 940 parish churches c.1300 as a proxy for the distribution of settlement and population.[72] After more than two centuries of population growth and settlement expansion, population densities ranged from a minimum of 5–10 per square kilometre in the highlands and islands of north-west Scotland to a maximum of over 75 per square kilometre in the most

---

69   All GIS analysis has been completed in ArcGIS 9.3 and version 10 Copyright © 1999–2012 ESRI.

70   Note, however, that densities are puzzlingly thin in Hampshire, averaging 26 per square kilometre in contrast to the 46 per square kilometre of neighbouring Wiltshire (Table 2.4). Conceivably, the county may have been undertaxed and its population, consequently, underestimated.

71   *Taxatio*, pp. 272–94; Denton and Taylor, 'Ecclesiastical benefices of Llandaff diocese'; Williams-Jones (ed.), *Merioneth lay subsidy roll*; TNA, PRO E 179/242/48–60.

72   Gregory and Ell, *Historical GIS*, pp. 71–81; Watt *et al.*, 'Parish churches'.

crowded parts of East Anglia and the east midlands. Given the paramount economic importance of agriculture and limited development as yet of proto-industry, densities were typically higher in the arable east than the more pastoral west. Indeed, the absolute sparseness of population in both south-west and north-west England, two regions which in later centuries would display much economic and demographic dynamism, helps explain why the country's population remained below the five million threshold. Commerce, too, as reflected in the distributions of towns and major ports with at least 2,000 inhabitants, displayed a stronger orientation to the North Sea than the Irish Sea and Atlantic, thereby reinforcing the strong eastern bias to the focus of economic activity.[73] Bristol was the sole substantial city on Britain's west coast and Chester the only port-town of note anywhere to its north, both deriving much of their commercial significance from the trade they drove with Ireland.[74]

Everywhere, difficult environmental conditions depressed population densities. The peat fens of East Anglia, barren uplands of Exmoor and Dartmoor, high moorlands of the central Pennines, Cumbrian fells, mountain fastnesses of central Wales, and southern uplands of Scotland were all more thinly peopled than their surrounding districts (Figure 2.2). Even within 25 kilometres of London, and notwithstanding the city's pervasive demands for food, fuel and raw materials, densities sank to below the national average on the poor sandy soils of east Berkshire and west Surrey, and the acid sands and stiff clays of Wealden Kent and Surrey (Figure 2.2).[75] Scotland's central lowlands, with densities in excess of 20 per square kilometre, were only marginally less populous and densities in Fife, at 36 per square kilometre (Table 2.6), were superior and matched those prevailing in the Vale of York (Figure 2.2). At 56° North, this core region of the Scottish kingdom constituted one of the most northerly extensions of moderately high population density in Europe. Nurtured by more than a century of peace, the Tweed Valley on the Anglo-Scottish border was also well peopled. Broadly comparable densities prevailed in

73   Campbell, 'Benchmarking', pp. 906, 909–10 and 913–16.
74   D. T. Williams, 'Medieval foreign trade: western ports', in *An historical geography of England before AD 1800*, ed. Darby, pp. 266–97 (pp. 295–6); W. R. Childs, 'Ireland's trade with England in the later middle ages', *Irish Economic and Social History* 9 (1982), 5–33 (pp. 23–4 and 29).
75   B. M. S. Campbell, J. A. Galloway, D. J. Keene and M. Murphy, *A medieval capital and its grain supply: agrarian production and its distribution in the London region c.1300* (Historical Geography Research Series 30, 1993).

the English-dominated lands of the Welsh Marches, and in Pembrokeshire, where significant English and Flemish immigration had occurred, Welsh densities reached a peak of 40 per square kilometre.[76] Even low-lying Anglesey, bread basket of north-west Wales, had only seventeen people per square kilometre (Table 2.5). In the mountainous parts of the principality, however, densities were only a tenth of those prevailing in Norfolk, 300 kilometres to the east.

Population densities in the most crowded parts of Norfolk, south Lincolnshire, Huntingdonshire and Cambridgeshire were double the English, four to five times the Welsh and seven times the Scottish averages and comparable to the most populous parts of southern Luxembourg, Lorraine and Tuscany, where rural densities likewise reached 60–70 per square kilometre.[77] Some of the most revealing analyses of rural society have been of manors in these most congested parts of England, where morcellation was rife, land markets active, and reliance upon credit widespread.[78] Only the most fertile, intensively cultivated, proto-industrialised and urbanised parts of the Low Countries sustained higher rural population densities. Thus, by the early fourteenth century in South Brabant, along with much of Liège, Hainaut and the French provinces of Artois and Picardy, population densities sometimes exceeded 100 per square kilometre, levels seemingly unmatched in England or anywhere else in Europe at that time except perhaps Lombardy in northern Italy.[79]

---

76   J. Howells, 'The countryside', in *Pembrokeshire county history, II, Medieval Pembrokeshire*, ed. R. F. Walker (Haverfordwest, 2002), pp. 401–25 (pp. 405–8).

77   N. J. G. Pounds, *An historical geography of Europe 450 BC–AD 1330* (Cambridge, 1973), p. 337.

78   Examples include: A. DeWindt, 'A peasant land market and its participants: King's Ripton, 1280–1400', *Midland History* 4 (1978), 142–59; B. M. S. Campbell, 'Population pressure, inheritance, and the land market in a fourteenth-century peasant community', in *Land, kinship and life-cycle*, ed. R. M. Smith (Cambridge, 1984), pp. 87–134; R. M. Smith, 'Families and their land in an area of partible inheritance: Redgrave, Suffolk 1260–1320', in *Land, kinship and life-cycle*, ed. Smith, pp. 135–95; J. Williamson, 'Norfolk: thirteenth century', in *The peasant land market in medieval England*, ed. P. D. A. Harvey (Oxford, 1984), pp. 31–105; E. Clark, 'The decision to marry in thirteenth- and early fourteenth-century Norfolk', *Medieval Studies* 49 (1987), 496–516; C. Briggs, *Credit and village society in fourteenth-century England* (Oxford, 2009).

79   Pounds, *Historical geography of Europe*, p. 332; B. van Bavel, *Manors and markets: economy and society in the Low Countries, 500–1600* (Oxford, 2010), p. 283. Intensive rice cultivation sustained substantially higher population densities in the Yangtze Delta of eastern China, averaging around 160 per square kilometre at the end of the Song era c.1290: S. Yoshinobu, *Sodai Konan keizaishi no kenkyu* [*A study of the economic history*

Changes in the population geography
of Great Britain 1290 to 1801

The marked east–west gradient in population densities that was such a conspicuous feature of both Scotland and England in 1290 had largely disappeared by 1801, when the first census at last allows a reasonably accurate reconstruction of the population geography of the whole of Great Britain.[80] By the latter date the populations of England, Wales and Scotland had more or less doubled (Table 2.1) and in the process, as comparison between Figures 2.3A and 2.3B reveals, the map of population had been redrawn. These changes were the cumulative net outcome of socially and geographically selective patterns of mortality and processes of family formation and migration, as individuals variously responded to the altered economic opportunities created by the rise of proto-industry, growth of the metropolis, establishment of capitalist agriculture, opening up of trans-Atlantic trade, establishment of overseas colonies and, eventually, advent of factory-based production. This profound reconfiguration of the country's population geography bears compelling witness to the scale and significance of the economic transformation achieved over these five centuries, to which a trebling of GDP per capita over the same period provides further powerful testimony (Figure 2.4).

Both developments belie the impression of stasis conveyed by the lack of any sustained improvement in the real wage rates paid to agricultural and building labourers, as the gains made during the late fourteenth and fifteenth centuries were largely lost during the sixteenth and early seventeenth centuries.[81] Wage rates for unskilled labouring work, however,

---

of Song-dynasty Jiangnan] (Tokyo, 1988), pp. 146 and 148 (we are grateful to Dr Ting Xu for this reference).

80   Lawton, 'Historical geography', p. 228; 'Population density (persons per hectare) in 1801 for district/unitary authority', http://www.visionofbritain.org.uk/atlas/data_map_page.jsp?data_theme=T_POP&data_rate=R_POP_DENS_H&data_year=1801&date_type=1Y&u_type=MOD_DIST (accessed 2 September 2014).

81   G. Clark, A farewell to alms: a brief economic history of the world (Princeton, NJ, 2007), advances a pessimistic verdict on English economic progress before 1800. L. Angeles, 'GDP per capita or real wages? Making sense of conflicting views on pre-industrial Europe', Explorations in Economic History 45 (2008), 147–63, explains the divergence between GDP per capita and real wage rates after c.1750. J. Hatcher, 'Unreal wages: long-run living standards and the "golden age" of the fifteenth century', in Commercial activity, markets and entrepreneurs in the middle ages: essays in honour of Richard Britnell, ed. B. Dodds and C. D. Liddy (Woodbridge, 2011), pp. 1–24, offers one possible explanation of the

Figure 2.3. The population of Great Britain in 1290 and 1801

A: 1290　　　　　　　　　　　　B: 1801

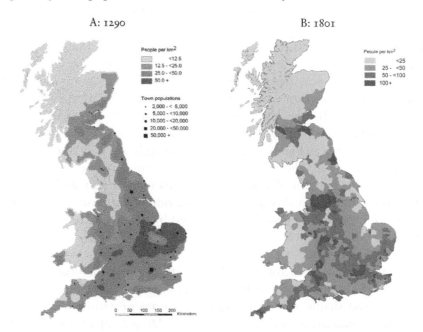

Sources: 1290: see text. 1801: R. W. Lawton, 'Historical geography: the industrial revolution', in *The British Isles: a systematic geography*, ed. J. Wreford Watson and J. B. Sissons (Edinburgh and London, 1964), pp. 221–44 (p. 228).

fail to capture the changes in employment structure taking place within the economy and associated growth of opportunities for augmenting household incomes through fuller engagement of household members in manufacturing and service activities.

In the late thirteenth century, England, and especially Wales and Scotland, had been relatively poor. Undeveloped agrarian economies and their respective population distributions consequently reflected the availability and quality of agricultural resources as mediated by the institutions that regulated access to land holdings. Thus, the highest rural population densities of over 60 per square kilometre occurred in regions not only well endowed with good arable land but also where, historically, free tenures, lax lordship, partible inheritance and, especially, active land

---

divergence between real wage rates and GDP per capita in the fifteenth century. Broadberry *et al.*, *British economic growth*, offers another.

Figure 2.4. English labourers' real wage rates and GDP per capita, 1275–1825

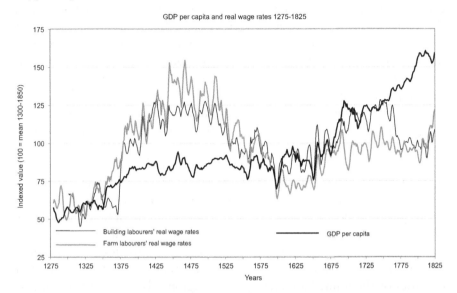

Sources: Building labourers' real wage rates: R. C. Allen, 'The Great Divergence in European wages and prices from the middle ages to the First World War', *Explorations in Economic History* 38 (2001), 411–47. Farm labourers' real wage rates: G. Clark, 'English prices and wages, 1209–1914', Global Price and Income History Group, University of California, Davis, 2006 (http://gpih.ucdavis.edu/Datafilelist.htm, accessed 2 September 2014). GDP per capita: Broadberry *et al.*, *British economic growth*.

markets together promoted maximisation of numbers on the land.[82] The manufacturing and service sectors as yet accounted for less than 40 per cent and perhaps as little as 30 per cent of employment.[83] Exports were mostly of unprocessed primary products – grain, hides, wool, lead and tin – and alien merchants handled the bulk of that trade.[84] Wealth was

---

82 Campbell, 'Agrarian problem'; C. T. Bekar and C. G. Reed, 'Land markets and inequality: evidence from medieval England', *European Review of Economic History* 17 (2013), 294–317.

83 S. N. Broadberry, B. M. S. Campbell and B. van Leeuwen, 'When did Britain industrialise? The sectoral distribution of the labour force and labour productivity in Britain, 1381–1851', *Explorations in Economic History* 50 (2013), 16–27.

84 B. M. S. Campbell, 'The sources of tradable surpluses: English agricultural exports 1250–1349', in *Cogs, cargoes and commerce: maritime bulk trade in northern Europe,*

highly polarised and the bottom third of all households lived a hand-to-mouth existence, subsisting on a bare-bones basket of consumables.[85] Five centuries later, agriculture employed less than a third of the labour force, the manufacturing and service sectors were both far more developed (affording greater earning opportunities for women), per capita national income had trebled and was rising strongly (Figure 2.4), and the transition to modern economic growth was well under way.[86] Fast population growth of 1.1 per cent per annum and steady GDP per capita growth of 0.5 per cent per annum were proceeding hand in hand.[87] The highest rural population densities of 50–200 per square kilometre were now associated with mining, proto-industrialisation, and the water-powered phase of factory production (Figure 2.3B). In the midlands and north, the new manufacturing towns of the steam-powered age were expanding apace and on the west coast, Glasgow, Liverpool and Bristol had emerged as major Atlantic ports serving dynamic and populous hinterlands. Their growth was however eclipsed by that of London, whose rise as both the capital of an expanded state and Europe's greatest international commercial entrepôt was writ large in the enhanced relative population densities of the immediate metropolitan region. Elsewhere, rural populations had been thinned as the advance of capitalist agriculture displaced smallholders from the land. The livelihoods of the most vulnerable were now protected by the poor law and a growing proportion of households were able to afford a respectability basket of consumables.[88]

1150–1400, ed. L. Berggren, N. Hybel and A. Landen (Toronto, 2002), pp. 1–30. Separate figures for denizen and alien exports are available from 1303–04: E. Carus-Wilson and O. Coleman, *England's export trade, 1275–1547* (Oxford, 1963); T. H. Lloyd, *Alien merchants in England in the high middle ages* (Brighton, 1982).

85   English households living below the poverty line and unable to afford a 'respectability' basket of consumables included those of most of the c.300,000 smallholders and c.240,000 cottagers and agricultural labourers, and almost all the c.160,000 non-agricultural labourers, rural craftsmen, paupers and vagrants, plus a majority of the c.50,000 miners, fishermen, sailors and men-at-arms. R. C. Allen, *The British industrial revolution in global perspective* (Cambridge, 2009), pp. 36–7, defines the 'respectability' and 'bare-bones' baskets of consumables.

86   Broadberry, Campbell and van Leeuwen, 'When did Britain industrialise?'.

87   Wrigley and Schofield, *Population history*, pp. 208–9; Broadberry *et al.*, *British economic growth*.

88   P. H. Lindert and J. G. Williamson, 'Revising England's social tables, 1688–1812', *Explorations in Economic History* 19 (1982), 385–408 (p. 388); R. C. Allen and J. L. Weisdorf, 'Was there an "industrious revolution" before the industrial revolution? An empirical exercise for England, c.1300–1830', *Economic History Review* 64 (2011), 715–29.

The elimination of rural congestion was one of the most notable developments that occurred between 1290 and 1801, with the result that in significant parts of the country rural populations actually fell. In the once bottom-heavy eastern English counties of Cambridgeshire, Huntingdonshire, Norfolk and Lincolnshire, population densities were substantially reduced and in 1801 were mostly below rather than above 50 per square kilometre (Figure 2.3B). Within these bread-basket counties, fewer but larger production units employed a smaller but more efficiently deployed workforce to produce significantly higher farm outputs both per unit area and per worker than those achieved by a combination of seigniorial and petty peasant producers in the middle ages.[89] The advance of agrarian capitalism, by promoting the engrossing rather than morcellation of holdings, had effectively dispossessed labour of land and thereby circumscribed opportunities for marriage and household formation.[90] Progressive elimination of common rights further diminished subsistence opportunities and reinforced active displacement of surplus population from the countryside by a combination of outmigration and emigration.

Another group of localities gained in population but by less than the national average. Often these supported densities of 50–75 per square kilometre by 1801, which were greater than those required by capitalist agriculture but less than those sustained by fully fledged capitalist industry. Typically these were regions which had thrived during the golden age of British proto-industrialisation, from the mid fifteenth to the mid eighteenth centuries, when manufacturing output had grown on average by 0.7 per cent per annum.[91] Handicraft production of textiles, leather goods, metal wares and pottery had boosted population densities in many regions relatively thinly peopled in the late thirteenth century, where the triad of cheap land, provisions and labour had subsidised the initial stages of manufacturing growth. Earnings from by-employments in turn boosted household incomes and helped perpetuate farm structures dominated by

89 B. M. S. Campbell and M. Overton, 'A new perspective on medieval and early modern agriculture: six centuries of Norfolk farming c.1250–c.1850', *Past and Present* 141 (1993), 38–105; L. Shaw-Taylor, 'The rise of agrarian capitalism and the decline of family farming in England', *Economic History Review* 65 (2012), 26–60.

90 J. Whittle, *The development of agrarian capitalism: land and labour in Norfolk 1440–1580* (Oxford, 2000).

91 P. Hudson, 'Proto-industrialization in England', in *European proto-industrialization*, ed. S. C. Ogilvie and M. Cerman (Cambridge, 1996), pp. 49–66; Broadberry *et al.*, *British economic growth*.

smallholdings. Demand for labour from successful industries attracted migrants and nurtured family formation whose legacies were the heightened population densities of the midland metalworking region and the cloth-working districts of East Anglia, the Weald, the west country, west Yorkshire and central Scotland (Figure 2.3B). Within these regions, occupational profiles were significantly more diversified than in areas of capitalist agriculture but in many cases were already narrowing dramatically under the impact of factory-based industrialisation.[92]

Finally, there were regions whose population densities had increased by more than the national average, often dramatically so, and whose growth was in many cases accelerating as a result of the centripetal forces of the industrial revolution.[93] Most, but not all, already supported densities in excess of the medieval maximum of 75 per square kilometre. Indeed, in the immediate environs of London, Bristol, Birmingham, Manchester, Edinburgh and Glasgow densities were at least twice as great. These were often actively industrialising regions, with, as in the case of the midlands, south Lancashire and west Yorkshire, and the central lowlands of Scotland, a long history of domestic manufacturing. Densities above 200 per square kilometre were symptomatic of the geographical concentration of factory production since 1782 made possible by the harnessing of steam power to rotary motion. The rise of these manufacturing centres, characteristically in areas with convenient access to cheap coal, drove fast-expanding regional economies which placed few obstacles in the path of high rates of natural increase other than the heightened mortality arising from overcrowded urban living conditions and dangerous industrial working conditions.[94] Greater Manchester is the clearest exemplar of these developments and almost nowhere was the demographic transformation between 1290 and 1801 as great: from a density of less than ten people per square kilometre, south Lancashire's population had grown

92   L. Shaw-Taylor, E. A. Wrigley, R. S. Davies, P. M. Kitson, G. Newton and A. E. M. Satchell, 'The occupational structure of England c.1710 to c.1871: work in progress', unpublished working paper, CAMPOP, 2010, available at http://www.hpss.geog.cam. ac.uk/research/projects/occupations/abstracts/ (accessed 29 July 2012). We are grateful for permission to cite this paper.

93   J. Stobart, *The first industrial region: north-west England c.1700–60* (Manchester, 2004).

94   R. W. Lawton, 'Population and society 1730–1914', in *An historical geography of England and Wales*, ed. Dodgshon and Butlin, 2nd edn (London, 1990), pp. 285–321 (pp. 296–301); E. A. Wrigley, 'English county populations in the later eighteenth century', *Economic History Review* 60 (2007), 35–69.

tenfold to well over 100 per square kilometre.[95] Metropolitan Middlesex and Surrey alone supported higher population densities.[96]

The metropolis grew twelvefold between 1290 and 1801 due to its enhanced political, administrative, financial, commercial, social and cultural importance as the capital of an enlarged realm. It achieved this, notwithstanding sometimes punitively high urban mortality rates, due to its magnetic attraction to migrants.[97] In fact, it was the sustained exodus of migrants to London that helped many of the country's demographically less dynamic regions shed excess numbers and maintain their equilibrium. Although the city was already exercising a powerful economic influence over much of south-eastern England by 1290, this was insufficient to elevate population densities within its immediately neighbouring counties much above average (Figure 2.2).[98] By 1801 this had ceased to be the case as the positive multiplier effects of a city approaching a million in population were felt throughout a greatly expanded hinterland.[99] Since the reign of Elizabeth I the city's growth had, of course, been facilitated by the shipping of 'seacoal' down the east coast from Newcastle.[100] A further manifestation of the capital's gathering gravitational attraction was, therefore, the build-up of population densities on the Northumberland and Durham coalfield to levels far above those prevailing in the late thirteenth century when coal had been mined on no more than a small scale for mostly local consumption (Figures 2.3A and 2.3B).[101]

Wales was the part of Great Britain least affected by all these developments and remained characterised by a thinly peopled, mountainous and pastoral interior fringed by higher densities in the north-west, the

95   Estimates for Lancashire's total population are: 1290–67,800 (this chapter, Table 2.4); 1377–43,100 (Broadberry *et al.*, *British economic growth*); 1600–183,700, 1700–232,500, 1750–317,200, 1801–703,100 (Wrigley, 'Rickman revisited', p. 721).

96   County densities calculated from Wrigley, 'Rickman revisited', p. 721.

97   Wrigley, 'Simple model', pp. 45–9; Wrigley and Schofield, *Population history*, pp. 166–70; J. Landers, *Death and the metropolis: studies in the demographic history of London, 1670–1830* (Cambridge, 1993).

98   Campbell *et al.*, *A medieval capital and its grain supply*.

99   Wrigley, 'Simple model'.

100   J. Hatcher, *The history of the British coal industry, I, Before 1700: towards the Age of Coal* (Oxford, 1993), pp. 39–47, 77–96 and 483–97.

101   Hatcher, *British coal industry*, pp. 72–7. S. Hipkin, 'The coastal metropolitan corn trade in later seventeenth-century England', *Economic History Review* 65 (2012), 220–55, considers the impact of the voracious demand for fodder crops generated by London's burgeoning overland trade.

Marches and south Wales. Prevailing population densities everywhere remained within the medieval range and nowhere exceeded 100 per square kilometre. In Scotland, too, the ancient contrast between the Highlands and Lowlands persisted, although by 1801 it was far more deeply etched, as industrialisation and urbanisation elevated densities in the more developed regions around Edinburgh and Glasgow to over 125 per square kilometre. At the same time, depopulation ensured that the Highlands retained their status as probably the most extensive area of sparse population in Great Britain, with densities ranging from 10 per square kilometre in Argyll down to 7 per square kilometre in Inverness and Ross and Cromarty, and barely 4 per square kilometre in Sutherland (Figures 2.3A and 2.3B). In England, too, the upland fastnesses of Bodmin Moor, Dartmoor, Exmoor, and especially the northern Pennines, together with the New Forest and Romney Marsh, all remained relatively empty of people.

By 1801, within the geographical constraints set by climate, topography, terrain and soils, Great Britain's population geography reflected above all the country's economic geography. Commercial agriculture, handicraft industries supplying national and international markets, concentrated urban demand, access to water power and fossil fuels, and predominant patterns of international trade all shaped the distribution of population as it had evolved over many generations and was now fast adjusting to industrial revolution.[102] In 1290 the range of economic influences was far narrower and their effects were more muted, except insofar as agricultural land quality exercised a general bearing upon the densities of population that could be supported. Rather, key demographic decisions to marry, remain celibate, or migrate were powerfully shaped by an array of historically entrenched institutional factors which affected access to land, occupational and geographical freedom of movement and, thus, the ability to form new households. These included the structure of lordship as it was mapped onto the population via estates and manors, the personal status of individuals and specifically whether they were free or servile, the nature and divisibility of tenures and competitiveness of entry fines and rents, the strength of custom and opportunities for exploiting common rights, and whether or not the land in question was subject to forest law.[103]

102 J. Langton and R. J. Morris (eds), *Atlas of industrializing Britain 1780–1914* (London and New York, 1986).
103 On lordship, manors and estates see: E. A. Kosminsky, *Studies in the agrarian history of England in the thirteenth century*, trans. R. Kisch, ed. R. H. Hilton (Oxford, 1956). On manors, free versus villein tenures, and common rights and rents: Campbell and Bartley,

The strong path-dependency element to many of these distinctively medieval institutions explains why in England the distribution of population in 1290 (Figure 2.2) was still, in broad outline, much the same as that in 1086, with the highest densities in a broad wedge of eastern counties and lowest in the south-west and north-west. Institutional factors also explain many of the localised discontinuities in the distribution of population between these two dates, as colonising areas of weak lordship and predominantly free tenures attracted migrants in quest of land from manors where the supply of holdings was tightly regulated.[104] The rapid growth of population in the hundred of Stoneleigh in Warwickshire's forested district of Arden is a classic example of this type of development.[105] In a pattern repeated in many other parts of the country, coexistence of smallholding, local woodland and pastoral resources, and an open social structure meant that this area saw early development of proto-industries, as manufacturing fastened onto excess rural labour.[106] The institutional fabric of medieval society thus shaped economic and demographic developments for centuries to come.

Towards a comparative historical population geography of Great Britain

Tracking the successive stages by which Britain's environmentally and institutionally bound population geography gave way to one in which economic influences were uppermost is a task for the future. Modern technology, especially GIS, enables far more sophisticated spatial analysis

Eve of the Black Death. On tenures and rents: J. Kanzaka, 'Villein rents in thirteenth-century England: an analysis of the Hundred Rolls of 1279–80', *Economic History Review* 55 (2002), 593–618. On royal forests: C. R. Young, *The royal forests of medieval England* (Leicester, 1979).

104   J. Z. Titow, 'Some differences between manors and their effects on the condition of the peasant in the thirteenth century', *Agricultural History Review* 10 (1962), 1–13. The once almost empty Fenland attracted significant numbers of migrants from the surrounding 'uplands': H. E. Hallam, 'Population density in medieval Fenland', *Economic History Review* 14 (1961), 71–81.

105   J. B. Harley, 'Population trends and agriculture developments from the Warwickshire Hundred Rolls of 1279', *Economic History Review* 11 (1958), 8–18.

106   A. Watkins, 'The woodland economy of the forest of Arden in the later middle ages', *Midland History* 18 (1993), 19–36; V. H. T. Skipp, *An ecological case study of the forest of Arden 1570–1674* (Cambridge, 1978).

than the laborious manual choropleth mapping undertaken at a scale no finer than the hundred or registration district by Darby, Lawton, and their collaborators and students. As demonstrated here, GIS also offers a method of extending analysis beyond England to include Wales and Scotland, with their often very different sources of evidence. Yet, for the time being, Darby and Lawton's fundamental work remains to be superseded. Systematic replotting of the vill-level population data contained in the Domesday Survey of 1086 is long overdue and although detailed mapping of the first census of 1801 is well advanced it is not yet complete for the whole of Great Britain.[107] The value of both exercises would be enhanced if they were undertaken within a common GIS capable of accommodating other equivalent cross-sectional data, of which those for 1755/61 are a prime candidate.[108] This would permit mapping and analysis on a strictly consistent and comparable basis in terms of class intervals, territorial units and boundaries, or, in the case of potential mapping, the points and kernel shapes and radii employed. Temporal comparison will then be possible using the precise tool of map overlay rather than crude device of visual comparison.[109] This is a logical extension of what Darby, in a very different technological age, was attempting to achieve.

107   Mapping (per square mile) of the parish-level returns for England and Wales is currently in progress at CAMPOP, 'The population geography of England and Wales c.1379–1911', Figure 4b, http://www.hpss.geog.cam.ac.uk/research/projects/occupations/ englandwales1379-1911/ (accessed 30 July 2012).

108   Combining Webster's Scottish census of 1755 with Wrigley's reworking of Rickman's estimates for England in 1761, if extended to include Wales, would provide a detailed picture of the distribution of Great Britain's population of around eight million on the eve of the great changes brought about by the industrial revolution: A. J. Youngson, 'Alexander Webster and his "Account of the number of people in Scotland in the year 1755"', Population Studies 15 (1961), 198–200; M. Anderson, 'Guesses, estimates and adjustments: Webster's 1755 "Census" of Scotland revisited again', Journal of Scottish Historical Studies 31 (2011), 26–45; Wrigley, 'English county populations'; M. Satchell, L. Shaw-Taylor and E. A. Wrigley, 'The population density of England by hundred, 1761', http://www.hpss.geog.cam.ac.uk/research/projects/occupations/englandwales1379-1911/ figure6/figure6a-small.html (accessed 25 July 2012). At CAMPOP, P. Kitson has also been engaged in mapping English population at a parish level using data from the Compton Census of 1676 and hearth tax returns of 1670: http://www.hpss.geog.cam.ac.uk/research/ projects/occupations/englandwales1379-1911/figure4/figure4a-small.html (accessed 25 July 2012).

109   For an example of the application of this technique see: K. C. Bartley and B. M. S. Campbell, 'Inquisitiones Post Mortem, GIS, and the creation of a land-use map of pre Black Death England', Transactions in GIS 2 (1997), 333–46.

3

Mobility and Mortality: How Place of Origin Affected the Life Chances of Late Medieval Scholars at Winchester College and New College Oxford

REBECCA OAKES

Detailed examination of factors affecting mortality patterns among the medieval population of England has long presented a challenge to the historian. In the period preceding the commencement of parish records in 1538, life events were not systematically recorded so as to provide adequate data from which the demographic regime of medieval England can be accurately reconstructed. However, a range of sources has survived which enable analysis of certain demographic characteristics among particular communities or groups.[1] The payments of customary fines recorded in manorial court rolls, for example, have enabled the examination of marriage patterns, illegitimacy and mortality within particular communities, albeit within the constraints of available data.[2]

---

1 See for example M. Ecclestone, 'Mortality of rural landless men before the Black Death: the Glastonbury head-tax lists', *Local Population Studies* 63 (1999), 6–29; T. H. Hollingsworth, 'A note on the medieval longevity of the secular peerage 1350–1500', *Population Studies* 29 (1975), 155–9; J. T. Rosenthal, 'Mediaeval longevity and the secular peerage, 1350–1500', *Population Studies* 27 (1973), 287–93; J. C. Russell, *British medieval population* (Albuquerque, 1948); S. L. Thrupp, 'The problem of replacement-rates in late medieval English population', *Economic History Review* 18 (1965), 101–19.
2 See for example L. R. Poos, *A rural society after the Black Death: Essex 1350–1525* (Cambridge, 1991), pp. 89–130; Z. Razi, *Life, marriage and death in a medieval parish: economy, society and demography in Halesowen, 1270–1400* (Cambridge, 1980). For discussion of the problems encountered in the use of manorial court rolls see in particular L. R. Poos, Z. Razi and R. M. Smith, 'The population history of medieval English villages: a debate on the use of manor court records', in *Medieval society and the manor court*, ed. Z. Razi and R. M. Smith (Oxford, 1996), pp. 298–368.

Medieval mortality in particular has also been investigated through the examination of closed communities, such as monasteries. Case studies have focused upon institutions with good surviving records, which allow the individuals resident within them to be followed, usually from the point of their recruitment until their deaths. This has enabled detailed examination and analysis of mortality rates and levels of life expectancy among the communities of monks at Christ Church Canterbury, Westminster Abbey and Durham Cathedral Priory across the period c.1390 to c.1540.[3] The advantage of such studies is that the size of the populations within which deaths are identified, and the approximate ages of the individuals within these groups, are more easily determined, making analyses of mortality and life expectancy for such samples more secure.

This chapter presents another such study of an institutional community, in this instance following medieval scholars through their educational careers at Winchester College and New College Oxford, and beyond into their post-university employment.[4] William of Wykeham, Bishop of Winchester, founded 'St Mary's College of Winchester in Oxford' (known as New College) in 1379 and its sister institution 'St Mary's College of Winchester near Winchester' (Winchester College) three years later. The two colleges had multiple purposes, acting as chantry foundations to provide prayers and masses for the benefit of Wykeham's soul after death, as well as being charitable foundations to provide education and training to seventy 'poor scholars'.[5] He intended that young boys between the ages of eight and eighteen would receive an education in grammar at Winchester College before continuing to New College to pursue their university education.[6] Places at New College were restricted to those who

3   B. F. Harvey, *Living and dying in England 1100–1540: the monastic experience* (Oxford, 1993); J. Hatcher, 'Mortality in the fifteenth century: some new evidence', *Economic History Review* 39 (1986), 19–38; J. Hatcher, A. Piper and D. Stone, 'Monastic mortality: Durham Priory 1395–1529', *Economic History Review* 59 (2006), 667–87.

4   R. H. A. Oakes, 'Mortality and life expectancy: Winchester College and New College Oxford, c.1393–c.1540' (unpublished Ph.D. thesis, University of Southampton, 2009).

5   W. A. Harwood, 'The College as school: the case of Winchester College', in *The late medieval English college and its context*, ed. C. Burgess and M. Heale (Woodbridge, 2008), pp. 230–52; G. Fitch Lytle, 'The social origins of Oxford students in the late middle ages: New College, c.1380–c.1510', in *The universities in the late middle ages*, ed. J. Ijsewijn and J. Paquet (Louvain, 1978), pp. 426–54.

6   See *Statutes of the colleges of Oxford: with royal patents of foundation injunctions of visitors, and catalogues of documents relating to the University, preserved in the Public Record Office, printed by desire of Her Majesty's Commissioners for Inquiring into the*

had first attended Winchester College for a period of at least one year and had proved themselves to be academically capable of further study. Those going on to New College had to do so by the time they were nineteen, although in most instances progression to New College occurred when boys were sixteen or seventeen years of age. Ultimately Wykeham intended that these scholars would supply a need for suitably trained recruits to enter the ranks of the clergy that had been greatly depleted by plague and war.[7] The emphasis upon education ensured the survival of these two institutions at the Reformation, and they have continued to function as educational establishments to this day. As a result of their unbroken operation a remarkable amount of medieval source material has survived, including admission registers, hall book accounts and details of student deaths or departures.[8] The combination of these materials has enabled scholars to be followed through their educational career at the two colleges. A range of biographical source materials have also been used to provide details of their subsequent careers, along with dates of death or last observation for the 2,692 individuals enrolled at Winchester College across the period 1393–1540.[9]

The methodology employed to study the scholars of these two communities is most closely analogous with that applied to the monastic datasets, and mortality rates and levels of life expectancy have been calculated for this population group in a previous study.[10] The unusual survival of data relating to the place of origin of these scholars also provides a

State of the University of Oxford, 3 vols (London, 1853), vol. 1, New College Statutes, rubric 2.

7   W. J. Courtenay, 'The effect of the Black Death on English higher education', Speculum 55 (1980), 709–14; R. L. Storey, 'The foundation and the medieval College 1379–1530', in New College Oxford 1379–1979, ed. J. Buxton and P. Williams (Oxford, 1979), pp. 3–43 (pp. 6–7).

8   These include WCA 21490a Registrum Primum, 1393–1686; WCA 22812–71 Hall books, 1395–1519; NCA 9654 Liber Albus, 1399–1450; NCA 9746–9 Registrum Protocollorum, 1450–1578 (4 vols).

9   Sources include A. B. Emden, A biographical register of the University of Oxford to AD 1500, 3 vols (Oxford, 1957–59); A. B. Emden, A biographical register of the University of Oxford AD 1501–1540 (Oxford, 1974); J. Foster, Alumni Oxonienses: the members of the University of Oxford 1500–1714, 4 vols (Oxford, 1891–92); ODNB online. See Oakes, 'Mortality and life expectancy', pp. 17–35 for a fuller description of the sources used.

10   Oakes, 'Mortality and life expectancy'; R. H. A. Oakes, 'Adolescent mortality at Winchester College 1393–1540: new evidence for medieval mortality and methodological considerations for historical demography', Local Population Studies 88 (2012), 12–32.

unique opportunity to explore the relationships between place of origin, geographical mobility and longevity for the late medieval period. The analysis of these data in particular forms the basis of this chapter.

The importance of place

The aforementioned studies of monastic communities highlight the possibility that place of origin may have affected the survival and life chances of the men recruited to the three urban monastic institutions.[11] Indeed, this is a logical hypothesis given what we know about early modern populations and the links between increasing density of settlement and associated increases in mortality rates.[12] As well as enabling the more rapid transfer of infectious diseases such as plague, problems with sanitation and water supply may also have been more frequently encountered in urban centres. While many of the diseases associated with urban living are not ones to which lifelong immunity can be acquired, it might be reasonably assumed that those who survived a childhood in such conditions were perhaps among the stronger or healthier members of the urban population. Surviving childhood in an area of high-density population might thus demonstrate the resilience of an individual, which might increase their chances of surviving their later years of life in a similar environment. Individuals who had grown up in areas of lower density population, however, might find movement into such surroundings more detrimental to their health, through exposure to pathogens they had not previously encountered or demonstrated the strength to resist.[13]

11   Harvey, *Living and dying*, p. 143; Hatcher, 'Mortality', p. 36; Hatcher, Piper and Stone, 'Monastic mortality', p. 682.
12   See for example A. Hinde, *England's population: a history since the Domesday survey* (London, 2003), p. 195; R. M. Smith, 'Plagues and peoples: the long demographic cycle 1250–1670', in *The peopling of Britain: the shaping of a human landscape*, ed. P. Slack and R. Ward (Oxford, 2002), pp. 177–210 (pp. 197 and 202–3); E. A. Wrigley and R. S. Schofield, *The population history of England, 1541–1871: a reconstruction* (London, 1981), pp. 165–6 and 415; E. A. Wrigley, R. S. Davies, J. E. Oeppen and R. S. Schofield, *English population history from family reconstruction, 1580–1837* (Cambridge, 1997), pp. 201–6.
13   See for example R. Davenport, L. Schwarz and J. Boulton, 'The decline of adult smallpox in eighteenth-century London', *Economic History Review* 64 (2011), 1289–314. They suggest that a decline in adult smallpox mortality in eighteenth-century London might in part be attributed to increasing endemicisation of smallpox outside of the city,

The interpretations of the monastic data suggest that recruits to the urban monasteries would have encountered such a scenario, and that when entering such environments, those originating from the neighbouring countryside might have been more at risk, and may plausibly have 'suffered from a lack of immunity to urban ailments'.[14]

The mortality rates and life expectancy profiles for the three monasteries in part perhaps reflect the relative severity of risk from their local urban disease pools. The monks of Durham, a number of whom lived in external rural cells, experienced lower rates of mortality and had noticeably higher levels of life expectancy than the monks at Canterbury and Westminster. At Canterbury, where there was a great through traffic of pilgrims and traders, peaks in mortality rates were more severe and life expectancy was appreciably lower. The monks of Westminster, close to the capital and to the seat of government, fared least well. They experienced the highest rates of mortality and lowest levels of life expectancy, and were certainly disadvantaged by their proximity to London.[15] This situation may have been aggravated at Westminster in the later part of the fifteenth century, when age at profession fell to ensure that demand for new recruits was met. Novices may subsequently have spent less time in the almonry school preparing for their profession as monks, and consequently had less exposure to the local disease environment before their full admission to the monastery.[16] This may explain observed increases in mortality at Westminster among the younger age groups of monks in particular, and in turn might go some way to explaining the precipitous drop in life expectancy from the mid fifteenth century.[17]

Investigation of the possible relationship between place of origin and

and hence prior exposure to the disease at younger ages within the London hinterland from which migrants were generally drawn.

14 Hatcher, Piper and Stone, 'Monastic mortality', p. 682.

15 Hatcher, Piper and Stone, 'Monastic mortality', p. 675. Harvey notes that the mortality profile of Westminster, and the years of apparent epidemic disease there, do not always seem to correlate with those identified for London in J. M. W. Bean, 'Plague, population and economic decline in England in the later middle ages', *Economic History Review* 15 (1963), 423–37 (see Harvey, *Living and dying*, p. 142). Bean used contemporary chronicles and occasional references found in governmental records to compile his list of plague epidemics (Bean, 'Plague', pp. 427–31).

16 R. Bowers, 'The almonry schools of the English monasteries c.1265–1540' in *Monasteries and society in medieval Britain*, ed. B. Thompson (Stamford, 1999), pp. 177–222; Harvey, *Living and dying*, pp. 74–5, 121–2 and 143.

17 Harvey, *Living and dying*, pp. 127–9, 138–41, figure IV.5 and appendix IV.

longevity within an urban environment has been difficult to undertake for
the monastic samples. In these communities, place of origin of members
can often only be inferred from locative surnames, and caution is needed
in this respect.[18] By the period of this study there is good reason to believe
that surnames had become more fixed, and that locative surnames may
have been retained by families long after they had migrated from the place
to which the surname referred.[19] However, investigation of a possible
link between place of origin and movement into an urban environment
is possible using the Winchester College dataset, as the place of origin
of scholars was systematically recorded as an item of information in its
own right. This allows more secure analysis of the impact of place of
origin on life expectancy, and testing of the hypothesis that those from
outside of the urban environment in which the colleges were situated were
more likely to succumb to 'urban' diseases. The analyses presented here
are limited to investigating whether deaths at Winchester College or New
College Oxford were more frequently observed among those who had not
originated from similar urban environments than among those who had
previously experienced living in such conditions.

The Winchester data

The 2,692 scholars enrolled at Winchester College in the period 1393–1540
have been followed through Wykeham's educational system, and beyond
into their post-Oxford employment.[20] Place of origin, along with details
relating to age and other distinguishing personal information, has proved a
valuable tool in ensuring more accurate record linkage between individuals
with the same or similar names who appear in different record sets. Even
within the medieval documents themselves, the colleges frequently used a
scholar's place of origin as a means of distinguishing him from others of
the same or similar names.

   In 1486, Richard Smyth was admitted to Winchester College. His time at
Winchester and New College can be traced through the numerous archival
records that have survived at these two institutions. Indeed, the records

18   J. Greatrex, 'Who were the monks of Rochester?', in *Medieval art, architecture and
archaeology at Rochester*, ed. T. Ayers and T. Tatton-Brown (Leeds, 2006), pp. 205–17;
E. H. Pearce, *The monks of Westminster* (Cambridge, 1916).
19   Harvey, *Living and dying*, p. 75.
20   Oakes, 'Mortality and life expectancy'; Oakes, 'Adolescent mortality'.

are so good that his attendance at Winchester can be attested on an almost weekly basis, through reference to the college hall books.[21] These books were compiled by the fellows of the college, and listed the names of all those eating in hall in order to track expenditure on food. Richard Smyth's first appearance in the dining hall was recorded in the first week of the fourth term, sometime around the last week of June.[22] At the time of his admission, three other scholars at Winchester College shared his surname. To avoid confusion this group of boys were frequently distinguished by their seniority, and referred to in the hall books as Smyth *minimus*, Smyth *minor*, Smyth *major* and Smyth *maximus*.[23] However, on occasion, these boys were also distinguished from one another by reference to their place of origin; so we find Smyth of Adderbury, Smyth of Devizes, Smyth of Heyford and Smyth of Henley.

This example demonstrates how place of origin can be used as a means of distinguishing between individuals with the same, or similar, names particularly for the purposes of record linkage. However, the recording of place of origin for scholars enrolled at Winchester College and New College Oxford went beyond being a mere tool to differentiate between those with similar names. Indeed this information formed one of the key criteria for determining which scholars were eligible for admission, and in what order they were to be admitted. An election was held annually to determine the names of those to be admitted to Winchester College and New College Oxford over the coming year to fill vacancies as they arose, with these lists of names recorded on an election roll.[24] All potential scholars had to demonstrate a required level of academic ability, fall below a designated level of income, meet the age criteria for admission, and not be suffering from any illness or condition that might prevent them from taking holy orders.[25] From the pool of eligible candidates, Wykeham's statutes gave preference to scholars originating from estates held by the colleges, followed by those from the diocese of Winchester, and then to those from a range of counties in a specified order. The counties were Oxfordshire, Berkshire, Wiltshire, Somerset, Buckinghamshire, Essex,

21 WCA 22812–71 Hall books, 1395–1519.
22 WCA 22851 Hall book, 1486.
23 WCA 22851 Hall book, 1486.
24 WCA 21587–92, Election rolls (various dates).
25 T. F. Kirby, *Annals of Winchester College from its foundation in 1382 to the present time* (London, 1892), appendix XI, 'The statutes', Rubric 2, pp. 457–8; N. Orme, *Medieval schools: from Roman Britain to Renaissance England* (Yale, 2006), p. 225.

Middlesex, Dorset, Kent, Sussex and Cambridgeshire, and after these, 'any other parts of the realm'.[26]

Only six election rolls have survived for Winchester College from the late medieval period.[27] However, the importance given to the place of origin of scholars for their admission to both colleges meant that this piece of information was also usually recorded at their admission to each institution.[28] A place of origin has thereby been accurately identified for 1,999 of the 2,692 scholars in this sample (74 per cent). A further 166 scholars (6 per cent) had a place of origin recorded, but the information given was not adequate to allow it to be distinguished from other places of similar or identical name. One example of this problem is Thomas Cheyney, admitted in 1501: while we know that he came from Houghton, the county of his origin is not stated in the documents. He could, therefore, have originated from Houghton in Hampshire or Houghton in Devon. In the case of the remaining 527 scholars (20 per cent), place of origin was either omitted from the documentary records, or illegible through damage or deterioration of the document.

The data regarding place of origin has been standardised to modern Ordnance Survey nomenclature and spellings, and linked to six-figure national grid references.[29] In total, 663 unique places of origin were accurately identified among the sample group. Figure 3.1 plots these locations and shows the diverse geographical spread of scholars by their stated place of origin. As might be expected from the aforementioned recruitment preferences, these locations are predominantly within the southern counties of England. There is, however, a wide scattering of the data into the midlands, as well as a couple of named locations further to the north and in the east of England. There was also one recruit (not shown in Figure 3.1) who came to Winchester from as far afield as Calais, which at that time was held by the English.

The plotted distribution of origins in Figure 3.1 is reassuring in terms of

26   Kirby, *Annals*, appendix XI, 'The statutes', Rubric 2, p. 457; Orme, *Medieval schools*, p. 226. The counties listed were those in which the colleges held estates, roughly in order of their value. Note the absence of Hampshire in this list, which fell within the diocese of Winchester and hence had already been accounted for higher up in the order of preference.
27   WCA 21587–92, Election rolls. The surviving rolls are for the years 1408, 1410, 1413, 1441, 1496 and 1508.
28   See admission records in WCA 21490a Registrum Primum, 1393–1686; NCA 9654 Liber Albus, 1399–1450; NCA 9746–9 Registrum Protocollorum, 1450–1578.
29   I would like to thank Dr Max Satchell of CAMPOP for guidance with the GIS mapping software. His time and patience are greatly appreciated.

Figure 3.1. Map showing the places from which scholars were recruited to
Winchester College

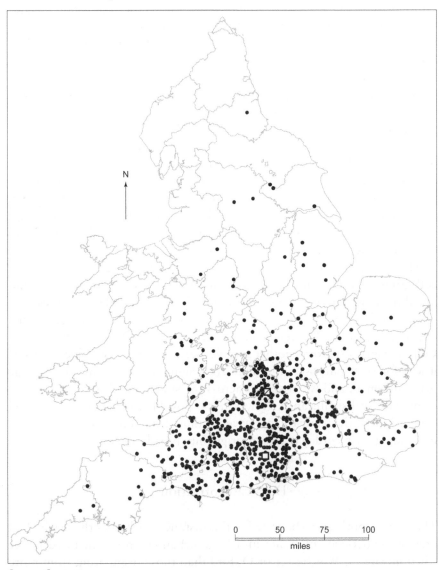

Source: See text.

Note: The location of Winchester is marked with an open square and that of Oxford with
a hatched square. Both of these cities were also the place of origin of a number of scholars
recruited to the college.

data validation. There is no apparent clustering in major towns, as might be expected if the nearest urban centre was being recorded for convenience, rather than an exact place of origin. Those scholars who did state a major town or city as their place of origin, such as London, Bristol or Winchester for example, frequently gave the parish from which they originated. This extra level of precision suggests that they were indeed coming from these urban centres rather than simply giving the name of their nearest major town.

Given that the statutes gave preference to those from particular areas, it is conceivable that an element of fabrication may have occurred if families wanted to get their son into Winchester College, for example by claiming to come from a college estate close to the place in which they actually lived. This might again have led to geographical clustering around college estates. However, the data plotted in Figure 3.1 also diverge from the pattern that would be expected if scholars had only been admitted from these estates.[30] It may well have been the case that the local parish priest or lord was required to support the application of potential scholars, and that details were thereby supplied accurately.

The data presented in Figure 3.1 demonstrate that recruitment to the colleges was from a wide area, and that scholars were drawn from beyond just those places to which preference was given in the college statutes.

It would be impossible to test whether those scholars originating from any one specific place had better chances of survival when moving to Winchester College than those from another specific locale. The data available are insufficient for such purposes: the numbers originating from any one specific place are small, and when spread across the study period would no longer be of statistical significance. However, it is possible to make a more general comparison of the relative experiences of those from different types of place by dividing the recorded places of origin into broad categories.

Data categorization

The basic hypothesis to be tested in this instance is whether those who had previous experience of living in a large urban environment fared better when moving to Winchester or Oxford than those originating from more

---

30 For details regarding the location of college-owned estates see J. H. Harvey, 'Introduction', in *Winchester College muniments*, ed. S. Himsworth, 3 vols (Chichester, 1976), pp. vii–xvii and F. W. Steer, *The archives of New College, Oxford: a catalogue* (London, 1974).

rural locales. For the purposes of testing this hypothesis, the different places of origin given by scholars in the records have been grouped into categories that reflect the type and nature of the settlements. However, defining these categories is not a straightforward task.

The distinction between urban and rural settlements is by no means clear for this period, and the characteristics of different settlement types have been the subject of much research and debate.[31] Legal status, for example, is a misleading guide as to what constituted a town or urban centre in late medieval England. Many places enjoyed the legal status of 'borough' during this period, but did not develop into urbanised areas, while conversely some undoubtedly urban centres never acquired this legal status.[32] Westminster is one example of the latter, which was under the governance of the abbot and monks of Westminster until the Reformation.[33] Despite its undoubtedly urban characteristics Westminster would thereby be excluded from the category of urban centres if only those places with legal borough status were to be included in that group. Contemporary terminology can be similarly misleading, and it is not possible to rely upon medieval terms such as 'vill' in order to identify towns, as this term could also be employed to describe places seemingly lacking in urban characteristics.[34] Legal status and contemporary description therefore seem inappropriate as methods of categorisation in this context, as these factors fail to define adequately the characteristics of a location that might have impacted upon the health of its inhabitants and their potential longevity.

A more appropriate and relatively straightforward measure to use in this instance is the relative size of the population within the different settlements. It is possible to divide the settlements into broad categories using collated quantitative data on population derived from the 1377 poll tax to enable simple comparisons of likely levels of environmental risk.[35]

31 See for example, G. Astill and A. Grant (eds), *The countryside of medieval England* (Oxford, 1988); C. Dyer (ed.), *The self-contained village? The social history of rural communities, 1250–1900* (Hatfield, 2007); K. Giles and C. Dyer (eds), *Town and country in the middle ages: contrasts, contacts and interconnections, 1100–1500* (Leeds, 2005); D. M. Palliser (ed.), *The Cambridge urban history of Britain, 1: 600–1540* (Cambridge, 2000).

32 C. Dyer, 'Small towns 1270–1540', in *Cambridge urban history of Britain*, ed. Palliser, pp. 505–38 (p. 505).

33 G. Rosser, *Medieval Westminster 1200–1540* (Oxford, 1989), p. 226.

34 C. Dyer, 'Small towns', p. 505.

35 A. Dyer, 'Appendix: ranking lists of English medieval towns', in *Cambridge urban history of Britain*, ed. Palliser, pp. 747–70; W. G. Hoskins, *Local history in England* (London, 1959), pp. 174–8.

Examination of the 1377 poll tax data has led to the places of origin of scholars given in the Winchester College records being divided into four main categories: London, greater towns, provincial towns and what, for convenience, will be termed 'rural' settlements. London was unique among English cities of the time for its size, density of population and its role as a major centre of both domestic and international trade and commerce.[36] In total, only 123 scholars were enrolled from the metropolis, but they were placed into a separate category to allow for specific analysis of the experiences of this group.

Those defined as the category of 'greater towns' comprise the twenty-three places listed as such by Kermode in *The Cambridge urban history of Britain*.[37] These greater towns had a taxpaying population in excess of 1,600 people at the time of the 1377 poll tax.[38] Their inclusion in this group is, however, based upon more than just the size of their population. Kermode also suggests that these towns were:

> distinguishable from market towns by the scale and intensity of their urbanity: physical size and appearance, complex internal economic and social structures, sophisticated government and regional significance.[39]

The more detailed descriptions of such places indicate environments in which people were 'living cheek-by-jowl', and where the proximity of dwellings to sites of manufacture and trade resulted in 'dirty and crowded conditions'.[40] Their regional significance may also have contributed to a greater degree of communication with other settlements and a greater through traffic of people. It is worth noting that both Winchester and Oxford appear within this list: according to the poll tax data, Winchester had a population of around 2,500 taxpayers in 1377 making it the

36   C. M. Barron, 'London 1300–1540', in *Cambridge urban history of Britain*, ed. Palliser, pp. 395–440 (p. 395).

37   J. Kermode, 'The greater towns 1300–1540', in *Cambridge urban history of Britain*, ed. Palliser, pp. 441–66 (pp. 442–3, see tab. 18.1). Edinburgh, also listed by Kermode, is excluded from this figure as college recruitment took place only from within the realm of England during this period.

38   A poll tax return for Chester does not survive. Kermode includes it within the list of greater towns, although its estimated population in Dyer, 'Ranking lists', is lower than for the rest of the 'greater towns' at somewhere between 1,178 and 1,340 taxpayers.

39   Kermode, 'The greater towns', p. 441. These factors may contribute to the inclusion of Chester within Kermode's list.

40   Kermode, 'The greater towns', p. 456.

fourteenth largest settlement in England by this measure; Oxford had a similarly sized population of 2,357 taxpayers and was ranked as the sixteenth largest settlement.

The third grouping includes all other settlements listed by A. Dyer in the rankings of provincial towns based upon their taxpaying populations in the 1377 poll tax data (other than those already assigned to the category of greater towns).[41] The size and relative regional importance of these provincial towns are highly variable, and there may be good reason to break this group down further for future analysis. For example, Southampton, a significant port town engaged in international trade with a taxpaying population in 1377 of 1,152, is unlikely to be a fair comparison with Writtle in Essex, with its much smaller community of 600 taxpayers.[42] However, for the purposes of the present study it was decided to leave all of these provincial towns in one group.

The fourth category, which for convenience has been termed 'rural', includes any place that is not listed in A. Dyer's provincial town rankings for 1377, and thereby falls below the level of Sheffield, with its 555 taxpayers. The designation of 'rural' is perhaps misleading in this context, as the group inevitably includes a fair number of places that might be better defined as small towns.[43] Again, the issue of where the dividing line should lie between places of different size is obscure. At what point does a provincial town become a small town? How do some of these small towns differ from villages, and indeed how do villages vary in terms of their settlement type and networks of trade and communication?[44] Without detailed qualitative examination it is impossible to divide the data presented here into more precise units. It should be noted that the 166 scholars mentioned earlier for whom a place of origin could not be accurately identified are included within this group. Although their place of origin could not be identified accurately enough for inclusion in Figure 3.1, usually due to the omission of the county in which their place of origin was located, none of the settlements mentioned in these instances could have been confused with those specified by Kermode or A. Dyer in the town ranking lists used above.

41 Dyer, 'Ranking lists', pp. 758–60.
42 Dyer, 'Ranking lists', p. 759.
43 Dyer, 'Small towns'. C. Dyer, for example, suggests that small towns could be arbitrarily defined as containing between 300 and 2,000 inhabitants, which would put some of the provincial towns within this category. Such alternative definitions form the basis of continuing research.
44 See for example the discussions in Giles and Dyer (eds), *Town and country*.

A final category into which scholars have been placed is that of
'unknown' origin. This comprises the 527 individuals mentioned above for
whom place of origin was either not recorded or illegible. Given the size of
this group, it is worth highlighting that the data analyses that follow might
be significantly altered if these individuals fell disproportionately within
one of the other previously mentioned categories. While it is important
to bear this caveat in mind, it seems unlikely that this would be the case.
Illegibility caused by damage or deterioration of the documents is relatively
random in its nature and might equally affect individuals from any place
of origin. Omission of information often affected a whole intake year,
perhaps with the scribe intending to return to the list of names at a later
date to insert the relevant details. Annual cohorts of recruits usually came
from a variety of backgrounds, and the annual breakdown of recruitment
across the broad categories remained fairly similar to that of the study
period as a whole. It is assumed, therefore, that the individuals categorised
as 'unknowns' are a random and representative subsample of the whole
study group, rather than one of the other categories in particular.

The categories designated here suffice for the purposes of this
study, which primarily seeks to examine whether individuals from an
environment similar to that of Winchester or Oxford fared better when
moving into those urban centres than did individuals from outside of the
group of greater towns. The inclusion of a division between provincial
towns and other smaller units provides a means of testing for any
difference between size of settlement and possible variation in experiences. It is likely that the settlements will represent a continuum of a range
of characteristics, and that these characteristics will have varied over time
and across different geographical regions, making simple classification
into types problematic.[45]

Mortality analyses

A number of simple tests were devised in order to assess the hypothesis
that those from outside of urban centres similar in nature to Winchester
or Oxford may have fared less well in terms of life chances than scholars

---

45 I would like to thank Professor Chris Dyer for discussing this issue with me, and for
sharing his insights into definitions of small towns within some of the southern counties
of England relevant to my research.

moving to those locations from similar types of settlement. These tests comprised:

1. Analysis of deaths at Winchester College, to determine if they more commonly occurred among any particular group of scholars;
2. Analysis of deaths at New College Oxford, to see if they more commonly occurred among any particular group of scholars;
3. Analysis of age at last observation, to see if any particular group of scholars were more commonly observed exceeding the estimated average life expectancy for the sample.

Deaths at Winchester College

Of the 2,692 individuals tracked over the course of the study period, 128 were observed to have died while they were resident as scholars at Winchester College. These deaths have been broken down into categories according to the place of origin of those scholars. These data are given in Table 3.1, along with the total number of scholars from the sample group that fall into each category of origin. Aside from noting deaths, the Winchester records also frequently gave details as to the departure of scholars, either to continue their studies at New College or to pursue other employment opportunities. The numbers from this group of Winchester College 'survivors' divided by place of origin category are also given in Table 3.1. A further group of individuals were not recorded as having died, but have no record of their departure cause. These individuals do not appear at New College, and the reason for their exit from Winchester College is unspecified. Over the course of the study period there were some years of defective registration, where departures and deaths appear to have gone unrecorded. These unspecified departures are from such years, and it cannot be determined whether this group contributed deaths to the sample, or whether they left Winchester College alive to follow other career paths.[46] Although there are a number of scholars falling within this unspecified departure category, the fate of a reasonably large proportion is known (c.80 per cent of the group; Table 3.1) and it is assumed here that this is an adequate subsample to consider the fate of the group as a whole. For this reason, the group of 'unspecifieds' are listed separately in Table 3.1, and have been excluded from the analyses that follow.

A simple comparison of the numbers of deaths in each group is inappropriate, as this would fail to take into account the very different

---

46   This is discussed further in Oakes, 'Adolescent mortality'.

Table 3.1. Breakdown of Winchester College sample by category of place of origin

	London	Greater Towns	Provincial Towns	Rural	Unknown origin	Total
Deaths	4	5	8	81	30	128
Survivors	80	173	159	1217	377	2006
Unspecifieds	39	48	42	309	120	558
Total in sample	123	226	209	1607	527	2692
Total (excl. Unspecifieds)	84	178	167	1298	407	2134

Source: WCA 21490a Registrum Primum, 1393–1686.

Table 3.2. Percentages of deaths at Winchester College compared with overall percentages for each origin group

	London	Greater Towns	Provincial Towns	Rural	Unknown origin	Total
Total (N) excl. Unspecifieds	84	178	167	1298	407	2134
Total %	3.9	8.3	7.8	60.8	19.1	100
Deaths (N)	4	5	8	81	30	128
Deaths %	3.1	3.9	6.3	63.3	23.4	100

Source: WCA 21490a Registrum Primum, 1393–1686.

subsample sizes recruited from each of the different types of settlements. As the breakdown clearly shows, a higher proportion of scholars were recruited from the rural group (60.8 per cent) than from all other groups combined. Instead, it is more appropriate to compare the percentages of deaths occurring per group with the percentage that each group comprises of the total sample size. This allows a comparison of how the proportion of deaths differs to what might be expected if the deaths had been divided among the different categories in the same proportions as that of the total sample size. These figures are given in Table 3.2.

Table 3.2 shows that there were relatively fewer deaths among those coming from London, the greater towns and provincial towns than might be expected if deaths were equivalent in proportion to the size of these individual groups. This was particularly true for those coming from the greater towns, with the proportion of deaths observed among this group just under half of the proportion that they contribute to the intake of scholars to Winchester College as a whole. Conversely, a slightly higher proportion of deaths were observed among the rural group than the proportion of scholars provided to Winchester College by these settlements.

The apparent variation between the relative size of each group and the percentage of deaths attributed to each of them is in many instances quite small. It is worth noting, for example, that the proportion of deaths of scholars from London is very close to the relative contribution that the group makes to the overall sample size. However, it does appear that those recruited to Winchester College from smaller, more rural settlements were disadvantaged to a slight degree when moving into an urban area than those with previous experience of such an environment. Furthermore, Table 3.2 appears to show a possible advantage experienced by those coming from the greater towns, with a far lower proportion of deaths among this group. Changes in mortality rates over time cannot explain these patterns,[47] as the relative proportion of scholars recruited from each type of settlement remained fairly constant across the study period. Although the sample sizes are relatively small, these data appear to support the hypothesis that those from the greater towns fared better when moving into a similar environment than those from smaller settlements.[48]

Deaths at New College

Similar analyses have been undertaken for the group of scholars in the sample who continued their studies at New College Oxford. Table 3.3 gives the number of scholars from each settlement type, and the numbers from each group who are known to have died at New College or survived their time there. Although recording of deaths was much more systematic at New College, there were still some scholars for whom cause of departure from the college was not specified. The numbers of these 'unspecifieds' are given in Table 3.3, and again, these individuals are excluded from the analyses that follow.

47 Annual mortality rates at Winchester College are discussed in full in Oakes, 'Adolescent mortality'.
48 A chi-squared test indicates that there is a significant association between the variables ($X^2 = 2.97$; $P < 0.1$), and that the distribution of the data in Table 3.2 may not be the product of chance.

Table 3.3. Breakdown of New College sample by category of place of origin

	London	Greater Towns	Provincial Towns	Rural	Unknown origin	Total
Deaths	10	20	22	115	49	216
Survivors	32	74	68	544	162	880
Unspecifieds	18	23	24	160	57	282
Total in sample	60	117	114	819	268	1378
Total (excl. Unspecifieds)	42	94	90	659	211	1096

Sources: WCA 21490a Registrum Primum, 1393–1686; NCA 9654 Liber Albus, 1399–1450; NCA 9746–9 Registrum Protocollorum, 1450–1578 (4 vols).

Table 3.4. Percentages of deaths at New College compared with overall percentages for each origin group

	London	Greater Towns	Provincial Towns	Rural	Unknown origin	Total
Total (N) excl. Unspecifieds	42	94	90	659	211	1096
Total %	3.8	8.6	8.2	60.1	19.3	100
Deaths (N)	10	20	22	115	49	216
Deaths %	4.6	9.3	10.2	53.2	22.7	100

Sources: WCA 21490a Registrum Primum, 1393–1686; NCA 9654 Liber Albus, 1399–1450; NCA 9746–9 Registrum Protocollorum, 1450–1578 (4 vols).

Once more, examination was made of the proportions of deaths among each origin group, as compared with the proportion of the total sample that each group comprised. These percentages are given in Table 3.4. What is striking in this table is the fact that the proportion of deaths from those among the urban groups is higher than might be expected given their overall contribution to the sample size. At New College it would appear that those from the group designated as 'rural' fared better than those who originated from any of the towns, with fewer than expected 'rural' scholars being observed among those who died at the college.

The reasons for this remain unclear. However, it should be highlighted that all of the scholars attending New College had first completed their studies at Winchester College. Consequently, all New College scholars, regardless of their initial place of origin, had experience of living in one of the greater towns. This may have levelled the playing field, and the variations between the observed proportions of deaths and the proportion that each group contributed to the sample size might be better explained by other factors. The hypothesis that those originating from London and the greater towns fared better than those from other areas when entering the environment of one of the greater towns does not appear to hold in this instance.[49] However, the lack of association between place of origin and observed deaths is perhaps unsurprising given the previous exposure of all scholars to an urban environment of a similar kind.

Age at last observation
The final analysis to be included in this chapter is that of age at last observation. The purpose of this test is to see whether those from any particular place of origin were more or less likely to live beyond the average life expectancy as calculated for this sample group. Previous analysis of life expectancy for those from Winchester College has shown that, across the period as a whole, those scholars attaining the age of twenty-five could expect to live on average for a further 30.4 years. Life expectancy at age twenty-five did vary across the period, from a high of 35.2 for those enrolled at Winchester College in the period 1405–29, to a low of 27.1 years for those enrolled a century later in the period 1505–29,[50] but for the purposes of this chapter the average life expectancy across this whole period of 30.4 years at age twenty-five will be used for the entire group.

Age at death is not known for every individual within the sample group, but where this has not been identified, an age at which an individual was last observed alive can be given. As a large number of scholars did not progress to New College Oxford, and thereby disappear from observation around the age of eighteen, it was decided to exclude this group from the following analyses, and focus only upon those attending New College. The sample was divided according to whether the individuals were last

---

49 A chi-squared test shows that the null hypothesis of no association between these variables cannot be rejected ($X^2 = 1.09$), and that the distribution of the data in Table 3.4 may thus be the product of chance.
50 See Oakes, 'Mortality and life expectancy', chap. 6, pp. 195–210.

Table 3.5. Age ranges at which scholars attending New College were last seen alive

Age at last observation	London	Greater Towns	Provincial Towns	Rural	Unknown	Total
Under 55	54	106	96	692	226	1174
55 +	6	11	18	127	42	204
Total (N)	60	117	114	819	268	1378
% under 55	90.0	90.6	84.2	84.5	84.3	85.2
% 55+	10.0	9.4	15.8	15.5	15.7	14.8

Sources: WCA 21490a Registrum Primum, 1393–1686; NCA 9654 Liber Albus, 1399–1450; NCA 9746–9 Registrum Protocollorum, 1450–1578 (4 vols).

observed at an age below fifty-five, or when aged fifty-five or above (i.e. whether they had reached the expected age of 25 + 30.4 years). Table 3.5 shows the number of scholars in each of these two age categories at the time of their last observation, divided into groups according to their place of origin.

Table 3.5 shows the majority of all groups tending to be last observed before reaching the age of fifty-five. Fewer of those from London and the greater towns were observed over this age than were seen from the provincial towns and from rural areas. It should be noted that many of these individuals were not recorded as having died at these ages. Instead we are examining age at last observation, and using it as a guide to assess whether there were any notable variations in the longevity of those with different places of origin. The differences observed in Table 3.5 are slight, and the lack of any major trend in the data suggests that the origins of the scholars did not provide a key to their longevity. Subsequent life experiences are far more likely to explain the length of time for which these individuals were observed alive: thus it may be less where they came from, and more where they ended up, that determined their longevity. Among the sample are those who went on to secure high-powered positions, reaching the ranks of bishop, archbishop, or chief administrators for the crown. However, the group also contains a large number of individuals who did not rise above the rank of parish priest. The variability in their life experiences was no doubt of more consequence than was their place of origin. Their employment patterns will undoubtedly have affected our ability to trace these individuals through their subsequent careers, and age at death is more likely to have been recorded for those who went on to the more illustrious of careers.[51]

Context and interpretations

The data presented here suggest that some association may be inferred between the origins of scholars admitted to Winchester College and mortality among this group, with those from urban areas slightly under-represented among those who died while in residence at the college. This would seem to support the hypothesis that those who moved into urban environments from less urbanised areas may have been at a disadvantage as a result of having no previous exposure or conferred immunity to urban disease pools.

On moving to Winchester to attend St Mary's College these individuals were undoubtedly placing themselves in a higher risk urban setting. Although it was situated just outside of the city wall, so as to be outside of the jurisdiction of the mayor and corporation of Winchester, the college was restricted to a relatively small site located between a Carmelite friary, the college of St Elizabeth and the Sustren Spital (maintained by the cathedral priory).[52] The lack of physical space and the size of the college community meant that the scholars shared rooms with as many as eleven other boys, with those under the age of fourteen sleeping two to a bed.[53]

Perhaps more alarmingly, and to the very obvious detriment of the health of the community, the college obtained its water from a rather dubious stream, which ran through the college grounds. This water had been channelled through the city from the river Itchen and served St Mary's Abbey (Nunnaminster) and St Swithun's priory before flowing out of the city wall to the college. This water was used for cooking and cleaning, with a small outside conduit in Chamber Court near the kitchen. Not only did the water first flow through the grounds of two religious houses, but was also downstream from the areas of the town in which tanning and butchery took place. Problems of effluence in the water

51 See discussions of this issue in Oakes, 'Mortality and life expectancy', chaps 2 and 6.
52 D. Keene, 'Town into gown: the site of the College and other College lands in Winchester before the Reformation', in *Winchester College sixth centenary essays*, ed. R. Custance (Oxford, 1982), pp. 37–76.
53 This calculation is based upon the number of available rooms allocated to the scholars and the size of the college community.

supply were noted in the fifteenth century. A grille was fitted to catch this waste, although this did not solve the problems of contamination.[54] In 1483, William Waynflete, Bishop of Winchester and former headmaster of Winchester College, obtained the right for water to be brought into the college by a conduit from Segryme's well at the bottom of St Giles's Hill.[55] While causes of death were not recorded at either Winchester College or New College Oxford, this measure seems undoubtedly to have helped at Winchester as mortality rates appear to have been lower in the period post-1483.[56]

If life at Winchester College was unfavourable, there was perhaps only marginal improvement for those scholars who continued their studies at New College. Once again the college was squeezed into the available space, this time in a notoriously unsavoury part of the city where 'malefactors, murderers, whores and thieves' were to be found.[57] The area had long been in decay, and it has been suggested that the arrival of the Black Death in 1348 was largely responsible for the desertion of this section of the city, although evidence also indicates that rents in this location had been declining before this date.[58] Sand and gravel pits were noted as a common feature in this largely uninhabited area, and the college was built right up against the city wall. A ditch ran outside of this wall, and was full of rotting waste.[59]

Despite the apparent disadvantages of the location, the New College community was blessed with a relative amount of space and comfort, the site being larger than that at Winchester. The overall community was also slightly smaller in number, as after their two-year probationary period scholars were made full fellows of the college. The fellows were responsible for the governance of the college, and fulfilled the roles of bursar, seneschal of hall, and other administrative posts. At Winchester, a dedicated group of adult fellows had been appointed to undertake these roles, and so had enlarged the size of the community to be housed on-site. The contrast with Winchester College may be most clearly seen in the accommodation provided, with fellows being housed no more than four

54 Kirby, *Annals*, p. 8, n. 2.
55 Kirby, *Annals*, pp. 205–7; T. F. Kirby, *Winchester scholars* (London, 1888), p. xvii.
56 Oakes, 'Adolescent mortality', pp. 24–31.
57 G. Jackson-Stops, 'The building of the medieval College' in *New College*, ed. Buxton and Williams, pp. 147–92 (p. 153); VCH, *Oxfordshire*, vol. 3, p. 144.
58 Jackson-Stops, 'The building', p. 153; VCH, *Oxfordshire*, vol. 3, pp. 144–5.
59 Jackson-Stops, 'The building', p. 153; VCH, *Oxfordshire*, vol. 3, pp. 144–5.

to a room, each man being provided with his own bed and study area, close to a window for light and ventilation.[60] The college also benefited from its own well within the grounds from which it could draw water. A latrine block was also provided, albeit situated in rather close proximity to the kitchen garden. A cess pit was enclosed beneath, which was periodically cleaned.[61]

Given the relatively improved conditions to be found at New College, and that the scholars had first survived their time at Winchester, it seems unsurprising that no association has been found between mortality observed at New College and the place of origin of those scholars. Perhaps surprising is the slight disadvantage that those originating from urban environments appear to have suffered. However, the weak association between these variables suggests that other factors might provide a better explanation as to mortality patterns observed at New College. Such explanations are beyond the scope of the present chapter, but examination of factors such as the period of time spent at Winchester, or the period of exposure to the Oxford environment forms the basis of continuing research.

It would seem that moving beyond Winchester weakened any likely association between mortality patterns and place of origin. This is hardly surprising, as the continued survival of scholars indicates their success in coping with the risks of urban living. That this association may have weakened over time is perhaps to be expected, as the individuals would have been exposed to a whole range of different environments and conditions throughout their individual subsequent career paths. This is a probable explanation for the apparent lack of correlation between place of origin and longevity. The probability of an individual being last observed above the age of fifty-five is much more likely to have been determined by the risks they encountered in later life, and hence by their subsequent employment patterns and standards of living.

Conclusions

This chapter has demonstrated the usefulness of place of origin data, and provided empirical evidence for the medieval period linking mortality within two urban institutional communities to the place of origin of

60   Jackson-Stops, 'The building', pp. 183–5; VCH, *Oxfordshire*, vol. 3, p. 150.
61   Jackson-Stops, 'The building', pp. 178–80; VCH, *Oxfordshire*, vol. 3, pp. 154 and 157.

its members. Institutional life was likely to have held its own dangers, associated with the extent to which the members of such a community were living in close proximity and the consequent ease with which disease might be communicated. However, it has been possible to show here that there may be some correlation between place of origin and initial survival in an urban area. It seems that in such circumstances, as hypothesised in the monastic studies, those from similar urban environments fared better than those who had no previous exposure to such a setting. However, the data also suggest that any association between place of origin and ability to survive in an urban environment may have weakened over time, and in the case of the Winchester scholars no association could be established between a subsequent move to a different urban environment and place of origin. Rather it would seem that an initial move to an urban setting created a risk, but that following survival of such a move it was subsequent life experiences that may have become more important in determining mortality risks and longevity.

4

Family and Welfare in Early Modern Europe: a North–South Comparison

JULIE MARFANY

The relationship between family and welfare in Europe has long been and continues to be a central theme for historians, anthropologists, sociologists and demographers. Its importance has been given added weight in recent decades by policy debates on the future of welfare provision in many European countries, including Britain.[1] Both current debates and the historiography of the last two decades or so have tended to characterise family forms and welfare regimes in Europe in terms of a north–south (perhaps more accurately a north-west/south-east) divide.[2] Put simply, northern Europe tends to be associated with nuclear family forms, 'weaker' family ties, and relatively generous provision of poor relief, both overall but also, and particularly in the case of England, in rural areas. By contrast, southern Europe, and also often eastern Europe, are associated with extended family forms, 'stronger' family ties and less generous poor relief provision, restricted in the main to urban areas. The relationships between these variables are complex, yet have serious implications both for our understanding of economic development in Europe and for social policy, both past and present. This chapter aims to offer

---

1 P. Horden and R. Smith, 'Introduction', in *The locus of care. Families, communities, institutions and the provision of welfare since antiquity*, ed. P. Horden and R. Smith (London and New York, 1998), pp. 1–18; P. P. Viazzo, 'Family, kinship and welfare provision in Europe, past and present: commonalities and divergences', *Continuity and Change* 25 (2010), 137–59.

2 While some historians have tried to stress the complexity and variation of welfare provision across Europe, the north–south divide still persists to a large extent. See Viazzo, 'Family, kinship and welfare provision'.

a critical reflection on the current state of historiography and some of the claims made for different welfare regimes across Europe. It addresses the interrelationship between welfare regimes and family forms and ties and the merits of different welfare systems, including the comparison of rural and urban poor relief. In doing so, it hopes to highlight some of the distinctive features of the English poor law. While the chapter draws on a wide secondary literature on southern Europe, it also presents some preliminary research findings for Catalonia, a region for which little work has yet been done on poor relief.

North–south divides

England's poor laws were undeniably unique in Europe. While other countries occasionally experimented with the funding of relief via taxation, England was the only state where a series of national statutes from 1572 onwards provided for compulsory relief of the poor by the inhabitants of the parish, to be funded via local rates, implemented in almost all parishes by the end of the seventeenth century.[3] Relief took the form of work for the able-bodied (theoretically), and both regular and casual payments in cash and kind. While there is now an emerging consensus that the introduction of the poor laws did not see a decline in traditional charitable giving, as discussed below, the poor laws came to be central to English poor relief, in both theory and practice. While England stands out, however, poor relief provision is perceived to have been superior across northern Europe compared with the south. First, levels of expenditure were supposedly higher. Second, historians echo contemporary, usually Protestant, claims that relief was often better administered. Third, relief was supposedly more widely available in rural areas. According to Peter Lindert's estimates, England and the Dutch Republic were the countries spending the highest share of national income (around 1.75 per cent) on their poor prior to 1795, ahead of France, though he provides no comparative data for southern Europe.[4] Certainly, the parlous state of French poor relief by the 1790s has been stressed by several

3   J. Innes, 'The state and the poor. Eighteenth-century England in European perspective', in *Rethinking Leviathan. The eighteenth-century state in Britain and Germany*, ed. J. Brewer and E. Hellmuth (Oxford, 1999), pp. 225–80.
4   P. H. Lindert, 'Poor relief before the welfare state: Britain versus the Continent, 1780–1880', *European Review of Economic History* 2 (1998), 101–40.

historians, perhaps most forcefully by Olwen Hufton, in her pioneering work on the subject:

> For antiquarians and Catholic historians, it has always been possible to be impressed by the range of institutions, produced by the efforts of the pious, which characterised formal relief before the Revolution ... This ... should not cloud the main issue, the total inadequacy of formal relief anywhere.[5]

In these assessments, local charity was haphazardly administered and difficult to sustain. Similarly, poor relief in England prior to the Reformation and the introduction of the poor laws (often seen as related events) has also been attacked as inadequate and indiscriminate.[6] Historians working on other regions of southern Europe have echoed these sentiments, and have even gone so far as to deny the existence of poor relief in rural areas at all. For Catalonia, despite acknowledging that 'little is known of rural poor relief', Henry Kamen has nonetheless asserted that 'there is no doubt' that the only ongoing provision in the early modern period was collections for the poor in churches.[7] Such confidence is, however, the result of taking a relative lack of evidence to be a reflection of reality. As Paolo Viazzo commented some years ago, the comparative history of European poor relief is 'plagued' by the problem that evidence is usually available for rural areas in the north and urban areas in the south.[8] It is certainly the case that evidence of poor relief practices in southern Europe is easier to obtain for the large welfare institutions of the cities. Nonetheless, as will be discussed below, historians have been able to demonstrate that rural poor relief was certainly not inexistent in southern Europe, and that further efforts to ferret out evidence from archives would be well repaid.[9]

---

5   O. H. Hufton, *The poor of eighteenth-century France* (Oxford, 1974), pp. 173–4. See also C. Jones, *Charity and Bienfaisance: the treatment of the poor in the Montpellier region, 1740–1815* (Cambridge, 1982).

6   See the discussion and reappraisal in C. Dyer, 'Poverty and its relief in late medieval England', *Past and Present* 216 (2012), 41–78.

7   H. Kamen, *The phoenix and the flame. Catalonia and the counter reformation* (New Haven, 1993), p. 203.

8   P. P. Viazzo, 'Family structures and the early phase in the individual life cycle. A southern European perspective', in *Poor women and children in the European past*, ed. J. Henderson and R. Wall (London, 1994), pp. 31–50.

9   See, for example, B. Pullan, 'Charity and poor relief in early modern Italy', in *Charity, self-interest and welfare in the English past*, ed. M. Daunton (London, 1996), pp. 65–89.

Differences in welfare provision, while they are of intrinsic interest to historians, also have far greater importance in terms of their implications for family formation and demography. Various historians have described family forms in Europe as subject to a north–south divide or, again, perhaps a north-west/south-east divide, following John Hajnal's classic 'line from Leningrad to Trieste'.[10] Hajnal thought that Mediterranean Europe had much in common with Eastern Europe in terms of family formation and household structure. Northern or north-western Europe was thus characterised by a tendency to form nuclear households, late marriage for both sexes but especially women, high proportions of solitary households, particularly among the elderly, and high levels of migration. By contrast, while nuclear families were to be found in many areas of France, Spain, Portugal and Italy, extended family forms were more common than in the north, with couples continuing to live in the parental household after marriage, early marriage (at least for women) and the elderly more often resident with kin. Beyond the question of family forms, which could and did vary, is the question of family ties. In a seminal article of 1998, David Reher views southern European families, past and present, as subject to much stronger ties of loyalty than northern ones, reflected in differences between north and south in the frequency with which the elderly reside with kin or in institutions, the proportions of young people leaving home at different ages and before marriage, and the proportion of solitary households to be found in the population.[11] For example, the recent *Survey of Health, Ageing and Retirement in Europe* (SHARE), found that, in 2004, only 1 per cent of Swedes and 4 per cent of Danes in the oldest age group of the population lived with a child, compared with 23 per cent of Italians and 34 per cent of Spanish, with similar patterns evident in frequency of contact between kin and financial transfers between generations.[12]

10   J. Hajnal, 'European marriage patterns in perspective', in *Population in history. Essays in historical demography*, ed. D. V. Glass and D. E. C. Eversley (London, 1965), pp. 101–43. Hajnal describes this simply as a 'European marriage pattern', but concedes that 'significant departures from the European pattern may probably be found not only as one proceeds eastwards but on the southern edge of Europe as well' (p. 103). See also J. Hajnal, 'Two kinds of pre-industrial household formation system', *Population and Development Review* 8 (1982), 449–94; P. Laslett, 'Characteristics of the Western family considered over time', in *Family life and illicit love in earlier generations*, ed. P. Laslett (Cambridge, 1977), pp. 12–49.
11   D. S. Reher, 'Family ties in Western Europe: persistent contrasts', *Population and Development Review* 24 (1998), 203–34.
12   See http://www.share-project.org/. Eleven countries contributed to the survey: Austria,

More important than these differences between family forms and family ties, however, are the claims that have been made for the significance of such differences. Hajnal had already suggested that there might be a relationship between the different household formation patterns of Europe, particularly north-west Europe, compared with those of Asia and Africa, and the different economic trajectories followed by these regions. Bolder still are the more recent claims of Jan de Vries and others that the explanation for northern Europe's early transition to a capitalist, industrialised economy is to be found in part in the supposedly greater dynamism of the nuclear family.[13] According to de Vries, the 'industrious revolution' claimed by him as a precursor to the industrial revolution was possible only in north-west Europe, since this region combined the requisite institutional features, namely open markets and a system of nuclear family formation that promoted independence and individualism. By contrast, 'the claustrophobic bonds of extended kinship' prevented a similar industrious revolution from occurring in southern Europe.[14]

However, as Richard Smith and Peter Solar have pointed out, what may be most important in this regard is not family forms and ties themselves, but the factors underpinning and supporting them.[15] In the English case, particular emphasis has to be placed on the poor law, and the extent to which it created a safety net that enabled the nuclear family to function and, above all, allowed labour to move freely by guaranteeing individuals support in times of hardship. Rather than restricting movement, the settlement laws made entitlement to relief relatively easy to obtain and, furthermore, were administered rationally in the sense that parishes frequently agreed between themselves to pay for the poor to remain in their parishes of residence rather than of settlement when the former option made more sense economically.

Belgium, Denmark, France, Germany, Greece, Italy, the Netherlands, Spain, Sweden and Switzerland.

13 J. de Vries, *The industrious revolution. Consumer behavior and the household economy, 1650 to the present* (Cambridge, 2008); T. De Moor and J. L. van Zanden, 'Girl power: the European marriage pattern and labour markets in the North Sea region in the late medieval and early modern period', *Economic History Review* 63 (2010), 1–33.

14 De Vries, *Industrious revolution*, p. 18.

15 P. M. Solar, 'Poor relief and English economic development before the Industrial Revolution', *Economic History Review* 48 (1995), 1–22; R. M. Smith, 'Social security as a developmental institution? The relative efficacy of poor relief provisions under the English old poor law', in *History, historians and development policy: a necessary dialogue*, ed. C. A. Bayly, V. Rao, S. Szreter and M. Woolcock (Manchester, 2011), pp. 75–102.

Other beneficial features of the English poor laws will be discussed below. For the moment, what remains to be considered is the other side of the relationship between welfare and family forms, that is, how different family structures affected the demand for welfare. An important concept here is that of 'nuclear family hardship'.[16] Peter Laslett proposed that the nuclear family form dominant in northern Europe was more vulnerable to poverty than the extended family forms of southern Europe, since extended families could draw on a wider range of kin for support. Most at risk were the elderly, since high levels of migration and the preference for nuclear household formation meant an absence of kin able to offer support in old age. This is not to say, however, that the extended family was cushioned from hardship.[17] Extended families could not always offer protection in times of need. Viazzo and others have shown that they were often hardest hit in the early stages of the life cycle, when burdened with young children and often also with elderly parents.[18] This life-cycle difference is adduced as an explanation for the greater levels of abandonment of children in southern Europe.

Any future comparative research into poor relief in Europe must therefore address several key questions. What relief was available in rural areas? How adequate or otherwise was it? Were some welfare regimes more generous in terms of provision than others and why? If poor relief was concentrated in cities, what effect did that have on rural and urban populations alike? How were welfare practices adapted to different patterns of life-cycle poverty across Europe? In all of this, it must be remembered that welfare regimes were not static. All areas of Europe witnessed growing numbers of poor over the eighteenth century in particular, prompting fierce debates as to the best manner in which to respond to poverty, a debate in which the participants were frequently well aware of, and interested in, how other states dealt with their poor.[19] The

16   P. Laslett, 'Family, kinship and collectivity as systems of support in pre-industrial Europe: a consideration of the "nuclear-hardship" hypothesis', *Continuity and Change* 3 (1988), 153–75; M. Pelling and R. M. Smith, 'Introduction' in *Life, death and the elderly: historical perspectives*, ed. M. Pelling and R. M. Smith (London, 1991), pp. 1–38.

17   K. A. Lynch, *Individuals, families and communities in Europe, 1200–1800* (Cambridge, 2003).

18   Viazzo, 'Family structures', pp. 36–7; S. Cavallo, 'Family obligations and inequalities in access to care in northern Italy, seventeenth to eighteenth centuries', in *Locus of care*, ed. Horden and Smith, pp. 90–110.

19   J. Innes, 'State, church and voluntarism in European welfare, 1690–1850', in *Charity, philanthropy and reform: from the 1690s to 1850*, ed. H. Cunningham and J. Innes (New York, 1998), pp. 15–65.

remainder of this chapter will consider these questions in more detail, and will attempt to highlight similarities as well as differences between northern and southern Europe.

Types of welfare provision in southern Europe

Local hospitals

In answer to the first question as to what poor relief was available in rural areas of southern Europe, a fairly lengthy list can be drawn up, even if very little in-depth discussion can be provided as yet. Best known, in that more evidence survives, are the hospitals, often medieval endowments, offering shelter and a degree of medical care to local and transient poor. As mentioned above, the focus has traditionally been on the large, wealthy hospitals of the cities, but many smaller towns and even villages also had hospitals. In 1791 there were 1,961 hospitals in France of which 1,034 were in settlements with populations of fewer than 2,000.[20] The capacity of these institutions varied: 768 French hospitals had ten beds or fewer, for example. Likewise, their revenues also varied, but many were well run and offered a degree of medical care and nursing to their residents. Daniel Hickey suggests that smaller French hospitals tended to have 'modest means' but to be relatively free from debt compared with larger institutions.[21]

Catalonia had an estimated 201 hospitals at the end of the eighteenth century. Precise quantification is impossible, since none of the sources available provides complete geographical coverage.[22] The figure may therefore underestimate the total number of institutions, although by the same token, it is not clear that all the hospitals included in this count were

---

20 M. Jeorger, 'La structure hospitalière de la France sous l'Ancien Régime', Annales HSS 32 (1977), 1025–51.

21 D. Hickey, Local hospitals in ancien régime France. Rationalization, resistance, renewal, 1530–1789 (Montreal, 1997).

22 The two main sources are the 1787 census of Floridablanca, which included the breakdown by age, sex and marital status of those resident in hospitals, distinguishing patients from staff, and an unpublished survey of schools, hospitals, prisons and the like carried out by the Barcelona authorities over the autumn and winter of 1813–14. The latter included questions on date and purpose of foundation, income, current state, impact of the war and future improvements needed, but is patchy in terms of geographical coverage as a result of the French occupation. For 1787, returns for the Barcelona and Tortosa districts are missing, but we know how many hospitals there were in the cities themselves.

Table 4.1. Hospitals in Catalonia according to the 1787 census, by population size

Population size	% population of Catalonia	Number of hospitals	% hospitals
<1,000	42	12	12.9
1,000–1,999	18	29	31.2
2,000–4,999	16	24	25.8
5,000–9,999	9	16	17.2
>10,000	14	12	12.9

Source: J. Iglésies (ed.), *El cens del comte de Floridablanca 1787 (part de Catalunya)*, 2 vols (Barcelona, 1969–70).
Note: Tortosa estimated at >10,000 inhabitants.

still functioning as such by this point. Table 4.1 provides the breakdown of locations with hospitals according to population size in 1787. A high proportion of hospitals, though not quite as high a proportion as in France, were in small places of under 2,000 inhabitants, the smallest being Les Pobles d'Aiguamurcia, a village of 299 inhabitants. At the top end of the scale, the figures are distorted by the seven hospitals in Barcelona (population 92,385).

Estimates of capacity are impossible to calculate, since no source records this systematically. Some idea of size is provided by the figures for patients in 1787, which record only those present in the hospital at the time of the census, not the number of beds available. That beds might well be empty is illustrated by the hospital at Reus, which had between twenty and twenty-five beds, but only seven patients in 1787.[23] Nonetheless, the figures at least give minimum estimates. Table 4.2 shows the breakdown for the ninety-one hospitals recorded in the 1787 census where detailed patient numbers are available. As can be seen, just under a third of hospitals had no patients at all on the census date, while just under 43 per cent had between one and nine. At first blush, these figures suggest a rather minimal role for hospitals in the provision of relief. However, provision was largely a reflection of income. Table 4.3 provides figures for income for those hospitals included in the 1813–14

23 P. Anguera, *Hospital de Sant Joan de Reus, 1240–1990* (Reus, 1990), pp. 21–6.

Table 4.2. Catalan hospitals according to number of patients recorded in 1787 census

Number of patients	Number of hospitals	% hospitals
0	28	30.8
1–4	26	28.6
5–9	13	14.3
10–19	7	7.7
20–49	8	8.8
50–99	3	3.3
100+	6	6.6
	91	100.0

Source: As Table 4.1, but excluding the two hospitals in Tortosa, for which only overall totals survive.

Table 4.3. Income per year for Catalan hospitals where income recorded, 1813–14

Income per year (*lliures*)	Number of hospitals	% hospitals
<50	19	33.3
50–99	11	19.3
100–199	12	21.1
200–499	11	19.3
500+	4	7.0
	57	100.0

Source: Arxiu General de la Diputació de Barcelona, *lligalls* 12 and 13.

survey where a precise value was given or a figure could be estimated.[24] A third of the hospitals included here had an income of under fifty *lliures* a year. Rough estimates based on surviving hospital accounts for the 1770s suggest expenditure of ten *sous* per patient per day, to include food,

24 The years 1813–14 were ones of high prices, but hospitals were asked for the value of income in 'normal' years. For most, this was in the form of fixed cash rents. The Catalan unit of account was the *lliura* (pound), divided into twenty *sous* (shillings). In turn, one *sou* equalled twelve *diners* (pence).

medical care and fuel.[25] An annual income of fifty *lliures* thus amounts
to a hundred days of care for one patient at 1770s prices. Many hospitals
were thus circumscribed by income. The 1813–14 figures are skewed
towards smaller and poorer hospitals because many towns did not send
back returns. Nonetheless, the picture is unlikely to be too distorted. The
majority of hospitals were medieval foundations intended to offer shelter
to the transient poor and pilgrims, rather than extensive care and, as such,
did not have large endowments. Provision of care is further discussed
below.

Endowed charities
Many areas, including England, had various types of endowed charity,
usually to provide clothing or bread doles for the poor, though we lack
systematic studies that would allow us to assess their relative importance
across different areas.[26] Endowed charities (*causes pies*) were particularly
significant in Catalonia. Some provided clothing, as in Vilafranca del
Penedès, where a fund endowed by Pau Janer distributed cloth to twenty-
four paupers each year.[27] Bread doles, however, were more common. The
diocese of Girona alone had eighty-eight documented in a survey of
1772–74.[28] Just to cite two examples of these, the village of Sant Feliu de
Guíxols had bread doles on Christmas Eve and Easter Sunday, endowed
with an annual income of sixty-eight *lliures* in cash and more in kind.[29] The
small town of Figueres had a charity founded in 1533, which began distributing bread at the start of Lent every year, and continued to do so every day
until funds ran out. While most bread doles appear to have been distributed
only once or twice a year, usually on particular feast days or anniversaries,
some of the larger ones, such as those of Barcelona and Girona, gave out
weekly or more frequent alms for several months of the year.

25 Hospital accounts of Cadaqués in AHG, *Hospici*, 676; Castelló d'Empúries and
Figueres in AHG, *Hospici*, 677; and Vic, figures in A. Pladevall, I. Prades and F. Rocafiguera,
Hospital de la Santa Creu de Vic (Vic, 2000), pp. 68–9.
26 For English examples, see J. Broad, 'Parish economies of welfare, 1650–1834',
Historical Journal 42 (1999), 985–1006. For northern Italy, see Pullan, 'Charity and poor
relief', pp. 71–2.
27 *El corregiment i partit judicial de Vilafranca del Penedès a l'últim terç del segle
XVIII. Respostes al qüestionari de Francisco de Zamora de Manuel Barba i Roca*, ed.
A. Sabaté (Vilafranca del Penedès, 1991), p. 37.
28 AHG, *Hospici*, 676, 677 and 2340. See also M. Borrell, *Pobresa i marginació a la
Catalunya il·lustrada* (Santa Coloma de Farners, 2002), pp. 509–17.
29 Ibid., pp. 80–5 and 509–17.

The most common type of *causa pia*, however, was the dowry fund, described by Stuart Woolf as a 'ubiquitous symbol of ancien régime charity' in southern Europe.[30] While some were restricted to providing dowries for the founder's family only, or for the daughters of guild or confraternity members, many were aimed at providing dowries for poor girls of the parish, usually one a year, selected by some form of lottery. In the Girona diocese alone, thirty-seven dowry funds for poor girls were established over the early modern period.[31] No attempts at quantification have yet been carried out for other dioceses, but numerous examples can be cited. Geroni Cornet, a merchant, endowed a dowry fund which was instituted in 1700, to provide a generous dowry of a hundred *lliures* (where the standard amount was often 25–30 *lliures*) to a poor girl born in the town of Igualada, chosen annually by lottery from the fifty women deemed to be the poorest.[32] Agustí Fages, rector of Castellbisbal, left money in his will for a dowry fund, instituted in 1780, to provide dowries for poor girls either born in Castellbisbal or who had been in domestic service there for five years.[33] Jaume Sosciats, a priest, left provision for a dowry fund, instituted in 1731, to provide dowries for three poor girls from Guissona.[34]

Almsgiving

Hardest to document, yet undoubtedly a major contribution to the 'economy of makeshifts' of the poor across Europe, was almsgiving.[35] This included bequests of clothes to the poor, distributions of alms at funerals

---

30 S. Woolf, *The poor in western Europe in the eighteenth and nineteenth centuries* (New York, 1986), p. 32.

31 Arxiu Diocesà de Girona, *Institucions de causes pies*, vols 1–28. See also Josep. M. Marquès, 'Fundacions de causes pies al bisbat de Girona (s.XVI–XIX)', *Pedralbes* 8 (1988), 513–23.

32 Arxiu Parroquial d'Igualada, *caixes* 13 and 15, 'Causa pia Geroni Cornet'.

33 ADB, *Institucions causes pies*, vol. 12, fols 320v–331r.

34 ADB, *Institucions causes pies*, vol. 13, fols 120r–129r.

35 For a discussion of almsgiving in Catalonia, see J. M. Puigvert, *Església, territori i sociabilitat (s.XVII–XIX)* (Vic, 2000), pp. 188–94; Borrell, *Pobresa*, pp. 80–7. For France, see Hufton, *Poor of eighteenth-century France*, pp. 194–216. Even in England, almsgiving remained important long after the introduction of the poor laws. See I. K. Ben-Amos, '"Good works" and social ties. Helping the migrant poor in early modern England', in *Protestant identities. Religion, society and self-fashioning in post-Reformation England*, ed. M. McClendon, J. P. Ward and M. MacDonald (Stanford, 1999), pp. 125–40; I. K. Ben-Amos, *The culture of giving. Informal support and gift-exchange in early modern England* (Cambridge, 2008), pp. 126–34.

and after mass, on the doorsteps of churches, convents, monasteries and wealthy houses, as well as hospitality and shelter to travellers and pilgrims. The Riembau family, fairly well-to-do peasant farmers from the parish of Sant Hipòlit de Voltregà, in central Catalonia, recorded in their account books various sums spent on alms at funerals, in both cash and kind, including donations of grain to the hospital of Vic as well as alms to the poor at the church door.[36] At the funeral in 1752 of Francesc Quatrecases, a peasant from Pruit, a small village near Vic, around 650 paupers received alms according to Quatrecases' son.[37] The monastery of Sant Pere de Rodes, in a particularly isolated and mountainous part of north-east Catalonia, offered shelter to all passers-by, and gave bread and sardines to poor visitors as well as distributing small rations of bread to beggars after mass. Despite its location, the monastery sometimes witnessed as many as a hundred paupers a day asking for relief by the late eighteenth century according to one account.[38] It is clear that, while some almsgiving such as that at funerals was on a one-off basis, many alms were given out frequently and with some regularity, as discussed below.

Mutual aid, networks and self-help

Despite certain views of the extended family, a common feature of southern Europe was the provision of aid through networks often going beyond the larger family unit. Italian and Spanish confraternities traditionally filled a welfare role from medieval times onwards, through assistance in sickness, at funerals and with dowry payments.[39] Aid was not exclusively for members, however; many confraternities also ran hospitals and distributed alms. While greater concentrations of confraternities were to be found in towns, they also proliferated in the countryside. Quantifying the volume of relief they provided is impossible, and there is some debate as to how far they continued to play a welfare role during the eighteenth century, though there is a suggestion that in Spain at least,

---

36   Arxiu Episcopal de Vic, Arxiu patrimonial Mas Riembau, 22, *Llibre de comptes (1660–1791)*, fols 78 and 80.

37   'Llibre de comptes i notes de Joan Quatrecases, Vicenç Quatrecases i Francesc Quatrecases (1696–1812)', reproduced in *Guerra, pau i vida quotidiana en primera persona*, ed. R. Ginebra (Vic, 2005), pp. 121–233 (p. 198).

38   F. de Zamora, *Diario de los viajes hechos en Cataluña*, ed. R. Boixareu (Barcelona, 1973), pp. 345–6.

39   M. Flynn, *Sacred charity: confraternities and social welfare in Spain, 1400–1700* (Basingstoke, 1989).

some of the 25,038 confraternities in existence in 1771 were beginning to take on the characteristics of mutual aid societies rather than the wealthier, more hierarchical organisations of earlier periods. In addition, the seventeenth and eighteenth centuries saw in Catalonia the creation of confraternities, both lay and religious, and often female, whose role was the direct assistance of the poor through the running of hospitals, provision of nursing and other types of care. Patients at the hospital of Mataró were cared for from 1791 by a local confraternity of both men and women.[40] In Solsona, a group of local women provided and washed all the linen used by the hospital.[41] Similarly, the village council of Olot elected two female administrators each year to take care of linen and clothing.[42] Arbúcies had a confraternity of Charity, modelled on the Saint Vicent de Paul order, consisting of seventy-two women including spinsters, married women and widows, founded in 1738.[43] Care of the sick in the parish of Verdú from 1615 until as late as 1936 fell to the confraternity of Our Lady of Solitude, members of which were all the widows of the parish.[44]

Other forms of mutual aid or self-help were the *monti di pietà* in Italy or *montes de piedad* in Spain, early forms of credit and later savings banks for the poor, often operating as pawnbrokers, though these seem only to have been a feature of larger cities in Spain. What was common in rural parishes in Spain and Italy was the equivalent in the form of a public granary, known as *botigues de blat* or *pòsits* in Catalan, *pósitos* in Spanish and *monti frumentari* in Italian, which loaned out grain for planting and for consumption to be repaid with interest after harvest.[45] While Pullan describes these as being in decline in northern Italy by the eighteenth century, they proliferated in Spain, arguably stimulated by the liberalisation of the grain trade in 1765. In 1773, there were 8,090 *pósitos* across Spain, with 1,854 (23 per cent) of these founded since 1751.[46] As

---

40 R. d'Amat i de Cortada, Baró de Maldà, *Calaix de sastre*, ed. R. Boixareu, 11 vols (Barcelona, 1987–2005), vol. 1, p. 279.
41 de Zamora, *Diario*, pp. 144–6.
42 J. Reventós and J. M. Marquès, *Els hospitals de les comarques gironines* (Barcelona, 2001), pp. 122–3.
43 Ibid., pp. 177–9.
44 J. Reventós, *Història dels hospitals de la Terra Ferma* (Lleida, 2002), pp. 91–5.
45 Pullan, 'Charity and poor relief', pp. 73–4; G. Anes, 'Los pósitos en la España del siglo XVIII', in *Economia e 'ilustración' en la España del siglo XVIII* (Barcelona, 1969), pp. 71–94.
46 Anes, 'Los pósitos', tab. 1 between pp. 80–1.

yet, however, there are almost no case studies of how individual granaries functioned in practice and how successful their welfare role was in this period.[47]

How adequate was poor relief?

Hufton is therefore right that one should be impressed by the range of resources available, even if little has been done as yet to offer a detailed picture. More controversial, perhaps, is her claim that such resources were inadequate to deal with the problem of poverty. While some, more localised studies, such as that by Jones of the Montpellier region, support her claim to an extent, other historians have been less damning. Daniel Hickey concedes that the revenues of the *bureaux de charité* were 'erratic' and that initiatives could be hard to sustain, but nevertheless argues that local elites could respond effectively to poverty, noting an increase in charitable donations for some areas over the eighteenth century, and greater expenditure upon outdoor relief.[48] Moreover, as has been noted by Marco van Leeuwen, the situation in France at the end of the eighteenth century should not perhaps be taken as typical either of earlier periods or of Europe as a whole.[49] The same caveat applies to Lindert's data, described above, which also exclude much charitable giving at a time when, in England at least, charity seems to have been flourishing.[50] Indeed, Colin Jones questions if the sums transferred by formal poor relief could ever have surpassed those transferred through charity anywhere in Europe prior to the nineteenth century.[51]

More importantly, as van Leeuwen also notes, any assessment of poor relief as 'inadequate' depends on what poor relief was intended to achieve. Taken as the sole means of support for families, poor relief was probably inadequate everywhere, except perhaps England, but there was

47   For one case study, see M. Bofarull, 'Una mena de mont de pietat (El "llibre de la botiga" d'Albinyana)', *Miscellània Penedesenca* 6 (1983), 13–28.

48   Hickey, *Local hospitals*, pp. 100–33 and 185–7.

49   M. H. D. van Leeuwen, 'Giving in early modern history: philanthropy in Amsterdam in the Golden Age', *Continuity and Change* 27 (2012), 301–43.

50   J. Innes, 'The "mixed economy of welfare" in early modern England: assessments of the options from Hale to Malthus (c.1683–1803)', in *Charity, self-interest and welfare*, ed. Daunton, pp. 139–80.

51   C. Jones, 'Some recent trends in the history of charity', in *Charity, self-interest and welfare*, ed. Daunton, pp. 51–63 (p. 52).

rarely the expectation, again except perhaps under the English poor law, that relief was intended to be a permanent source of income that covered all of a household's needs.[52] Rather, in most instances, it was devised as a supplement to other sources of income, part of Hufton's 'economy of makeshifts', or as a means to survive a short-term crisis. While some of those advocating reforms to Spanish poor relief in the eighteenth century argued for the suppression of many alms and charitable foundations on the grounds that one or two bread doles a year did nothing to relieve the poor, others took the view that patching together small grants and gifts could make a contribution to a household's survival strategies, and provide a means of getting by during winter months or after poor harvests.[53] Similarly, while most hospitals had limited income, their role in providing shelter, food and medical care to both local and transient poor was still crucial. Wardens ensured that foundlings in particular were transferred from parish to parish until they reached one of the foundling hospitals. For the local poor, medical care where provided was increasingly sophisticated by the late eighteenth century and, above all, was free. Catalonia saw increasing professionalisation of medical care, especially nursing, with the recruitment by many hospitals of the Daughters of Charity.[54] Hospitals also covered the significant cost of burial. Their role is nicely summed up by the statement from Llançà, in north-east Catalonia, where the hospital had only around twelve *lliures* income, but nonetheless tried to offer medical care to poor labourers from the village, 'to prevent them from using up what little money they have, and their families from ending up on the streets'.[55] Here, the local doctor and surgeon offered their services for free, and the apothecary provided medicines at half-price.

Alongside the issue of 'inadequacy', however, lie other questions concerning the merits of different schemes of poor relief. One fierce criticism of much *ancien régime* poor relief, particularly almsgiving, in southern Europe was that it was 'indiscriminate' in nature and thus served to create or at least reinforce the very problem of poverty by encouraging the idle poor to engage in vagrancy and other disruptive behaviour.

---

52 Indeed, some historians question the generosity of even the English poor law. See in particular S. Hindle, *On the parish? The micro-politics of poor relief in rural England c.1550–1750* (Oxford, 2004).

53 See the discussion in Borrell, *Pobresa*, pp. 391–7 and 499–505.

54 On the Daughters of Charity, see J. Reventós, *Els hospitals i la societat catalana* (Barcelona, 1996), pp. 95–7 and 120–3.

55 AHG, *Hospici*, 676.

Accounts by travellers from northern Europe inevitably feature the stereo-
typical description of the hordes of beggars crowding around the door
of the church or convent, a stereotype about which some members of the
clergy were becoming increasingly sensitive by the end of the eighteenth
century.[56] There were claims, for example, that households in Girona sent
their servants to claim bread doles as a means of paying lower wages,
and that crowds engaged in unseemly pushing and shoving at funerals
in order to get a share of handouts.[57] In both France and Spain, there
were complaints that many beggars roamed the countryside extorting
alms from remote households through threats of violence.[58] In response,
many proposals for reform, adopted earlier and with more enthusiasm in
France, advocated the building of large poorhouses in towns into which
the poor of the surrounding area could be admitted. In Spain, this growing
preference among some thinkers for indoor relief in large institutions has
often been characterised by historians as part of a general enlightened
trend towards centralisation and secularisation of poor relief, education
and the like.[59]

One should not rush, however, to accept such evaluations at face value.
Other contemporaries and historians alike have suggested that 'indiscriminate' is too harsh a judgement. Almsgiving was not always indiscriminate, in Catalonia at least: anecdotal evidence suggests it was often
distributed in an orderly fashion, to known recipients. One eighteenth-
century traveller described the distribution of alms by the convent of the
Mercenarios in Vic, where the poor queued according to a set order.[60]
Similarly, the alms distributed by the monastery of Sant Pere de Rodes,
described above, could only be claimed once every fortnight. According
to the mayor of Vilafranca del Penedès, nineteen wealthy families in the
town distributed alms to the poor from their doors, but on set days and at
set times.[61] In many rural areas of southern Europe, almsgiving may have
been an important means of reinforcing seigneurial ties, and seems at the

56   See, for example, J. Townsend, *A journey through Spain in the years 1786 and 1787*, 3
vols (London, 1791), vol. 1, pp. 366 and 378–9; vol. 2, pp. 6–9, 84–5, 98 and 278; and vol. 3,
pp. 16–18, 57–60 and 251–4. For criticism of indiscriminate charity among clerics by other
clerics, see F. A. Lorenzana, *Cartas, edictos y otras obras sueltas* (Toledo, 1786), pp. ii–iii.
57   Borrell, *Pobresa*, pp. 537–9.
58   Hufton, *Poor of eighteenth-century France*, pp. 201–10; Borrell, *Pobresa*, pp. 30–3.
59   W. J. Callahan, 'The problem of confinement: an aspect of poor relief in eighteenth-
century Spain', *Hispanic American Historical Review* 51 (1971), 1–24.
60   de Zamora, *Diario*, p. 58.
61   M. Llorca Agulló, 'Informe del Alcalde Mayor (1786)', reproduced in *El Penedès*

very least to have been part and parcel of the kind of paternalism required of those of higher social status.[62] A Catalan noble described in his diary the regular distribution of alms on the feast day of his patron saint, when he also provided a dinner for his tenants, as a duty that was expected of him.[63] Similarly, on a visit to his country estate in 1794, he distributed alms in the village.[64] Even further down the social scale, charity remained a duty that was owed to those less fortunate, particularly where ties of kinship or neighbourliness existed. In his memorandum book, a peasant from a tiny village near Vic recorded that, in the year of harvest failure of 1764, his household had fed twenty-five to thirty poor every evening, up to sixty-five on one occasion, 'many of whom were known to us, or kin'.[65] His son later explained his family's ability to weather the difficult years of 1788–91 and pay for rebuilding of the house without going into debt by the fact that, throughout, they had kept up their support for the poor, thus God had shown them charity.[66] Similarly, peasants from the Penedès district saw almsgiving as 'a duty inherited from their forebears; and in the recent years of scarcity, some insisted upon fulfilling this'.[67]

Moreover, outdoor relief at the local level could be adapted to fit the needs of families and maintain the independence and unity of households *in situ*. This is one of the merits often emphasised by champions of the English poor law, but there are indications that relief could function in a similar manner in France and Spain. Even Hufton offers some rare praise for the locally administered *ateliers de charité* introduced by Turgot, describing them as a 'sympathetic and highly imaginative recognition that the problem of poverty was a family problem'.[68] In Spain, much of the opposition to the large urban workhouses or *hospicios* stemmed from the conviction that local poor relief funds were best deployed locally to help the poor in their own parishes, rather than transferring funds and

durant la segona meitat del segle XVIII: textos inèdits, ed. R. Arnabat and B. Moreno (Vilafranca, 2006), pp. 53–96.

62 K. Norberg, *Rich and poor in Grenoble, 1600–1814* (Berkeley, 1985), pp. 153–6 and 255–7.

63 d'Amat i de Cortada, *Calaix de sastre*, vol. 3, p. 275 and vol. 4, p. 249.

64 Ibid., vol. 2, p. 224.

65 'Llibre de comptes de Joan Quatrecases', p. 182.

66 Ibid., p. 124.

67 M. Barba i Roca, 'Apéndice a las respuestas al interrogatorio sobre Villafranca del Penedès (1790)', reproduced in R. Arnabat, *Manuel Barba i Roca (1752–1824): entre l'humanisme i la Il·lustració* (Vilafranca del Penedès, 2006), pp. 253–63 (p. 263).

68 Hufton, *Poor of eighteenth-century France*, p. 184.

poor alike to the *hospicios* which, like their French equivalents, were often (though not always) inefficient and costly.[69] Instead, local parishes by the eighteenth century were increasingly redirecting funds from endowed charities such as bread doles towards other forms of giving, such as payments to poor families. These efforts were actively sanctioned by the government in a law of 1785, which provided for the bringing together of regular almsgiving and different endowed funds at the parish or neighbourhood level under the administration of a single body, the *Juntas de Caridad*, along the lines of the French *bureaux de charité*.[70] Much more work needs to be done to determine how widespread and active these bodies were. In Spain, the legislation envisaged that these would be urban institutions, to be created in provincial and district-level towns, and most examples that have hitherto come to light are urban.[71] The best-known examples for Catalonia are those of Barcelona and Vilafranca del Penedès, a district capital. The Barcelona committee was initially set up on an *ad hoc* basis following the harvest failure of 1764 and again in 1799–1804, which were years of high prices. Prominent on the committee were cotton manufacturers, concerned to provide relief for their workforce, many of whom were unemployed as a result of the wartime blockade on overseas trade and to avoid urban unrest. The committee's main activity was to run soup kitchens for the poor, financed through collections, raffles and charity balls.[72] It went on to set up the permanent institution of a new workhouse in 1803.

The Vilafranca *Junta* was founded in 1799 under the auspices of a local enlightened lawyer, Manuel Barba i Roca, with the aim of undertaking a long-term reform of local administration of poor relief.[73] Within two years, it was running a regular soup kitchen for poor families throughout the winter months and a school for poor girls as outdoor relief for an

69 On opposition to the *hôpitaux généraux* and the *hospicios*, see Hufton, *Poor of eighteenth-century France*, pp. 149–59; Callahan, 'The problem of confinement', pp. 13–16 and 21–2; Borrell, *Pobresa*, pp. 391–7 and 499–505.

70 Hufton, *Poor of eighteenth-century France*, pp. 159–73; J. Soubeyroux, 'El encuentro del pobre y la sociedad: asistencia y represión en el Madrid del siglo XVIII', *Estudios de Historia Social* 20–1 (1982), 7–225 (pp. 126–59).

71 Soubeyroux, 'El encuentro', pp. 126–7, n. 3, documents *Juntas* in Granada, Zamora, Torrelavega and Villanueva de los Infantes, as well as Barcelona.

72 P. Vilar, *La Catalogne dans l'Espagne moderne*, 3 vols (Paris, 1962), vol. 2, pp. 410–18; A. Simon, 'Barcelona i Catalunya durant la crisi de subsistències de 1763–1764', in *La població catalana a l'edat moderna. Deu estudis* (Bellaterra, 1996), pp. 193–210.

73 Arnabat, *Manuel Barba i Roca*, pp. 127–61 and 269–79.

unstated number of households. The emphasis was very much on self-help and efficiency: labourers were relieved by employing them to plant potatoes and other vegetables for the soup kitchen, and girls were provided with clothing that would enable them to find work in domestic service. In 1804, the *Junta* offered a prize, advertised in the Barcelona newspapers, to anyone who could invent a machine for pureeing potatoes for Rumford soups, the soups having been eulogised by Barba i Roca the previous year as an economical means of feeding the poor.

For Catalonia, an intriguing example has come to light of a rural *Junta de Caridad*, founded in the small village of Batea in south-west Catalonia in 1786.[74] Accounts survive for only two years, 1786 and 1789. What is striking, however, is that at the end of both years the committee was in credit, simply through bequests and collections in church. In 1786, only 3 per cent of expenditure went on indoor relief in the small local hospital. Of the rest, 43 per cent was spent helping thirty-seven households through short-term periods of illness by paying for food, and the remaining 54 per cent was spent on daily pensions to a crippled artisan, a poor widow with four children, another two widows and a young woman. In addition, the relatives of two orphan children were being paid to look after them and to ensure they were being educated. Most interestingly, the committee had brought two local girls back from the Barcelona Misericòrdia workhouse, and was paying them to teach cotton spinning and carding to others. The accounts for 1789 are even more impressive. The fund was not only in credit at the start of the year, but had almost doubled the amount by the end. Again, expenditure on the hospital was minimal: just 4.5 per cent including the salary of the warden. The bulk of expenditure had gone on outdoor relief, either temporary help with illness or regular pensions to widows, orphans and labourers 'burdened with children', including milk for two babies, but also on the school for poor children. A new expense had been the purchase of five oilskins to loan to local families for carrying oil up from the mill to their houses (the local economy was based on grain and olives).

Batea is, of course, just one example of poor relief at the local level in southern Europe. In the absence of additional evidence, as yet it is impossible to say how often local poor relief was generously funded

---

74 Arxiu General de la Diputació de Barcelona, *lligall* 13, 'Articulo sobre establecimiento de la Junta de Caridad de la villa de Batea'. The village of Batea is missing from the 1787 census, but in 1845 had around 2,400 inhabitants.

and sensitively administered, and how often communities struggled to amass resources or lacked the individuals capable of administering them efficiently. Poor relief in southern Europe could share many of the merits of English poor relief in terms of helping poor households to survive without splitting them up or consigning them to workhouses. It clearly could in some places, such as Batea, function well.[75] The difference is that, in England, local efforts were sanctioned and given structure and direction by a national scheme of legislation, based on a system of compulsory taxation that effectively avoided the danger that some parishes would offer relief and others not (the 'free rider' problem).[76] A key question for further research into poor relief in southern Europe is therefore how far the absence of a system based on compulsory taxation affected the ability of parishes to raise revenue for the poor. Richard Smith has suggested that the consolidation of the poor laws permitted a sustained increase in the sums raised and expended upon poor relief over time.[77] This brings us back to the question raised earlier with reference to Lindert's work, namely, the relative generosity of poor relief across Europe. It would appear that government relief expenditure at least was greater in England and the Dutch Republic than elsewhere. It remains an open question, however, whether greater generosity was the result of more efficient systems of raising revenue, a greater willingness to give to charitable causes, or of greater levels of overall wealth in these societies. As Smith shows effectively, however, what is most striking about comparisons between England and France is the much higher levels of relief provided in rural areas compared with urban in England than in France.[78] Calculations made by one contemporary in 1792 suggested that the amount of relief raised in rural areas amounted to £1 per 2.6 inhabitants, compared with £1 per 6 inhabitants in large towns.[79] That the burden of relief could be so effectively borne by the countryside in England is testimony to the strength of the agrarian economy although, at the same time, it may also reflect the greater need for support among a labouring class that was far more numerous than

75   Hickey also stresses the extent of local dynamism that existed in France. Hickey, *Local hospitals*, pp. 122–33.
76   R. M. Smith, 'Charity, self-interest and welfare: reflections from demographic and family history', in *Charity, self-interest and welfare*, ed. Daunton, pp. 23–49.
77   Smith, 'Social security', pp. 81–2.
78   Ibid., pp. 84–6.
79   J. Howlett, 'On the population and situation of the poor in England', *Annals of Agriculture* 18 (1792), 573–81 (tab. on p. 578).

its continental equivalents. Nonetheless, at least until the late eighteenth century, England possessed a class of ratepayers capable of supporting the rural poor. The smaller size elsewhere of this 'middling sort' group may be significant in explaining differences in welfare provision. Part of the strength of rural provision under the English old poor law may also be due to the greater tendency of the English aristocracy and wealthy elites to maintain a continued presence in rural areas, rather than gravitating to the towns permanently. An additional question for studies of poor relief in southern Europe would be precisely to ascertain which groups within rural communities did take responsibility for the welfare of the poor. So far, considerable emphasis has been placed on the 'pivotal' role of the parish priest, but by the eighteenth century, he may have been joined by 'enlightened' figures within communities, such as Manuel Barba i Roca.[80]

A particular insight of recent work has been to recognise the demographic implications of extensive poor relief in rural areas, namely, preventing excessive migration to urban areas in times of crisis, and thus indirectly keeping overall mortality levels lower, given how severe the urban penalty was in early modern Europe.[81] Harvest failures in southern Europe were correlated with rises in mortality, particularly in towns, in contrast to England, where parish-based poor relief combined with government intervention in grain markets prevented rising prices from translating into rising mortality. Moreover, the support offered by the old poor law to illegitimate children arguably created a unique situation whereby illegitimacy ratios were lower in towns than in the country. The converse is certainly true of France: Jean-Pierre Bardet has shown that illegitimacy ratios in Rouen were of the order of 20 per cent, compared with only 2 per cent in the surrounding Normandy countryside.[82] Bardet estimates that some 70 per cent of urban illegitimate births were to immigrants. Given that such illegitimate children were then likely to be abandoned at foundling hospitals, with a consequently much higher risk of mortality, the final effect was to raise urban infant mortality rates still

---

80 The description of the priest's role as 'pivotal' comes from Hufton, *Poor of eighteenth-century France*, p. 183. Similar claims are made by Norberg, *Rich and poor in Grenoble*, pp. 193–4; Puigvert, *Església*, pp. 88–110 and Pullan, 'Charity and poor relief', pp. 77–9. In Catalonia at least, priests also had an important role as the endowers of many charitable funds.

81 Smith, 'Social security'.

82 J.-P. Bardet, *Rouen aux XVIIe et XVIIIe siècles: les mutations d'un espace social* (Paris, 1983).

further. Whether the same effect can be demonstrated for Italy or Spain remains to be seen. Overall illegitimacy ratios were far lower in Spain, and caution needs to be exercised when considering what proportion of foundlings were illegitimate.[83] Nonetheless, it would seem to be the case that illegitimate children in both Spain and Italy almost invariably ended up in foundling hospitals.

More generally, English poor relief may have contributed directly and indirectly to keeping infant and particularly child mortality rates lower than elsewhere in Europe. The direct contribution took the form of relief payments to families burdened with young children, increasingly so over the eighteenth century.[84] The indirect contribution came in the form of payments to the elderly, which freed married couples from the obligation of caring for elderly kin, and left them able to invest more in their children instead, though it is worth noting in this context that nuclear households may have lost out in terms of the childcare that extended kin may have been able to offer. While difficult to test, the hypothesis that the poor law may have contributed to England's fertility-driven 'low pressure' demographic regime serves to underline still further the need for comparative studies of European poor relief and the effects of different systems.

This brings us back to the relationship between family forms and welfare provision. As discussed above, 'nuclear hardship' is perceived to have hit the elderly the most, a factor certainly recognised by the old poor law. The predominance at least until the eighteenth century of the elderly, particularly widows, among English poor law recipients, has been well documented.[85] Similarly, almshouses for the elderly far outnumbered other charitable foundations in the Dutch Republic.[86] More research needs to be done into how the elderly fared in southern Europe. It tends to be assumed that they were co-resident with kin, which was indeed the case in those

83 For Italian foundlings, see D. I. Kertzer, *Sacrificed for honor. Italian infant abandonment and the politics of reproductive control* (Boston, 1993). For Spanish foundlings, see the references and discussion in J. Marfany, 'Proto-industrialisation and demographic change in Catalonia, c.1680–1829' (unpublished Ph.D. thesis, University of Cambridge, 2003), pp. 220–30.

84 P. Slack, 'Dearth and social policy in early modern England', *Social History of Medicine* 5 (1992), 1–17.

85 R. M. Smith, 'Ageing and well-being in early modern England: pension trends and gender preferences under the English old poor law c.1650–1800', in *Old age from antiquity to post-modernity*, ed. P. Johnson and P. Thane (London, 1998), pp. 64–95.

86 H. Looijesteijn, 'Funding and founding private charities: Leiden almshouses and their founders, 1450–1800', *Continuity and Change* 27 (2012), 199–239.

areas where the extended family was the norm, but begs the question of what occurred in those areas characterised by nuclear families. The elderly were an obvious category to receive indoor support but, where the populations of hospitals have been analysed, the picture is mixed. Norberg found that around one-fifth of the inmates of the Grenoble *hôpital général* on the eve of the revolution were over sixty, but the same proportion were aged under five.[87] Marital status and absence of kin appear to have been more important than age: 75 per cent of the adult inmates were single men and women. The same is broadly true of the population of the Barcelona Misericòrdia workhouse in the 1760s to 1780s where, although those over sixty had a visible presence, they were actually slightly underrepresented in relation to the age structure of the Catalan population.[88] In terms of age, young women dominated, but in terms of marital status, it was widows who were the most overrepresented category, followed by spinsters. The elderly, therefore, also figure to some extent as a vulnerable category, even in areas of predominantly extended families, but less so than in England. However, these figures are only for indoor relief. Quantification of the proportion of outdoor relief the elderly may have received is impossible, though further research might shed some light on how prominent they were among recipients.

Viazzo is certainly right that the strain of poverty appears to have hit hardest when families were burdened with young children, as evidenced by the increasing abandonment of children, legitimate as well as illegitimate, in the face of rising prices over the eighteenth century. Confronted with growing numbers of abandoned children, Spanish reformers, backed by the Crown, called for the foundation of more foundling hospitals and reform of existing hospitals to counter the high mortality levels.

Girls and young women were another group increasingly targeted by formal relief programmes in Spain and Italy, a response to what Montserrat Carbonell has termed the growing 'feminisation of poverty' during this period.[89] Family breakdown, particularly the death of or abandonment by the male head of household, was frequently grounds for admission to orphanages or to poorhouses. It would be wrong to view families as abandoning daughters to these institutions. While in some instances women did spend many years in such places, often a stay in a workhouse

87 Norberg, *Rich and poor in Grenoble*, pp. 175–80.
88 M. Carbonell, *Sobreviure a Barcelona. Dones, pobresa i assistència al segle XVIII* (Vic, 1997), pp. 127–31.
89 Ibid., pp. 112–21. See also tab. 4 on p. 196.

seems to have been viewed as a temporary measure to alleviate the burden on the family and to provide the girl herself with training that would enhance her opportunities for earning a living, either as a domestic servant or in the textile trades. The case of the two young women reclaimed from the Barcelona Misericòrdia workhouse by the Batea charity committee in order to teach spinning shows that parishes did not lose sight of the girls who entered these institutions, and that they were considered to have acquired useful skills. Sandra Cavallo describes similar strategic uses of institutions during difficult periods and at difficult points in the life cycle by poor families in seventeenth- and eighteenth-century Turin.[90]

What would be of interest to discover for southern Europe is how other types of poor relief fitted into this pattern. In other words, did the kinds of local, primarily outdoor relief that have yet to be studied also target orphans, young women and widows, or was the range of recipients broader? Certainly dowry funds were also for the benefit of young women, arguably compensating for the relative lack of waged labour for females, and helped in the initial stages of setting up a household. As yet, however, there is little indication as to who were the main recipients of almsgiving and what criteria, if any, governed their selection.

Conclusion

This chapter has sought to survey differences in poor relief provision across Europe, with particular reference to the perceived north–south divide whereby southern poor relief was restricted to urban areas and supposedly inadequate both in terms of expenditure and the indiscrim-inate manner in which it was administered. By contrast, northern Europe, especially England, is argued to have benefited from generous expenditure on poor relief, which was more carefully targeted and, above all, widely available in rural areas. In turn, north–south divides in welfare provision can be seen as being closely bound up with differences in family forms and the strength of family ties. Whether nuclear families really were more dynamic than extended ones, as de Vries would have it, is debatable, but certainly poor relief provision, especially in England, may have played a vital role in sustaining the nuclear family by providing migrants and the elderly kin they left behind with a safety net. However, extended families

90   Cavallo, 'Family obligations', pp. 93–8.

were no less vulnerable to poverty, despite Laslett's claims; merely, poverty hit hardest earlier in the life cycle, when families were struggling with young children as well as with elderly kin. Indoor relief in southern Europe was therefore concerned much more with the young: foundlings, orphans and especially young women, but the limited evidence so far suggests a wider range of recipients of outdoor relief at the local level.

The chapter has questioned the view that poor relief in the south was restricted to urban areas, pointing to the evidence for a wide range of welfare in the countryside. It has also suggested that Hufton's view that rural poor relief was 'inadequate' may be unfair: not only is our knowledge of rural poor relief too thin to endorse such a claim but, more importantly, assessments of the adequacy of welfare depend very much on the degree to which poor relief was supposed to subsidise the household economy. Welfare in southern Europe was undoubtedly a patchwork of different institutional and individual gifts, but that is not to say that households could not and did not draw upon these different sources in order to make a significant contribution to their incomes. Urban institutions may well have taken more of the strain in difficult years, but the extent to which the balance was skewed between rural and urban poor relief remains to be seen.

None of this is to deny the unique features of the English old poor law. It is highly plausible that this system based on compulsory taxation and administered through local parishes can be credited with enabling aspects of economic growth, and with beneficial effects in terms of lower mortality. All that is proposed here is an investigation into the workings of rural poor relief elsewhere in Europe. Even in the absence of a framework such as the English poor law, some communities at least seem to have managed to respond to the problem of poverty with a certain degree of dynamism. How typical they were and how successful their efforts could be are questions that would merit further research and, ultimately, would serve to contextualise the achievements of the English poor law.

5

Support for the Elderly during the 'Crisis' of the English Old Poor Law

SAMANTHA WILLIAMS

In early modern England many elderly men and women faced deep poverty in old age.[1] A legal obligation to relieve the aged poor was enshrined in the Elizabethan poor law legislation of 1598–1601 (39 Eliz., c. 3; 39 Eliz., c. 4; 43 Eliz., c. 2).[2] Overseers were to dispense the money rated from local inhabitants for relief of the 'lame impotent old [and] blind'.[3] Under the old poor law, the aged were considered the most deserving of parochial relief. Those who could no longer work due to age and infirmity were generally preferentially treated by the parish authorities: they accounted for the largest group of recipients and they were allocated the largest regular cash payments (pensions), often for many years.[4] It has been

---

1   S. R. Ottaway, 'Introduction: authority, autonomy, and responsibility among the aged in the pre-industrial past', in *Power and poverty: old age in the pre-industrial past*, ed. S. R. Ottaway, L. A. Botelho and K. Kittredge (Westport, CT, 2002), pp. 1–12 (p. 1).

2   R. M. Smith, 'The structured dependence of the elderly as a recent development: some sceptical historical thoughts', *Ageing and Society* 4 (1984), 409–28 (p. 419); S. R. Ottaway, *The decline of life: old age in eighteenth-century England* (Cambridge, 2004), pp. 173–4; E. M. Leonard, *The early history of English poor relief* (Cambridge, 1900, repr. London, 1965), p. 140; P. A. Fideler, *Social welfare in pre-industrial England* (Basingstoke, 2006), pp. 99–101.

3   Fideler, *Social welfare*, p. 100. See also Ottaway, *The decline of life*, p. 173.

4   Smith, 'Structured dependence'; R. M. Smith, 'Ageing and well-being in early modern England: pension trends and gender preferences under the English old poor law c.1650–1800', in *Old age from antiquity to post-modernity*, ed. P. Johnson and P. Thane (London, 1998), pp. 64–95; M. Pelling and R. M. Smith (eds), *Life, death and the elderly: historical perspectives* (London, 1991); S. R. Ottaway, 'Providing for the elderly in eighteenth-century England', *Continuity and Change* 13 (1998), 391–418; Ottaway, *The decline of life*; D. Thomson, 'The decline of social welfare: falling state support for the elderly since early

argued by Susannah Ottaway that 'the care of the aged and important poor remained one of [the old poor law's] most closely guarded principles, and one of its least controversial doctrines'.[5]

Much of the research on the aged poor relates to the period before 1800, yet from the late eighteenth century the old poor law was in a prolonged 'crisis'. This chapter focuses upon this long period of difficulty and its implications for the aged poor. It is based on evidence from two communities: Campton and Shefford in east Bedfordshire. The study begins before the crisis, in the 1760s, and terminates with the Poor Law Amendment Act of 1834. The approach adopted – the creation of 104 'pauper biographies' of the elderly through nominal linkage between poor law sources and family reconstitution – provides unusually detailed evidence on the nature of relief to this group though the assembly of longitudinal pauper biographies.[6] 'Old age' has been defined as those aged sixty or above.[7] The methodology of pauper biographies provides evidence that cannot be found in the overseers' accounts alone; the account books for Campton and Shefford list recipients' names, the amount given in cash or the value of relief in kind, and, some reasons for relief (such as illness or unemployment). However, once linked to the family reconstitution, the researcher knows the family circumstances of recipients; for the elderly this would include information on their age, whether they had a living spouse, age at widowhood and remarriage, and the number of teenage or grown-up children they had. The main aim of the chapter is to provide more precise information on the family circumstances of elderly paupers; this is only possible at the microlevel. The biographies have been analysed

---

Victorian times', *Ageing and Society* 4 (1984), 451–82. Pat Thane and Lynn Botelho have offered alternative perspectives: P. Thane, *Old age in English history: past experiences, present issues* (Oxford, 2000); L. A. Botelho, *Old age and the English poor law, 1500–1700* (Woodbridge, 2004). See also: M. Pelling, 'Old age, poverty, and disability in early modern Norwich: work, remarriage, and other expedients', in *Life, death and the elderly*, ed. Pelling and Smith, pp. 74–101; T. Sokoll, 'Old age in poverty: the record of Essex pauper letters, 1780–1834', in *Chronicling poverty: the voices and strategies of the English poor, 1640–1840*, ed. T. Hitchcock, P. King and P. Sharpe (Basingstoke, 1997), pp. 127–54.

5   Ottaway, *The decline of life*, p. 173.

6   On methodology see S. Williams, *Poverty, gender and life-cycle under the English poor law, 1760–1834* (Woodbridge, 2011), pp. 30–4. This approach has also been adopted for the elderly by Smith, 'Ageing and well-being', p. 69; Ottaway, *The decline of life*, chaps 5–6.

7   Ottaway, *The decline of life*, pp. 7, 20–1, 26 and 59, and chap. 1 *passim*; Thane, *Old age*, pp. 21–7. See the discussion of the definition of old age in M. Pelling and R. M. Smith, 'Introduction', in *Life, death and the elderly*, ed. Pelling and Smith, pp. 1–38 (pp. 5–8).

both quantitatively and qualitatively, to show trends over time and to reflect upon individual life courses.

Between the seventeenth and late eighteenth centuries social welfare expanded; not only were the elderly a prominent group in the list of recipients but the value of relief to them increased in real terms.[8] Aged women, particularly widows, tended to significantly outnumber men.[9] This was a period when 9–10 per cent of the population was aged sixty or over.[10] However, expenditure on the poor increased rapidly from the late eighteenth century: annual national costs rose from an average of £689,971 for the three years ending in 1750, to £1,912,241 for the period 1783–85, to £4,077,891 in 1803, and to £7.9 million in 1818.[11] The crisis in providing for the poor – which was particularly evident in the south midlands, south and south-east – was due to many factors, including rapid population increase, parliamentary enclosure, the decay and decline of cottage industries (especially those of hand-spinning and weaving), the Revolutionary and Napoleonic Wars, harvest failures and post-war depression that brought with it widespread seasonal underemployment.[12] Attitudes towards the poor hardened and there were repeated calls for reform of the poor laws, finally resulting in the Poor Law Amendment Act of 1834.[13] There has been a strong and remarkably enduring assumption in the secondary literature on this crisis period that 1795 marked a decisive turning point in parish policy, with the Speenhamland decision to give relief to male heads of households scaled by the price of bread and the size of families, either as minimum wages or unemployment assistance. George Boyer has argued that the major function of poor relief in rural

---

8 T. Wales, 'Poverty, poor relief and the life-cycle: some evidence from seventeenth-century Norfolk', in *Land, kinship and life-cycle*, ed. R. M. Smith (Cambridge, 1984), pp. 351–404; W. Newman Brown, 'The receipt of poor relief and family situation: Aldenham, Hertfordshire 1630–90', in *Land, kinship and life-cycle*, ed. Smith, pp. 405–22; Botelho, *Old age*, chap. 4; S. Williams, 'Poor relief, labourers' households and living standards in rural England c.1770–1834: a Bedfordshire case study', *Economic History Review* 58 (2005), 485–519 (pp. 486–8).

9 Ottaway, *The decline of life*, pp. 179–80, 184–5 and 222–7; S. King, *Poverty and welfare in England 1700–1850: a regional perspective* (Manchester, 2000), chaps 6–7.

10 Smith, 'Ageing and well-being', pp. 70 and 88; Smith, 'Structured dependence', p. 414.

11 D. R. Green, *Pauper capital: London and the poor law, 1790–1870* (Farnham, 2010), pp. 26–7.

12 A. Kidd, *State, society and the poor in nineteenth-century England* (Basingstoke, 1999), p. 14. See also Fideler, *Social welfare*, chap. 6.

13 Ibid., pp. 13–29.

parishes from 1795 to 1834 was the payment of unemployment benefits to seasonally unemployed agricultural labourers.[14] The dependency ratio remained high, despite a contraction in the proportion of the population aged over sixty, due to a rapidly rising birth rate. In 1826, the dependency ratio reached a peak with 39.62 per cent of the population of England and Wales aged fourteen or under and 6.54 per cent aged sixty and above.[15] However, despite there being a fall in the proportion of the elderly in the population due to the increase in the number of children, life expectancy for those aged sixty-five and over improved over the 'long' eighteenth century.[16]

This chapter seeks to establish the impact of the crisis upon the elderly poor. A great deal of the discussion on this period has concerned relief to families and able-bodied unemployed men, but a small number of historians have shown that the growing crisis affected the aged in a variety of ways. Ottaway argues that up to 1800 the welfare net spread more widely and that parishes continued to accommodate the elderly while increasing relief to couples with young children. In fact, the dependency of the elderly increased, as rapid inflation and underemployment pushed older men and women from 'the margins of independent subsistence into dependent poverty'. The real value of the pension declined and more of the aged poor were accommodated in workhouses.[17] Richard Smith also finds a decline in the real value of pensions to the elderly after 1750, as well as a masculinisation of pensioners, most probably due to a growing number of families requiring relief and a shift in policy from the allocation of outdoor relief to elderly women to provision for them within a workhouse (such as in Terling, Essex, and also found by Ottaway).[18] Steven King's

14   G. R. Boyer, *An economic history of the English poor law, 1750–1850* (Cambridge, 1990), pp. 10–23. See also A. Armstrong, *Farmworkers: a social and economic history, 1770–1980* (London, 1988), pp. 69–70.

15   E. A. Wrigley and R. S. Schofield, *The population history of England, 1541–1871: a reconstruction*, 2nd edn (Cambridge, 1989), pp. 443–50 (tab. A3.1 at pp. 528–9).

16   E. A. Wrigley, 'British population during the "long" eighteenth century, 1680–1840', in *The Cambridge economic history of modern Britain, 1: Industrialisation, 1700–1860*, ed. R. Floud and P. Johnson (Cambridge, 2004), pp. 57–95, tab. 3.5, p. 80; E. A. Wrigley, R. S. Davies, J. E. Oeppen and R. S. Schofield, *English population history from family reconstitution, 1580–1837* (Cambridge, 1997), pp. 280–93, and particularly tab. 6.19 at p. 290.

17   Ottaway, *The decline of life*, pp. 10–12, 223, 227–32; Ottaway, 'Providing for the elderly', p. 409; King, *Poverty and welfare*, chap. 6.

18   Smith, 'Ageing and well-being', pp. 83–8; R. M. Smith, 'Charity, self-interest and

study is one of the few that continues until 1834. He finds that the elderly were squeezed in the south and east in the 1780s and 1790s – particularly the very old (aged seventy and over) – but that by 1820, elderly men were reclaiming their place in the relief rolls. There was less of a squeeze on the aged poor in the north and west, but pensions here were generally more meagre.[19] Both Alannah Tomkins and Ottaway argue that the hardening of attitudes towards the poor also extended to the elderly; the aged poor were increasingly perceived as an encumbrance and a parish burden.[20]

The aim of this study is to establish whether the elderly in Campton and Shefford were squeezed, either in the numbers on relief or in the quality of the care that they received, by an increase in pauperised male-headed families. The chapter calculates the age at which pensions commenced, the number and proportion of the elderly in receipt of parish relief over this period, whether the aged poor were moved from outdoor relief into a workhouse, and the value and relative generosity of relief over time. Given that the elderly had been perceived to be a particularly deserving group, did their numbers hold up with worsening economic conditions and an expansion in other groups also requiring help? The crisis might also have impacted negatively on the value and quality of the assistance given to the aged poor. Since regular weekly cash sums – 'pensions' – were the most valuable source of relief, the chapter will present some estimations on their value, but it will also assess the importance of additional assistance in kind given to the elderly, such as rent, fuel, clothing and shoes, care, nursing and burial costs.

**

Campton was a small, rural, and predominantly agricultural parish, with a population of 449 in 1831, while Shefford was Campton's neighbouring market town, with 763 inhabitants and a more varied occupational structure, with 40 per cent of families employed in manufacture.[21] Like

---

welfare: reflections from demographic and family history', in *Charity, self-interest and welfare in the English past*, ed. M. Daunton (London, 1996), pp. 23–49 (pp. 39–40). See Ottaway's in-depth study of Terling's workhouse: *The decline of life*, chap. 7.

19   King, *Poverty and welfare*, pp. 164–70 and 208–15.

20   A. Tomkins, *The experience of urban poverty, 1723–82: parish, charity and credit* (Manchester, 2006), p. 8; Ottaway, *The decline of life*, pp. 12–13.

21   *1831 Census*, Enumeration abstract (PP, 1833, XXXVI), pp. 2–3. A detailed study of these communities appears in Williams, *Poverty, gender and life-cycle*; Williams, 'Poor relief, labourers' households and living standards'.

Figure 5.1. Annual expenditure on poor relief in Campton (1767–1834) and Shefford (1794–1828), in pounds

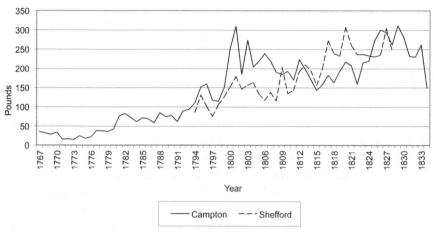

Source: See text.

Figure 5.2. Number of pensioners and all paupers, Campton and Shefford, by decade

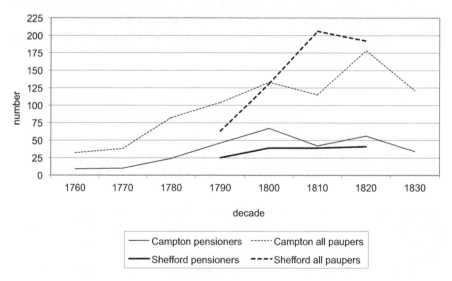

Source: See text.

elsewhere in the south and east, the crisis in Campton and Shefford was marked by rapidly rising expenditure and numbers claiming relief (Figures 5.1 and 5.2).[22] The cost of living was volatile in this period, with rapid inflation from the 1790s and deflation after Waterloo.[23] Parish overseers were unable to take advantage of the reduction in the cost of living after 1815 since the agricultural depression, and associated unemployment, kept spending high. It is evident that the 'problem' of poverty had significantly worsened.[24] In Campton and Shefford, parish officials responded to rising costs and the lengthening relief lists by reducing the proportion of expenditure allocated to relief in kind. The decline was far more severe in Campton, where relief in kind fell from 31 per cent of spending on the poor in the 1760s, to 17 per cent in the 1770s, to 7 per cent in the 1830s, while in Shefford it fell from 10 per cent in the 1790s to 8 per cent in the 1820s. The highest nominal pension sums also fell slightly from the 1820s, although they remained higher than they had been before 1800 and did not fall to the extent of the cost of living.[25] The parishes also sought to contain medical costs through medical contracts.[26]

There were 104 elderly paupers in total: sixty-two in Campton (1767–1834) and forty-two in Shefford (1794–1828).[27] Age information was available for almost 60 per cent of these aged paupers, while for the others either their family circumstances or their pauper 'careers' indicate that they too were old. John Ivory, for instance, was given occasional relief and

22 Williams, *Poverty, gender and life-cycle*, pp. 36–8; D. Eastwood, *Governing rural England: tradition and transformation in local government, 1780–1840* (Oxford, 1994), tab. 6.1 at p. 135; King, *Poverty and welfare*, chap. 6.
23 C. H. Feinstein, 'Pessimism perpetuated: real wages and the standard of living in Britain during and after the industrial revolution', *Journal of Economic History* 58 (1998), 625–58 (tab. 2 at p. 640).
24 Williams, *Poverty, gender and life-cycle*, pp. 36–8.
25 Ibid., pp. 39–40.
26 S. Williams, 'Practitioners' income and provision for the poor: parish doctors in the late eighteenth and early nineteenth centuries', *Social History of Medicine* 18 (2005), 1–28.
27 There were 104 elderly individual pauper biographies, counting couples as two people even if all payments were only paid to one spouse. The present chapter analyses the elderly pauper biographies in far more depth than in Williams, *Poverty, gender and life-cycle*, pp. 57, 64–5, 111–14, 140–4, 161 and 163. BLARS, P18/12/1–2, X514/1–3 Campton overseers' accounts (1767–1834), P70/12/1–2 Shefford overseers' accounts (1794–1828), and the family reconstitution for Campton-with-Shefford and Southill, CAMPOP. Other sources used were: BLARS, P70/8/1 Shefford's vestry minutes, P70/11/1–3 Shefford's ratepayers' books, and Campton-with-Shefford's baptism, marriage and burial registers.

Table 5.1. Age distribution of elderly pensioners, Campton and Shefford, 1760s–1830s

Age	Percentage
60–4	37
65–9	33
70–4	12
75–9	12
80 or over	6
[70 or over]	[30]

Source: See text.

then a regular weekly pension from 1795 until his burial on Christmas Eve 1797. He had grown-up children aged forty and forty-four, and so he was likely to have been in his mid-sixties.[28] In these two communities the most common age for a pension later in life was when recipients were in their sixties (70 per cent), but regular relief was awarded for others only when they were older, in their seventies (24 per cent) or even their eighties (6 per cent) (see Table 5.1). These figures highlight that the withdrawal from the labour market was a gradual process and that it was debility, rather than old age, which motivated a person to apply for a pension and for officials to grant it.[29] Parish dependency was gendered: women tended to be younger than men when they collected their first 'old age' pension. Four-fifths were in their sixties, with one-fifth in their seventies, such as Susannah Brawn who was aged seventy-four. In contrast, 50 per cent of men were in their sixties, 41 per cent in their seventies and 9 per cent in

28   In both communities just over 71 per cent of elderly paupers had family reconsti-tution forms and thus potential age information (baptism and burial dates, age at burial information, or information from the 1841 census). Of those, at least 82 per cent did have age information, which means that just over 58 per cent of all elderly paupers had accurate age information. It was also available from Campton's overseers' accounts which listed the age of pensioners in December 1834. For others without baptism dates but with first marriages, it was possible to estimate their age by using the average age at marriage in Campton and Shefford. Average age at marriage is given in S. Williams, 'Malthus, marriage and poor law allowances revisited: a Bedfordshire case study, 1770–1834', *Agricultural History Review* 52 (2004), 56–82 (pp. 79–80).
29   Smith, 'Ageing and well-being', p. 78; Ottaway, *The decline of life*, chap. 1; Sokoll, 'Old age in poverty', pp. 143–5.

their eighties. This confirms the results of other historians, who have also found that men were generally older when they came onto regular poor relief.[30]

Yet not all pensions commenced after the age of sixty in Campton and Shefford. Pensions were given to a small number of men and women in their fifties. Mary Rogers' pension, for instance, began when she was aged fifty-four following the death of her husband and she had two children under the age of fifteen, as well as other grown-up children. It could be argued that hers was a 'widow's pension' rather than an 'old age' one, but regular payments continued into her old age, until she was aged seventy-eight. One-third of recipients in their fifties were widows. In the other two-thirds of cases the beneficiaries were couples, such as William and Lucy Newman, and Thomas and Elizabeth Knight. Both couples had received relief earlier in their lives (when they were families) and were then allocated pensions again when they were in their fifties. In both cases they too still had adolescent children at home (as well as grown-up children) and in both instances the pensions were small at first but substantial at the point of the deaths of William and Thomas. These pensions then continued to Lucy (now aged fifty-nine) and Elizabeth (aged sixty-five), initially at reduced rates but rising again as they grew older. In all the instances where couples in their fifties were in receipt of a parish pension, when the husbands died the weekly sums continued to their widows. Another small group of women came on to long-term relief when they were widowed in middle age and they were responsible for dependent children, and their pensions continued without a break into their old age; this group lived particularly pauperised lives.

There are two ways in which regular relief to the elderly can be assessed: a snapshot approach per decade, and a longitudinal approach that follows each individual over their life courses. The first shows important trends over time, while the second reveals all the interactions between individuals and the parish authorities.[31] This section of the chapter pursues the first method and the decadal approach reveals that the number of elderly pensioners increased over time, except for the final period which was a

30 Ottaway, *The decline of life*, pp. 201–2; M. Barker-Read, 'The treatment of the aged poor in five selected West Kent parishes from settlement to Speenhamland (1662–1797)' (unpublished Ph.D. thesis, Open University, 1989), pp. 192–4; J. Pearson, '"Labor and sorrow": the living conditions of the elderly residents of Bocking, Essex, 1793–1807', in *Power and poverty*, ed. Ottaway, Botelho and Kittredge, pp. 126–42 (p. 126).
31 See Williams, *Poverty, gender and life-cycle*, chaps 2, 4.

Table 5.2. Number of elderly pensioners by decade in Campton and
Shefford, 1760s–1830s

Period	All pensioners	Elderly	Elderly as %	Men	Couples	Women
Campton						
1767–69	9	1	11	0	0	1
1770–79	9	4	44	1	1	2
1780–89	23	9	39	2	1	6
1790–99	41	9	22	3	0	6
1800–09	46	15	33	3	0	12
1810–19	39	19	49	1	7	11
1820–29	46	19	41	3	8	8
1830–34	29	14	48	2	5	7
Shefford						
1794–99	23	8	35	3	1	4
1800–10	35	12	34	4	3	5
1810–19	34	14	41	2	4	8
1820–28	42	17	40	1	4	12

Source: See text.
Note: The column 'all pensioners' enumerates groups of pensioners (couples, families,
lone parents) not individuals; total individuals would be men plus women plus couples
(counting as two individuals).

period of four (rather than ten) years for Campton (1830–34) (Table 5.2).[32]
The elderly accounted for a large proportion of all pensioners. In Shefford
the proportion increased, whereas in Campton there was more volatility,
but with an upward trend from the 1810s with the elderly accounting for
almost half of all pensioners in the 1810s and 1830s. Numbers rose faster
than population growth in the two communities,[33] perhaps a reflection
of the increased longevity for those aged over sixty-five.[34] The elderly
were heavily over-represented on the relief rolls: in 1841, 7–8 per cent
of Campton and Shefford's populations were aged sixty or over, but the

32   Ibid., p. 57.
33   Population rose from 316 in Campton and 474 in Shefford in 1801 to 449 and 763
respectively in 1831.
34   Wrigley, 'British population', tab. 3.5 p. 80; Wrigley *et al.*, *English population history*,
pp. 280–93, tab. 6.19 at p. 290.

aged poor accounted for 40–48 per cent of all pensioners between the late eighteenth and early nineteenth centuries; thus this age group were over-represented six times more than their proportional share of the popula-tion.[35] This is roughly in line with Richard Smith's findings that elderly pensioners were over-represented by between five to nine times their share of the population in the earlier period of 1663–1742.[36] Likewise, Ottaway found that the aged accounted for an average of 34 per cent of pensioners in the 1790s, but the figure could be as high as 41.8 per cent in agricultural areas.[37] Smith also estimated the proportion of those over the age of sixty who were likely to have a parish pension for some period prior to their deaths: in Whitchurch, Oxfordshire, at the end of the seventeenth century, the figure was between 40 and 50 per cent.[38] In Abson and Wick, near Bristol, in the period 1760–1803, 50 per cent of the elderly were in receipt of poor relief when they died;[39] in the early nineteenth century in Campton the proportion was around 50 per cent, but slightly lower in Shefford at around 30 per cent.[40] David Thomson's investigation into poor relief under the new poor law in Bedfordshire in the 1840s also revealed high levels of support for the elderly: of those aged seventy or more, two-thirds of women and half of men were pensioners; of those aged between sixty and sixty-nine, one-half of women and a 'significant minority' of men were regularly relieved.[41] These figures suggest some continuity, in the south and east at least, in the extent to which communities were prepared to support the aged over the eighteenth and nineteenth centuries.[42] This is

35   Williams, *Poverty, gender and life-cycle*, pp. 64–5.

36   Smith, 'Ageing and well-being', pp. 70 and 75.

37   Ottaway, *The decline of life*, pp. 184–9, 202–3 and 242–3. The proportion of the elderly on poor relief increased over the eighteenth century. Thane, on the other hand, finds a much lower proportion at 2.7 per cent in the 1790s for a variety of English parishes: *Old age*, pp. 147–8. See also King, *Poverty and welfare*, p. 168.

38   Smith, 'Ageing and well-being', p. 74.

39   M. E. Fissell, 'The "sick and drooping poor" in eighteenth-century Bristol and its region', *Society for the Social History of Medicine* 2 (1989), 35–58 (tab. 1 at p. 40).

40   S. Williams, 'Poor relief, welfare and medical provision in Bedfordshire: the social, economic and demographic context, c.1770–1834' (unpublished Ph.D. thesis, University of Cambridge, 1998), tabs 2.4 and 2.5 at p. 62.

41   D. Thomson, 'The welfare of the elderly in the past: a family or community responsi-bility?' in *Life, death and the elderly*, ed. Pelling and Smith, pp. 194–221 (p. 202).

42   In some areas elderly men came to dominate as union workhouse inmates: N. Goose 'Poverty, old age and gender in nineteenth-century England: the case of Hertfordshire', *Continuity and Change* 20 (2005), 351–84.

compelling evidence that the aged continued to be perceived as particularly deserving of relief despite the crisis in poor relief provision.

As elsewhere, there was an increase in the number of other groups of
pensioners (Table 5.2), some of whom were indeed families (with payments
to male household heads) who were allocated regular weekly sums, but
pensions to families were primarily restricted to particular periods of
hardship (1799–1802 and 1815–22).[43] Instead, it was largely female-headed
lone-parent families (as well as the elderly) who were given pensions.[44]
In terms of occasional payments, there was a massive rise in relief to
unemployed adult men and boys after 1815, although this never accounted
for more than 13 per cent of annual expenditure on the poor.[45] Single elderly
women were not squeezed out by either of these changes, however. In
Campton, the number of solitary aged women in receipt of a pension rose
slowly and then remained largely constant, while in Shefford the number
of elderly women increased in each decade. The predominance of elderly
women is clear. In both communities, the number of elderly men remained
at fewer than five while the number of elderly couples in receipt of pensions
rose. Thus, the illusion of 'masculinisation' is largely a product of analysis of
named recipients in overseers' accounts rather than of actual family circumstances. Pensions to families and elderly couples were usually paid to the
husband – and hence a masculinisation of names – but these payments also
benefited wives and, in the case of families, children. This is an important
point. Payments to aged couples were intended for the husband and his
wife; this is apparent in the sums allocated to couples, which were generally
higher than those for the single aged.[46] There is little evidence in Campton
and Shefford that elderly women were the casualties of the masculinisation
of outdoor relief given in pensions. Instead welfare provision appears to
have broadened to accommodate families in times of particular hardship
and elderly couples alongside solitary elderly men and women.

As we saw earlier, the usage patterns of indoor relief in workhouses
have also played a role in discussions about relief for the elderly in
this period. Ottaway has found that there were two usage patterns of
workhouses in rural and provincial communities in the eighteenth century.
In Terling, Essex, there was a dramatic rise in the proportion of the
elderly housed in the (small) workhouse: while the elderly had accounted

43   Williams, *Poverty, gender and life-cycle*, pp. 56–65.
44   Ibid., pp. 57 and 63–5.
45   Ibid., pp. 131–44.
46   Ibid., p. 64.

for no more than 25 per cent of inmates before 1790, by 1798 the figure was 82 per cent. Moreover, Terling was not unusual, with workhouses in Shropshire, Berkshire, Oxfordshire, and others in Essex also primarily housing the aged poor. However, Ottaway also found that in many other places the workhouse was used partly to house the aged and infirm, but also to accommodate poor children and the middle-aged, such as in the Halifax township of Ovenden.[47] Tomkins found a mix of ages in the urban workhouses of Oxford, Shrewsbury, and York, in the period 1723–82, as did MacKay and also Boulton and Schwarz for the huge metropolitan workhouse of St Martin-in-the-Fields, although there was an increase in the proportion of those aged sixty and over here in the 1800s and 1810s.[48]

There were 'workhouses' in Campton and Shefford but they were usually termed 'poor houses'. They were small and more like community houses, as described by John Broad.[49] There is a paucity of information on the people accommodated in these houses, but it would appear from what evidence there is that most of those living in Shefford's house were the transient – described as 'man' or 'woman' – not settled pensioners. There were forty-four payments to strangers at the workhouse (1810–28) with three exceptions: John Newman (age unknown) stayed in the house in the months while he awaited removal to Shillington; a one-off payment in 1811 for 'Refreshment to Jᵃˢ Humberstones [aged fifty-three] Family at the Workhouse'; and there was at least one longer-term elderly inmate, John Bowers (aged sixty-two) (and presumably his wife, Ann, aged sixty-four). The Justice of the Peace Samuel Whitbread and the parish overseer agreed in November 1811 that Bowers was to live in the poorhouse and to be given 4s a week. It would appear that Ann left the poorhouse some time after her husband's death, since in 1818 and 1824 the parish paid her poor rates, and she continued to receive a weekly pension.[50] The picture is

47   Ottaway, *The decline of life*, chap. 7.
48   Tomkins, *Experience of urban poverty*, pp. 45–50; L. MacKay, 'A culture of poverty? The St Martins in the Fields workhouse, 1817', *Journal of Interdisciplinary History* 26 (1995), 209–31; J. Boulton and L. Schwarz, '"The comforts of a private fireside"? The workhouse, the elderly and the poor law in Georgian Westminster: St Martin-in-the-Fields, 1725–1824', in *Accommodating poverty: the housing and living arrangements of the English poor, c.1600–1850*, ed. J. McEwan and P. Sharpe (Basingstoke, 2011), pp. 221–45.
49   J. Broad, 'Housing the rural poor in southern England 1650–1850', *Agricultural History Review* 48 (2000), 151–70; J. Broad, 'The parish poor house in the long eighteenth century', in *Accommodating poverty*, ed. McEwan and Sharpe, pp. 246–62.
50   *Samuel Whitbread's notebooks, 1810–11, 1813–14*, ed. A. F. Cirket (Bedfordshire Historical Record Society 50, 1971), entries 381 and 384.

slightly different in Campton, for which there is information on only three inmates of the poorhouse, all of whom were old: William Collip (exact age unknown but elderly), Ann Briant (exact age unknown but elderly) and Ann Herbert (aged sixty-four), who were accommodated towards the end of their lives. However, they continued to be listed in the overseers' accounts and so they did not 'disappear' from the relief lists as did the older women in Smith's study. There is evidence here of a small number of aged paupers (four in total) living in parish housing. Only a few elderly recipients were accommodated in other local workhouses. In the nearby parish of Cardington, there were thirty-two inmates in the workhouse in 1782, three of whom were elderly widowed women and two old married couples. The elderly were not confined to the house, since similar numbers were in receipt of outdoor relief. By 1808, the men in Cardington's workhouse were all elderly and there were still a few elderly women housed there.[51] The parish of Hawes owned a poorhouse and a cottage. In 1801 the poorhouse was divided into two parts, accommodating two families in each part: the first housed a middle-aged lone mother and her five children, as well as a lame father, aged forty-six, his wife and their four children; the second accommodated a middle-aged couple with their six children, plus Widow Ann Whitmore (aged sixty-one) and Sarah Whitmore (aged eighteen). The cottage housed one middle-aged couple and their six children.[52] Thus, poorhouses in east Bedfordshire were more like Ovenden's workhouse, with a mixture of ages of inmates, than the Terling house, which was primarily for the aged poor.

This next section of the chapter shifts to the second, longitudinal approach to the pauper biographies. Such a methodology reveals a great deal more about the lives of the elderly and it also adds a rich layer of detail to the quantitative evidence. Analysis of the pauper biographies shows patterns of poor relief receipt over entire lifetimes; this is the first study to undertake this approach. This methodology is rather less revealing about change over time, however, and so this section of the chapter assesses the life courses of those who became elderly pensioners and the quantity and quality of relief instead. At the point of an 'old age'

51   *The inhabitants of Cardington in 1782*, ed. D. Baker (Bedfordshire Historical Record Society 52, 1973), tabs 26 and 27 at pp. 47–8; BLARS, Whitbread Collection, W1/767. Eaton Socon, Bedfordshire, changed its policy frequently between workhouse provision and outdoor relief: F. G. Emmison, 'The relief of the poor at Eaton Socon, 1706–1834', *Bedfordshire Historical Record Society*, XV (1933), 1–98.
52   BLARS, Whitbread Collection, W1/762.

pension being awarded,[53] there were a total of 104 individuals in Campton and Shefford, of whom 42 were aged women, 14 were elderly men, and there were 24 couples (48 individuals).[54] As was apparent from Table 5.2, aged women dominated the lists until the 1810s, after which elderly couples also came onto relief. In both communities, of those persons who received a pension in their old age, almost two-thirds were given their first pension only when they were aged sixty or over. More women outlived their husbands than *vice versa*, but when one of the spouses of a pensioner-couple died, pensions generally continued to the remaining widow(er). This reveals that for most of the aged poor the commitment shown to a couple continued when a spouse died.

In just over one-third of cases, aged pensioners had also received a parish pension at some earlier point in their lives or their pensions had started while they were middle-aged and had been paid continuously from that point into their old age. Of those aged paupers who had previously been in receipt of a parish pension, nine had been relieved when they were part of a couple heading a family (receiving 'family allowances'), six were lone parents with children (most of whom were headed by women), and one woman, Sarah Odell, had been a middle-aged widow with adult children. A number of middle-aged widows with dependent children had their pensions paid into old age, such as Esther Merryweathers, who came on to long-term relief when her husband died (she was aged forty-two), leaving her with young children to care for, and she remained on relief for the next thirty-seven years, dying when she was aged seventy-nine. Many elderly pensioners, whenever their pensions began, had also previously received occasional relief in cash or in kind. This analysis – of the entire life courses of individuals who received pensions in old age – reveals that many of the poor managed to keep off regular relief until they were elderly. It was growing debility and associated impoverishment, plus the contracting labour market after 1815, which brought them on to relief. However, a significant minority (one-third) had required relief at that earlier poverty life-cycle point of parenthood, either as couple-headed families or lone parents. Not only does this highlight that life-cycle stress was an important cause of poverty, but, in the case of a third of families,

53   Some of these pensioners had also received a pension earlier in their lives.
54   Campton: 62 individuals, of whom 25 were women, 7 were men, and 15 were couples; Shefford: 42 individuals, of whom 17 were women, 7 were men, and 9 were couples.

such hardship meant that they fell into deep, longer-term poverty twice in their lifetimes.

This chapter has shown that both parishes were committed to the relief of elderly pensioners in terms of numbers, but were pensions sufficient to live on? The relative generosity of relief to the aged poor has generated considerable debate. Wales, Smith, Ottaway, Solar and Thomson point to substantial levels of assistance and a relatively high proportion of the aged receiving such benefits.[55] Pension values were particularly high in the first half of the eighteenth century when pension sums were rising while wages were static and prices falling.[56] Thane and King, on the other hand, have drawn a more pessimistic picture of the restricted nature of poor relief to the elderly and their reliance upon the wider 'economy of makeshifts'.[57] A regional pattern is evident in the value of relief, with the south and east appearing more generous than the north and west.[58] There were important shifts in the later eighteenth and early nineteenth centuries which meant that the value of relief was coming under pressure: pension sums frequently failed to keep pace with inflation and a greater proportion of expenditure was allocated to occasional relief.[59] What was the situation in the case study communities? Those aged sixty or over in Campton received the highest value pensions of any group of up to 51 per cent (lone elderly) and 62 per cent (couples) of neighbouring labouring households' adult-equivalent income in 1832, compared with lone, non-aged men and women, who received up to 45 per cent, lone parents

---

55   Thane, *Old age*; King, *Poverty and welfare*; Smith, 'Ageing and well-being'; P. M. Solar, 'Poor relief and English economic development before the Industrial Revolution', *Economic History Review* 48 (1995), 1–22; S. King, 'Poor relief and English economic development reappraised', *Economic History Review* 50 (1997), 360–8; P. M. Solar, 'Poor relief and English economic development: a renewed plea for comparative history', *Economic History Review* 50 (1997), 369–74; Thomson, 'The decline of social welfare'; Ottaway, *The decline of life*; Wales, 'Poverty, poor relief and the life-cycle'.

56   Smith, 'Ageing and well-being'; Ottaway, *The decline of life*, pp. 194–207 and 227–32.

57   P. Thane, 'Old people and their families in the English past', in *Charity, self-interest and welfare*, ed. Daunton, pp. 113–38; Thane, *Old age*, chap. 8; King, *Poverty and welfare*, chaps 6–7; S. King, 'Reconstructing lives: the poor, the poor law and welfare in Calverley, 1650–1820', *Social History* 22 (1997), 318–38 (pp. 330–2). See also S. King and A. Tomkins (eds), *The poor in England 1700–1850: an economy of makeshifts* (Manchester, 2003).

58   King, *Poverty and welfare*, chaps 6–7; Ottaway, *The decline of. life*, chap. 5.

59   Smith, 'Ageing and well-being'; Barker-Read, 'The treatment of the aged poor'; Ottaway, *The decline of life*, chap. 6; King, *Poverty and welfare*, chap. 6; J. Broad, 'Parish economies of welfare, 1650–1834', *Historical Journal* 42 (1999), 985–1006 (pp. 985–6).

30 per cent, and families 17 per cent.[60] Elderly couples always received higher mean pensions than single elderly men and women.[61]

The length of time that the elderly were in receipt of parish pensions is also important. Whether relief was paid for months, years or decades was a crucial factor in the household economies of the poor and it is another aspect of any assessment of the relative generosity of welfare payments. In Campton, 41 per cent of those receiving a pension for between five and ten years were elderly, the figure was 47 per cent in Shefford, and some of the elderly were on relief for more than ten years.[62] Such a long period of old-age 'dependence' on the parish might be a consequence of increasing longevity of those aged over sixty-five.[63] It would seem that these durations were longer than in Kent. In the seventeenth century, the 'pension lives' of the elderly were five years for men and eight years for women.[64]

When viewed at the individual level, elderly pensioners received 'welfare packages' of weekly pension payments, additional cash and relief in kind that were highly tailored, reflecting personal circumstances (including illness and growing debility), the seasons, and a volatile cost of living. There was no 'standard' old age weekly pension sum, but rather payments rose and fell as needs required. This finding is similar to that of Ottaway's study of Terling, Puddletown and Ovenden; Ottaway argues that relief to the aged came in the form of 'customised care packages'.[65] In Campton, William Barber and his wife Mary, for instance, were admitted to the pension list for nine months in February 1818, when they were aged sixty-seven and sixty-eight respectively. The size of their pension payments varied almost weekly, as the following range of sums indicates: 7s 6d, 5s 6d, 2s, 1s, 5s, 1s, 4s, 2s, 5s, 1s, 4s, 1s. After Mary died in June 1820, William received his own pension, as a widower now aged sixty-nine, until the overseers' accounts end in 1834. His weekly sum started at 5s a week, but the amount changed frequently, falling at times to 3s. The sum he received most often was 3s 6d. He also received additional

60 Williams, *Poverty, gender and life-cycle*, p. 65; Williams, 'Poor relief, labourers' households and living standards', pp. 506–11. Ottaway adopts a variety of approaches: *The decline of life*, pp. 229–32.

61 Williams, *Poverty, gender and life-cycle*, p. 64.

62 Ibid., p. 116.

63 Wrigley, 'British population', tab. 3.5 at p. 80; Wrigley *et al.*, *English population history*, pp. 280–93, tab. 6.19 at p. 290.

64 Barker-Read, 'The treatment of the aged poor', pp. 192–4.

65 Ottaway, *The decline of life*, pp. 189–90 and 232–7.

cash when he was ill, plus clothing, shoes and a new bedtick.[66] William did not necessarily receive more when his wife was alive, as an elderly couple, than when he was a widower. Instead, payments were bespoke. In the case of Ingram and Ann Chapman, higher payments to couples than the widowed are more evident. When they were aged sixty-seven and sixty-six respectively they were given weekly sums of 5s, 3s and 4s (1815–18); these payments were higher than the regular 2s a week that Ann was given when she was widowed. Her elderly widow's pension remained at the constant sum of 2s until her own death in January 1826. These pauper biographies make it clear that it is difficult to generalise about poor relief to the elderly. These cases also reveal that pension sums did not necessarily increase as a person aged, although this too did happen.

Relief in kind was worth an additional 8 per cent to pension values per pensioner. It is worth breaking down payments in kind into their constituent parts – rent, fuel, clothing and shoes, care and nursing, and burial costs – in order to establish the proportion allocated to the elderly.[67] Rather unusually, rent was paid only rarely by the Campton and Shefford parochial authorities.[68] Indeed, in 1814 Samuel Whitbread had to order the parish to pay the rent of 1s a week of Benjamin Bland, aged seventy.[69] Shefford paid the rent of twelve paupers, none of whom were old; Campton paid the rent of just eleven paupers, three of whom were elderly. In March 1785, Widow Ann Proyar's rent of 10s, to cover a quarter of a year, was paid and a further 10s 'bought Widdow Proyars Goods'. This compares with the 1s per week she was receiving in pension payments for six months. In another case, Campton's overseer paid the rent twice for John and Elizabeth Rogers, at £1 12s in 1775 and £1 1s in 1777. Their pension was between 3s and 3s 6d. The final case, of Richard Roberson, illustrates well the total benefits that some of the elderly might receive. He was in receipt of a pension in two periods, 1771–75 and 1790–92,

66   'Bedtick': 'A large flat quadrangular bag or case, into which feathers, hair, straw, chaff, or other substances are put to form a bed.' *OED* online.
67   Botelho has undertaken a similar exercise for the Suffolk parishes of Cratfield and Poslingford in the seventeenth century: *Old age*, tab. 4.3 at p. 119.
68   Other historians have found that rent was paid for the elderly: Barker-Read, 'The treatment of the aged poor', pp. 76–84; Ottaway, *The decline of life*, pp. 232–3. See also McEwan and Sharpe (eds), *Accommodating poverty*. Snell and Millar include rent in their calculations of the value of poor relief to lone-parent families: K. D. M. Snell and J. Millar, 'Lone-parent families and the Welfare State: past and present', *Continuity and Change* 2 (1987), 387–422 (pp. 405–8).
69   Williams, *Poverty, gender and life-cycle*, p. 141.

with occasional relief in between in 1784. In the first pension period his payments ranged from 1s to 1s 6d and he was allocated a regular sum of 2s 6d in the period 1790–92. His rent was paid only once, in 1791, a sum of £1 12s. During this last pension period, culminating in his death and burial, the parish also paid for two carers for 'doing for' him, stockings and shoes, fuel, the making of sheets, the provision of a bedtick and the cleaning of the bed, and his funeral. However, while these rent payments were significant sums in addition to pensions, the infrequency with which they were paid must lessen their importance in the wider care package provided to the elderly.

The provision of fuel could be important to the aged given that this group were more prone to sickness and death in the winter months. Fuel was worth, on average, 1–2s per individual fuel payment. Campton made hundreds of payments for fuel (628 payments, 1767–1834) but Shefford gave fuel far less frequently (fifty-nine payments, 1794–1828). Faggots and coals were generally given to pensioners (87 per cent) rather than occasional recipients (13 per cent) and in both communities, fuel was given to a core group of pensioners: forty-five individuals in Campton and just eight in Shefford. In Campton, 44 per cent of those in receipt of fuel were elderly and, of these, elderly widows (70 per cent) dominated over elderly couples or aged men. Of the forty-five individuals given fuel in Campton, just five individuals were given more than half of all the fuel payments (63 per cent) and four of these paupers were elderly: Widow Rogers, Sarah Lincoln, William Kilby and Widow Devereux. The other beneficiary, Mary Clark, was married with children, but fuel payments continued to be given to her after she was widowed and elderly. Widow Rogers was given fuel on ninety-seven occasions and William Kilby on 104 occasions. Thus, in terms of rent and fuel, relief was highly tailored and given in large part to specific individuals. Furthermore, rather less was provided by Shefford's overseers.

In terms of the allocation of parish clothing and shoes, the elderly accounted for the largest share of recipients – at 33 per cent – followed by lone parents (30 per cent). Elderly pensioners were also provided with caring services. For instance, 'doing for' was paid for by Campton's overseers on behalf of Sarah Lincoln weekly for almost three years between 1790 and 1793. Three different carers provided this service for her and they were paid between 6d and 9d per week. It might be expected that illness and growing debility, associated with old age, would mean that the elderly would loom large as recipients of care work, but in fact they comprised a smaller proportion of care recipients – at one fifth of those receiving care in Campton and one quarter in Shefford – than they were as beneficiaries of fuel and clothing/shoes. Nursing care was clearly distributed more evenly among all age groups. Nevertheless, the elderly would have benefited from the attendance of a contracted parish doctor and also from the growth of expenditure dedicated to medical relief.[70]

Parish burials were another payment in kind where it would be expected that the elderly would predominate. The expenses paid for funerals were comprehensive – for laying out of the corpse, the coffin, the cap, muffler and wool the body was wrapped in, the affidavit and church fees, and the bread, cheese and beer for the mourners – and could amount to as much as £1 16s 8d. Of all those buried at the parishes' expense in Campton and Shefford, 40 per cent were aged over sixty.[71] Although both Wales and Ottaway found that almost all of the elderly died on the parish,[72] in Campton and Shefford pensions were paid up to the point of death for the majority, but not all, of elderly pensioners (83 per cent). The authorities in Campton and Shefford did not pay for all the funerals of those dying on the parish, however, and such expenses were met in just over 70 per cent of cases. In 30 per cent of instances, therefore, burial costs were paid for by someone else – either relatives or through membership of a friendly society. Elderly pensioners who did not die on relief (17 per cent) fell into three groups: a small number of widows who had received couples' pensions with their husbands but once they were widowed the pension did not continue to them; a number of non-resident recipients who were receiving their pensions in another parish; and a number of pensioners whose payments simply stopped, there was no payment for a funeral in the overseers' accounts, and no burial recorded in the parish register.[73] It is possible that some widows were able to support themselves without parish pensions, or that they moved away. In the case of the non-resident, lump sum payments to overseers elsewhere might have covered funeral expenses,

70 Williams, 'Practitioners' income and provision for the poor'; S. Williams, 'Caring for the sick poor: poor law nurses in Bedfordshire, c.1770–1834', in *Women, work and wages in England, 1600–1850*, ed. P. Lane, N. Raven and K. D. M. Snell (Woodbridge, 2004), pp. 141–69; Williams, *Poverty, gender and life-cycle*, pp. 45–9.
71 Williams, *Poverty, gender and life-cycle*, pp. 41–2.
72 Wales, 'Poverty, poor relief and the life-cycle', fig. 11.1 at pp. 362–4; Ottaway, *The decline of life*, pp. 219, 227.
73 A number of the elderly were still in receipt of pensions at the end of the overseers' accounts (Campton 1834, Shefford 1828) and so it is not possible to know if they died on relief.

and in the cases of those with no entry in the burial register it is likely that the register was deficient.[74]

On the whole the aged poor received a significant share of relief in kind and they were often given tailored welfare packages. A detailed breakdown of relief in kind reveals a rather complicated picture, however. A high proportion of the fuel distributed by parish overseers was given to the elderly, especially aged widows, but further analysis also shows a concentration of fuel payments on a small core group of particular individuals. Very many of the elderly were buried at parish expense. This would seem to indicate that many of the labouring poor, and certainly most of those requiring a parish pension, could not save for their own funerals. A funeral costing £1 16s 8d, for instance, would represent almost one quarter of a pension of 3s per week paid over a year. The high number of parish funerals might also indicate that there was not the same fear of a pauper burial that was to develop under the new poor law. The elderly also received a significant proportion of the clothing and shoes that the parish distributed, but a rather smaller proportion of medical and nursing care. Rent payments were few and far between. In addition, as total expenditure rocketed in the two communities, relief in kind came under pressure and the proportion of spending devoted to payments in kind contracted from the 1810s.[75] Thus, although payments in kind could be valuable additions to a pension, it was the regular weekly pension that carried the most value.[76] Pensions to the elderly (62 per cent) plus relief in kind (8 per cent) totalled 70 per cent of neighbouring labouring households' adult-equivalent income per recipient. This is a high proportion, but it is worth keeping in mind that, although the elderly received the most 'generous' provision of any group, assistance did not equal the incomes of those independent of relief. Of all groups, the elderly were most likely to need to live off their pensions and yet – at 70 per cent of labouring incomes – the aged would have had to supplement their poor relief from elsewhere or else lead meagre lives.[77]

One of the most important findings of these case studies is the growth in the number of elderly couples in receipt of pension payments. This shift

74 P. Razzell, C. Spence and M. Woollard, 'The evaluation of Bedfordshire burial registration, 1538–1851', *Local Population Studies* 84 (2010), 31–54.

75 Williams, *Poverty, gender and life-cycle*, pp. 44–5.

76 The proportion of relief spent on pensions was reduced slightly (as occasional cash payments rose) but remained high at a minimum of 70 per cent, 1760s–1830s: Williams, *Poverty, gender and life-cycle*, p. 39.

77 Ibid., pp. 161–2.

dated largely after 1815 and it was a response by the parish authorities to the worsening economic situation in the south and east following the end of the Napoleonic Wars, with demobilisation, agricultural depression, and structural unemployment. Older men were increasingly crowded out of an overstocked agricultural labour market at younger ages and on to occasional and regular relief. The number of adult men (and boys) in receipt of occasional cash payments for periods without work rose rapidly after 1815 (and accounted for up to 45 per cent of occasional recipients by the 1830s) and the parish provided make-work schemes.[78] It is likely that farmers employed younger men rather than older ones; contemporaries certainly believed that men with young children were favoured by farmers to keep them off the poor rates.[79] E. H. Hunt has argued that pensions to older men in the context of overstocked labour markets (such as Bedfordshire) were essentially 'unemployment' or 'disability' pensions, rather than the 'old age' pensions claimed by David Thomson.[80] Nevertheless, it has to be recognised that the distinction between unemployment, disability, old age, and dependency was blurred and contingent. If it is assumed that Ottaway's finding – that the average age of all male pensioners was around seventy years old in the eighteenth century – had also held true for Campton and Shefford earlier in the eighteenth century, then it would appear that for some men the age of male dependency had decreased after 1815.[81] While this was not true in all cases, since half of all men were still expected to continue to work until they were in their seventies or even their eighties, many men (and their wives) had now become pensionable in their sixties.

Conclusion

This chapter has found that there was a strong and enduring commitment to the elderly poor in Campton and Shefford throughout the 'crisis of the old poor law'. There is little evidence that the hardening of attitudes extended to the aged.[82] Despite lengthening relief lists and soaring costs,

---

78   Ibid., fig. 15 at p. 133, tab. 13 at p. 134.
79   *Report from His Majesty's Commissioners for inquiring into the administration and practical operation of the poor laws* (PP, 1834, XXVII), p. 40.
80   E. H. Hunt, 'Paupers and pensioners: past and present', *Ageing and Society* 9 (1989), 407–30; Thomson, 'The decline of social welfare'.
81   Ottaway, *The decline of life*, pp. 201–2.
82   Tomkins, *Experience of urban poverty*, p. 8; Ottaway, *The decline of life*, pp. 12–13.

the number of the elderly relieved by the parish authorities increased between the 1760s and 1830s, the aged were over-represented in the relief lists, and this group received some of the highest, longest, and most tailored pensions. However, there were important shifts in the composition of aged pensioners as a result of the crisis. Before 1815 most elderly pensioners were solitary men and women, who were either single or widowed, but after 1815 the number of elderly couples increased markedly as a result of widespread un- and underemployment. Older men were increasingly marginalised by employers in this overstocked labour market and were pushed on to long-term relief. These pensions might be interpreted as a mixture of long-term unemployment benefits and recompense for increasing infirmity. Before the problems in the local economy these men had not been regarded as beyond work, however, and now found that they were. This finding has implications for contemporary concepts of masculinity, age, and the ability to work. It also suggests that, while local farmers and other employers marginalised older men, parish officers did not. This might have been a negative experience for the men themselves, since they were pushed out of the labour market and onto long-term parish dependence with lower incomes. However, the parish provided them with a safety net at a time when the net was under considerable strain. Even though parish officers were seeking ways to contain expenditure, the net was thrown wider to respond to the crisis in agriculture. The chapter also finds that elderly women were not marginalised and that the 'masculinisation' of relief – for pensioners at least – is a product of consulting the overseers' accounts alone and it is not evident when the actual family circumstances of the poor are known. Wives also benefited from pension payments. The pauper biographies also reveal that for some elderly pensioners (one-third) this was not their first pension. During this period of long drawn-out crisis, the poverty life-cycle points of childhood, parenthood and old age became more difficult to navigate without (sometimes repeated) assistance from the parish.

6

Indoors or Outdoors? Welfare Priorities and Pauper Choices in the Metropolis under the Old Poor Law, 1718–1824[1]

JEREMY BOULTON

Nothing is more apparently necessary to the common good, than that parochial charity should be given to some out-pensioners, by a weekly allowance, as well as to maintain the inhabitants of workhouses; but where the strictest enquiries are not made, it encourages some to be idle. I have seen such a pensioner begging in the streets; but upon enquiry found he was incapable of work, and that the allowances made him was not more than sufficient to pay his lodging: How then was he to live? It seems most reasonable that *such* persons should be received into the workhouse. Others there are who being aged and infirm, or having a number of young children to support, must be assisted in their own habitations, where they will live cheaper, and earn more by their labour, than being sure of their food and raiment, shut up within the wretched walls of a workhouse.

> Jonas Hanway, *The citizen's monitor: shewing the necessity of a salutary police, executed by resolute and judicious magistrates, assisted by the pious labours of zealous clergymen, for the preservation of the lives and properties of the people, and the happy existence of the state* (London, 1780), p. 103.

One of the most striking – and still not well understood – features of many eighteenth-century parish welfare systems is surely the survival of outdoor relief in parishes that built workhouses under the 1723 'Workhouse

---

1   All publications deriving from larger research projects inevitably accumulate a number of debts. I would, in particular, like to thank my colleague Leonard Schwarz, who is

Test Act'. That act was designed to deter those in need from applying for poor relief by applying the workhouse test. Those refusing to enter the new workhouses could, quite legally, be denied poor relief. The new workhouses would instil much needed work discipline, reduce the overall costs of poor relief and perhaps improve the morals and manners of those incarcerated. Workhouses spread quite rapidly in the eighteenth century. Hindle reports that by mid century around 600 were in existence, housing some 30,000 inmates, and by 1777 there were almost 2,000 workhouses in the country. It has been estimated that by 1782 'a third of all parishes, and probably more, either had their own or had access to one through incorporation or contract'.[2]

However, as Paul Slack pointed out some time ago, 'it is questionable ... whether deterrence worked in anything more than the shortest of short terms'. Moreover it was doubtful if workhouses ever succeeded in reducing overall spending on the poor in the long term. 'More often, outdoor relief for both impotent and able-bodied slowly returned, not only and inevitably in large towns such as Hull, Liverpool and Leeds, but in smaller places like Eaton Socon, Bedfordshire'.[3] Perhaps particularly surprising is the well-documented survival not merely of casual one-off payments but of regular parish pensions paid to the poor in their own homes – despite the fact that room might be available in the parish workhouse. As Richard Smith, Steve Hindle, Alannah Tomkins and others have demonstrated, it was indeed common in those parishes which built workhouses for outdoor pensions to either return or remain, albeit at reduced levels.[4]

co-director of the Pauper Biographies Project, for his support, and Romola Davenport for her typically insightful comments on an earlier draft. Other helpful comments were made by the editors and those attending the conference 'Population, economy and welfare, c.1200–2000: a conference in honour of Richard M. Smith', 16–18 September 2011. John Black, Peter Jones, Rhiannon Thompson and, latterly, Tim Wales collected some of the raw material on which this chapter is based. Alison Kenney and other staff at the City of Westminster Archives Centre (COWAC) have been exceptionally helpful and obliging since the Pauper Biographies Project commenced in 2004. I am also happy to acknowledge the support of ESRC, research grant RES-000-23-0250.

2 P. Slack, *The English poor law 1531–1782* (Basingstoke, 1990), p. 43 (quotation); S. Hindle, *On the parish? The micro-politics of poor relief in rural England, c.1550–1750* (Oxford, 2004), p. 187; S. and B. Webb, *English local government: English poor law history: part I. The old poor law* (London, 1927), pp. 243–5.

3 Slack, *English poor law*, p. 42.

4 R. M. Smith, 'Ageing and well-being in early modern England: pension trends and gender preferences under the English old poor law c.1650–1800', in *Old age from antiquity to post-modernity*, ed. P. Johnson and P. Thane (London, 1998), pp. 64–95 (pp. 86–7);

The survival of outdoor relief alongside indoor relief makes it very difficult for those attempting to uncover the history and estimate the monetary worth of parish poor relief in the eighteenth century. Where workhouses were built, the number of outdoor pensions granted and their average value may well have been reduced, even if not abolished altogether. This is because such institutions typically cared for those in their declining years, who might otherwise have existed on increasingly large pensions.

Early on in the eighteenth century, some (but not all) London parishes expected the erection of their workhouses to mean the end of out-pensions. Among the rules governing the poor of St Andrew Holborn in Shoe Lane, was one which stated explicitly:

> That no pension be allowed to any Pensioner out of the House, unless in Cases of Lunacy, Plague, Small-Pox, Foul-disease, or Idiotism: and that all the Money received or collected for the use of the Poor of this Parish, (Sacrament Money excepted) shall be brought to Account, and applied to the Support of this House, and the Maintenance of the Poor therein.[5]

At Tavistock in Devon, the opening of the workhouse in 1747 had the effect of reducing the average number of parish pensioners from 109 to 64 between 1735–36 and 1760–61, and the average weekly pension fell from 1s 3d to 1s 0d.[6] Tomkins in her study of parishes in Oxford, Shrewsbury and York similarly reported that:

> The distribution of out-relief in the three towns was never decisively ended by the use of the workhouse test in the mid-eighteenth century. As elsewhere, attempts to compel all of the poor to enter the house lasted only for short periods after which pension and other payments began again. Fluctuations in total overseers' spending, and the proportions of the total spent on either pensions or workhouses, illustrate the emphasis placed on different components of poor relief in each parish.[7]

Hindle, *On the parish?*, pp. 186–91; A. Tomkins, *The experience of urban poverty, 1723–82: parish, charity and credit* (Manchester, 2006), pp. 43–50.

5   *An account of the work-houses in Great Britain, in the year M,DCC,XXXII*, 3rd edn (London, 1786), p. 19. This order was repeated for the parish of Allhallows, Bread Street: ibid., p. 80.

6   Smith, 'Ageing and well-being', pp. 77, 84 and 89–90.

7   Tomkins, *Experience of urban poverty*, p. 43.

In the towns studied by Tomkins, parish pension lists were commonly reduced in size by the application of the workhouse test.[8] As Tim Hitchcock noted, 'in parish after parish the existence of these houses drove down the numbers of people dependent on relief by over fifty per cent'.[9] In Ware, Hertfordshire, shortly after the workhouse opened in 1724 it was reported that 'Two thirds of the Pensioners have left taking their Pensions'.[10] Barker-Read, in her fine study of five Kentish parishes, similarly noted that 'as parishes opened their new workhouses the pension lists disappeared from the overseers' accounts'. All pensioners were sent to the new workhouse in Cranbrook, but other Kentish towns retained some pensioners on out-relief. Within seven years, however, pension lists reappeared in all towns.[11] Attempts to measure average size of pension and the number of pensioners are subject to great uncertainty caused by the presence or absence of a parish workhouse and the ways in which such institutions functioned within the patchwork of local welfare systems that made up early modern England. The average level of outdoor pensions, in other words, would almost certainly be reduced if the parish housed some of its particularly decrepit poor in a workhouse.[12]

The fact that workhouses coexisted with outdoor relief in various

8   Ibid., pp. 43–5.
9   T. Hitchcock, 'Paupers and preachers: the SPCK and the parochial workhouse movement', in *Stilling the grumbling hive: the response to social and economic problems in England, 1689–1750*, ed. L. Davison, T. Hitchcock, T. Keirn and R. B. Shoemaker (Stroud and New York, 1992), pp. 145–66 (p. 146). See also, T. V. Hitchcock, 'The English workhouse: a study in institutional poor relief in selected counties, 1696–1750' (unpublished D.Phil. dissertation, University of Oxford, 1985), p. 211, reporting that 'at St Margaret's, Westminster, 108 people were listed as receiving collection from the parish in 1726, all of whom were offered the house when it opened. Only forty-one people eventually entered, the rest refusing to go into the house, choosing instead to give up their parish relief.'
10 *An account of the work-houses in Great Britain*, p. 125. For the halving of the outdoor poor at Maidstone, see ibid., p. 132. For the dismissal of pensioners at Whitechapel, see ibid., p. 10. Twenty men and women and eight children 'came into the House about Lady-Day 1725, and more are daily adding to the Number; while others chose to struggle with their Necessities, and to continue in a starving Condition, with the Liberty of haunting the Brandy-Shops, and such like Houses, rather than submit to live regularly in Plenty'.
11 M. Barker-Read, 'The treatment of the aged poor in five selected West Kent parishes from settlement to Speenhamland (1662–1797)' (unpublished Ph.D. thesis, Open University, 1989), pp. 220–1. For other examples, see also, S. and B. Webb, *The old poor law*, p. 245.
12 Smith, 'Ageing and well-being', p. 87.

forms, of course, is something of an elephant in the room for those who use workhouse admission registers *alone* to look at local patterns of poor relief. Although such studies can provide striking findings, it is frequently the case that little context can be provided regarding patterns of outdoor relief in those same localities. Similarly, those who use parish overseers' accounts without knowledge of expenditure on the workhouse may tell only part of a more complex story.[13] The 1803 Parliamentary returns confirm the obvious point for London.[14] For every hundred people in the workhouses of the capital (which was itself unusually reliant on indoor relief) there were often hundreds more relieved in their own homes, either 'permanently' or temporarily. As David Green has noted, 'In terms of numbers, though not necessarily cost, outdoor paupers far exceeded those receiving relief inside a workhouse or other institution.' Although interpreting the data from the 1803 returns is not straightforward, 'in London as a whole the outdoor poor comprised about 60 per cent of all permanent paupers'. Data on the total numbers relieved in St Marylebone (which then had one of the biggest workhouses in London) in the period 1821–33 show that the number of casual poor fluctuated enormously over time but was never less than 40 per cent of those relieved by the parish. Earlier, in 1791, the authorities of St Andrew Holborn 'above the bars' relieved a thousand persons yearly, of which only 280 were in the workhouse.[15] This is a particular problem for those looking at individual experiences within any specific welfare system, since those inhabiting a parish workhouse might have received various forms of out-relief while they were resident,

---

13   The excellent and perceptive recent essay on parish relief by Henry French is unusual in making reference to indoor relief: 'Living in poverty in eighteenth-century Terling', in *Remaking English society. Social relations and social change in early modern England*, ed. S. Hindle, A. Shepard and J. Walter (Woodbridge, 2013), pp. 281–315. See especially pp. 293, 300 and 308–9, where the possible impact of the workhouse on French's figures is discussed.

14   These national returns were made by overseers to a parliamentary committee. They are discussed in J. S. Taylor, 'The unreformed workhouse, 1776–1834', in *Comparative Development in Social Welfare*, ed. E. W. Martin (London, 1972), pp. 57–84.

15   D. R. Green, *Pauper capital: London and the poor law, 1790–1870* (Farnham, 2010), pp. 69–72; *Rules, orders, and regulations, for the government of the workhouse belonging to that part of the parish of St Andrew, Holborn, which lies above the Bars, in the county of Middlesex, and the parish of St George the Martyr, in the said county* (London, 1791), p. 40. See also, R. M. Smith, 'Social security as a developmental institution? The relative efficacy of poor relief provisions under the English old poor law', in *History, historians and development policy: a necessary dialogue*, ed. C. A. Bayly, V. Rao, S. Szreter and M. Woolcock (Manchester, 2011), pp. 75–102 (p. 89).

or more often in periods when they were outside.[16] Since length of stay in workhouses was usually short, it is very likely that many of those who experienced indoor relief sought other forms of outdoor poor relief.[17]

This chapter attempts to shed more light on the relationship between outdoor and indoor relief. It does this via a case study of one large metropolitan parish, that of St Martin-in-the-Fields, between 1718 and 1824. The principal focus will be on how the poor experienced indoor and outdoor relief, and how the form and nature of that relief changed over time. The aim of the chapter is to analyse the extent to which outdoor relief coexisted with indoor relief. Particular attention is paid in what follows to the immediate impact of the parish workhouse when it opened in 1725 since the later period has been, to some extent, covered in a previous publication.[18] Surviving documentation is exceptionally revealing about the transition from an outdoor to an indoor relief system in 1725 and about what actually happened to hundreds of parish pensioners faced with an unpleasant and probably unforeseen dilemma. As Hindle puts it, 'the workhouse test presented paupers with a stark choice between total and institutionalized dependence on the one hand and complete reliance

16   Rule 47 of the St Martin's workhouse in 1828 stated that 'when Pentioners apply for admission, they are required to assign their pensions before they are admitted': *Rules and regulations for the government of the workhouse, of the parish of St Martin in the Fields, and of the infant poor-house at Highwood Hill* (London, 1828), p. 14. This might have referred particularly to Chelsea out-pensioners, who are occasionally identified in the admission records. Around 100,000 men were in receipt of various military or civil service pensions in the 1840s: D. Thomson, 'Welfare and the historians', in *The world we have gained. Histories of population and social structure*, ed. L. Bonfield, R. Smith and K. Wrightson (Oxford, 1986), pp. 355–78 (p. 368). Caroline Nielsen of Newcastle University is currently completing an important Ph.D. thesis on the Royal Hospital Chelsea and its pensioners.

17   For some data on length of stay in the workhouse of St Marylebone, see A. Levene, 'Children, childhood and the workhouse: St Marylebone, 1769–1781', *London Journal* 33 (2008), 41–59 (pp. 49–50). Levene's findings resemble closely those found in St Martin's. Patterns shared by both institutions included a peak in lengths of stay for children aged between five and thirteen, and a marked tendency for the elderly to stay for relatively longer periods than other adults. It was rare for any age group to spend, on average, much more than a year in either workhouse. Those in their sixties spent on average just one year and four months in the St Marylebone workhouse.

18   J. Boulton and L. Schwarz, '"The comforts of a private fireside"? The workhouse, the elderly and the poor law in Georgian Westminster: St Martin-in-the-Fields, 1725–1824', in *Accommodating poverty: the housing and living arrangements of the English poor, c.1600–1850*, ed. J. McEwan and P. Sharpe (Basingstoke, 2011), pp. 221–45.

on their own resources on the other'.[19] This chapter begins by setting out the poor relief system as it existed on the eve of the introduction of the workhouse, sets out the dramatic changes that occurred in its first ten years of operation, and then surveys later interrelationships between indoor and outdoor relief. It ends by presenting a new model of how of eighteenth-century parish relief worked in practice.

The local welfare system of St Martin-in-the-Fields and the arrival of the workhouse

St Martin's was an enormous urban district of about 40,000 people in the early eighteenth century, located in the West End of London. Unfortunately for our purposes it lost the parish of St George Hanover Square, which was carved out in 1725. Although difficult to estimate exactly, our parish probably lost about one third of its population, and a significant number of wealthy parishioners, as a consequence of this division.[20]

The parish of St Martin's opened its workhouse in July 1725.[21] Before that date the parish spent huge sums of money (usually around £4,000 per year) on poor relief under three distinct headings. For fifteen years before the workhouse opened, about half of all expenditure went on parish pensions, paid to orphans or adult pensioners, and the remainder went on casual or 'extraordinary' relief. Its poor relief system before 1725 was dominated, therefore, like most of those in London, by outdoor relief. Parish pensions funded by a poor rate had actually been paid in the parish for over 150 years. A significant development from the late seventeenth century was the growth in the amount of money spent on extraordinary relief. Of particular importance within this growing category of expenditure was the development of a network of parish nurses. By the early eighteenth century, these individuals were providing shelter and care for a large number of local paupers in private nursing homes. In effect, therefore, these parish nurses acted as a sort of decentralised

---

19 Hindle, *On the parish?* p. 187. The extent of such dependence of course was limited by the relatively short stays made by many workhouse inmates.

20 A tiny part of the parish may have been lost to the small neighbouring parish of St Mary le Strand around the same time according to a note in the vestry minutes: COWAC, F2006/163 and 166.

21 For the standard account of the founding of workhouses in London, see Hitchcock, 'The English workhouse', especially chaps 4 and 8.

workhouse or local hospital.[22] Lastly, the parish maintained some seventy-two elderly almswomen in parish almshouses located, for most of our period, in Hog Lane, in the neighbouring parish of St Anne, Soho. These almswomen were selected by churchwardens, vestrymen and the local vicar from, as far as can be judged, the more respectable parish poor and the middling sort down on their luck. Their (relatively generous) stipends were funded partly by funds controlled by the churchwardens but also, until 1782, by the overseers of the poor and the vicar. The almshouses played a small but significant part in the care of elderly women in the parish throughout our period. Some 5 per cent of all women dying aged sixty or over died in the parish almshouses between 1747 and 1825 (see below Figure 6.5).[23]

The parish is a good place to look at poor relief. Its records are extremely rich, and include an almost complete set of workhouse admission registers, a rich set of settlement examinations and unbroken sets of vestry minutes. It has a good series of churchwardens' accounts, useful runs of overseers' accounts and some uniquely detailed burial books. Before 1726 there is also a good series of petty sessions records, intermingled with the settlement examinations. The former record the decisions of Justices of the Peace (JPs) relating to poor relief applications – a distinctive feature of poor relief in the parish in the early eighteenth century was the close oversight exercised by JPs over admissions to the pension lists.[24] Combining all these records to reconstruct the lives of the poor has been the principal aim of the *Pauper Biographies Project* since 2004.[25] There are, unfortunately, some gaps in coverage which particularly affect our knowledge of the outdoor poor. Payments to individual pensioners survive in the overseers' accounts only until 1780, and there are many gaps in coverage between 1725 and that date. After 1780 and until 1824, the overseers' accounts survive in a virtually unbroken series and include summarised payments to the 'casual' and 'settled' poor but they

22   J. Boulton, 'Welfare systems and the parish nurse in early modern London', *Family and Community History* 10 (2007), 127–51.
23   These are treated in detail in J. Boulton, 'The almshouses and almswomen of St Martin-in-the-Fields, 1683–1818', paper delivered to the 'Almshouses in Europe from the late Middle Ages to the Present – Comparisons and Peculiarities' conference, Haarlem, The Netherlands, 7–9 September 2011.
24   For this see also J. Kent and S. King, 'Changing patterns of poor relief in some English rural parishes circa 1650–1750', *Rural History* 14 (2003), 119–56 (pp. 143–4).
25   See http://research.ncl.ac.uk/pauperlives/ (accessed 28 July 2014).

contain no information about either pension size or numbers of payments and are not itemised by name.[26]

The parish yields robust numbers. It seems to have experienced a decline in population, from around 30,000–35,000 at the beginning of our period in 1725, to 22,000–25,000 in the late 1750s, and then a gradual recovery such that the population seems to have returned to its original size by the 1820s. The 1801 census population was 27,437.[27] It contained large numbers of poor and humble residents but also many substantial inhabitants, capable of raising large sums of money via the poor rate. Because of its size, and despite the large numbers of substantial parishioners, the overall profile of the parish in the eighteenth century could be argued to be reasonably representative of the metropolis. William Maitland's statistics (collected for the late 1720s and published for the first time in 1739) suggest that the parish was spending about £1.30 per 'house' per year on its poor, ranking it ninety-fifth out of 153 parishes in the capital. Statistics of spending by London parishes display a wide range of values and are not always easy to interpret, but the St Martin's figures are comparable to the overall spend per house in London which was £1.08.[28]

The application of the workhouse test resulted in the complete extinction of parish pensioners as an accounting heading in the overseers' accounts. In St Martin's, no regular parish pensions are recorded for at least fifteen years.[29] Orphan pensions (payments made to their carers – surviving parents, parish nurses and so on) were drastically cut back in number in 1725 and disappear completely from the overseers' accounts

26   After 1780, individual payments made to parish pensioners were recorded in separate books, which have not survived. Some information about payments authorised to the poor is contained in a series of discontinuous churchwardens' and overseers' minute books. These rarely make it clear whether payments were to 'casual' or 'settled' poor, and have not been included in this analysis.

27   See for some background, Boulton and Schwarz, '"The comforts of a private fireside"?'.

28   W. Maitland, *The history of London from its foundation by the Romans to the present time* (London, 1739). The Maitland data has a standard deviation of 0.706, and ranges from the generous £3.76 per house spent by the tiny city parish of St Benet Sherehog to the miserable £0.13 disbursed by St George the Martyr, Queen Square. There was a weak negative correlation (–0.4316) between the number of houses and the amount spent per house. I intend to discuss the parochial returns in more detail elsewhere.

29   Apart, that is, from the continuing maintenance of the parish almswomen, described above. The almswomen, and those receiving payments from charitable sources ('sacrament pensioners' and recipients of parochial charities), have also been excluded from this analysis.

Table 6.1. Number of orphan pensioners and parish pensioners recorded in the overseers' accounts of St Martin-in-the-Fields, 1724–80

Accounting year beginning	Individual orphan pensions	Individual parish 'pensioners' (those receiving regular payments, the 'settled poor')	Accounting year beginning	Individual orphan pensions	Individual parish 'pensioners' (those receiving regular payments, the 'settled poor')
1724	333	541	1750		239
1725	n/a	n/a	1751		228
1726	49		1754		206
1727	51		1765		159
1728	51		1766		139
1729	35		1767		122
1730	34		1768		182
1731	35		1771		121
1732	34		1772		105
1733	35		1773		77
1734	35		1774		63
1735	34		1775		144
1736	34		1776		116
1737	35		1777		158
1738	32		1778		132
1739	28		1779		90
1740	28		1780		55
1749		198	c.1794		240[1]

Sources: COWAC, F459a, F462, F465, F468, F472, F476, F478, F482, F485, F488, F492, F495, F498, F501, F504, F507, F2223, F526, F529, F535, F547, F549, F551, F553, F559, F561, F563, F565, F567, F569, F571, F573, F575 and F577.

Note: [1] The 1794 figure is from Frederick Morton Eden, *The state of the poor; or, an history of the labouring classes in England, from the Conquest to the present period*, 3 vols (London, 1797), vol. 2, p. 440, given as 'about 240 weekly out-pensioners'.

after 1740 (Table 6.1). Even allowing for the effects of the loss of Hanover Square, such changes represented a dramatic discontinuity in the local welfare system. Orphan pensions as a form of outdoor relief essentially disappeared forever after 1740. Parish pensioners relieved outdoors in their own homes seem to have returned by the late 1740s, although there are signs of regular payments to individuals in the extraordinary accounts in the early 1730s. It is also clear from Table 6.1 that the number of individuals paid outdoor pensions continued to fluctuate dramatically over time in the eighteenth century. Despite this, even if one assumes that one third of the pensioners in 1724 belonged to Hanover Square, the number of outdoor pensioners never recovered to pre-workhouse levels. Information on the average size of pensions and the number of payments reveal that neither recovered to levels found in 1724/5, at least before 1780 when such information is available.[30]

The erection of the workhouse therefore forced well over 800 pauper households to make an unpleasant choice. How did those on pensions cope with their abolition? Could they get by without cash doles? How many entered the new workhouse or were relieved in other ways? It is possible using the rich records of this parish to explore such questions in detail. We need to start by providing more context on the operation of poor relief before the workhouse. Table 6.2 sets out the role of local justices in authorizing and ordering poor relief payments, presumably undertaken under the authority of the Act of 1692.[31] Most of these decisions were taken in formal petty sessions, others were annotations made on settlement examinations by an individual JP.

In less than eight years, JPs sitting in the local vestry room made over 1,500 decisions relating to the payment of poor relief in this one parish. Clearly their influence was felt most strongly over the payment and augmentation of parish pensions. The numbers here demonstrate that a very high proportion of all new pensioners must have had their applications heard before a Justice.[32] It is striking that it was almost unheard of for justices to order a reduction or a cessation of relief, which suggests

30   If one third were resident in the area carved out as Hanover Square, then some 361 parish pensioners would have belonged to St Martin's in 1724/5.
31   Slack, *English poor law*, p. 62.
32   Thus, when the vestry wished to award a parish pension to a sexton's widow, it recorded in 1724 that 'some of his Majesties Justices of the Peace be desired to put her the said Widow Hussey on the Pencon at four shillings per Month to be received by her': COWAC, F2006/125.

Table 6.2. Petty sessions decisions relating to poor relief in St Martin-in-the-Fields, 1718–25

Petty Session Decision	Number of cases	% Cases
To be put on the parish pension	573	36.4
To be put on the orphan pension	458	29.1
To be put on extraordinary relief	233	14.8
Parish pension supplemented	156	9.9
Orphan pension supplemented	46	2.9
To be sent out of the parish	24	1.5
To be further examined	18	1.1
To be put in the workhouse	13	0.8
Pension to cease	7	0.4
Poor rate appeal	6	0.4
Referred to overseer	6	0.4
To be paid arrears on orphans pension	5	0.3
Extraordinary payments to cease	4	0.3
Referred to next meeting	4	0.3
To be put out apprentice	4	0.3
To be paid arrears of pension or wages	2	0.1
Pension reduced	2	0.1
Payment not to trouble parish further	2	0.1
To be passed to another parish	2	0.1
Orphan pension reduced	2	0.1
To be sent to a Hospital	2	0.1
Recommended to churchwarden	2	0.1
Entertaining inmates	1	0.1
To be sent to a parish nurse	1	0.1
Not to trouble the parish	1	0.1
	1574	100

Sources: COWAC, F5013, F5014, F5015, F5016, F5017, F5018 and F5019.

that they were not working, in practice, to reduce the local burden of poor relief. It also demonstrates that, in this parish, cutting or reducing pensions was rarely used as a crude form of social engineering.[33] Only a tiny fraction of extraordinary payments could have been so influenced by these magistrates given the fact that thousands of such payments took place each year in the parish, both before and after 1725. In the twenty years or so after 1725, although the workhouse quickly came to comprise the bulk of parish spending on the poor, extraordinary payments usually comprised between one quarter and one third of total parish expenditure.[34]

Another striking feature of petty sessions activity in the parish is that pensions were still being authorised in the parish even as the workhouse was being built in the parish churchyard. As late as May 1725, eighteen applicants were granted new pensions or had their pensions restored or continued, even though the entire pension system was to cease operation within a few months. As far as can be judged in the absence of their accounts, no pensions were paid out by overseers after 28 July 1725. The vestry explicitly recorded their decision to cease paying pensions. In June 1725 it was:

> Ordered that the Overseers be desired to acquaint the severall Pentioners and Orphans of this parish on the next pay day that the last payment that shall be made to them will be on the 28th day of July next And that they do then prepare to come in and be provided for in the Workhouse.[35]

And on 26 July:

> Ordered that all the Pentioners of this Parish ordered to be lodged maintained and Employed in the House erected in the new Church yard of this Parish for that purpose be Lodged maintained & Employed therein without making any distinction or shewing any favour to any one in particular.

---

33 See the discussion of this point in J. Boulton, 'The poor among the rich: paupers and the parish in the West End, 1600–1724', in *Londinopolis. Essays in the cultural and social history of early modern London*, ed. P. Griffiths and M. S. R. Jenner (Manchester and New York, 2000), pp. 197–225.
34 See the overseers' accounts: COWAC, F462, F465, F468, F472, F476, F478, F482, F485, F488, F492, F495, F498, F501, F504, F515 and F519/348.
35 COWAC, F2006/191.

Ordered that no Person or Persons whatsoever shall from & after the
28th of this Instant July receive Reliefe or Collection from this Parish
who shall refuse to be Lodged, kept maintained and Employed in the
aforesaid house And that no Overseer of the Poor of the said parish do
from and after the said 28th day of this instant July give any more relief
to any such person of any of the Parish Monies.[36]

In August 1725, the overseers were meeting with the churchwardens
'about Affairs of the Workhouse' and they are known to have spent 15s
in December 1725 on a meeting 'Examining the Poor and Ordering and
placing them in the workhouse'.[37]

The last petty sessions meetings recorded in the examination books in
September and November 1725 were the only ones at which the workhouse
test can be seen in explicit operation. Thirteen applicants, some of them
described as 'late' pensioners, were offered workhouse places rather than
outdoor relief. Mary Carr, for example, 'was late a Pentioner applied for
relief Ordered that she go into the Workhouse, or else not to be relieved'
on 27 September 1725. Penelope Reed, likewise, 'Late a Pentioner applied
for relief, Ordered that she be sent to the Work House'. Biographical
information can be used to amplify such bald statements. Penelope,
for example, had been receiving a parish pension of 6s a month since a
petty sessions decision in May 1721. Like most poor law applicants in
the parish, her settlement examination survives in the voluminous parish
archives. She had been examined around February 1721:

Penelope Reed aged 60 Lodging at Mrs Lambs in Shandois Street says
she is the Widow of John Reed who dyed about 25 years agoe, was
Married to him at St Martin's Church about 30 years agoe, never kept
house, never a yearly servant, never was Apprentice, was in the Horse
Guards in King Charles time and dyed after King James came to the
Crown, his Father kept house in Suffolk Street and he lived with his

---

36 COWAC, F2006/196–7. The vestry were to meet at the workhouse at this last payment
to give the 'necessary orders and directions'.

37 COWAC, F83/30, 32 and 34. On 25 March 1725, the vestry 'Ordered that the Clerk of
this Vestry Examine the Severall books of the Settlements of the poor of this Parish to find
what poor belong to the two outwards of the said Parish': F2006/173. A vestry committee
was given responsibility on 29 March 1725 to oversee the affairs of the new workhouse and
also to 'Examine the Accounts of the Extraordinary Disbursements of the Overseers of
the Poor' – another sign that it was not envisaged that monthly pensions would be paid
after the workhouse was completed: F2006/176.

Father there and after she Married him they lived there till he dyed, she has one Child Mary 25 with a relation Esqr Congrove at Frame in Staffordshire, she was Apprentice at the New Change in the Strand to Mr Wansell before King Charles dyed, was Married from thence, he kept house in Durham Yard, never lived out of this Parish since her Apprenticeship, she was about 20 when she was bound.

As far as one can tell from the workhouse admission records, this 64-year-old widow refused to enter the workhouse in 1725, and disappears from our view.[38] How common was it for pensioners to go it alone in this way?

Since we have a full set of workhouse admission registers from the opening of the institution until the end of 1729 it is possible, although technically exacting, to find out how many of those known to have been receiving pensions in 1724/5 moved to the workhouse after that date. Since the 1726/7 overseers accounts also survive, it is also possible to see how many former parish pensioners moved from regular parish pensions to payments on the extraordinary account in the following accounting year. In order to add some much needed flesh to what are rather dry bones, illustrative case studies will be deployed.[39] Although every effort has been made to make the nominal linkage as accurate as possible, there will be a small margin of error caused by the difficulty of correctly linking people with common forenames and surnames across different classes of record.

Who were the parish pensioners? Overwhelmingly, and typically, they were female. The sex ratio of our pensioner population (which counts only those named as receiving pensions and thus underestimates wives) in 1724/5 was 31 males per hundred females. The average age of a sample of pensioners listed in a census of the poor in 1716 was 65.75. That population consisted largely of the elderly – just 18 per cent were under sixty, although there were a large number of unknown ages.[40]

Of the 541 individual parish pensioners receiving payments in 1724/5 only 170 can be found entering the workhouse at any time between the

38   For references to Penelope Reed, see COWAC, F5014/146 and 190; F5018/573; F454/162; F459a/225. She does not appear in the workhouse admission registers. For an earlier, briefer examination, see F5008/97. Her husband was then described as a tailor.

39   For similar biographies, see Smith, 'Ageing and well-being', pp. 79–83.

40   COWAC, F4539. There were 63 males to 227 females in this population, a sex ratio of 28 per hundred, very similar to that of 1724/5. All told there were 295 pensioners listed in this 1716 list, just 192 of whom had ages listed.

Table 6.3. Workhouse destinations of those on parish pensions in
St Martin-in-the-Fields, 1724–25

Total estimated parish pensioners in parish of St Martin-in-the-Fields 1724/5 (less Hanover Square)	361	%
Entered the workhouse for first time in 1725	102	28.3
Entered the workhouse for first time in 1726	28	7.8
Entered the workhouse for first time in 1727	20	5.5
Entered the workhouse for first time in 1728	11	3.1
Entered the workhouse for first time in 1729	9	2.5
Total entering workhouse for first time between 1725 and 1729	170	47.1

Sources: COWAC, F459a (overseers' accounts 1724/5), F4002, F4007, F4073, F4074 and
F4077 (workhouse admission registers and day books).

end of July 1725 and August 1729. If we assume that one third of those
original pensioners found themselves in the new parish of Hanover
Square, then that suggests that 170/361 (47 per cent) at most moved to the
workhouse after losing their regular outdoor relief.[41] Table 6.3 presents
the information in more detail.

Table 6.3 actually suggests that no more than 28 per cent of pensioners
entered the local workhouse in the year that their pensions ceased. Others
spent months and sometimes years before entering. The overall figure of
47 per cent is very similar to the situation found in Tavistock. There, only
fourteen of the original thirty-one pensioners (45 per cent) entered the
workhouse in 1747. The remainder lost their doles and presumably got by
thereafter without recourse to regular parish relief.[42]

There was a similar reluctance to send orphan children to the
workhouse. Orphans were children who had lost one or both parents and
were usually aged between three and fourteen, with an average age of
about nine.[43] The carers received pensions. As noted in Table 6.1, orphan

41   A committee of the local vestry were 'to meet the Gentlemen of the parish of
St George Hannover Square about settling the Poor belonging to that Parish' in April 1725:
COWAC, F2006/179.
42   Smith, 'Ageing and well-being', p. 89.
43   Information on orphans' ages can be found in a census of the poor taken in 1716: 171
out of 181 ages were listed: COWAC, F4539/11–77.

Table 6.4. Workhouse destinations of those receiving orphan pensions in St Martin-in-the-Fields, 1724–25

Total estimated orphan pensioners in parish of St Martin-in-the-Fields 1724/5 (less Hanover Square)	222	%
Entered the workhouse for first time in 1725	54	24.3
Entered the workhouse for first time in 1726	19	8.6
Entered the workhouse for first time in 1727	6	2.7
Entered the workhouse for first time in 1728	6	2.7
Entered the workhouse for first time in 1729	9	4.1
Total entering workhouse for first time between 1725 and 1729	94	42.3
Total continued on the orphan pension in 1726	19	8.6

Sources: COWAC, F459a, F462 (overseers' accounts 1724/5, 1726/7), F4002, F4007, F4073, F4074 and F4077 (workhouse admission registers and day books).

pensions were drastically curtailed on the opening of the workhouse. Table 6.4 shows that less than one third of these children were sent to the workhouse in the year that it opened, and that overall only 42 per cent entered the workhouse at some point before the end of 1729.

More could be said about what happened to those ejected from the pension lists. Many of the former orphans were removed by parents or sent out on parish apprenticeships. Many of the elderly pensioners admitted, of course, died in the workhouse. Others simply left it again. A telling example here is that of the pensioner Diana Lothlaine, or Lathlane. This individual had been examined by the parish authorities at the beginning of 1709:

> Diana Lathlane sayes she knowes not whether she is a Widow of Andrew Lathlane a fringe & Lacemaker who was a houskeeper in Rose Street aboute 20 years ago in King James time, she sayes. John Jerman li[vd] next door to her, she sayes she nor her husband never was houskeepers since, nor never livd out of the parish since but kept shop in Bedford Street in this parish & payd Taxes. She has no children to be provided for, she lives at Burdetts in Feather Ally, her husband went away about 7 year ago to the East Indias.

Marginal notes reveal that Lothlaine then had one adult child, Charlotte, and that she had married her husband at St Marylebone church thirty years previously. By 1714 she was receiving a regular pension worth 4s 4d a month. In 1716 she was listed, aged sixty-seven, as one of the parish pensioners in the census of that year. Her pension payments increased as she got older, advancing to 6s per month by 1720, and were increased again to 8s per month at petty sessions in 1724. Lothlaine entered the workhouse at the stated age of seventy-six in October 1725, but left just nine days later. According to the workhouse discharge register she then 'went o[u]t: again to try to maintain herself'.[44] Other former pensioners clearly preferred a lengthy stay in the new workhouse to life outside. Winifred Ball, for example, had been granted a pension of 5s per month after her examination sometime in 1717:

> Winifred Ball aged 58 yeares sayes she was marryd to Robert Ball a Sawyer deceased about 22 year ago. He never kept house, he was about 21 when she marryd. He was Apprentice to John Watkins in Scotland Yard and Roger Watkins Sawyer in Bedfordbury. He was not quite out of his Apprenticeship when he marryed [*underlined in original*], he was a servant to Mr Bernard at Low Layton & so was she 2 or 3 year, [& lived] the[re] about half a year and after that he learnd the Trade of a Sawyer. He was a Shropshire man, he had a brother Thomas Ball Corn chandler in Old Soho, deceased 24 year ago – at Low Layton.

Winifred spent eight years on the pension without any change in her stipend. She entered the workhouse in September 1725 when she was said to be seventy-six years old, stayed for six months and then 'Left ye House' in March 1726. Just twelve days later Winifred returned for a stay of just over four months, leaving for the second time in July 1727. She returned in the middle of September 1727 for the third and last time, staying for over twelve *years*. She died in the workhouse in January 1740 at the supposed age of ninety.[45]

Of particular interest is the extent to which former parish pensioners succeeded in applying for regular or irregular outdoor relief on the extraordinary books. It is probable, after all, that applications that led to repeated payments was the means by which pensioners regained their

---

44 For Diana Lothlaine's biography, see COWAC, F5001/43; F5017/112c; F4002/11; F4539/43; F444/154; F445/148; F446/140; F447/153; F449/167; F451/180; F452/167; F454/159; F459a/220.

45 For Winifred Ball's biography, see COWAC, F5010/77; F4002/29, 91; F4073; F447/148; F449/162; F451/174; F452/160; F454/153; F459a/209.

presence on outdoor relief. Regular payments to individuals on the extraordinary account became *de facto* pensions. To what extent, however, do the thousands of payments on the extraordinary account contain *former* parish pensioners?

The results are striking. Of the 541 parish pensioners in 1724/5, some 145 (27 per cent) can be found receiving one or more payments on the extraordinary account in 1726/7. Of these, 53 also entered the workhouse at some point between 1725 and 1729. This means that in addition to the 102 former pensioners who entered the parish workhouse in 1725, another 88 or so received some temporary relief in the following financial year *without* entering the institution. What was this extraordinary relief worth to our hapless former pensioners? The average monthly parish pension was about 7s per month in 1724/5. Only three former parish pensioners received payments exceeding that sum in 1726/7. One (possible) former pensioner was paid a large sum to make a one-way trip to Ireland. Of the other two individuals, one received thirty individual payments amounting to a monthly pension of nearly 8s in one year, this despite the fact that she had applied for relief in November 1725 'on the Pention applied for Relief Ordered she be maintained in the house Erected for the poor'. This may have been preparatory to getting her into an almshouse place when one fell vacant.[46] The still more fortunate Elizabeth Kibblewhite received a large *de facto* monthly pension of 10s per month throughout the accounting year. Elizabeth may have been favoured due to the fact that she was thought to be a centenarian, which belief might also have kept her out of the workhouse.[47] Overall, however, accessing extraordinary relief did not usually make up for the loss of a regular monthly pension. Only 20 out of 145 former pensioners received handouts worth 2s 6d per month or more in the extraordinary accounts. Just under half of them received

46 This was one Mary Mullins (a not uncommon name) who seems to have moved from a pension in 1724/5 to an almshouse place in 1728, which she held until 1733. Mullins had had a parish pension of 8s a month since 1721. For her pension and almshouse place see COWAC, F454/160; F459a/222; F468/138; F472/126; F476/158; F478/198; F482/170; F485/172b. See also F5019/42. For her payments in the extraordinary account in 1726/7, see F462/230–41, 243–5, 247–8, 250–2 and 328.

47 For Elizabeth Kibblewhite's pauper biography see COWAC, F462/230–2, 234, 236, 238, 240, 243, 246, 248 and 251. She was listed as aged 101 in a petty sessions meeting in 1724 when it was 'Ordered that the Overseers write for on the Extraordinary for the said Elizabeth Kibblewhite 4s' which might have increased her pension: F5017/222a. Kibblewhite had been receiving pension payments of 8s per month since 1708. She seems to have been occupying an almshouse place in 1707: F4509/36.

only one or two payments and just over half received a total cash benefit of 5s *a year* or less.

Since extraordinary relief seems commonly to have coexisted with indoor relief and may have contained large numbers of regular payments to particular individuals, it is worth investigating it a little further. How extensive were these one-off payments? It is worth recalling here that our only currently available year, 1726/7, was a period when the parish workhouse was still relatively small (see Figure 6.1). As we shall see, the relative part played by the workhouse in parish relief increased very significantly after this time. Nonetheless, even in 1726/7, twice as much was spent on maintaining the workhouse as was expended on extraordinary relief.[48] The 1726/7 accounting year ran from 22 April 1726 to 12 April 1727. During that exact period the parish workhouse, with about 250 people then inhabiting the institution at any one point in time, admitted 599 individuals and discharged 539. Another laborious nominal linkage exercise enables us to group extraordinary payments by individual recipient. Putting aside payments to anonymous individuals and administrative payments, the overseers made 4,552 payments to 1,322 named individuals during this time.[49] Although the average payment was just 27.3d, this still meant that eighty-one individuals received a total of 30s per year or more: ninety-seven individuals received at least twelve payments in the accounting year. One could go further, but this brief analysis does confirm the potential importance of outdoor relief noted above by David Green and others. It is easy to see how regular payments might 'creep' back into parish accounts – they may never, in fact, have entirely gone away.

It is also striking that parish overseers did not necessarily follow local policy decisions. In a number of cases, paupers were given regular relief by overseers in direct contradiction to earlier rulings made by justices, and certainly against the whole notion of the workhouse test. One can only assume that the annual rotation of the overseers' office, poor communications, a past history of rate-paying, and perhaps humanitarian and charitable sentiments explain such action. Take, for example, Philip and Hester New. This couple were awarded a joint pension of 12s per year in August 1723, following Philip's settlement examination in the previous month:

48   The extraordinary account also covered payments to hospitals, parish apprenticeship costs, tradesmen's bills and other headings which are not treated here.
49   Something like 124 other individuals were maintained in hospitals by the parish in 1726/7.

Philip New aged 69 years lodging at a Barbers Shop the upper end of Bull Inn Court saith he was married to Hester his wife at St. Sepulchres Church: about 38 years agoe. He is a staymaker kept house in Harvey Court 23 years and paid £20 per annum Rent and all Taxes for many years. Saith he left the same last Christmas never kept house since has 4 Children. Simon thirty married he is a mans Taylor keeps house in Edwards Street in old Soho. Sarah 28 singlewoman at home Quilter. Honor 27 married to James Roy he is a polisher and lives in Cranborne Street. & Hester 25 singlewoman Quilter at home.[50]

It is interesting, although something that is unfortunately rarely visible in our records, that this aged couple had two adult children at home, and two married children in the immediate neighbourhood. Such a support network might have enabled this elderly couple to retain residential independence into their old age.[51] Following their examination, Philip and Hester New duly appear as parish pensioners in 1724. After the abolition of pension payments in 1725, Philip appeared at petty sessions, 'late a Pentioner applied for relief, Ordered that he be no otherwise provided for than in the Workhouse'. However, despite this ruling, not only did the couple remain outside the workhouse, but they were paid regular sums of 2s 6d or so every week from November 1726 until the end of April 1727 by the parish overseers.[52]

This analysis has demonstrated quite clearly that the introduction of the parish workhouse had a dramatic impact on the volume of welfare delivered to parish pensioners, both adult parish pensioners and orphaned children. Many of these individuals were clearly reluctant to enter the institution. Something like one half never entered at all and less than a third entered in the year that their pensions ceased. A not inconsiderable number of pensioners turn out to have received relief on the extraordinary account, but in most cases such payments did not replace the pensions they had lost. It was a feature of the extraordinary accounts that individual paupers could be awarded regular payments, spread out over the entire year.

We do not know, as yet, whether the experience of St Martin's was

50   COWAC, F5016/318.

51   M. Pelling, *The common lot. Sickness, medical occupations and the urban poor in early modern England* (London, 1998), pp. 140, 165.

52   For Philip New's biography see COWAC, F5016/318 and 331; F5018/574; F462/239, 240, 164, 241, 242, 243, 244, 245, 246, 169, 247, 248, 249 and 250–2; F459a/223.

duplicated in other London parishes, but it would be very surprising if it was not. Given the enthusiasm with which most of London's parishes adopted indoor relief, this suggests that the decades after 1725 must have been extremely hard for many former metropolitan pensioners.[53] How these individuals, often elderly females, coped without recourse to regular outdoor relief that they had received sometimes for years, remains unclear. Presumably they eked out a living in the economy of 'makeshift and mend'. It may also be that the relatively low food prices in the 1720s and 1730s facilitated adjustment to a life without a parish pension.[54] We now know that many applied for short-term relief from the parish. Other strategies would have included migration at what were often relatively advanced ages. Settlement laws might have made the residential mobility of the poor elderly more likely in the eighteenth century.[55] Not everybody could cope. One of our pensioners, Elizabeth Alva, with a parish stipend that rose from 4s per month in 1717 to 8s per month by 1724, 'hanged herself in St Giles's parish' in July 1725.[56]

It has already been noted that, as was commonly the case elsewhere, parish pensions were being paid in quite large numbers by the late 1740s (see Table 6.1). This suggests an easing of restrictions over welfare and a less rigorous approach to the workhouse test. It certainly suggests that for some reason overseers, and very occasionally local JPs, were more willing to order regular out-relief, as long as it did not become too expensive.[57]

53 For a recent discussion of London workhouses under the old poor law, see D. R. Green, 'Icons of the new system: workhouse construction and relief practices in London under the old and new poor law', *London Journal* 34 (2009), 264–84 (pp. 264–9). For workhouses before 1750, see Hitchcock, 'The English workhouse'.
54 L. D. Schwarz, *London in the age of industrialisation: entrepreneurs, labour force and living conditions, 1700–1850* (Cambridge, 1992), pp. 168–73.
55 K. Snell, 'Parish registration and the study of labour mobility', *Local Population Studies* 33 (1984), 29–43 (pp. 33–7). Elderly Londoners might have left the city in significant numbers. An estimate of net immigration in eighteenth-century London revealed 'a net outflow above the age of forty': J. Landers, *Death and the metropolis: studies in the demographic history of London, 1670–1830* (Cambridge, 1993), p. 183. For migration of the elderly in Elizabethan Norwich, see Pelling, *The common lot*, pp. 140–1.
56 COWAC, F83/28; F447/159; F449/161; F451/173; F452/159; F454/153; F459a/209.
57 It was extremely rare for examining JPs to order regular out-relief after 1725. From a sample of 192 examinations carried out by the JP Daniel Gach between 1744 and 1750, just three included annotated orders for outdoor relief. One effect of the building of workhouses, therefore, was to significantly *reduce* the day-to-day influence of JPs over the granting of out-relief. In our sample of over 12,000 transcribed examinations 1725–94, Gach seems to have been the *only* JP who made such orders; see COWAC, F5038/251;

Table 6.1 also revealed marked fluctuations in the total number of pensions paid. Can we explain these patterns?

To answer this question we need to make a brief survey of the course of outdoor and indoor relief during the eighteenth century. We should start by observing that the size of parish workhouses fluctuated significantly over time.[58] Figure 6.1, which is based on averages of fortnightly counts of the number of inmates in the workhouse, shows how the parish workhouse changed in size in the eighteenth and early nineteenth centuries. After its initial construction, average numbers of inmates (which conceal marked winter peaks and summer troughs) rose to a peak of just under 500 in 1741. Average numbers then declined to 336 in 1752 and then rose slowly to around 400 where they remained until 1771. The workhouse was rebuilt and greatly extended in 1772, after which there was clearly a renewed enthusiasm for indoor relief. Average numbers of inmates doubled in the decade after 1771 to reach a peak of 800 in 1784. Thereafter indoor relief shrank again with average numbers of inmates falling to around 500 in the early nineteenth century, only to experience a resurgence following the end of the Napoleonic Wars (Figure 6.1).

The balance between outdoor relief and indoor relief changed significantly over time. It seems reasonable to conclude that the first resurgence in outdoor pensions seen in Table 6.1 was associated with the period of decline in use of the workhouse in the 1740s. There were fewer parish pensioners in the 1760s than there seemingly had been in the early 1750s, something which might be related to the gradual increase in workhouse numbers. What is certain, however, is that the redevelopment of the workhouse in 1772 was responsible for a dramatic shift away from outdoor pensions, in the years 1772 to 1774. That local policy was hostile to the granting of outdoor pensions at this time can be verified independently. Jonas Hanway, famous reformer and philanthropist, visited the St Martin's workhouse shortly after its rebuilding. After claiming that the new building was not big enough for 'for so vast a number as six hundred paupers, and upwards', Hanway went on to remark, presumably following conversations with local officials, that 'It is an established maxim, that it is prejudicial to give money to out-pensioners'.[59] We do not have pensioner

F5039/13 and 149. JPs continued to have limited involvement in the granting of 'extraordinary' relief: just 200 or so (around 4 per cent) of 4,731 payments in 1726/7 were made by order of petty sessions; see F462/162–327.

58   Green, 'Icons of the new system', pp. 265–9.
59   Hanway, The citizen's monitor, p. 173.

Figure 6.1. Average number of inmates in the parish workhouse of
St Martin-in-the-Fields, 1725–1818

Source: COWAC, F491, F2212, F2213, F4003–6, F4008–14 and F4016–26.

counts after 1780, but prejudice against granting such payments seems to
have diminished considerably if Eden's reported figure of 240 or so outdoor
pensioners recorded in 1794 is correct. The implied growth in pensioners
between 1780 and 1794 (Table 6.1) roughly coincides with falling numbers
of workhouse inmates, perhaps reflecting an increasing aversion to indoor
relief at this time.[60] Notwithstanding the growth of outdoor pensions to
the early 1790s, St Martin's (unusually, even for London) still relieved 60
per cent of its 'permanent poor' indoors in 1803.[61]

In the absence of itemised pension lists after 1780 it is difficult to unpick
the implications of these changes in local policy towards the poor. One
approach is to investigate spending on the outdoor poor in more detail.
The money paid to the outdoor poor listed in the overseers accounts is
sometimes broken down further between money spent on 'casual', that is,
temporary relief, and that spent on 'settled poor', who were those receiving

60   Slack, *English poor law*, pp. 43–4.
61   *Abstract of answers and returns under Act for procuring returns relative to expense
and maintenance of the poor in England* (PP, 1803–04, XIII), pp. 724–5.

Figure 6.2. The ratio between expenditure on the 'settled' and 'casual' poor

Source: COWAC, F547, F549, F551, F553, F559, F561, F563, F565, F567, F569, F571, F573, F575, F577, F611, F613, F615 and F617.
Note: Five-year moving averages. The higher the ratio, the greater the relative amount spent on the settled poor.

regular pensions. Between the mid-1760s and 1780 it was common to spend as much on 'casual' relief as on the 'settled poor'. By the end of the eighteenth century, spending on the settled poor outstripped that spent on the casual poor by factors of between four and nine to one (Figure 6.2). Since there was no marked increase in the total sums spent on the outdoor poor until the early nineteenth century (Figure 6.3), this changing ratio suggests that more of the casual poor were being sent to the workhouse in the last two decades of the century, refused poor relief altogether or granted regular pensions.

A technique by which to assess the changing balance between indoor and outdoor relief is presented in Figures 6.3 and 6.4. The two figures represent the actual spend on the workhouse and on 'casual' and 'settled poor' in the overseers' accounts between 1765 and 1824 (Figure 6.3), and the ratio between the sums of money spent (Figure 6.4). The ratios in Figure 6.4 have been smoothed using a five-year moving average. Although

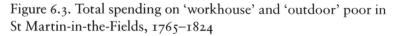

Figure 6.3. Total spending on 'workhouse' and 'outdoor' poor in
St Martin-in-the-Fields, 1765–1824

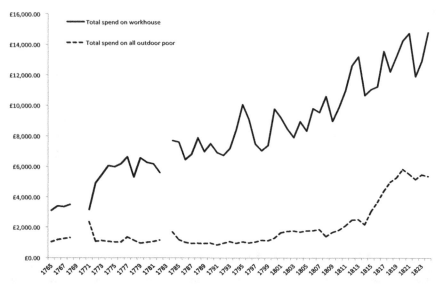

Source: COWAC, F547, F549, F551, F553, F559, F561, F563, F565, F567, F569, F571, F573,
F575, F577, F579, F581, F585, F587, F589, F591, F593, F595, F597, F599, F601, F603, F605,
F607, F609, F611, F613, F615, F617, F619, F621, F623, F625, F627, F629, F631, F633, F635,
F637, F639, F641, F643, F645, F647, F649, F651, F653, F655, F657, F659, F661, F663 and F665.

one can sometimes quarrel about which costs to assign to the workhouse
in the surviving accounts, the general picture seems reasonably clear.
Figure 6.3 shows that overall spending on the workhouse more than
quadrupled (4.8) in monetary terms between 1765 and 1824. In the same
period, spending on the outdoor poor increased overall by a factor of
more than five (5.1). As the changing ratios in Figure 6.4 imply, however,
whereas spending on the indoor poor jumped after the 1771/2 rebuilding
and then increased more or less steadily to 1824, spending on the outdoor
poor remained at a plateau of around £1,000 a year until the beginning of
the nineteenth century. Spending on the outdoor poor then increased to
about £1,800 a year in 1805, increased to around £2,000 or so in the next
five years and surged ahead after 1815, such that spending was over £5,000
a year by 1819.

If Figure 6.3 is deflated by the Phelps Brown–Hopkins cost-of-living
data to allow for price inflation, then *real* expenditure on indoor relief

Figure 6.4. Ratio of expenditure on workhouse to expenditure on outdoor poor in St Martin-in-the-Fields, 1765–1824 (five-year moving average)

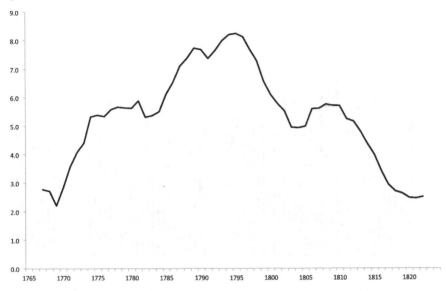

Source: See Figure 6.3.

stagnated in 1780s, after doubling in the decade following the rebuilding.[62] Indoor relief costs actually fell in real terms in the last five years of the eighteenth century and then stagnated again until real spending surged once more following the crisis produced by demobilisation in 1815. Inflationary pressures may thus explain why numbers in the workhouse declined after peaking around 1785 (Figure 6.1). Spending on outdoor relief stagnated in real terms until 1785 or so, *declined* to a nadir around 1800, and then stagnated again until a resurgence in real spending on the outdoor poor around 1815.

Figure 6.4 reflects, first, the greater emphasis on outdoor relief before the workhouse was rebuilt in 1772, and clearly shows the increasing relative spend on indoor relief until the end of the eighteenth century. A renewed emphasis on outdoor relief in spending can be seen after that date. Such expenditure is partly reflected in the changing number of inmates in the workhouse depicted in Figure 6.1. A peak in spending on indoor relief in

---

62 For this series, see E. H. Phelps Brown and S. V. Hopkins, 'Seven centuries of the prices of consumables, compared with builders' wage rates', *Economica* 23 (1956), 296–314.

Figure 6.5. Percentages of females dying aged sixty or more in St Martin-in-the-Fields who died in the workhouse or in almshouses, 1748–1825

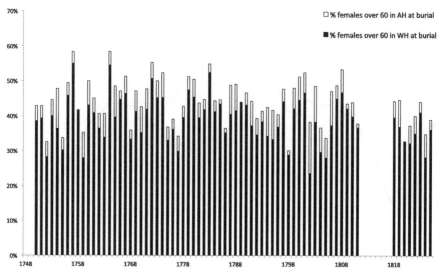

Sources: COWAC, 419/123, 419/233–7, 419/238–44, Accession 419/265–9, F2465, F2467 and F2469.

1795 may reflect a surge in workhouse costs, possibly associated with a sharp increase in poverty in that year. The one exceptionally low ratio in Figure 6.4 found in 1771 reflects the greater resort to out-relief during the period when the workhouse was being rebuilt. During that year some of the inmates were temporarily lodged elsewhere.[63]

Parish expenditure on outdoor and indoor relief clearly fluctuated – sometimes dramatically – over the eighteenth century. Hidden within total expenditure on outdoor relief, there were also significant changes in the way such relief was delivered. In some periods the parish invested relatively more money in regular pensions rather than short-term one-off payments; in other periods it invested much more heavily in casual relief. Such changes in this one local welfare system must have had very significant

63 For such short-term changes elsewhere see Tomkins, *Experience of urban poverty*, p. 43. During the rebuilding, the parish hired a temporary house in Brownlow Street. The parish paid 'one Years Window Tax for the House in Brownlow Street hired for the Use of the Poor of this Parish' in 1771, as well as sums of money for the watch, water supply and 'Cleansing the necessary': COWAC, F559.

implications for its local poor and particularly the poor elderly. There is some evidence for example, presented elsewhere, that the proportion of the local elderly resident in the workhouse at any one time increased after the 1772 rebuilding.[64]

The observation that workhouses reduced levels of outdoor relief by taking in the potentially burdensome elderly, sick and dying is also amply born out. Something like 15–20 per cent of *all* those dying in the parish died in the workhouse after 1725. This phenomenon was particularly marked among the elderly and particularly among elderly females, those most at risk of pauperism and most likely to be in need of expensive care towards the end of their lives. Figure 6.5 illustrates this morbid role of the parish workhouse by setting out the proportions of elderly women (aged sixty or more) who died there. It was usual for 30–40 per cent of *all* elderly women to die in the parish workhouse and in some years more than 50 per cent did so. A further 5 per cent or so died in parish almshouses.[65]

Conclusions

There can be little doubt that workhouses distorted patterns of poor relief in the eighteenth century. The evidence presented here shows quite clearly that the number of outdoor pensions and the volume of outdoor relief fluctuated significantly over the eighteenth century and that their number never recovered to pre-workhouse levels. Historians of welfare must surely do more to uncover the dynamic relationship between indoor and outdoor relief, particularly when their arguments revolve only around changes in the volume and level of outdoor relief.

What is also clear, however, is that the influence that this workhouse had on outdoor relief was not always predictable or consistent. The dramatic abolition of parish pensions in 1725 proved to be relatively short-lived. As other studies have found, parish pensions returned, but why? One of the wider questions this research raises is why *outdoor* pensions proved such a resilient form of poor relief.

64   Boulton and Schwarz, '"The comforts of a private fireside"?', pp. 229–30.
65   The medical role of the St Martin's workhouse is explored in detail in J. Boulton, R. Davenport and L. Schwarz, '"These ANTE-CHAMBERS OF THE GRAVE"? Mortality, medicine and the workhouse in Georgian London (1725–1824)', in *Medicine and the Workhouse*, ed. J. Reinarz and L. Schwarz (Rochester, NY, 2013), pp. 58–85.

Explaining the survival of parish pensions is particularly difficult given the huge investment represented by the building and especially the running costs of the workhouse. Indoor relief was more expensive than outdoor relief. Between 1765 and 1824, for example, the workhouse of St Martin's absorbed the gigantic sum of £482,099 out of a total poor relief expenditure by the overseers of £771,319 (63 per cent), easily dwarfing the money spent on outdoor relief (see Figure 6.3).[66] A satisfactory answer to this attachment to outdoor relief in the face of this huge investment would probably require a detailed analysis to undercover the backgrounds of parish pensioners: were they thought too respectable to enter workhouses, for example?[67] The attitudes of local officials to both indoor and outdoor relief would also be important. The attachment of overseers to out-relief may explain many decisions to continue out-payments. Even the usually triumphalist *Account of workhouses*, which was intended to advertise the savings that new workhouses made, included reports that revealed the survival of regular outdoor relief. The Maidstone report blamed overseers explicitly for the continuation of outdoor pensions.[68] More work, too, is clearly needed on the nature and experience of workhouse life and on the attitudes of the parish poor to such institutions. It may be, too, that parochial authorities in London welcomed the deterrent effect that workhouses represented to the casual and immigrant poor. What is certain is that any explanation for their continual use in London must encompass the survival of significant volumes of outdoor relief in its various forms.[69]

Another point that is worth highlighting is the very significant welfare

66   For similar proportions for the Kentish parish of Tonbridge, see Barker-Read, 'The treatment of the aged poor', p. 222. For the greater relative cost of indoor relief in the nineteenth century, see M. Rose, 'The allowance system under the new poor Law', *Economic History Review* 19 (1966), 607–20 (p. 613).

67   It may be significant that some West End workhouse regulations made separate provision for those inmates who had seen better days. The regulations of the parish of St Brides in 1731, for example, ordered that 'The Poor that have been formerly Housekeepers in repute, are lodged in the best Apartments, and eat at a different Table, that they may not be incommoded by the noise of the common Poor, who are clamorous, and unaccustomed to good Manners'. Similar provision was reported by the workhouse of St Margaret, Westminster, *An account of the work-houses in Great Britain*, pp. 23 and 64. The Webbs argued that overcrowding and the unregulated mixing of social groups within workhouses 'increased the reluctance of the Justices to allow Overseers to compel the respectable poor to enter the workhouse': S. and B. Webb, *The old poor law*, p. 250.

68   *An account of the work-houses in Great Britain*, p. 132.

69   For this, see Tomkins, *Experience of urban poverty*, pp. 36–78.

problem represented by London's adoption of large-scale indoor relief in the first half of the eighteenth century. Particularly when workhouses were first built, but also at other points in the eighteenth century, large numbers of often elderly poor faced cuts to or abolition of their outdoor relief. Although many either entered the workhouse or survived on lower volumes of casual relief, many others seem to have got by without recourse to parish relief at all. Was this because London's economy provided more opportunities? Was it peculiarly easy for even elderly women to maintain themselves in the eighteenth-century capital? Alternatively, did they leave the capital and seek succour in other parishes, perhaps with relatives? Do we need to know more about the migration patterns of the aged poor in this period?

Given the complexities it might be helpful to summarise this chapter in diagrammatic form. Figure 6.6 sets out a schematic representation of how the poor relief system operated after the workhouse was built in 1725. The diagram is intended to clarify the various routes to relief within what Paul Slack once dubbed the 'machine' of welfare. It should be noted that an 'application' here is shorthand for a variety of different pathways to welfare. Paupers facing destitution might have been removed from other parishes and delivered to overseers, they might have applied at the workhouse door, been found on the streets by beadles, relieved by individual ward overseers or occasionally by local magistrates. Many poor relief decisions were made by the Board of Guardians (churchwardens and overseers) who governed the workhouse for most of the eighteenth century. By the later eighteenth century, the process of application itself had become heavily bureaucratic with admission to the workhouse requiring a printed ticket signed by an overseer.[70] Any decision, of course, would have also taken into account the poor law resources available. The diagram has only a dotted arrow linking a decision to the granting of a pension. This is to illustrate the likelihood that weekly or monthly pensions were not paid for the first twenty years or so after a workhouse was integrated into the local poor law machinery.

There are a number of features of the system worth noting. Poor relief applicants were, of course, only a subset of the total number of those in need. As the diagram indicates, an unknown number of individuals must have been deterred from applying for parish poor relief. Some would have

70   For a surviving example, see http://research.ncl.ac.uk/pauperlives/esrcprojectdetails.htm (accessed 28 July 2014).

Figure 6.6. Schematic diagram illustrating potential outcomes from a single poor relief application under the old poor law in a parish operating the workhouse test

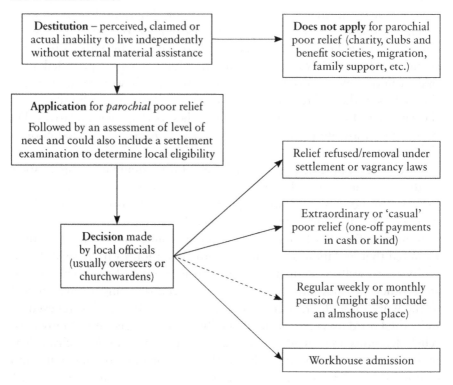

feared being sent to the workhouse and others would have known that they possessed no legal settlement in the parish and so were at risk of removal. Such individuals sought alternative, non-parochial, forms of relief, which might include leaving the parish voluntarily to seek work or aid from family or friends. Others would have returned voluntarily to their parish of settlement. Moreover, not all applications for relief were successful – an unknown number must have been turned down. It is, unfortunately, rare for failed poor relief applications to be recorded.[71]

71   J. Boulton, 'Going on the parish: the parish pension and its meaning in the London suburbs, 1640–1724', in *Chronicling poverty: the voices and strategies of the English poor, 1640–1840*, ed. T. Hitchcock, P. King and P. Sharpe (Basingstoke, 1997), pp. 19–46 (pp. 26–33).

It is also the case, of course, that practice on the ground was more blurred than the neat schema in Figure 6.6. It was common, for example, to delay many settlement examinations until *after* a pauper had been admitted into the workhouse.[72] Some workhouse applicants might find themselves given causal relief immediately prior to admission to the workhouse – this was especially likely given that paupers were rarely admitted on Sunday. In 1828, paupers seeking admission to the workhouse with a magistrate's order out of office hours were to 'receive 6d [*and*] a quarter of a loaf with cheese until the following morning'.[73] Nor, of course, does the diagram portray subsequent movement between the various boxes in the diagram. Failed applicants might reapply and those who preferred alternative coping strategies to parish relief might find them inadequate. Paupers removed under settlement laws might, nonetheless, return and reapply for poor relief. Those receiving regular pensions might find themselves in the workhouse – particularly at the end of their lives. Those on extraordinary relief might later qualify for regular pensions. Workhouse inmates might find themselves on extraordinary relief after discharge, and those on casual relief might later be admitted to the institution.

In the absence of family reconstitution evidence for the parish, it is difficult to relate this dynamic welfare system closely to the demography of this huge metropolitan parish.[74] We have already seen that the workhouse played a significant part in relieving the poor, particularly at the end of their lives (Figure 6.5). Perhaps the most obvious demographic impact was on migration. Figure 6.6, at a number of points, links outmigration to applications for poor relief. Failure to qualify for poor relief in an urban environment is likely, in the absence of alternatives, to have led to enforced or voluntary outmigration. To the extent that workhouses increased the

---

72 J. Boulton, 'Double deterrence: settlement and practice in London's West End, 1725–1824', in *Migration, settlement and belonging in Europe, 1500–1930s: comparative perspectives*, ed. A. Winter and S. King (Oxford and New York, 2013), pp. 54–80.

73 *Rules and regulations for the government of the workhouse, of the parish of St Martin in the Fields*, pp. 13–14.

74 Romola Davenport is conducting a limited reconstitution of the parish, see http://research.ncl.ac.uk/pauperlives/Infantmortalityproject.htm (accessed 28 July 2014). For recent work on the possible relationships between the poor law and English demography see Smith, 'Social security', and M. Kelly and C. Ó Gráda, 'The poor law of old England: institutional innovation and demographic regimes', *Journal of Interdisciplinary History* 41 (2011), 339–66.

level of deterrence in the system, therefore, they may have worked to increase the overall level of migration among the poor.

Figure 6.6 has more implications for perceived *depth* of need. Paul Slack long ago suggested that poverty could be conceived of as being either 'shallow' or 'deep'.[75] This chapter suggests that a tripartite division is a better way of conceptualizing parochial relief. Paupers required total care, long-term support or short-term relief. Those admitted to the workhouse were considered unable to maintain themselves independently and, in effect, received *total care* (food, shelter, clothing) for the duration of their stay. Those receiving outdoor pensions or regular casual relief were receiving income supplements – not total care. Such people were perceived to be in *chronic long-term need* but not yet at the stage of *total care*. Those receiving temporary 'casual' relief required only *short-term support* until their circumstances either improved or deteriorated further. This suggests that changes in the balance between different types of relief in the diagram, and portrayed in Figures 6.2–6.4, may have been driven by changes in, or local perceptions of, the levels and types of necessity among applicants. Thus, for example, the rising number of pensions identified in Table 6.1 between 1780 and c.1794, and implied by the changing ratio between settled and casual poor (Figure 6.2), could suggest that there was thought to be relatively more *chronic* need at the end of the eighteenth century, but less need to provide short-term outdoor relief. The fall in the number of workhouse inmates from around the 1780s to the early nineteenth century also suggests that there was less need for total care in this same period.

Explaining local patterns of poor relief can be a challenging exercise. London, in particular, may not necessarily be the ideal laboratory for identifying changes in the nature and treatment of poverty due to the countervailing forces that affected its economy. Thus, for example, its wage-earning population was undoubtedly impoverished – even physically stunted – by the fall in real wages after 1750. However, the amount of *total care* required might actually have fallen due to the beneficial effects of the fuller employment caused by heavy military recruitment in London, particularly – but not exclusively – during the Revolutionary and Napoleonic Wars (1792–1815).[76] The apparent 'retreat' from indoor relief

75 P. Slack, *Poverty and policy in Tudor and Stuart England* (London, 1988), p. 39.
76 Schwarz, *London in the age of industrialisation*, pp. 95–101. The proportion of men of military age admitted to the St Martin's workhouse declined sharply in periods of prolonged warfare, see J. Boulton, 'The poor in crisis: price shocks, mortality

at the end of the eighteenth century might also reflect disenchantment among local policy-makers about its effectiveness and relatively high cost.[77] Poor law historians talk frequently about the efficacy and relative 'generosity' of relief – this chapter argues that more attention should be paid to exactly how such relief was delivered.

surges, economic depression, bankruptcies – and warfare: London "crises" and a parish workhouse, 1740–1825', unpublished paper delivered to the 'Coping with Crisis Conference: Re-evaluating the role of crises in economic and social history', Durham University, 26 July 2013.

77   Slack, *English poor law*, pp. 43–5.

7

Population Growth and Corporations of the Poor, 1660–1841

S. J. THOMPSON

The publication, in 1798, of T. R. Malthus's *An essay on the principle of population*, marked a turning point in contemporary attitudes to the English poor laws. Malthus's *Essay* condemned the institutional framework established by the 1601 Act for the Relief of the Poor for generating unsustainable population growth. The apparent failure of the poor laws to remove the poor's distress was not, Malthus claimed, due to fraud or mismanagement, as other critics of the system had argued, but was an intrinsic feature of their design and operation.[1] The fundamental weakness of the poor laws – especially in the wake of the Speenhamland decision of 1795 to vary able-bodied relief according to family size and bread prices – was their tendency to 'increase population without increasing the food for its support' by enabling poor men to 'marry with little or no prospect of being able to support a family in independence.' Malthus argued that the 'prospect of parish provision' was so powerful a stimulus to marriage that population would inevitably and inexorably outpace the means of subsistence, thereby depressing not just household-level, but also aggregate-level, living standards. Welfare transfer payments reinforced the 'want of frugality observable among the poor'. For Malthus, the poor were a class of people who stood in stark contrast to 'petty tradesmen and small farmers' because the poor 'seldom think of the future' and lacked 'both the power and the will to save'.[2]

Malthus's claims concerning the labouring poor's susceptibility to

---

1 [T. R. Malthus], *An essay on the principle of population* (London, 1798), pp. 74–5.
2 Ibid., pp. 83, 85–6.

improvident marriages and fertility-driven welfare-dependency resonated powerfully with parliamentarians and political economists in the thirty years or so prior to the passage of the 1834 Poor Law Amendment Act. Historians have disagreed over how far the 'new' poor law should be seen as a wholly Malthusian measure.[3] But there can be little doubt that the Poor Law Commissioners agreed with Malthus's first *Essay* in regarding the poor as powerless to resist post-Speenhamland incentives to marry and multiply. As the authors of the *Report* put it, under the existing system the income of a single man 'does not exceed a bare subsistence; but he only has to marry, and it increases. Even then it is unequal to the support of a family; but it rises on the birth of every child.'[4] Central to this shared way of thinking was the assumption that population growth was regulated by the supply of poor law allowances: cutting off that supply by abolishing the poor laws altogether would, Malthus believed, check the growth of population and raise living standards. What neither Malthus nor the Poor Law Commissioners appeared willing to consider was the possibility that family allowances under the old poor law were a demand-led response to demographic and economic processes – rising fertility, altered dependency ratios and short-term price shocks – that were occurring 'upstream' of England's institutional welfare arrangements.

Numerous scholars have sought to test Malthus's hypothesis about the fertility-enhancing effects of poor law allowances using parish register, census and poor law expenditure data at both county and parish level. Huzel compared vital rates in selected parishes to try to determine the demographic impact of allowance policies between 1801 and 1832. He showed that marriage and birth rates rose in a majority of his seventeen sampled rural parishes following the abolition of allowances, apparently confounding Malthusian expectations.[5] These findings were subsequently challenged by Boyer who employed two different regression models to show that between 1826 and 1830 child allowances had a positive effect on birth rates across a sample of 214 south-eastern parishes.[6] Williams

---

3   See J. P. Huzel, *The popularization of Malthus in early nineteenth-century England: Martineau, Cobbett and the pauper press* (Aldershot, 2006), pp. 42–4 for an overview of the historiographical debate over Malthus's influence.

4   *Report from His Majesty's Commissioners for inquiring into the administration and practical operation of the poor laws* (PP, 1834, XXVII), pp. 32–3.

5   J. P. Huzel, 'The demographic impact of the old poor law: more reflexions on Malthus', *Economic History Review* 33 (1980), 367–81.

6   G. R. Boyer, 'Malthus was right after all: poor relief and birth rates in southeastern

has, in turn, questioned Boyer's emphatic claim that 'Malthus was right' by using a longitudinal, micro-historical analysis of two Bedfordshire parishes, Campton and Shefford, to demonstrate that child allowances were typically temporary expedients, limited in duration to periods of 'exceptionally high prices'.[7] If Williams's findings apply more widely across southern England, it seems hard to sustain the view that temporary and discretionary child allowances can have been a determining factor in household-formation decisions. Nonetheless, the Malthusian hypothesis has recently been reasserted by Greif and Iyigun. They have offered strong support to Boyer's conclusions on the basis of a multi-variate analysis of the determinants of county-level per capita poor relief assessments. They found that 'aid to the poor generated faster rates of population growth – but only in the 19th century'. Prior to that time, however, Greif and Iyigun found evidence of a negative relationship between poor relief and population growth.[8]

There is, it seems clear, a marked lack of consensus regarding at least two central aspects of the relationship between welfare provision and demographic change. First, was there a positive or negative association between poor relief and population growth? Secondly, did administrative changes to the poor laws cause population growth, or were they a response to it? This chapter addresses both of these questions through a reappraisal of the spatial and temporal development of local corporations of the poor during the long eighteenth century. My aim in what follows is not to demonstrate a statistically significant relationship between welfare transfer payments and population growth in general, or birth rates in particular, since doing so would fail to resolve the question of causation. Instead, I will use the history of corporations of the poor to illustrate the degree to which the eighteenth-century welfare regime was responsive to economic and demographic change. In doing so, I seek to emphasise the inherent flexibility of the poor law system in this period, in contrast to those who, inspired by Malthus's first *Essay*, have sought to draw a monochromatic picture of the demographic implications of welfare

England', *Journal of Political Economy* 97 (1989), 93–114. Unlike Huzel, Boyer controlled for a variety of other socio-economic variables including male agricultural incomes, population density per acre, infant mortality, housing, allotments and cottage industry.

7   S. Williams, 'Malthus, marriage and poor law allowances revisited: a Bedfordshire case study, 1770–1834', *Agricultural History Review* 52 (2004), 56–82 (p. 74).

8   A. Greif and M. Iyigun, 'What did the old poor law really accomplish? A redux', IZA DP No. 7398, May 2013, p. 16 (http://ftp.iza.org/dp7398.pdf, accessed 3 March 2014).

provision. What is required, I would suggest, are more nuanced interpretations that integrate robust statistical evidence with a fuller understanding of the dynamics of welfare policy-making at a national, regional
and parochial level.

The remainder of this chapter is divided into three sections. The first
provides a brief introduction to the existing literature on corporations of
the poor before turning to a quantitative analysis of all poor relief legislation, both local and general, enacted between 1660 and 1841.[9] In the
second section, I relate the tempo of local legislation to other indicators
of economic and demographic change, principally through a consideration of the growth of London and the changing urban hierarchy. In
addition, qualitative evidence derived from local petitions for poor law
corporations is presented that suggests that changes to the welfare regime
were 'downstream' of population growth. Finally, I employ evidence from
the most heavily incorporated English county, Suffolk, to try to determine
if different poor law policies were associated with systematic differences
in demographic behaviour.

'For the better regulation of the poor': the chronology
and geography of poor relief statutes, 1660–1841

Writing in the early twentieth century, the Webbs observed that the 125
or so corporations of the poor established between 1696 and 1833 had
'been almost ignored by historians'. They attributed this neglect to the
fact that corporations were established under local acts of parliament.[10]
Nearly a century later, eighteenth-century historians remain reluctant to
study this particular body of statutes systematically, with some notable
exceptions.[11] Consequently, the Webbs' discussion of corporations is

9   Cf. J. Innes, *Inferior politics: social problems and social policies in eighteenth-century
Britain* (Oxford, 2009), p. 101: 'It is evident that general and local legislation did not
constitute two independent streams of legislation. On the contrary, in numerous instances
the one can only be fully understood in the context of the other'.
10   S. Webb and B. Webb, *English local government: statutory authorities for special
purposes* (London, 1922), p. 109.
11   See especially S. Lambert, *Bills and acts: legislative procedure in eighteenth-century
England* (Cambridge, 1971); Innes, *Inferior politics*; P. Langford, *Public life and the
propertied Englishman 1689–1798* (Oxford, 1991); J. Hoppit, 'Patterns of parliamentary
legislation, 1660–1800', *Historical Journal* 39 (1996), 109–31; J. Hoppit (ed.), *Failed legislation, 1660–1800: extracted from the Commons and Lords journals* (London, 1997);

still the most exhaustive available, at least with respect to the legal and administrative principles around which these statutory authorities were organised.[12] The Webbs singled out corporations for special attention because they appeared to be harbingers of 1834, noting that '[i]t was from these statutory Poor Law Authorities that was derived the machinery of administration by committees, for unions of parishes, through salaried officials, with the workhouse in the background'.[13]

This characteristically whiggish interpretation of corporations has not gone unchallenged. Paul Slack, for example, has treated the formation of corporations not as a pioneering step on the road to modernity and uniformity, but as a remnant of early modern Puritanism's promotion of 'the common weal'. According to Slack, the fourteen urban corporations formed in the period 1696–1712 'constitute a cluster of instances of local reformation', which in a majority of places built upon a pre-existing tradition of godly reform.[14] Moreover, Slack's account – with its emphasis on the sectarian and partisan character of these early urban corporations – is an important corrective to the Webbs' story of a steady march towards a national, secular and bureaucratic welfare system. Indeed, Slack observes that parliament repeatedly blocked attempts to make corporations the administrative norm across the country.[15] But it should be noted that the pre-1712 corporations discussed by Slack represent only a tiny fraction of the '125 Incorporated Guardians of the Poor' identified by the Webbs.[16]

Given the large number of corporations established over the course

J. Hoppit, 'The landed interest and the national interest, 1660–1800', in *Parliaments, nations and identities in Britain and Ireland, 1660–1850*, ed. J. Hoppit (Manchester, 2003), pp. 83–102; J. Innes, 'Legislating for three kingdoms: how the Westminster parliament legislated for England, Scotland and Ireland, 1707–1830', in *Parliaments, nations and identities*, ed. Hoppitt, pp. 15–47.

12 Webb and Webb, *Statutory authorities*, pp. 107–51.

13 Ibid., pp. 109–10.

14 P. Slack, *From reformation to improvement: public welfare in early modern England* (Oxford, 1999), p. 103; cf. P. Slack, *Poverty and policy in Tudor and Stuart England* (London, 1988), p. 197: 'It makes sense, therefore, to see the Corporations as lineal descendants of the Puritan municipal projects of the early seventeenth century'.

15 Slack, *Reformation*, pp. 117–18, 143–4. See also J. Innes, 'The "mixed economy of welfare" in early modern England: assessments of the options from Hale to Malthus (c.1683–1803)', in *Charity, self-interest and welfare in the English past*, ed. M. Daunton (London, 1996), pp. 139–80 (pp. 151–2, 154–5 and 160–3).

16 Webb and Webb, *Statutory authorities*, p. 109. I have identified at least 140 corporations established between 1696 and 1833, but classification is not straightforward.

of the long eighteenth century, it is difficult to define the administrative structure of the 'typical' corporation. Broadly speaking, however, certain common features can be identified before turning to the analysis of their chronological development. Outdoor relief was rejected in favour of workhouses for 'maintaining and employing the poor'. Because workhouses were capital intensive, incorporating statutes often enabled several parishes to unite to form a 'body politick or corporate' with powers to buy and sell property and to borrow money secured against the poor rates. The local ratepayers elected guardians to run the corporations on their behalf. The guardians, who were drawn from among the Justices of the Peace and principal inhabitants, were invested with the authority to set the rates, hear and determine relief applications, and pass by-laws. In addition, the guardians were responsible for appointing executive officers, or directors, to whom the day-to-day running of the workhouse was delegated. While urban corporations were often established to share the cost of poor relief more equally across the incorporating parishes so that resources could be transferred from rich parishes to poor parishes, rural corporations were funded according to fixed parish quotas which were based upon the relative (or even absolute) cost of poor relief in the period immediately before incorporation.[17]

When and where were corporations established during the long eighteenth century? To answer this question it is necessary to isolate acts of incorporation from among the many thousands of statutes passed by parliament. Analysing the scope and content of poor relief legislation is hardly novel. Eighteenth-century writers including Richard Burn and Sir Frederick Eden digested those statutes that were regarded as particularly important.[18] The Webbs referred somewhat dismissively to the method of Sir George Nicholls in his *History of the English Poor Law* (1854) as 'describing one after another ... the fourscore or so general statutes, initiated, not by Ministers, but by private members, in addition to the hundred or more Local Acts'.[19] Subsequent historians have taken the

---

17   This discussion draws on J. Cary, *A proposal offered to the committee of the Honourable House of Commons, appointed to consider of ways for the better providing for the poor, and setting them on work* (London, n.d., ?1700) and Langford, *Public life*, p. 241.

18   R. Burn, *The history of the poor laws* (London, 1764); F. M. Eden, *The state of the poor, or, an history of the labouring classes in England, from the Conquest to the present period*, 3 vols (London, 1797).

19   S. Webb and B. Webb, *English local government: English poor law history: part I. The old poor law* (London, 1927), p. 149.

Webbs' rough estimate of the number of local acts for granted, even where they have stated the number of general acts with greater precision.[20] One purpose of this section, then, is to improve on the Webbs' estimates by quantifying the passage of both local and general poor relief legislation during the long eighteenth century.

Classifying legislation is a time-consuming task and this analysis builds on the path-finding work of Julian Hoppit and Joanna Innes.[21] Hoppit and Innes devised a comprehensive coding scheme based on 10 major categories, 31 subcategories and 177 particular descriptors.[22] The most relevant codes for present purposes begin '62' ('Poor law and poverty'). A preliminary analysis of all statutes passed between 1660 and 1832 returned 369 acts with this code. A further eleven acts had a secondary coding beginning '62'. To test the robustness of the coding scheme, I compiled an independent dataset based on statute titles. By using a variety of keyword searches (with variants of: 'poor', 'relief', 'employment', 'workhouse', 'settlement', 'bastardy', 'apprenticeship', 'vagrancy', 'rogues', 'idle', 'labourers', 'charity', 'labourers', 'wages', 'rates', etc.) a larger dataset was created of around 800 statutes, covering the period 1660–1841. This second dataset was then coded according to my own classification scheme. After excluding legislation relating to Scotland and Ireland, as well as charities, friendly societies and debtor legislation, a dataset comprising 141 general and 299 local statutes was created.[23]

If we compare these totals with the estimates provided by the Webbs, it is immediately apparent that they underestimated the volume of general and particular legislation by a considerable margin. Most strikingly,

20 S. King, *Poverty and welfare in England 1700–1850: a regional perspective* (Manchester, 2000), p. 18 notes that 'in total 264 general acts and more than 100 local acts impinged directly upon the poor and the administration of their communal relief between 1601 and 1850'.

21 I am grateful to Joanna Innes for supplying me with a machine-readable version of the dataset of failed bills underlying Hoppit (ed.), *Failed legislation* and a machine-readable dataset of public and private statutes, 1660–1832, classified according to the same coding scheme. I have constructed an independent dataset of the titles of all public and private statutes, 1660–1841, based on the Parliamentary Archives catalogue, *Portcullis*.

22 Hoppit (ed.), *Failed legislation*, pp. 30–2.

23 The exclusion of Scotland and Ireland is justified on the grounds that the Westminster parliament did not legislate for these kingdoms at the beginning of the period. The exclusion of charity and friendly society statutes is more arbitrary, but limitations of space prevent a full consideration of this material.

Table 7.1. Poor relief bills and acts, 1660–1841

	No. sessions	General poor relief legislation			Local poor relief legislation			All acts	All failed bills	% success
		Acts	Failed bills	% success	Acts	Failed bills	% success			
1660–79	19	3	20	13.0	1	11	8.3	531	1,301	29.0
1680/1–1698/9	15	3	12	20.0	9	6	60.0	725	1,058	40.7
1699/1700–1719/20	22	10	26	27.8	11	12	47.8	1,384	891	60.8
1720/1–1739/40	22	9	6	60.0	4	5	44.4	1,258	570	68.8
1740/1–1759/60	21	8	8	50.0	24	5	82.8	1,967	580	77.2
1760–1779/80	22	3	15	16.7	64	14	82.1	3,897	1,046	78.8
1780/1–1800	22	22	29	43.1	59	40	59.6	4,454	1,579	73.8
1660–1800	143	58	116	33.3	172	93	64.9	14,216	7,025	66.9
1800–20	22	39	-		75	-		7,556	-	
1821–41	22	44	-		52	-		5,942	-	
1800–41	44	83			127			13,498		
1660–1841	187	141			299			27,714		

Sources: Portcullis; J. Hoppit (ed.), *Failed legislation, 1660–1800: extracted from the Commons and Lords journals* (London, 1997).
Note: % success = 100 × (Acts / (Acts + Failed bills)).

there were nearly three times as many local acts passed during the period 1660–1841 than has generally been supposed. In addition, as Table 7.1 makes plain, the overwhelming majority of local poor relief acts (250/299, or 83 per cent) were passed after the accession of George III.

The pattern of legislative action reported here deserves further comment, not least because existing discussions have tended to focus on the pre-1712 local acts, largely to the exclusion of later developments. This is perhaps not surprising since these were the trailblazers and it is generally assumed that subsequent corporations were closely modelled on the Bristol template. Table 7.1, however, reveals a number of different trends. The period as a whole can be divided into four, albeit unequal, phases. During the late seventeenth and early eighteenth centuries (1680/1–1719/20) there was roughly one local poor relief bill for each parliamentary session (38 bills in 37 sessions). In the second phase, 1720/1–1739/40, the demand for local poor relief legislation decreased sharply: only nine bills were presented in 22 sessions. The inclusion of failed bills in Table 7.1 indicates that this was a 'real' decline rather than simply a function of a higher failure rate. The demand for local legislation roughly halved in this subperiod. Intriguingly, the 1720s and 1730s was the only time after 1688 when general poor relief statutes exceeded local ones. In addition, these two decades saw the highest success rate – 60 per cent – for relief legislation of a general nature.

The third phase, 1740/1–1779/80, witnessed a dramatic reversal. There was a sustained take-off in the demand for local poor relief legislation, especially after 1760 (29 bills in 21 sessions during the 1740s and 1750s; 78 bills in 22 sessions during the 1760s and 1770s). This subperiod also witnessed the highest success rates, with more than four-fifths of local poor relief bills reaching the statute book. At the same time, however, both the number and success rate of general statutes declined markedly. In the final phase, 1780/1–1841, there was a step change in the frequency of parliament's recourse to general legislation. Nearly three-quarters of all general poor relief statutes in the dataset were passed in the final third of the 181-year period. In addition, the relative balance between general and local acts began to shift away from local poor law measures such that by the 1820s and 1830s, 46 per cent of all poor relief legislation was of a general nature, compared with less than 5 per cent in the 1760s and 1770s. This change is perhaps symptomatic of the growing perception, at least among the governing classes, that the statutory relief of poverty demanded a one-size-fits-all approach.

Table 7.2. The formation, amendment and repeal of local poor relief authorities

	New local act	Amending act	Repeal	Total
1660–1679	1	1	0	2
1680/1–1698/9	8	1	0	9
1699/1700–1719/20	8	3	0	11
1720/1–1739/40	1	3	0	4
1740/1–1759/60	15	9	0	24
1760–1779/80	44	18	2	64
1780/1–1800	28	28	3	59
1800–20	28	44	3	75
1821–41	16	30	6	52
1660–1841	149	137	14	300

Source: As Table 7.1.
Note: The 1662 'Act for the better relief of the poor of this kingdom' (the 'Settlement Act') is treated as a local act for the purposes of this table because it contained provisions relating to the City of London Corporation of the Poor. In Table 7.1 it was included in the general column.

This preliminary analysis provokes several further questions. First, to what extent were late-eighteenth-century local acts simply amending existing corporations of the poor? There is clearly a significant discrepancy between the Webbs' estimate of 125 corporations and the nearly 300 local acts passed in this period. Secondly, what types of communities applied for local legislation? Were they distributed evenly across England and Wales, or confined to particular regions? Finally, to what extent was the demand for local legislation driven by demographic or economic change?

Table 7.2 indicates that over the period as a whole, there was an almost even split between local acts that granted new statutory powers (149) and acts that either amended or repealed such powers (151). Demand for new local acts peaked in the first two decades of George III's reign, when forty-four individual parishes or groups of parishes successfully secured parliamentary sanction for the better 'government and regulation', 'relief and employment', or 'maintaining' of the poor. Thereafter, the passage of Thomas Gilbert's Act for the Better Relief and Employment of the Poor in 1782 provided an alternative mechanism for either single parishes or

Table 7.3. The regional geography of local poor relief acts

County	No. statutory authorities	Total no. local acts
Middlesex (including Cities of London and Westminster)	44	112
Suffolk	12	28
Surrey	18	25
Norfolk	8	19
Gloucestershire	5	16
Kent	11	16
Devon	5	15
Worcestershire	3	7
Wiltshire	5	6
Yorkshire East Riding	2	6
Essex	3	5
Shropshire	4	5
Durham	2	4
Warwickshire	3	4
Hampshire	2	3
Lancashire	2	3
Shropshire, Montgomeryshire	1	3
Sussex	3	3
Cornwall	1	2
Herefordshire	1	2
Leicestershire	2	2
Lincolnshire	1	2
Oxfordshire	2	2
Somerset	1	2
Bedfordshire	1	1
Cheshire	1	1
Derbyshire, Leicestershire, Nottinghamshire	1	1
Dorset	1	1
Hertfordshire	1	1
Huntingdonshire	1	1
Shropshire, Denbighshire	1	1
Staffordshire	1	1
TOTAL	149	300

Source: As Table 7.1.
Note: No local acts were obtained by parishes in Berkshire, Buckinghamshire, Cambridgeshire, Cumberland, Monmouthshire, Northamptonshire, Rutland, Westmorland, Yorkshire North Riding or Yorkshire West Riding.

groups of parishes to fund workhouse construction.[24] Notwithstanding Gilbert's efforts, however, it is noteworthy that just under half of all *new* local acts were passed *after* Gilbert's Act.[25] This suggests, in other words, that Gilbert Unions and Local Corporations were being formed simultaneously in the closing decades of the old poor law: the former were manifestly not a substitute for the latter.[26] By the early nineteenth century, meanwhile, an increasing proportion of local acts were amending existing powers, rather than creating new ones. Overall, the data presented in Table 7.2 suggest that the Webbs' figure of 125 local corporations needs to be revised upwards to almost 150.

Geographically, local poor relief acts were not confined to a particular region, but nor were they found in all English counties (Table 7.3). One of the striking features of Table 7.3 is the large number of acts – over one third of the total – that regulated Middlesex parishes. If one also includes the Surrey legislation, which governed parishes no further south than Croydon, then nearly half (46 per cent) of all local poor relief acts related to London and its immediate hinterlands. Although a recent historian of London poor relief has noted the existence of 'a bewildering array' of local acts in the capital, sustained discussion of their chronological development, scope or coverage is conspicuously thin.[27]

24   22 Geo. III, c. 83. The act is reprinted in Eden, *State of the poor*, vol. 3, pp. clcccii–ccix.
25   Eden, *State of the poor*, vol. 1, p. 366 noted that 'few incorporations of parishes have taken place under this Act'. The Webbs suggested that as many as 924 parishes united into sixty-seven unions as a result of this legislation: Webb and Webb, *The old poor law*, p. 171. This is repeated in J. R. Poynter, *Society and pauperism: English ideas on poor relief, 1795–1834* (London, 1969), p. 12, and King, *Poverty and welfare*, p. 25. The Webbs derived their estimate from Appendix A, No. 2, *Ninth Annual Report of the Poor Law Commissioners* (PP, 1843, XXI).
26   A. Digby, *Pauper palaces* (London, 1978), p. 46 notes that 'Gilbert's Act slowed the incorporating movement in Norfolk' because 'it was very much cheaper to set up a Gilbert Union of parishes than to seek incorporation under an expensive local act of Parliament'. A decade earlier, Poynter (*Society and pauperism*, p. 12) observed that Gilbert Unions 'were hardly more successful in the long run than earlier ventures, and did not even supersede the old practice of seeking reform by local act'. Further research is needed to establish how far post-1782 corporations departed from the provisions of Gilbert's Act.
27   D. R. Green, *Pauper capital: London and the poor law, 1790–1870* (Farnham, 2010), p. 82. Elsewhere, Green comments that the powers of parochial vestries 'had multiplied and grown in complexity from the mid-eighteenth century as a result of innumerable local acts' (p. 87).

Local corporations of the poor, urban growth and demographic change

For present purposes, it is only possible to offer a brief sketch of the legislative patterns found in the capital. Although the hundred or so parishes of the City of London had been incorporated as early as 1647, by an 'Ordinance for the relief and employment of the poor, and the punishment of vagrants and other disorderly persons', subsequent eighteenth- and early-nineteenth-century legislation dealt almost exclusively with single parishes, or parts of parishes, lying outside the City.[28] This is quite unlike the pattern found in most of the pre-1712 urban corporations, where several contiguous parishes typically united.

In terms of the micro-geography of metropolitan relief acts, Figure 7.1 presents clear evidence of what might be described as 'domino effects'. That is to say, when one parish obtained a local act, those immediately surrounding it soon followed suit. In the West End, for example, St Martin-in-the-Fields obtained a poor relief, street cleansing and watch act in 1749.[29] Two years later, the neighbouring parish to the south of St Martin's, Westminster St Margaret's, united with its own southerly neighbour, Westminster St John the Evangelist for the purpose of the 'better relief and employment of the poor ... and for cleansing the streets, and repairing the highways'.[30] This was followed by the parish sandwiched between the two detached parts of St Margaret's, St George Hanover Square, in 1753.[31] Then, in 1756, the parishes lying immediately to the west, Kensington, and to the north, Marylebone, also obtained local acts.[32] Similar waves of statute-making occurred in George III's reign so that by 1800 virtually all of the parishes bordering the City, not to mention outlying districts, including St John Hampstead to the west and

---

28   The only parishes to be united for poor relief purposes were Westminster St Margaret and St John the Evangelist (1751, to which St James Piccadilly, the Liberties of Saffron Hill, Hatton Garden, Ely Rents and the Precinct of the Savoy were added in 1835); St Andrew Holborn (above the Bars) and St George the Martyr (1766); and St Giles in the Fields and St George Bloomsbury (1774). See 25 Geo. II, c. 23; 6 Geo. III, c. 100; 14 Geo. III, c. 62.

29   23 Geo. II, c. 35. St Martin-in-the-Fields had previously obtained an act 'for the better improving a certain Piece of Ground ... for the Use of the Poor, and for other purposes' in 1702 (1 Anne Stat. 2, c. 21), hence it is shaded in black in Figure 7.1.

30   25 Geo. II, c. 23.

31   26 Geo. II, c. 97. The title of this act was virtually identical to that uniting St Margaret's and St John the Evangelist.

32   29 Geo. II, c. 53 and c. 63.

Figure 7.1. Metropolitan parishes with local acts

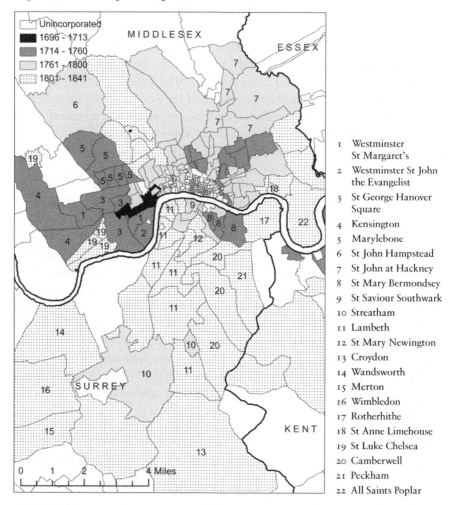

1   Westminster
    St Margaret's
2   Westminster St John
    the Evangelist
3   St George Hanover
    Square
4   Kensington
5   Marylebone
6   St John Hampstead
7   St John at Hackney
8   St Mary Bermondsey
9   St Saviour Southwark
10 Streatham
11 Lambeth
12 St Mary Newington
13 Croydon
14 Wandsworth
15 Merton
16 Wimbledon
17 Rotherhithe
18 St Anne Limehouse
19 St Luke Chelsea
20 Camberwell
21 Peckham
22 All Saints Poplar

Source: As Table 7.1. I am grateful to Max Satchell for supplying me with electronic boundary data.
Note: The boundary data are based upon 1851 census units rather than ancient parishes; each number represents one parish. Only parishes referred to in the main text are numbered, with the exception of St Martin-in-the-Fields, which is shaded in black (see n. 29).

St John at Hackney to the east, had acquired local acts.[33] Altogether there were over thirty statutory poor law authorities operating in Middlesex at the beginning of the nineteenth century.

South of the Thames, meanwhile, fewer parishes petitioned for local legislation before 1800. Parishes within the Bills of Mortality like St Mary Bermondsey and St Saviour Southwark, as well as outlying parishes like Richmond (not shown on Figure 7.1) and Streatham successfully obtained acts, but bills promoted by the inhabitants of Lambeth failed in 1783 and 1792.[34] Between 1808 and 1816, a swathe of half a dozen urban or urbanizing Surrey parishes, beginning with St Mary Newington, sought acts 'for better assessing and collecting the Poor and other Rates ... and for regulating the Poor thereof'.[35] Following a brief hiatus, a further five Surrey parishes – Croydon, Wandsworth, Merton, Wimbledon and Rotherhithe – secured similarly titled local acts between 1825 and 1829.[36]

Explaining these legislative patterns is less straightforward than describing them. However, it is plausible to suppose that the demand for local legislation may be taken as a proxy for London's suburban expansion in the century after 1750. Local relief acts, I would suggest, were a response to the stresses and strains of population growth. The face-to-face administrative structures and rural assumptions of the old poor law were ill-equipped to deal with sprawling urban centres, where labour markets operated according to different rules and rhythms. The workhouse represented, in material form, the ambition of the principal inhabitants and ratepayers to acquire new legal powers to regulate the lives of not dozens, but hundreds, or even thousands, of their poorer neighbours.[37]

33   39 & 40 Geo. III, c. xxxv; 4 Geo. III, c. 43.

34   31 Geo. II, c. 45; 31 Geo. III, c. 19 (St Mary Bermondsey); 14 Geo. III, c. 75 (St Saviour Southwark); 6 Geo. III, c. 72; 25 Geo. III, c. 41 (Richmond); 30 Geo. III, c. 80 (Streatham). St George Southwark and St John Southwark also obtained local acts (23 Geo. III, c. 23; 26 Geo. III, c. 114).

35   St Mary Newington (48 Geo. III, c. xxi), Lambeth (50 Geo. III, c. xix) and Southwark Christ Church (51 Geo. III, c. xxxii) were all within the Bills of Mortality; Clapham (51 Geo. III, c. cvii) and Camberwell (53 Geo. III, c. clxii) were not, but bordered Lambeth to the west and east respectively. Mitcham (56 George III, c. v) lay to the south of Streatham.

36   6 Geo. IV, c. lxxvi; 7 Geo. IV, c. lxiii; 9 Geo. IV, c. i; 9 Geo. IV, c. ii; 10 Geo. IV, c. cxxxi. While Croydon (1821 pop. 7,801), Rotherhithe (1821 pop. 12,114) and Wandsworth (1821 pop. 5,644) were clearly urbanised by the mid-1820s, Merton (1821 pop. 905) and Wimbledon (1821 pop. 1,914) were little more than large villages.

37   It is important to emphasise the legal dimension since many metropolitan parishes had already built workhouses before petitioning parliament for additional statutory powers. See

Trends in local relief legislation correspond reasonably well with what is already known about the metropolis's demographic and physical growth. The initial incorporation of the City's parishes in the mid seventeenth century coincided with the tail end of London's 'first heroic age' of explosive demographic growth, 1500–1650.[38] From around 1660 – when the Corporation went into temporary abeyance due to the confiscation of its property by Charles II – the growth of London was slowing down and this trend continued during the early eighteenth century.[39] Schwarz has even suggested that London's population may have declined in the second quarter of the century.[40] For Landers, meanwhile, 'it is overwhelmingly likely that demographic expansion virtually ceased in the 1730s and 1740s, and the population of 1750 probably exceeded that of 1730 by less than 3 per cent'.[41] During this period of relative demographic stagnation there was a corresponding dearth of local statutes in Middlesex. Only a handful of acts were obtained, two for St Martin-in-the-Fields (1702; 1749), another for St Botolph without Aldgate in 1741 and one for Bethnal Green in 1745.

After 1750, however, evidence from foreign trade, coal imports and building activity points to a sustained physical and demographic expansion of the metropolis. Schwarz estimates that London's population grew by as much as 50 per cent at the end of the eighteenth century.[42] By the end of the period covered by this chapter, in the 1830s, the process of suburban growth had resulted in 'a contiguous mass of housing from Limehouse to Chelsea, on the northern side of the Thames, linked by half a dozen bridges to a matching southern expanse stretching from Camberwell to Peckham'.[43] This cumulative thickening of the built environment is clearly discernible in Figure 7.1, although arguably stretched even further west

T. V. Hitchcock, 'The English workhouse: a study in institutional poor relief in selected counties, 1696–1750' (unpublished D.Phil. dissertation, University of Oxford, 1985), Appendix, pp. 258–83 for a detailed chronology of workhouse foundations by county.

38   L. D. Schwarz, *London in the age of industrialisation: entrepreneurs, labour force and living conditions, 1700–1850* (Cambridge, 1992), p. 2.

39   The Interregnum Corporation was revived without new statutory backing in 1698 at the suggestion of the Lord Mayor, Sir Humphrey Edwin. See S. M. MacFarlane, 'Social policy and the poor in the later seventeenth century', in *London 1500–1700: the making of the metropolis*, ed. A. L. Beier and R. A. P. Finlay (London, 1986), pp. 252–77 (p. 262).

40   Schwarz, *London in the age of industrialisation*, p. 128.

41   J. Landers, *Death and the metropolis: studies in the demographic history of London, 1670–1830* (Cambridge, 1993), p. 84.

42   Schwarz, *London in the age of industrialisation*, p. 128.

43   Landers, *Death and the metropolis*, p. 51.

and south than Landers' comments might suggest. For example, although St Anne Limehouse obtained a local relief act in 1809, the district immediately to the east, the 'Hamlet' of Poplar and Blackwall, followed suit in 1813. In 1811, this so-called hamlet was home to 7,708 inhabitants; ten years later this figure had risen to 12,208.[44] What I am arguing, in other words, is that in London at least, the accumulation of local relief acts tends to confirm the pattern of urban growth that previous historians have identified using wholly independent proxies. A trickle of Middlesex statutes in the first half of the eighteenth century was followed by a steady stream from 1750. On average, just over one Middlesex statute was passed each year between 1750 and 1841.[45]

If we now consider the legislative trends beyond Middlesex and Surrey, the first half of the eighteenth century saw considerable activity in regions that were experiencing more rapid population growth than the metropolitan core. Wrigley has estimated that twenty counties experienced faster population growth rates than Middlesex during the first half of the eighteenth century. This was in complete contrast to the seventeenth century, when Middlesex's population grew by 84.4 per cent, compared with only a 55.6 per cent increase in the second fastest-growing county, Northumberland.[46] Although places that obtained local poor relief acts before 1750 were located in counties growing both slower and faster than Middlesex, it is noteworthy that the county with the highest frequency of statute-making in this period – Gloucestershire – was the second fastest-growing county in England at this time.[47] Much of this growth must have been driven by the expansion of Bristol, which probably more than doubled in size between 1700 and 1750, overtaking Norwich to become the country's second city. Although pre-census estimates are necessarily approximate, it is possible that Bristol increased its share of the Gloucestershire population from around 15 per cent in 1700 to 24 per cent in 1750.[48]

44   *1811 Census*, Enumeration abstract (*PP*, 1812, XI), p. 194; *1821 Census*, Enumeration abstract (*PP*, 1822, XV), p. 192.
45   1750–1800: 56 statutes; 1800–41: 48 statutes.
46   See tab. 4, in E. A. Wrigley, 'Rickman revisited: the population growth rates of English counties in the early modern period', *Economic History Review* 62 (2009), 711–35 (p. 723).
47   Bristol obtained four local acts (1696, 1713, 1717 and 1743) to Gloucester's two (1702 and 1726).
48   See tab. 1 in E. A. Wrigley, 'Urban growth and agricultural change: England and the Continent in the early modern period', *Journal of Interdisciplinary History* 15 (1985), 683–728 (p. 686) and tab. 3 in Wrigley, 'Rickman revisited', p. 721. Bristol grew from 21,000 to 50,000, while Gloucestershire grew from 139,448 to 206,599.

Table 7.4. The changing English urban hierarchy and the number of local acts, 1662–1841

	Population (c.1662)[1]	Year of first local act [or failed bill]	No. local acts		Population (1841)[2]	Year of first local act [or failed bill]	No. local acts
London[3]	310,941	1662	45	London[4]	1,948,417	1662	133
Norwich	14,216	1711	4	Manchester*	311,269	1790	1
York	14,201	[1730]		Liverpool	286,487	1831	2
Bristol	13,482	1696	8	Birmingham*	182,922	1783	2
Newcastle	11,617			Leeds*	152,074		
Oxford	11,065	1771	1	Bristol	125,146	1696	8
Cambridge	10,574	1697		Sheffield*	111,091	[1791]	
Exeter	10,307	1697	5	Wolverhampton*	93,245		
Ipswich	9,774			Newcastle	70,337		
Great Yarmouth	9,248			Hull	67,308	1697	5
Canterbury	7,671	1727	3	Bradford*	66,715		
Worcester	7,046	1703	5	Norwich	61,846	1711	4
Deptford*	6,919	1754	1	Newington[5]*	54,606	1808	2
Shrewsbury	6,867	1784	2	Sunderland*	53,335	1791	2
Salisbury	6,811	1770	2	Bath	53,196	1815	2
Colchester	6,647	1697	2	Portsmouth	53,032	[1674]	2
Hull	6,600	1697	5	Nottingham	52,360	[1701]	5
TOTAL			83				161

Sources: Table 14.4 in J. Langton, 'Urban growth and economic change: from the late seventeenth century to 1841', in *The Cambridge urban history of Britain, 2: 1540–1840*, ed. P. Clark (Cambridge, 2000), pp. 453–90 (pp. 473–4); *Portcullis*; Hoppit (ed.), *Failed legislation*.

Notes:

¹ Based on the Hearth Tax returns.

² Based on size, density and nucleation criteria defined by C. M. Law, 'The growth of urban population in England and Wales, 1801–1911', *Transactions of the Institute of British Geographers* 41 (1967), 125–43. As a result, figures differ from those reported in the 1841 census.

³ Cities of London and Westminster, their Liberties and the Borough of Southwark.

⁴ London Division, *1851 Census*, Enumeration abstract (*PP*, 1852–53, LXXXV).

⁵ Although (St Mary) Newington was part of the 1851 Census London Division (and its population is included in the 1841 London total), Langton enumerated it separately in his 1841 hierarchy. I have adjusted the number of local acts so that the two Newington statutes were not double counted.

* Enfranchised by the Great Reform Act in 1832. All other towns listed were parliamentary boroughs before 1832.

Another way of trying to determine whether local acts were a response to urbanisation is by considering the English urban hierarchy. Table 7.4 reports the size and rank order of the largest English towns at the beginning and end of the period. This table implies that any relationship between settlement size and the establishment of statutory poor law authorities is far from straightforward. Demography alone cannot account for different administrative and institutional configurations, nor would anyone familiar with the capricious nature of eighteenth-century parliaments expect it to. Nonetheless, it is striking that in both urban hierarchies, a clear majority of England's largest towns and cities were successful in securing peculiar local powers at some point during the long eighteenth century. Three-fifths of all local poor law acts passed during this period regulated the towns and cities listed in Table 7.4.[49]

Moreover, it would appear that places that were not represented in parliament were not unduly disadvantaged when it came to establishing statutory authorities. Had the unreformed parliament been entirely indifferent to the claims of rapidly urbanizing – and unrepresented – communities, we would expect to find a quite different pattern in Table 7.4. Over half the towns listed in the 1841 hierarchy were not parlia-mentary boroughs before 1832, yet this did not prevent the inhabitants of Manchester, Birmingham, (St Mary) Newington and Sunderland from acquiring statutory powers for the relief of the poor between 1783 and 1808. Meanwhile, the failure of Sheffield's inhabitants to obtain 'a Bill for taking down … the present Workhouse for the said Township, and erecting a new one instead thereof, sufficiently large and commodious for the Reception and Employment of the Poor' in February 1791 cannot be attributed to the absence of parliamentary representation. Like Deptford, Birmingham and Manchester before, and Sunderland and Newington after, Sheffield's petition was referred to a committee on which at least one of the relevant county MPs sat.[50] Given that long-standing boroughs

---

49   This is based on adding the total number of acts in the 1841 panel (161) to the acts for Oxford, Exeter, Canterbury, Worcester, Shrewsbury, Salisbury and Colchester, all of which had dropped out of the hierarchy by 1841. Deptford's act is included in the 1841 London total.

50   CJ, xlvi, 18 Feb. 1791, p. 191. Sheffield's petition was referred to a committee which included William Wilberforce and Henry Duncombe, both of whom sat for Yorkshire. The petitions from Sunderland (received three days after Sheffield's on 23 Feb. 1791) and St Mary Newington (CJ, lxiii, 25 Feb. 1808, pp. 109–10) were treated in exactly the same way, whereas those from Birmingham (CJ, xxxix, 27 Jan. 1783, p. 111) and Manchester

such as York, Portsmouth and Nottingham all failed to obtain local legislation earlier in the period, it would appear that borough representation was neither a necessary, nor sufficient, condition of legislative success.

So far the analysis has been concerned with identifying an association between urban growth and the establishment of local poor law corporations at a relatively superficial level. The remainder of this section considers in what sense, if any, Malthus's views about the demographic impact of welfare transfer payments were shared by the principal inhabitants who petitioned parliament for statutes of incorporation. To what extent did the communities that were early adopters of the workhouse and guardians of the poor blame indiscriminate outdoor relief policies for generating unsustainable population growth? One way of answering this question is to examine the expressly declared purpose of local poor relief statutes as recorded in the petitions that preceded legislative action. The following discussion is based upon a 10 per cent random sample of the 149 local corporations established during the long eighteenth century.

Table 7.5 provides an abstract of fifteen local petitions presented to the House of Commons with a view to obtaining a local poor relief statute. It would clearly be unwise to place too much interpretative weight on the arguments articulated in what were, after all, highly formal documents drawn up to satisfy proper parliamentary procedure.[51] Petitions were recorded in the *Journal of the House of Commons* according to the clerks' stylistic conventions with the result that we have only a partial insight into the objectives of the petitioners. Nonetheless, it is possible to detect shifting attitudes and priorities. Although the workhouse was a persistent feature of petitioners' demands throughout the period, its functions became increasingly inclusive. Whereas the earliest workhouses were intended as 'schools of industry', those of the late eighteenth century were promoted for the 'general reception' of the poor.

For two places in the sample – King's Lynn and Gloucester – no petition was printed in the *Commons Journal*. It is possible to reconstruct the aims of these statutes from other evidence, including the statutes that

(*CJ*, xlv, 1 Mar. 1790, p. 194) were referred to committees that contained only one of the relevant county's MPs.
51   Lambert, *Bills and acts*, p. 153 notes that for local bills, 'the petition … was always considered by a committee before leave to introduce a bill was given'. See also J. G. Hanley, 'The public's reaction to public health: petitions submitted to parliament, 1847–1848', *Social History of Medicine* 15 (2002), 393–411 for a helpful survey of parliamentary petitioning more generally during this period.

Table 7.5. Declared purpose and scope of fifteen randomly selected poor law incorporation statutes

Place	No. parishes	Principal category of pauper to be relieved	Powers sought	Date of petition
King's Lynn (12 & 13 Will. III, c. 6)	2	Poor children	Workhouse; assistants; street lighting	No petition printed in *CJ*[1]
Gloucester (1 Anne Stat. 2, c. 11)	10	Poor children	Workhouse	No petition printed in *CJ*[2]
St Paul Shadwell (10 Geo. III, c. 56)	1	Manufacturers and labouring persons	New workhouse; power to rate owners of subdivided houses	24/01/1770 (*CJ*, xxxii, p. 617)
New Sarum (10 Geo. III, c. 81)	3	General poor	Consolidation of rates	09/02/1770 (*CJ*, xxxii, p. 677)
Southampton (13 Geo. III, c. 50)	6	Children; general poor	Consolidation of rates; workhouse for whole town; sharing cost of maintaining roads	29/01/1773 (*CJ*, xxxiv, p. 82)
Hartismere, Hoxne and Thredling Hundreds (19 Geo. III, c. 13)	63	Aged, infirm and diseased; able and industrious; profligate and idle; children	Workhouse for general reception of poor	03/12/1778 (*CJ*, xxxvii, p. 12)
Westbury (26 Geo. III, c. 23)	1	General poor	Additional overseer	06/03/1786 (*CJ*, xli, p. 297)
London Saint Bride Fleet Street (32 Geo. III, c. 64)	1	Aged, infirm and diseased; industrious; idle and refractory; infant poor	Workhouse for general reception of poor; repair of church	24/02/1792 (*CJ*, xlvii, p. 425)
Tewkesbury (32 Geo. III, c. 70)	1	Exceedingly numerous poor	Workhouse for general reception	17/02/1792 (*CJ*, xlvii, p. 396)
Montgomery and Pool (32 Geo. III, c. 96)	15	Very numerous poor	United district with workhouse for general reception	05/03/1792 (*CJ*, xlvii, p. 495)

Place	No. parishes	Principal category of pauper to be relieved	Powers sought	Date of petition
Bedford (34 Geo. III, c. 98)	5	All the poor	Workhouse for general reception	21/02/1794 (CJ, xlix, p. 210)
Aldbourne (39 & 40 Geo. III, c. xlviii)	1	Exceedingly numerous poor	Additional overseer; workhouse to compel poor to work	06/03/1800 (CJ, lv, p. 270)
Chatham St Mary (42 Geo. III, c. lvi)	1	Very numerous poor	Enlarge existing workhouse	26/02/1802 (CJ, lvii, p. 178)
Saint Pancras (44 Geo. III, c. xlvii)	1	Very numerous poor	Directors of Poor; new workhouse; paid collectors of rates	03/12/1803 (CJ, lix, p. 27)
Bromley St Leonard (51 Geo. III, c. cxxv)	1	General poor	Workhouse; removal of coal dust	31/01/1811 (CJ, lxvi, p. 60)

Sources: Table 7.2., column 2 (New local acts)

Notes:

[1] *Reasons for passing the bill for better employing the poor of Lynn; in answer to some pretended reasons lately publish'd against it* (London, 1701).

[2] 1 Anne Statute 2, c. 11.

followed, as well as broadsides published for and against the proposals.[52] In both King's Lynn and Gloucester, the promoters placed particular emphasis on making provision for poor children (who, along with the elderly, were *the* classic victims of 'nuclear hardship').[53] The King's Lynn workhouse was spacious enough to accommodate 'more than 100 Poor Children of both Sexes', who 'before were Naked, Surfeited, and almost perished with Diseases'. In Gloucester, meanwhile, 'a considerable number of Poor Children … have been lately and now are exercised in Readeing, Writing, and Working'.[54] Petitioners after 1750, by contrast, tended to be far less precise when referring to the poor persons most likely to benefit from local incorporation. Children were only explicitly mentioned in the petitions from the inhabitants of Southampton and the Suffolk Hundreds of Hartismere, Hoxne and Thredling. Far more common in the late eighteenth century were references to 'the general poor', or simply 'the poor'. The most common adjective used to describe the poor was 'numerous'. In only two cases – St Bride's and Hartismere, Hoxne and Thredling – do we find petitioners drawing a distinction between 'deserving' (aged, infirm and diseased) and 'undeserving' (idle and refractory) poverty.

In terms of specifying a link between population growth and poor relief, the petitioners remained largely silent. Marriage and family size are *never* mentioned, either positively or negatively. Indeed, poverty is largely taken for granted; it is not principally viewed as the outcome of individual or familial imprudence. Five of the petitions (St Paul Shadwell, Westbury, Tewkesbury, Aldbourne, and St Pancras) note how 'populous' the parish in question is but this is not attributed to defects of the existing poor law administration. There is, in other words, no evidence in the petitions of a Malthusian or proto-Malthusian model of hardship in which the institutional flaws of the poor laws are presented as the root cause of poverty.

Indeed, it could be argued that the outstanding characteristic of these

---

52 See Slack, *Reformation*, pp. 103–6 for a discussion of the political background to the King's Lynn and Gloucester corporations.

53 R. M. Smith, 'Charity, self-interest and welfare: reflections from demographic and family history', in *Charity, self-interest and welfare*, ed. Daunton, pp. 23–49 (p. 27); cf. P. Laslett, 'Family, kinship and collectivity as systems of support in pre-industrial Europe: a consideration of the "nuclear-hardship" hypothesis', *Continuity and Change* 3 (1988), 153–75 (p. 154).

54 *Reasons for passing the bill for better employing the poor of Lynn; in answer to some pretended reasons lately publish'd against it* (London, 1701); Preamble, 1 Anne Stat. 2, c. 11.

petitions is their clear recognition of the collectivity's welfare obligations. If anything, it would seem that the petitioners – usually comprising the clergy, churchwardens, overseers and principal inhabitants – were seeking a more formal specification of the community's duties *vis-à-vis* the poor. For example, the inhabitants of St Paul Shadwell applied for the power to rate the landlords and leaseholders of subdivided dwellings because they believed these individuals were evading their parochial responsibilities. Elsewhere, in Southampton and Salisbury (New Sarum), we find evidence of a supra-parochial commitment to sharing the costs of poor relief according to the relative wealth of individual parishes. Moreover, it would appear that these two incorporation proposals were not driven by a desire to reduce aggregate relief expenditure. It is only from the late 1770s that comparative statements concerning the increasing cost of poor relief find their way into the petitions sampled here.[55] Crucially, however, the principle of rate-based welfare provision was not challenged, either before or after the publication of Malthus's first *Essay* in 1798.

This does not, of course, preclude the possibility that petitioners misunderstood the dynamics of welfare policy, poverty and population growth in their own communities. But the absence of a Malthusian analysis, especially in the early-nineteenth-century petitions, suggests that in some of the country's most populous parishes it was the sheer demand for relief from across a very wide spectrum of age groups, rather than the poor laws' alleged encouragement to early marriage, which threatened to overwhelm the poor law authorities. Faced with unprecedented economic and demographic change, which was transforming the English urban hierarchy, local elites took advantage of eighteenth-century parliaments' permissive disposition to experiment with new models of administration and new modes of relief. Sometimes the corporations proved to be short-lived, while others survived the legislative upheavals of 1834.[56] Although there was considerable diversity of experience – which must

55 Eight petitions (Hartismere, Hoxne and Thredling, Westbury, St Bride's, Tewkesbury, Montgomery and Pool, Bedford, Aldbourne, and Chatham) refer either to the 'great' and 'burthensome' expense, or the 'annual' increase of the poor rates.
56 Of the fourteen original corporations established between 1696 and 1712, only those in Bristol, Norwich, Hull, Exeter and Plymouth were still active in the mid nineteenth century. In addition to these five, a further eighteen incorporated unions and fourteen single parish corporations that were established after 1712 were operating in 1852. Nearly one in eight people (11.6 per cent) in England and Wales lived under the jurisdiction of poor law corporations at the time of the 1851 census. By comparison, only 1.1 per cent of the population lived in Gilbert Unions at the same date: see *Return of each Parish and*

necessarily undermine any attempt to specify a simple causal relationship between transfer payments and population growth – this discussion has drawn attention to patterns of institutional development in London and elsewhere that lend tentative support to the view that the eighteenth-century welfare regime was downstream of urban growth. It was not the poor law which caused population growth in towns but growth did prompt new approaches to poor relief. In the final section of the chapter the analysis shifts to rural corporations to assess whether incorporated parishes experienced distinctive demographic regimes compared with their unincorporated neighbours.

Population and poor relief in rural Suffolk

It should be noted that Malthus himself never endorsed local corporations as an alternative to the parochial system established in 1601. Malthus referred to workhouses only a handful of times in the second *Essay*. When he did so, he revealed himself to be sceptical of their benefits, observing that

> the quantity of provisions consumed in workhouses, upon a part of the society, that cannot in general be considered the most valuable part, diminishes the shares that would otherwise belong to more industrious and more worthy members, and thus, in the same manner, forces more to become dependent.[57]

Later in the same chapter, Malthus struck a somewhat paradoxical note while reflecting upon the demographic implications of outdoor and indoor relief. 'Those who are not deterred for a time from marriage', Malthus wrote,

> are either relieved very scantily at their own homes, where they suffer all the consequences arising from squalid poverty; or they are crowded together in close and unwholesome workhouses, where a great mortality almost universally takes place, particularly among young children ... A very great part of the redundant population occasioned by the poor

---

Township in England and Wales in which Poor are managed under Gilbert's Act or Local Act (PP, 1852, XLV); *1851 Census*, Enumeration abstract (PP, 1852–53, LXXXV).
57   T. R. Malthus, *An essay on the principle of population* (London, 1803), p. 410.

laws, is thus taken off by the operation of the laws themselves, or at least by their ill execution.[58]

In this passage at least, Malthus retreated from the first *Essay*'s emphatic insistence that the poor laws encouraged population growth. He implied that the net effect of the poor laws could have been to increase the relative pressure within the demographic system – higher fertility counteracted by higher mortality – without increasing the absolute number of people. Towards the end of the second *Essay*, Malthus argued that the 'terrific forms of workhouses and parish officers' might explain why the poor laws 'do not encourage marriage so much as might be expected from theory'.[59]

Malthus's theorising on the demographic repercussions of workhouses provides an appropriate starting point for a preliminary analysis of the relationship between population change and poor relief in the county most affected by the late-eighteenth-century incorporation movement, namely, Suffolk. *Ceteris paribus*, a Malthusian would expect to find higher marriage ages and thus slower population growth rates in areas where poor relief was conditional upon entry into the workhouse since couples could have no rational expectation of future child allowances. Suffolk provides an ideal testing ground for Malthusian reasoning since the county was relatively homogenous in economic terms, being dominated by agriculture, but divided into roughly equal halves in poor relief terms.

Beginning with the hundreds of Colneis and Carlford in 1756, much of eastern Suffolk had been incorporated by 1780.[60] The ten corporations established by this date were all modelled, to a greater or lesser extent, on the example of Colneis and Carlford. In place of the parochial system of management by overseers, up to twenty-four Directors of the Poor and up to thirty-six Acting Guardians of the Poor were elected from among the local clergy, landowners and substantial occupiers to administer poor relief in

---

58   Ibid., p. 416.

59   Malthus, *Essay* (1803), p. 575. See also the discussions of this passage in R. M. Smith, 'The social policy: Malthus, welfare and poverty', in *Visiting Malthus: the man, his times, the issues*, ed. A.-M. Jensen, T. L. Knutsen and A. Skonhoft (Oslo, 2003), pp. 80–99 (p. 94) and Poynter, *Society and pauperism*, p. 155.

60   Colneis and Carlford hundreds (29 Geo. II, c. 79); Blything Hundred (4 Geo. III, c. 56); Bosmere and Claydon Hundred (4 Geo. III, c. 57); Samford Hundred (4 Geo. III, c. 59); Mutford and Lothingland Hundred (4 Geo. III., c. 89); Wangford Hundred (4 Geo. III, c. 91); Loes and Wilford hundreds (5 Geo. III, c. 97); Stow Hundred (18 Geo. III, c. 35); Hartismere, Hoxne and Thredling hundreds (19 Geo. III, c. 13); Cosford Hundred (19 Geo. III, c. 30).

the incorporated hundreds. Directors generally held office for life and were required to own land within the hundred. Acting Guardians, by contrast, served for up to three years at a time and could be owners or occupiers.[61] Controlling relief costs was a central priority for the incorporated hundreds in Suffolk. To achieve this, the local acts typically contained a clause stating that the assessments of individual parishes should not exceed 'the Sum which shall have been expended for the Relief and Support of the Poor ... upon an Average of Seven Years' prior to the passage of the act.[62]

Individual- or household-level analysis of the relationship between Suffolk poor relief policies and demographic behaviour is beyond the scope of this chapter. The age, marital status and family circumstances of poor law pensioners can only be reliably established using family reconstitution techniques.[63] What is attempted here is more modest. Parliament's insatiable appetite for parish-level data on population and poor rate expenditure in the early nineteenth century provides us with a rich, albeit neglected, data source for examining aspects of the relationship between population and welfare at various scales of analysis.[64]

Table 7.6 compares population growth rates, crude marriage rates, age structure and levels of poor relief expenditure across Suffolk. Uniquely among the early-nineteenth-century censuses, the 1821 census reports age structure at hundredal level. It is around 97.1 per cent complete for Suffolk.[65] For the sake of clarity, Table 7.6 only gives the percentage of the population aged under fifteen since this is a proxy for the proportion of dependent children within the population. The data presented here allow us to investigate Malthus's hypothesis that the 'terrific' form of the workhouse acted as a restraint on population growth in Suffolk's incorporated hundreds due to the 'great mortality ... particularly among young children' that he believed was a consequence of indoor relief.

---

61   19 Geo. III, c. 30. See also Webb and Webb, *Statutory authorities*, pp. 126–35 for a fuller discussion of the constitutional structure of the Suffolk and Norfolk incorporations.
62   See, for example, 18 Geo. III, c. 35.
63   R. M. Smith, 'Ageing and well-being in early modern England: pension trends and gender preferences under the English old poor law c.1650–1800', in *Old age from antiquity to post-modernity*, ed. P. Johnson and P. Thane (London, 1998), pp. 64–95 (p. 74); Williams, 'Malthus', p. 61.
64   See S. J. Thompson, 'Census-taking, political economy and state formation in Britain, c.1790–1840 (unpublished Ph.D. thesis, University of Cambridge, 2010), pp. 134–58 for a discussion of John Rickman's role as both producer and interpreter of census and poor law data.
65   *1821 Census*, Enumeration abstract, p. 324.

At first glance, it seems doubtful that Suffolk's Hundred Houses did much to reduce population growth rates in the incorporated half of the county between 1781 and 1821. Indeed, what is particularly striking about the population growth figures is that incorporated hundreds were growing faster, on average, than their unincorporated neighbours. Seven of the top ten fastest growing Suffolk hundreds were incorporated under local acts. The slowest growing hundreds, by contrast, tended to be unincorporated. This finding runs directly counter to Malthus's hypothesis about the effect of workhouses on population growth.

Further doubt is cast upon Malthus's argument by the data on age structure and crude marriage rates. It will be recalled that Malthus's principal objection to the poor law was based upon his conviction that rural overseers' adoption of allowance scales after 1795 tended to lower marriage ages and encourage larger family sizes. While Table 7.6 provides no direct evidence on marriage age or family size, it does suggest that there were no systematic differences in the proportions of dependent children among the populations of the different Suffolk poor relief regimes. Indeed, the share of the population under fifteen looks remarkably invariant across the county as whole, at around 40 per cent. Meanwhile, the crude marriage rate also appears to have been relatively stable in incorporated and unincorporated hundreds alike, hovering around 7–8 per thousand.

By contrast, Table 7.6 suggests that there was far less uniformity in poor rate expenditure per capita across the county's hundreds.[66] At the extremes, the hundred of Babergh were spending nearly eight times the sum being spent in Mutford and Lothingland. Demographically, there is little to distinguish between them if one compares the proportions of the population under fifteen or the crude marriage rates. What does distinguish them, however, are their historic rates of growth. Mutford and Lothingland was the fastest growing hundred in the county between 1781 and 1821 whereas Babergh was the slowest. More generally, Table 7.6 implies that there may have been a negative correlation between population growth rates and poor relief expenditure per capita in 1821.[67] To a Malthusian this is hard to reconcile because the poor laws allegedly created the poor they were designed to relieve. If, however, the quest for the causes of population growth is redirected away from the welfare

66 The coefficient of variation for each variable is as follows: share of the population under 15: 0.02; crude marriage rate: 0.11; poor rate expenditure per capita: 0.28.

67 The correlation coefficient, r, between population growth rates and poor relief expenditure per capita is –0.52.

Table 7.6. Poor rate expenditure and selected demographic measures for Suffolk, 1821

	Pop. (1781)	Pop. (1821)	Pop. growth, 1781–1821 (%)	Crude marriage rate (average of 1820, 1821, 1822)	Pop. under 15 (%)	Total expenditure on the poor	Poor rate expenditure per capita
Unincorporated Hundreds							
Babergh	19,001	21,784	14.6	7.9	40.0	£30,106.40	£1.38
Blackbourne	9,930	13,089	31.8	7.7	39.7	£12,750.10	£0.97
Hartismere[1]	13,608	16,186	18.9	8.0	38.8	£17,818.25	£1.10
Hoxne[1]	13,012	15,458	18.8	8.0	40.6	£19,634.10	£1.27
Lackford	7,679	11,521	50.0	8.3	39.6	£8,799.00	£0.76
Plomesgate	7,647	10,616	38.8	8.2	39.8	£10,392.65	£0.98
Risbridge	12,396	14,719	18.7	8.2	41.2	£16,834.35	£1.14
Thedwestry	7,106	9,278	30.6	6.8	39.6	£8,009.55	£0.86
Thingoe	4,591	5,724	24.7	7.9	38.5	£5,321.40	£0.93
Thredling[1]	2,375	3,166	33.3	5.3	39.8	£3,362.65	£1.06
Subtotal	97,345	121,541	24.9	7.8	39.9	£133,028.45	£1.09
Incorporated Hundreds							
Blything	17,834	22,903	28.4	6.6	40.9	£15,232.05	£0.67
Bosmere and Claydon	10,446	12,100	15.8	6.8	39.0	£8,219.25	£0.68
Carlford	4,222	5,966	41.3	7.9	41.4	£7,256.35	£1.22
Colneis	2,874	4,169	45.1	7.9	42.2	£4,374.25	£1.05

	Pop. (1781)	Pop. (1821)	Pop. growth, 1781–1821 (%)	Crude marriage rate (average of 1820, 1821, 1822)	Pop. under 15 (%)	Total expenditure on the poor	Poor rate expenditure per capita
Cosford	6,897	9,478	37.4	7.5	39.6	£9,825.90	£1.04
Loes	8,132	12,208	50.1	7.4	39.1	£12,275.10	£1.01
Mutford and Lothingland	7,774	13,565	74.5	8.8	39.9	£2,469.50	£0.18
Samford	8,366	10,629	27.0	6.4	41.3	£7,926.40	£0.75
Stow	5,395	7,536	39.7	7.3	38.7	£6,182.40	£0.82
Wangford	9,602	12,594	31.2	6.2	39.7	£8,679.45	£0.69
Wilford	4,486	6,718	49.8	7.3	39.8	£6,592.75	£0.98
Subtotal	86,028	117,866	37.0	7.1	40.1	£89,033.40	£0.76
Boroughs							
Bury St Edmunds	7,559	9,999	32.3	8.2	38.5	£6,445.45	£0.64
Ipswich	5,373	17,186	219.9	9.6	38.1	£13,248.05	£0.77
Sudbury	3,491	3,950	13.1	9.4	36.1	£3,052.35	£0.77
Suffolk	199,796	270,542	35.4	7.7	39.8	£244,807.70	£0.90
England	7,206,143	11,261,437	56.3	8.3	39.1	£6,674,938.00	£0.59

Sources: Tables A2.6, A2.7 in E. A. Wrigley, The early English censuses (Oxford, 2011); 1821 Census, Enumeration abstract (PP, 1822, XV), pp. 324–5 and 427–9; 1821 Census, Parish Register abstract (PP, 1822, XV), pp. 113–17 and 145; 1831 Census, Parish Register abstract (PP, 1833, XXXVIII), pp. 312–24 and 412; Report from the Select Committee on Poor Rate Returns (PP, 1822, V), pp. 162–9 and 238.

Notes: [1] Although Hartismere, Hoxne and Thredling were incorporated by 19 Geo. III, c. 13, no workhouse was ever built and the corporation was never constituted.

regime and towards the labour market then a negative association between population growth and poor law expenditure is easier to comprehend. As Wrigley has recently argued, it is at least conceivable that hundreds which grew most rapidly in this period were those where demand for secondary and tertiary workers was highest. The slowest growing hundreds, on the other hand, were more likely to be dominated by agricultural production.[68] One implication of this might be that tight agricultural labour markets – where seasonal unemployment was increasingly the norm – produced higher per capita welfare bills relative to hundreds where manufacturing and/or services were expanding vigorously.

However, there is also another, more political, explanation for the higher relief bills in the unincorporated hundreds of Suffolk. As was noted above, the Suffolk corporations were established with the explicit intention of imposing a cap on poor relief assessments so that no parish would contribute more than the average of the last seven years' assessments immediately preceding incorporation. It is therefore possible that the lower expenditure figures found in the incorporated hundreds did not reflect lower levels of poverty, or demand for welfare, but were a function of the inflexible nature of the incorporations themselves.

There is certainly contemporary testimony which would support such an interpretation. Henry Stuart, the assistant commissioner appointed by the Royal Commission of Inquiry into the Poor Laws, remarked that

> The county of Suffolk is exclusively agricultural, there being no kind of trade or manufacture carried on within it, beyond the ordinary handicraft trades required for the purposes of husbandry, and to supply the daily wants of the inhabitants … The *general circumstances of the population being throughout so much alike*, the chief variety that is to be found in the practical operation of the Poor Laws within the county, arises from a difference in the manner of administering them.[69]

One consequence of Suffolk's different administrative arrangements which Stuart highlighted was that 'the pressure of the poor-rate in those

---

68   E. A. Wrigley, 'Coping with rapid population growth: how England fared in the century preceding the Great Exhibition of 1851', in *Structures and transformations in modern British history*, ed. D. Feldman and J. Lawrence (Cambridge, 2011), pp. 24–53 (pp. 44–9).

69   *Report from His Majesty's Commissioners for inquiring into the administration and practical operation of the poor laws* (PP, 1834, XXVIII), Appendix A, p. 333. My emphasis.

parts of the country where it is under parochial management, will be observed to be uniform and heavy', whereas 'in the incorporated districts, it will be seen that the burthen is comparatively light'. As Table 7.6 indicates, this pattern was at least a decade old. In 1821, the unincorporated hundreds spent £0.33 – or 43 per cent – more per capita than the incorporated districts. In seeking to account for these expenditure differences, Stuart was emphatic that poor law administration, rather than local topographic, economic or demographic conditions, was the key. The Hundred Houses were only part of the story, however. Indeed, Stuart noted that 'although the workhouse was the great recommendation of the system' it was quickly found that 'the benefits to be derived from it had been greatly overrated; profit there was none'.[70]

Much more significant, Stuart suggested, was the fact that acts of incorporation established a common fund, whose managers 'guarded with more jealousy' compared with their parochial counterparts.[71] In Mutford and Lothingland, where expenditure was so low, Stuart described how the directors and guardians exercised 'an inflexible and vigilant system of management'. This was greatly aided by the magistrates' refusal to 'intermeddle' in the Board's decisions.[72] Notwithstanding his obvious admiration for the incorporated system, Stuart was nevertheless critical of the inequality of assessment *within* incorporations. This defect arose from capping of parochial assessments at a level no higher than the pre-incorporation average.[73]

It is possible to observe the effects of parochial capping by looking at the relationship between parish size and poor rate expenditure. In the absence of an incorporating statute, parochial poor rate expenditure was strongly correlated with the number of inhabitants living in the parish (Figure 7.2A). Around three-quarters of the variation in expenditure can be explained by parish population size. It might be argued that this is not a particularly interesting finding. Total expenditure on the poor is self-evidently a function of the total number of people – and therefore paupers – living in a particular community. What is striking, however, is the decreased explanatory power of this simple model when applied to the data for incorporated parishes (Figure 7.2B).

70   Ibid., p. 355.
71   Ibid., p. 356.
72   Ibid., pp. 362–3.
73   Ibid., p. 356.

Figure 7.2. The relationship between parish size and poor rate expenditure, 1821

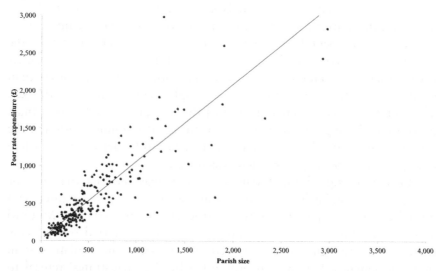

A) Unincorporated parishes

$EXP_{(unincorporated)} = 1.0318POP_{1821} + 22.836$ $R^2 = 0.7316 (n = 252)$

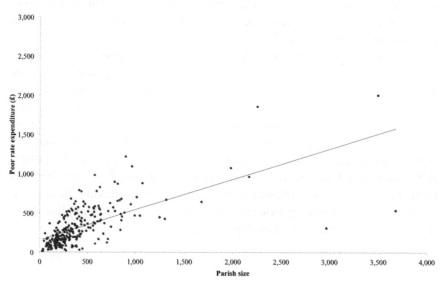

B) Incorporated parishes

$EXP_{(incorporated)} = 0.387POP_{1821} + 158.86$ $R^2 = 0.4416 (n = 242)$

Source: As Table 7.6.

Less than half the variation in total poor rate expenditure in the incorporated parishes can be explained by variations in parish size.[74] This discrepancy – as well as the gentler gradient of the line of best fit – is due, I would argue, to the legal constitution of the Suffolk corporations. Because the local acts sought to fix individual parishes' assessments according to a pre-incorporation average, and provided no mechanism for varying the level of contribution short of an amending act, poor rate assessments ossified. By 1821, when the Suffolk incorporations were all at least forty years old, out-of-date assessments and uneven population growth produced the pattern visible in Figure 7.2B. In the unincorporated parishes, by contrast, overseers (and magistrates) retained administrative autonomy and outspent their incorporated counterparts by a considerable margin.

Three important implications follow from the results reported in Figure 7.2. First, the perceived failure of the Suffolk incorporations – both in the eyes of contemporaries and subsequent historians – needs to be set within its regional context. Certainly, the Hundred Houses, like other corporation workhouses, did not generate the profits promised by their most enthusiastic promoters.[75] Judged on their own terms, the corporations manifestly failed, but judged by reference to their immediate neighbours – as Figure 7.2 demonstrates – the incorporated hundreds were more effective at controlling costs. Whether or not the poor would have regarded this as a mark of success is debatable, but there is no doubt that the principal inhabitants who petitioned parliament between the 1750s and 1770s regarded cost control as a major priority.[76]

Secondly, local discontent relating to the operation of the Suffolk corporations, especially in the 1820s, was not about the *absolute* cost of corporations, but the *relative* costs borne by individual parishes within corporations. The distribution of expenditure data in Figure 7.2B, which is arguably more curvilinear than linear, implies that costs rose most sharply at small parish population sizes (population <250). As population size increases, the distribution flattens out. This suggests that incorporation

74   Even if the possibly anomalous hundred of Mutford and Lothingland is excluded from the model, the value of R^2 does not exceed 0.65.

75   For late-seventeenth-century projections of a profit-generating workhouse system, see J. Bellers, *Proposals for raising a college of industry* (London, 1696) and J. Cary, *An essay on the state of England in relation to its trade, its poor, and its taxes* (Bristol, 1695), pp. 157–9.

76   See p. 216, above.

might be advantageous for large and/or expanding parishes, but relatively more expensive for small rural parishes. By contrast, the distribution of expenditure in unincorporated parishes is more obviously linear: in other words, there was no financial advantage associated with relief administration in large parishes. The flaws of the Suffolk corporations are exemplified by the Loes and Wilford Guardians' decision to seek disincorporation in 1826 owing to the 'great and unequal burthen on the several Parishes composing the Incorporation'.[77] Five years earlier, in 1821, the writing was already on the wall: the smallest parish in the corporation, Boulge (pop. 44), was spending the most per head (£3.34), while the second largest parish, Melton (pop. 861), was paying the least (£0.53).[78]

Thirdly, the comparative Suffolk evidence reminds us that any attempt to clarify the historical relationship between population change and poor relief must pay attention both to the extent of legal and institutional heterogeneity within the eighteenth-century welfare regime at any given moment, as well as the dynamic nature of relief practices across time. It is surely naïve to suppose that either an unambiguous confirmation or refutation of Malthus's hypothesis is empirically attainable given the high degree of variation observed within a single county's expenditure data, let alone nationally. Nonetheless, it is an intriguing and noteworthy feature of Figure 7.2 that the correlation between relief expenditure and population size is *strongest* in the sample of parishes whose vestries enjoyed maximum administrative autonomy. On the one hand, this reflects the absence of the statistical 'noise' generated by the incorporations' assessment-capping clause, but on the other it implies that the demand for relief, which was in some senses predictable given a prevailing age structure and settlement size, exercised a very powerful influence over parish rating and relief practices. Moreover, it could be argued that the relatively slow population growth rate observed in western Suffolk between 1781 and 1821 (around half the national average), implies that its comparatively high per capita expenditure (nearly twice the national average) had few, if any, pro-natalist effects. The more rapid population growth of eastern Suffolk in the same period – where indoor relief was the norm and relief bills were typically lower – suggests that other, more significant, economic and demographic processes must have been at work in this period.

77   7 Geo. IV, c. i; *CJ*, lxxxi, 10 Feb. 1826, p. 31.
78   *Report from the Select Committee on Poor Rate Returns* (PP, 1822, V), p. 169; *1821 Census*, Enumeration abstract, p. 322.

This inference is, I would argue, entirely consistent with the evidence presented in the first two sections of this chapter. Beginning with the City of London in the second half of the seventeenth century, parish elites in urbanizing communities across England lobbied parliament to grant new powers for the 'better relief and employment of the poor'. Not surprisingly, such lobbying tended to occur only after population growth and economic change had begun to put the structures of the Elizabethan welfare regime under pressure. To suggest that the causes of demographic and economic expansion were wholly, or even largely, endogenous to the welfare regime hardly seems plausible given that all parishes were obliged to provide poor relief, but only a minority experienced the explosive growth of the towns listed in Table 7.4. Even if the eighteenth-century poor laws did create marriage incentives, it seems highly likely that these were severely attenuated by successive waves of internal migration which accompanied the expansion and contraction of England's various regional labour markets.

Finally, it is perhaps appropriate to conclude by noting that the historical debate over the demographic effects of the poor law has to a large extent missed Malthus's later qualifications of the position he set out so emphatically in the first *Essay*. As he put it in an appendix to the third *Essay*, 'I will not presume to say positively that [the poor laws] tend to encourage population ... it will readily occur to the reader, that ... it must be extremely difficult to ascertain, with any degree of precision, what has been their effect on population'.[79]

79   T. R. Malthus, *An essay on the principle of population*, 2 vols (London, 1806), vol. 2, p. 547.

8

Charity and Commemoration: a Berkshire Family and their Almshouse, 1675–1763

NIGEL GOOSE AND MARGARET YATES

In comparison with the volume of research dedicated to the history of formal, state-sponsored poor relief, research into the history of philanthropy is in its infancy. Within the gamut of private philanthropy, a particularly neglected topic among academic historians is the English almshouse, although there are a considerable number of popular (and often pictorial) almshouse histories, many of which command academic respect. This neglect is perhaps surprising, given the ubiquity and longevity of these institutions. This chapter provides a contribution towards rectification of this situation by focusing upon the Raymond almshouses founded by Philip Jemmett in the late seventeenth century in Newbury, Berkshire, and placing this institution within the wider context of the historical geography of almshouse foundation as revealed in recent publications and hitherto unpublished research. We therefore combine a macro-historical approach, informed by close attention to regional and local variation, with a micro-historical approach via a case study of a particular institution and the family with which it was associated.

Almshouses originated in medieval England as places that provided care for the sick poor, usually attached to a monastery. Their original focus on travellers or monks was extended in the twelfth and thirteenth centuries to include lay people who were sick or feeble, commonly housed in separate establishments administered by the monks and lay brethren. Specific care was provided for lepers in distinct institutions called lazar houses, some 250 of which were founded in the medieval period. Hospitals were also established by non-monastic benefactors – the crown, clergymen, the aristocracy and gentry, urban livery companies and guilds or individual merchants.[1] The diverse origins of the modern almshouse resulted in an array of terminology in the medieval period: spitalhouses, bedehouses, Godshouses, and a range of other descriptors were used, as well as the terms hospital and almshouse. Many were multi-purpose, and had not yet evolved into the residences for the (usually) elderly poor that is the modern almshouse characteristic. From the late fifteenth century, English parishes started to play a fuller role in the relief of the poor, and parish fraternities increasingly accumulated stocks of land or animals, gave doles to the poor and sometimes (especially in market towns) established almshouses too. Just why these developments took place at this time is unclear, but it has recently been argued that there may have been a demographic imperative behind this growth in foundations. Research on the demography of late medieval monasteries has revealed a dramatic deterioration in life expectancy in the last third of the fifteenth century, and if this can be generalised to the population at large it suggests that the capacity of families to deliver care to their members was probably at rock bottom, with charitable or semi-public provision in the form of almshouses and parish houses stepping in to fill the gap. So while tenancy arrangements had long made provision for elderly ex-tenants, the late fifteenth century saw an increase in the setting up of maintenance contracts with non-kin, often endorsed in manorial courts, as well as the growth of charitable provision.[2] By the end of the fifteenth century, almshouses, so often shrouded in terminological confusion and of uncertain purpose in the earlier middle ages, had emerged in their modern form: as privately endowed establishments, specifically intended to provide accommodation for local, elderly people who had fallen into poverty on account of their age or ailing health.

1   R. M. Clay, *The mediaeval hospitals of England* (London, 1909), pp. xvii–30; C. Dyer, 'Poverty and its relief in late medieval England', *Past and Present* 216 (2012), 41–78; W. H. Godfrey, *The English almshouse* (London, 1955), pp. 15–20; J. A. A. Goodall, *God's house at Ewelme. Life, devotion and architecture in a fifteenth-century almshouse* (Aldershot, 2001); B. Howson, *Houses of noble poverty. A history of the English almshouse* (Sunbury-on-Thames, 1993), pp. 17–33; N. Orme and M. Webster, *The English hospital 1070–1570* (New Haven and London, 1995), pp. 15–68; C. Rawcliffe, *Urban bodies: communal health in late medieval English towns and cities* (Woodbridge, 2013). The best recent general survey can be found in S. Sweetinburgh, *The role of the hospital in medieval England. Gift-giving and the spiritual economy* (Dublin, 2004), pp. 19–67.
2   R. M. Smith, 'Situating the almshouse within demographic and familial changes 1400–1600', lecture delivered to 'The almshouse conference', University of Hertfordshire, St Albans Campus, 22 September 2007.

The number of institutions described as almshouses or hospitals has been cautiously estimated by Nicholas Orme and Margaret Webster to be 585 for the period 1501–30.[3] On the basis of a long-term research project, Marjorie McIntosh has identified a total of 1,005 hospitals or almshouses *operating at some point* between 1350 and 1599, their number rising to a peak of 617 in the 1520s, followed by a dramatic reduction as a consequence of the dissolution of the monasteries when as many as 260 hospitals and endowed almshouses were closed. Despite steady recovery from the 1560s, by the end of the sixteenth century just 479 were in operation.[4] McIntosh's research ends at 1600, but the work of W. K. Jordan has revealed that, in his ten sample counties containing 3,033 parishes, 387 permanently endowed almshouses had been established in the period 1480–1660, and a further seventy-one without a stock for maintenance. Assuming his sample was typical of the country as a whole, there were perhaps a thousand almshouses in existence by the later seventeenth century, and hence at this date approximately 10 per cent of English parishes had ready access to accommodation for the elderly poor.[5]

What proportion of the population benefited from almshouse provision? McIntosh estimates that they housed 5,000–6,400 people in the 1520s, falling to 2,500–4,500 in the 1590s.[6] Our own estimates, based upon the assumption of an average almshouse capacity of eight to ten residents and shown in Table 8.1, suggests a total almshouse population of perhaps 5,000–6,000 in the 1520s, 3,800–4,800 by the end of the sixteenth century, and 8,000–10,000 by the end of the seventeenth century. Of more significance than the total number of residents, however, is the proportion of the 'at risk' population that they catered for – that is, the proportion of those aged sixty or over in the population at large. Table 8.1 assumes a population of 2.5 million in the 1520s, and uses the earliest information we have on age structure, that for 1541, which suggests that approximately

3 Orme and Webster, *English hospital*, tab. 1, p. 11.
4 M. K. McIntosh, 'Local responses to the poor in late medieval and Tudor England', *Continuity and Change* 3 (1988), 209–45 (p. 228); M. K. McIntosh, *Poor relief in England 1350–1600* (Cambridge, 2012), pp. 124–7 and Appendix D.
5 W. K. Jordan, *Philanthropy in England 1480–1660. A study of the changing pattern of English social aspirations* (London, 1959), pp. 27 and 261–2; N. Goose, 'The English almshouse and the mixed economy of welfare: medieval to modern', *The Local Historian* 40 (2010), 3–19 (pp. 7–8).
6 McIntosh, *Poor relief in England*, p. 127.

Table 8.1. Proportion of the elderly in almshouses in England and United Kingdom, c.1520–2012

Date	No. almshouses	No. residents (8 each)	No. residents (10 each)	% of the elderly (age 60+)	
1520	617	4,936	6,170	2.32–2.90	England
1600	479	3,832	4,790	1.22–1.52	England
1660	1,019	8,152	10,190	1.80–2.24	England
1870*	1,336	10,688	13,360	0.71–0.88	England
1943	1,500	12,000		0.21	UK
2012	2,600	36,000		0.28	UK

Sources: 1520 and 1600: M. K. McIntosh, *Poor relief in England 1350–1600* (Cambridge, 2012), pp. 124–7 and Appendix D; 1660: W. K. Jordan, *Philanthropy in England 1480–1660. A study of the changing pattern of English social aspirations* (London, 1959), pp. 27, 261–2; 1870: Digests of Endowed Charities (PP, 1867/8–1877, various); 1943: Nuffield Foundation, *Old people: report of a survey committee on the problems of ageing and the care of old people* (London, 1947); 2012: The National Almshouse Association, http://www.almshouses.org/ (accessed 3 August 2014).

Notes: Estimated populations age 60+ all taken from E. A. Wrigley and R. S. Schofield, *The population history of England, 1541–1871: a reconstruction* (London, 1981), tab. A3.1. *30 per cent added to number of places with an almshouse in 1870 to allow for multiple institutions in towns.

8.5 per cent of the population were sixty or over.[7] At this date, therefore, between 2.32 and 2.90 per cent of the relevant age group could be accommodated in almshouses. By the end of the sixteenth century, largely as a consequence of significant population growth, that proportion had fallen to between 1.22 and 1.52 per cent. Slower population growth between 1600 and 1660, allied to the continued growth of foundations, produced a revival to between 1.80 per cent and 2.24 per cent of the 'at risk' age group by the third quarter of the seventeenth century.

The above figures are, of course, no more than estimates, and present averages across the country as a whole, but it is important to note that almshouse provision varied considerably from place to place and from region to region, and hence their contribution to the social welfare of the elderly poor could be very patchy indeed. McIntosh noticed that

7   E. A. Wrigley and R. S. Schofield, *The population history of England 1541–1871: a reconstruction* (London, 1981), p. 528.

'the number of hospitals and almshouses per county varied widely', and that between 1350 and 1539 very few institutions specifically identified as almshouses were situated in the north or north-west, while the highest proportion were located in East Anglia and the south-east, with a secondary cluster in the south-west and west.[8] From a more localised perspective, Ian Archer's analysis of seventeen parishes and towns in possession of almshouses for various years within the period 1589–1710, which also defines the 'at risk' population as those aged over sixty, concludes that only 3 per cent could be accommodated in London's almshouses in 1598, but as many as 23 per cent in Bray, Berkshire, in 1640, while most parishes in his sample stood closer to a figure of 10 per cent.[9] And, of course, as Jordan's data revealed, approximately 90 per cent of English parishes had no almshouses at all located within their boundaries. The precise historical geography of almshouse foundation, however, remains to be discovered, and work on this topic is currently in progress.

In 2005 the Almshouse Project was established, a research initiative proposed by Nigel Goose and adopted by the Family and Community History Research Society (FCHRS).[10] The project's intention was to investigate national provision of almshouse accommodation on a county by county basis. The endowment of an almshouse is a highly visible form of charitable giving, requiring relatively substantial investment, the establishment of a trust and the construction or adoption of a physical building. However, while historians have written extensively about both formal and informal poor relief, the role played by the almshouse in the history of the poor has been largely ignored. Indeed, as Alannah Tomkins has argued, it may be that their image 'has been over-determined' by the idealism of their founders and their quaint present-day appearance as part of our 'heritage'.[11] Perhaps this is why historians have not taken them seriously. Whatever the reason, it is a simple fact that there is not a single, substantial academic study of the place of the English almshouse within the 'mixed economy of welfare' for any period in English history after 1500.

8   McIntosh, *Poor relief in England*, p. 70.
9   I. W. Archer, 'Hospitals in sixteenth- and seventeenth-century England', in *Hospitals and institutional care in medieval and early modern Europe*, ed. M. Scheutz, A. Sommerlechner, H. Weigl and A. S. Weiss (Vienna, 2008), pp. 53–74 (tab. 4, p. 65).
10   Seed-corn funding was kindly provided by the Economic History Society.
11   A. Tomkins, 'Almshouse *versus* workhouse: residential welfare in eighteenth-century Oxford', *Family and Community History* 7 (2004), 45–58 (p. 46).

The FCHRS project, coordinated by Anne Langley, has involved a team of over sixty volunteer researchers, one of whom is Sue Lambert, whose M.Phil. on seventeenth-century Berkshire almshouses was awarded in 1997.[12] But apart from the formidable research efforts of its volunteers, the project has also inspired research into hitherto largely untapped sources, prominent among which are the *Digests of endowed charities*, compiled by the Charity Commission and focusing mainly upon the years between 1861 and 1875, which are published among the parliamentary papers.[13] These are far more systematic, more comprehensive than the better-known, earlier, Brougham Commission reports, and give breakdowns of the amount of endowed charity dedicated to different uses. Even though by the early Victorian period endowed charity may have been giving way to 'associational' or 'subscription' charity, the sums involved remained significant. What is more, they record the accumulated charitable endowments of several centuries, and are therefore of as much relevance – perhaps more – to early modern England as they are to the nineteenth century which spawned them.[14]

The Charity Commissioners' *Digests* for 1861–76 indicate a total annual charitable spend from endowments slightly less than £2.2 million and, as our best 'guesstimates' suggest that total charitable expenditure was by now well in excess of £7.5 million, the proceeds from endowed charities stood well below the sums raised by subscription.[15] Charitable giving by endowment had far from ceased, however: comparison of the Brougham Commission totals which relate to the period 1819–37 with the *Digests'* data relating to 1861–76 show an increase of just under £1 million – partly due to the discovery of hitherto invisible charities, partly to the growth of income over time, but also due to the establishment of new endowments, the number of which was 4,805 producing additional income of £226,952 per annum. If we assume a rate of return on capital of 4 per cent, this represents additional endowments to the value of £5,673,800. In 1895 the Charity Commission confirmed their continuation, recording thirteen

12   S. Lambert, 'Seventeenth-century Berkshire almshouses' (unpublished M.Phil. dissertation, University of Reading, 1997).

13   Digests of Endowed Charities (*PP*, 1867/8–1877, various).

14   They have been introduced at a number of academic conferences, most recently N. Goose, 'The historical geography of philanthropy in England and Wales to the Victorian era', Economic History Society Annual Conference, Robinson College, Cambridge, 1–3 April 2011, and are presently being systematically analysed with a view to publication.

15   A. Kidd, *State, society and the poor in nineteenth-century England* (Basingstoke, 1999), p. 67.

new trusts of over £100,000 each during the two previous decades, and an average of 500 new endowments each year.[16] Nevertheless, between the eighteenth century and the mid-Victorian period, voluntary charity had overtaken charity by endowment, and as population growth in the respective English counties varied so widely between the late eighteenth and late nineteenth centuries, we must be very wary in estimating relative levels of generosity from these data.

The data for 1870 presented in Table 8.1 are compiled from this source, and reveal that – despite further growth in the number of almshouses – the proportion of the elderly population that they catered for had fallen substantially, a product of rapid population growth from the later eighteenth and into the later nineteenth centuries. Considerable variation, both in philanthropic activity generally and in almshouse provision in particular, is evident from this source, however, as shown by the complete county data for England and Wales presented in Table 8.2. Employing population totals for each county from the nearest census to the date the respective county data were compiled – either 1861 or 1871 – makes it possible to calculate the annual returns from endowed charities per capita. For England and Wales as a whole that figure stood at £0.07, or 7 (new) pence. For Cornwall, however, the figure was just 1 penny, for Lancashire and Wales as a whole 2 pence, and for both Cheshire and Sussex 3 pence. At the other end of the spectrum stood Rutland, with an annual income per capita from endowed charities of 31 pence, Bedfordshire with 18 pence, Gloucestershire (including Bristol) with 16 pence and Berkshire – the focus of this chapter – with 15 pence.

These figures will, as noted above, have been affected by relative rates of population growth since the later eighteenth century, however, and might be particularly misleading if subscription charities grew more rapidly in some counties than in others. Recalculation of county returns for endowed charities on the basis of county populations in 1761 taken from the recent work of Tony Wrigley, shown in the final column of Table 8.2, does produce a rather different rank order, and in particular elevates industrial Lancashire from near the foot of the table to closer (but still below) the national average (19 pence against the average for England as a whole of 24 pence).[17] Still, however, considerable variation is evident,

16   D. Owen, *English philanthropy 1660–1960* (London, 1964), pp. 469ff; G. Finlayson, *Citizen, state and social welfare in Britain 1830–1990* (Oxford, 1994), p. 134.
17   E. A. Wrigley, 'English county populations in the later eighteenth century', *Economic History Review* 60 (2007), 35–69.

Table 8.2. Expenditure on endowed charities and almshouses 1861–76: England and Wales

County	Date	Pop. 1861 or 1871	% pop. age 60+	Endowed charity per capita (£)	Almshouse expenditure per capita age 60+ (£)	% endowed charity on almshouses	No. localities supporting almshouses	% localities supporting almshouses	Endowed charity per capita (£) pop. base 1761
Beds	1861–63	135,287	7.68	0.18	0.64	27	15	15	0.47
Berks	1862–63	176,256	8.86	0.15	0.62	36	28	20	0.27
Bucks	1862–64	167,993	8.88	0.10	0.20	19	32	19	0.17
Cambs	1863–64	176,016	9.15	0.12	0.17	13	16	12	0.27
Cheshire	1862–63	505,428	6.57	0.03	0.07	16	10	5	0.11
Cornwall	1863–64	369,390	8.60	0.01	0.02	18	13	9	0.03
Cumb	1864–65	205,276	8.64	0.03	0.02	5	7	6	0.06
Derbys	1869–70	379,394	7.39	0.05	0.14	20	29	12	0.17
Devon	1865–67	584,373	9.68	0.08	0.10	13	44	12	0.15
Dorset	1863–64	188,789	9.19	0.07	0.19	24	22	15	0.14
Durham	1869–70	685,089	5.35	0.03	0.24	47	15	17	0.15
Essex	1863–64	404,851	8.47	0.07	0.16	19	38	13	0.14
Glos	1864–65	485,770	8.80	0.06	0.12	18	26	11	0.37
Bristol	1869–70	182,552	7.03	0.26	0.95	25			
Hants	1869–71	514,684	8.16	0.05	0.22	39	18	8	0.14
Heref	1864–66	123,712	11.84	0.13	0.32	30	18	10	0.19
Herts	1862–63	173,280	8.45	0.11	0.30	23	26	21	0.20
Hunts	1863–64	64,250	8.77	0.07	0.12	15	9	13	0.13
Kent	1861–63	733,887	7.57	0.09	0.53	46	58	18	0.28
Lancs	1865–68	2,429,440	5.28	0.02	0.05	11	17	4	0.19

County	Date	Pop. 1861 or 1871	% pop. age 60+	Endowed charity per capita (£)	Almshouse expenditure per capita age 60+ (£)	% endowed charity on almshouses	No. localities supporting almshouses	% localities supporting almshouses	Endowed charity per capita (£) pop. base 1761
Leics	1862–63	237,412	8.92	0.12	0.46	34	26	15	0.27
Lincs	1864–66	412,246	8.89	0.12	0.27	21	59	14	0.27
London cos	1865–66					54		20	
London pars	1875–76	74,897	7.13	1.35	2.05	11	21	20	
Westminster	1875–76	246,606	6.31	0.11	0.55	30	5	50	
Middx	1861–63	1,839,799	6.20	0.03	0.11	26	42	44	0.31
Monmouth	1863–65	174,633	6.78	0.04	0.10	17	5	7	n/a
Norfolk	1862–64	434,798	10.27	0.12	0.33	29	22	5	0.20
Northants	1870–72	243,891	8.79	0.13	0.34	23	34	13	0.25
Northumb	1869–71	386,646	6.92	0.07	0.32	31	5	7	0.19
Notts	1869–70	319,758	8.61	0.08	0.32	36	20	10	0.27
Oxon	1869–70	177,975	9.49	0.12	0.28	23	21	10	0.21
Rutland	1863–64	21,861	10.10	0.31	1.40	46	7	21	0.42
Salop	1862–63	240,959	9.24	0.11	0.31	25	17	9	0.20
Somerset	1869–71	463,483	10.09	0.06	0.16	29	36	11	0.12
Staffs	1865–66	746,943	5.87	0.04	0.09	13	19	10	0.18
Suffolk	1871–74	348,869	10.30	0.12	0.31	26	32	9	0.24
Surrey	1861–63	831,093	6.75	0.09	0.37	29	31	21	0.42
Sussex	1862–64	363,735	8.42	0.03	0.10	25	23	17	0.12
Warks	1872–74	684,189	6.28	0.09	0.25	17	16	8	0.57
Coventry	1872–74	37,670	8.31	0.41	0.91	18			
Westm	1864–65	60,817	8.98	0.12	0.15	11	3	3	0.20

(ctd)

County	Date	Pop. 1861 or 1871	% pop. age 60+	Endowed charity per capita (£)	Almshouse expenditure per capita age 60+ (£)	% endowed charity on almshouses	No. localities supporting almshouses	% localities supporting almshouses	Endowed charity per capita (£) pop. base 1761
Wilts	1867–69	257,177	9.99	0.08	0.38	46	28	14	0.12
Worcs	1873–75	338,837	7.99	0.11	0.36	26	13	8	0.31
Yorks ER	1872–75	312,262	8.01	0.11	0.52	37	14	7	0.36
Yorks NR	1873–75	293,278	8.15	0.04	0.14	26	19	7	0.09
Yorks WR	1873–76	1,830,815	5.97	0.05	0.20	25	69	16	0.25
Anglesey	1872–74	51,040	11.95	0.04	0.06	19	6	10	n/a
Brecknock	1862–65	61,627	8.87	0.04	0.08	17	3	6	n/a
Cardigan	1862–65	72,245	9.96	0.01	0.00	0	0	0	n/a
Carmarthen	1862–65	111,796	9.52	0.02	0.03	14	2	5	n/a
Carnarvon	1872–74	106,121	9.23	0.02	0.06	29	5	10	n/a
Denbigh	1872–74	105,102	9.12	0.06	0.17	26	9	16	n/a
Flint	1872–74	76,312	9.12	0.02	0.01	2	1	3	n/a
Glamorgan	1862–65	317,752	5.43	0.01	0.00	0	0	0	n/a
Merioneth	1872–74	46,598	9.81	0.02	0.05	20	3	8	n/a
Montgom	1872–74	67,623	10.65	0.02	0.00	1	3	6	n/a
Pembroke	1862–65	96,278	10.17	0.03	0.02	6	1	3	n/a
Radnor	1862–65	25,382	9.33	0.03	0.00	0	0	0	n/a
Total Eng & Wales		21,204,242	7.40	0.07	0.26	26	1061	12	0.07
England		20,066,366	7.33	0.08	0.28	27	1028	12	0.24

Sources: *1861 Census*, Population Tables, England and Wales, Vol. II pt I, Summary Tables (*PP*, 1863, LIII pt I), pp. x–xiii; General Digest of Endowed Charities (*PP*, 1867–68, LII pt I; 1867–68, LII pt II; 1868–69, XLV); 1761 county population totals from E. A. Wrigley, 'English county populations in the later eighteenth century', *Economic History Review* 60 (2007), 35–69.

Cornwall remaining at the foot of the table with just 3 pence per capita, while other counties performing badly include Cumberland (6 pence), Yorkshire North Riding (9 pence) and (once again) Cheshire (11 pence). At the top we now find Warwickshire at 57 pence – more than double the national average – Rutland still performs well (42 pence), as does Bedfordshire (47 pence), while Berkshire, at 27 pence, now drops back much closer to the national average.

In terms of almshouse provision there are similarly stark variations. The percentage of endowed charity devoted to almshouses was nothing at all in Cardiganshire, Glamorgan and Radnorshire, while among the English counties Cumberland spent only 5 per cent, Lancashire 11 per cent and Staffordshire 13 per cent. At the top of the rankings stood Durham on 47 per cent, while Kent, Wiltshire and Rutland all devoted 46 per cent of their total endowed charity spend to almshouses. The number of parishes (or, in the north, townships) able to benefit from almshouse provision at all also varied widely. The same three Welsh counties, self-evidently, contained no almshouses at all, while in Denbighshire 16 per cent did so as compared with a national average of 12 per cent for England and Wales as a whole. In England, almshouses were clustered thickly in Westminster and Middlesex, with almost half of the identifiable localities here containing at least one almshouse, while they were to be found in only 4 per cent of Lancashire localities, 5 per cent in Cheshire and (surprisingly) Norfolk, and 6 per cent in Cumberland. Outside of London and Middlesex, the rankings were headed by Hertfordshire, Rutland and Surrey with almshouses in 21 per cent of localities, closely followed by Berkshire on 20 per cent.

Why there was such regional variation, and why provision varied geographically in the manner that it did, is impossible to answer with confidence at present. A recent attempt to calculate correlation coefficients for a number of potentially related variables – lay and clerical wealth in the early sixteenth century, population density in the eighteenth century and the number of market towns in each county – proved depressingly inconclusive, the strongest correlation (between population density and endowed charity) standing at just 0.41.[18] These and many other variables will need to be considered before these data can be fully explained. However, the

18   N. Goose, 'Accommodating the elderly poor: almshouses and the mixed economy of welfare in England in the second millennium', *Scandinavian Economic History Review* 62 (2014), 35–57.

results presented here, allied to regional analysis of the breadth and depth of formal poor relief, offer an early indication that there may have been a distinct geography of social welfare, with much of the south and south-east performing better than much of the north, north-west and south-west, a possibility that is more fully discussed elsewhere.[19]

What does seem clear is that proximity to London was one factor at work. In his magisterial study of philanthropy in England, W. K. Jordan waxed lyrical about the charitable impulses of the mercantile classes in general, but noted in particular the 'incredible generosity of London's benefactors'.[20] As we will see from the following discussion of almshouse provision in Berkshire, the relationship between the county's mercantile community and commerce in the capital was of great significance to philanthropic provision in the county.

In the third quarter of the nineteenth century, almshouses were to be found in twenty-eight different localities in Berkshire, representing 20 per cent of all localities in the county identified in the *Digest*, compared with the 12 per cent found nationally.[21] The county's total annual return from endowments in the period 1862–63 when its *Digest* was compiled was £26,994, and of this total £9,683 was devoted to the support of 'almshouses their inmates and pensioners'. Thus almshouse charities accounted for almost 36 per cent of total charitable endowments, which compares to just 27 per cent for England as a whole, or 26 per cent for England and Wales. Berkshire was thus particularly rich in almshouse endowments, standing in joint seventh place among all English and Welsh counties.[22] Employing the proximate census population total, Berkshire's annual return from its endowed charities stood at £0.15 per capita, which compares with £0.08 for England as a whole, and £0.07 for England and Wales (Table 8.2). Expenditure on almshouses per capita of the 'at risk' population – that is, those aged sixty-plus – stood at £0.62, which compares with just £0.28 for England or £0.26 for England and Wales.

---

19   N. Goose, 'Regions 1700–1870', in *The Cambridge economic history of modern Britain, 1: 1700–1870*, ed. R. Floud, J. Humphries and P. Johnson, 2nd edn (Cambridge, 2014), pp. 149–77.

20   Jordan, *Philanthropy in England*, p. 241.

21   This does not indicate that there were twenty-eight almshouses in the county, for individual foundations are not identified in the *Digest*, merely the total spend under this heading. As the larger towns are very likely to have possessed more than one almshouse, this total is a minimum one.

22   Counting the East Riding of Yorkshire as a separate county.

If we take our base population as 1761, to allow for the relative decline of giving by endowment and the rapid population growth experienced by the industrializing counties, Berkshire's endowed spend per capita rises to £0.27 per capita, but now stands much closer to the national total of £0.24. For almshouses alone, however, per capita expenditure stood at £0.10, still substantially above the national total of £0.06, and ranking it in joint sixth place among all English counties. So, Berkshire was relatively well endowed with funds dedicated to almshouses and their pensioners, and this was true of the county both in the mid-Victorian period, as well as in the mid eighteenth century.

For the seventeenth century, Sue Lambert has identified twenty almshouses in Berkshire founded during that century alone, situated in thirteen different localities. If the total number of discrete places was the same as those identified in the Victorian *Digest* for the county, then a minimum of 12 per cent of localities supported at least one almshouse, and this would suggest that Berkshire was better endowed than the average for the counties included in W. K. Jordan's sample.[23] Of these foundations, six were endowed by merchants, four more by tradesmen or artisans and one by a member of the professional classes – John Hall, apothecary, of Reading. Many of these, and particularly the merchants, had close connections with London, and apparently were resident there when they made their wills. James Smith, for example, who endowed an almshouse in Maidenhead, described himself as 'of London, esquire', and was a member of the Company of Salters. William Goddard, 'sometime a citizen and fishmonger of the City of London', was living in Westminster when he drew up the letters patent that founded an almshouse for forty residents in Bray, known as Jesus Hospital, and he made the Company of Fishmongers trustees and governors of the charity.[24] However, of particular interest for our present purpose are the Raymond almshouses in Newbury founded by Philip Jemmett.

The story begins with a 'local boy made good' who returned to the area of his childhood, erected an almshouse in his birthplace and endowed it handsomely. Its subsequent history was as a family concern until, perhaps due to a lack of male heirs, it was granted to the Corporation of Newbury in 1763 to ensure that the institution and its charity would continue in perpetuity. Could one argue that this was an act of commemoration for

23 S. Lambert, 'Seventeenth-century Berkshire almshouses', in *Almshouses in England and Wales c.1350–1900*, ed. N. Goose, A. Langley and H. Caffrey (forthcoming). Jordan, of course, included all foundations across the period 1480–1660.
24 Ibid.

the family? Certainly as we will show, commemorative monuments were a
feature of their legacies. Yet the almshouses do not bear the name of their
founder, Philip Jemmett, but that of his heir, Raymond.

Philip Jemmett was born in Newbury in 1616, the son of a brewer.[25] In
1635 he was apprenticed to Josias Centre, citizen and brewer of London,
and successfully completed his apprenticeship in 1642.[26] He appears to have
made a success of being a brewer and had apprentices of his own. Jemmett
was active in the Brewers' Company holding various offices including steward
in 1659, auditor and renter warden, but appears to have avoided acting as
master of the Company as in 1668 he was excused serving, and in 1671 paid
a fine for another to replace him.[27] Meanwhile, he was also active in the city,
serving as alderman of Dowgate between 21 March and 7 May 1667 when
he paid a fine of £420 to be discharged, and as common councilman for
Portsoken 1666–67.[28] He had taken on lease several properties including, in
1662, houses at Garlickhithe in Thames Street for which he paid a large entry
fine of £1,300 to the Company. These properties were subsequently damaged
in the Great Fire,[29] and in 1667 he attempted to renegotiate the terms of
his lease as the houses had been burnt.[30] Indeed in 1671 he was acquitted
of arrears of rent while the houses remained unbuilt.[31] Nevertheless, in the
same year he was buying up several large landed estates in Berkshire and
may have had cash-flow problems rather than being impoverished.

During his lifetime Jemmett amassed a sizeable landed estate. In
addition to the London properties already mentioned, in 1663 he bought
copyhold and freehold estates in Hornsey in Highgate, Middlesex;[32] in
1669 and 1674–75 he purchased properties in Hertfordshire.[33] He began
buying lands in Berkshire in 1669, that is, Henwick in Thatcham and
other estates from John Winchcombe, with final conveyance two years

---

25   Baptised 8 September 1616 as son of Phillip Jemmett. BRO, D/P89/1/1.
26   Brewers' Company, MS 5445/16, court 17 December 1635. Phillipp Jemmatt the son
of Phillipp Jemmatt of Newbury brewer.
27   Brewers' Company, MS 5446/1, No. 1: 7, 81; No 2: 3, 4, 93, 431. Additionally he acted
as auditor 1675–77 and apprentices were bound to him in 1662, 1664, 1667 and 1669.
28   A. B. Beaven, The aldermen of the city of London, 2 vols (London, 1908–13), vol. 1,
p. 141; J. R. Woodhead, The rulers of London 1660–1689 (London, 1965), p. 98.
29   Brewers' Company, MS 5446/1, No. 1: 112, 124.
30   Brewers' Company, MS 5446/1, No. 2: 52. MS 5445/20, court 5 November 1667.
31   Brewers' Company, MS 5446/1, No. 3: 53, 196.
32   T. F. T. Baker (ed.), A history of the county of Middlesex, 6: Ossulstone Hundred
(London, 1969), pp. 146–9.
33   Hertfordshire Archives and Local Studies, E1806, DEGA/36395.

later in 1671 when he also purchased Farnborough.[34] In this same year he purchased the large manor of Kintbury Amesbury and resided there.[35] Together these formed the basis of the family estate and would pass to his only surviving child, his daughter Anne as heir.[36] Jemmett's interests now included those of a country gentleman and in 1674 he was made high sheriff of Berkshire and the Brewers' Company presented him with a brace of bucks to mark the occasion.[37] Other offices he held included farmer of Irish revenues between 1669 and 1675.[38]

As he established himself in landed society his involvement in the Brewers' Company declined, as reflected in the fine he received from the Brewers' court for absence in 1670.[39] Nevertheless he maintained his London connections and was chosen as the Company's auditor in 1675, 1676, and 1677.[40] In fact, in a deed of endowment of the Raymond Charity he was referred to as being 'Philip Jemmett late of the parish of St Buttolph without Bishopsgate London esquire deceased'.[41]

It is within this London–Berkshire context that we turn now to his charitable activities. In 1663, together with fellow brewer William Carpenter, he administered the gift of a friend and established a charity that would provide money for stockings and shoes for two poor London brewers.[42] Jemmett's own benefaction for poor brewers is viewed in the context of a Company in decline, along with many other livery companies, and adversely affected by the Great Fire of 1666 which destroyed their Brewers' Hall.[43] By his will of 1676 he bequeathed £100 to the Company for its stock, and an additional £100 to be invested to pay £6 per annum to four poor freemen or women of the Company at 7s 6d each per quarter. These doles were distributed from 1679, being paid from the profits of various houses belonging to the Company in Shoe Lane.[44]

34 VCH, *Berkshire*, vol. 3, pp. 22 and 313–14.
35 Ibid., p. 207.
36 Jemmett had married Elizabeth, daughter of Lancelot and Anne Grimshaw of St Mary Aldermary London, and it was their daughter Anne who married Sir Jonathan Raymond in 1661. Society of Genealogy, *Boyd's inhabitants of London*, 15781.
37 Brewers' Company, MS 5446/1, No. 3: 334, 337.
38 Woodhead, *Rulers of London*, p. 98.
39 Brewers' Company, MS 5446/1, No 2: 341, 348.
40 Brewers' Company, MS 5446/1, No 3: 442, No 4: 1, 65.
41 BRO, N/QR1/1/1–2.
42 Brewers' Company, MS 5462, f. 33.
43 M. Ball, *The worshipful company of brewers. A short history* (London, 1977).
44 Brewers' Company, MS 5445/22, ff. 127–8, 194, 325, 428. An indenture of covenant

Newbury had been a successful town manufacturing cloth in the fifteenth and sixteenth centuries but had fallen on hard times and was experiencing economic decline in the seventeenth century. Nevertheless, there was a longer history of almshouses and other provision for the poor of the town, so philanthropic activity was not reserved solely for times of hardship.[45] Prior to writing his will in January 1676, Jemmett had built 'at his own proper costs and charges' twelve almshouses with their appurtenances in Newbury.[46] These he bequeathed to his grandson Jemmett Raymond in trust to house twelve poor people of Newbury (unmarried) chosen by his grandson or his heirs and for each to receive 12d a week from income derived from lands, including the Globe Inn in Newbury. In addition, Jemmett bequeathed £600 to his son-in-law Jonathan Raymond to be invested in lands and tenements, income from which would be used to increase the dole to 2s per week.[47] Thus we have the beginning of the family charity and almshouses that they would administer and maintain until 1763. Jemmett died at Kintbury in 1678 and was buried, along with his wife, in what was to become the family vault with a memorial erected to him in the chancel of the parish church.[48]

Philip Jemmett's daughter Anne, acting as executrix, ensured her father's wishes were carried out in both charitable contexts. In June 1679 she settled by indenture of covenant the £200 on the Company to fulfil his wishes to establish that charity.[49] She was active with her husband and son in setting up two trusts related to the Newbury almshouses.[50] Furthermore by her will of 1709 she left an additional legacy of £400 to her son, Jemmett Raymond,

was drawn up between the Company and Philip Jemmett's daughter and executrix Anne on 23 June 1679 ratifying this bequest. MS 5462A, ff. 182–4.

45   Lambert, 'Seventeenth-century Berkshire almshouses' (1997), p. 19.

46   BRO, N/QR1/1/1. This will does not survive and details have been taken from the various indentures related to the charity.

47   BRO, N/QR1/1/1.

48   BRO, D/P78/1/1, 26 June 1678. Among the parish documents is a plan dated 1753 of the family vault in the chancel providing details of the persons buried and position of their coffins, including Philip Jemmett and his wife, but not the location of the entrance to the vault.

49   Brewer' Company, MS 5462A, ff. 182–4.

50   TNA, PROB 11/511. Anne Raymond's will mentions two indentures to set up trusts of 24 November 1703 and 18 April 1705 which relate to the Newbury almshouses and charity. In addition, the charity commissioners refer to a lease and release of 9 September 1707 between Jonathan and Jemmett Raymond and Roger Geater of Barton regarding the endowment, but Anne was not named in this action. BRO, N/QR1/1/1.

to purchase lands and from this income to pay the twelve poor people of Newbury an additional 6d each weekly, and to provide for further expenses whenever necessary, particularly as payments for fuel to the almspeople.[51] She died at Henwick and was buried at Kintbury in 1709 next to her father in the family vault as requested in her will.[52]

Jemmett's son-in-law, Jonathan Raymond, was also a master brewer and had been described by Le Neve as 'a very weak silly man but gott a great estate', presumably through his marriage to Anne.[53] He was knighted on 20 October 1679 when described as of Barton Court and Kintbury, and sheriff of London;[54] as Brewer 1681–96 and master 1679–80; MP for Great Bedwyn 1690–95;[55] and alderman for Bishopsgate in 1681, 1683 and 1685.[56] He was discharged 24 September 1696 on the plea that his affairs required him to reside wholly in the country.[57] Indeed, the parish documents record his active participation in events in Kintbury such as when acting as 'allower' or auditor of the churchwardens' accounts in 1684, and again in 1699.[58]

Jonathan Raymond fulfilled his late father-in-law's wishes and invested the £600 in lands and tenements in Newbury and probably also in two bonds of £100 each in the East India Company.[59] At this time the income from the impropriate tithes of Kintbury were added to the charity, together with rents from various properties in Kintbury parish. As a result, the cash dole to the almspeople was increased to 2s, and became 2s 6d in 1709 as a result of Anne's bequest. Moreover, each almsperson was to be provided with a new gown of blue cloth each year. A grant of 40s (subsequently increasing to £5) was made annually to the vicar of Newbury, who was to find and pay a suitable person to read prayers to the almspeople twice a week. Jonathan Raymond died in 1711 and was buried at Kintbury. As a

---

51 TNA, PROB 11/511. The will was made with the express consent of her husband who signed a memorandum to this effect.

52 BRO, D/P78/1/1. Her monument in Kintbury parish church records that she died 17 June 1709 age 64.

53 Beaven, *Aldermen of London*, vol. 2, p. 192.

54 W. A. Shaw, *The knights of England*, 2 vols (London, 1906), vol. 2, p. 254.

55 E. Cruickshanks, S. Handley and D. W. Hayton (eds), *The House of Commons 1690–1715*, 5 vols (London, 2002), vol. 5, pp. 258–9.

56 Beaven, *Aldermen of London*, vol. 1, p. 42; vol. 2, p. 108.

57 Beaven, *Aldermen of London*, vol. 1, p. 42.

58 BRO, D/P78/5/1.

59 BRO, N/QR1/1/1 and income from the bonds are mentioned in the charity's ledger BRO, N/QR3/1.

result of Anne and Jonathan Raymond's activities, the family charity had been increased significantly.[60]

Philip Jemmett's grandson, Jemmett Raymond the elder, was born in 1662 and, on the death of his parents, had been the recipient of the family lands and estates, including the almshouses and charitable trust. His principal residence appears to have been at Kintbury as, from 1686 onwards and while his father was still alive and active, his name appears in the parish records when acting as countersignatory to various accounts, including the accounts of overseers of the poor in 1690, and his signature is often evident at the head of lists of signatories, above that of the vicar.[61] He was knighted in 1680 in London, a year after his father.[62] He married for the first time in 1687 the heiress Elizabeth Brown from whom he acquired Wolverton in Hampshire, but she died in 1688 aged seventeen, nine days after the birth of their only son, also Jemmett.[63] In 1704 he was married for the second time: Elizabeth Skylling was daughter of Henry Skylling of Draycott in Wiltshire by whom he had several sons and daughters who predeceased him, save for a daughter Elizabeth.[64] The second Elizabeth died in 1754 and was buried at Kintbury.[65] His will was made in 1743 and proved in 1755 in which he left the estates at Henwick, Shaw and Harwell to his wife for life and then to his daughter Elizabeth; the remaining estates (unspecified but which would have included the almshouses and charity) to his son and executor, Jemmett the younger. Jemmett Raymond the elder wished to be buried in the parish church of Kintbury 'in a private and decent manner'.[66] He and his two wives are commemorated in a monument, erected by order of his son and by the latter's widow, which records that 'Sir Jemmett lived in great hospitality and esteem to the 93rd year of his age'. He was succeeded by his son, Jemmett Raymond the younger (1688–1767) who died childless. Perhaps it was in recognition of the end of the Raymond line and to perpetuate the charity that he granted the family's almshouses and endowments in trust to the Corporation of Newbury on 18 March 1763.[67]

60   Their monument in Kintbury parish church states that they were married 11 June 1661 and had six sons and five daughters, although not all survived to adulthood.
61   BRO, D/P78/5/1.
62   Shaw, *Knights of England*, vol. 2, p. 254.
63   VCH, *Hampshire and the Isle of Wight*, vol. 4, pp. 270–2.
64   Details taken from monument in Kintbury parish church.
65   BRO, D/P78/1/2.
66   TNA, PROB 11/815.
67   BRO, N/QR1/1.

At this point it is possible to see the full extent of the charity and its endowments. In summary, they included the twelve almshouses with their gardens and fuel sheds; grounds containing over an acre of land lying to their south; the Globe Inn; lands in Newbury purchased from the borough by Jemmett Raymond and formerly the church almshouses; impropriate tithes from Kintbury; income from rents from lands there; a garden ground in Newbury on the Island with the profits from the associated watercourses in the vicinity of the weaving shops; meadows in Speen; and two bonds of £100 each of the East India Company.[68]

The almshouses and charity were to be administered by a Receiver and Treasurer elected annually by the mayor, aldermen and capital burgesses.[69] It was anticipated that there would be surplus income derived from the investments over and above the requirements for the maintenance of the almshouses and their residents. Jemmett Raymond ordered, therefore, that a fund of no less than £400 principal money be maintained against future eventualities, which would be employed subsequently to fund the erection of additional Raymond almshouses by the Corporation.

The Corporation would take over the responsibilities previously undertaken by the family, including, and in association with the vicar, the selection of suitable poor persons of Newbury (six men and six women) as almspeople when a vacancy arose either through death, or eviction for 'irreligious, immoral or disorderly behaviour'.[70] These people were to be respectable unmarried men and women of the town who had been born and had lived in Newbury for the majority of their lives. While the women were usually widows, the men tended to be skilled craftsmen such as carpenters, tailors, butchers, and there was also a millwright and a hair dresser.[71] Respectability lay in their regular contributions to the town's poor rates and many had done so for over thirty years before entry. As elsewhere, these persons were usually aged around sixty on entry, although they could be younger: Hannah Ely was forty-six, while Richard Gough was older, being seventy-two on entry. It was assumed that they would remain in the almshouses for the rest of their lives, which for Hannah Ely was a period of over thirty years. Their cash doles were paid regularly, their blue gowns were made by a local tailor each year, the twelve almshouses were maintained and repaired, and the almspeople received regular deliveries

68   BRO, N/QR1/1. The properties are described in great detail.
69   BRO, N/QR1/1.
70   BRO, N/QR1/1/1.
71   BRO, N/QR8/1/1.

of peat for fuel and further assistance when they were ill. Their spiritual wellbeing was addressed through the regular prayers read to them twice weekly by the vicar or another suitable person, and a Bible and prayer-book were purchased in 1769 for this purpose.[72]

The charity and almshouses had been actively managed by the family and Jemmett Raymond the younger continued to do so for the rest of his life, appointing the almspeople and managing the finances. His activities relating to income and expenditure are recorded in the charity's ledger, including a one-off payment of £1 6s 0d in May 1763 for a dinner for the almspeople, perhaps to celebrate the grant of the charity.[73] The ledger demonstrates his involvement, with records of his payments of the land tax, collection of rents and tithes, payment for repairs to the almshouses of timber, bricks, and for labour, payments of the cash doles and gowns for the almspeople.[74]

In the codicil to his will of September 1763 Jemmett Raymond the younger bequeathed (among other things) £200 to Mr Thomas Henshaw of Chieveley, his heir and executor, to be paid out of his personal estate for the erection of a monument in Kintbury church to the memory of his father and his two wives with three busts – unless in the meantime he and his wife had undertaken the work. His charitable concerns included bequests of £20 to the poor of Kintbury, £15 to the poor of Thatcham, £10 to the poor of Wolverton and £5 to the poor of Farnborough. Perhaps this was in proportion to the size of the estates in these places.

He also appears to have been infatuated with the widow Elizabeth Craven whom he eventually married at some point between 1755 and 1756.[75] Elizabeth was the daughter of John Staples of Ash Park, Berkshire, and was first married in 1719 to Charles Craven esquire (1682–1754), previously Governor of South Carolina, with a marriage portion of £6,000 given by her father.[76] She married Jemmett Raymond within a year or two of being widowed.

72   BRO, N/QR3/1.
73   BRO, N/QR3/1.
74   BRO, N/QR2/1.
75   In his first will of 1755 he was described as of Wolverton and made bequests to Mrs Elizabeth Craven a widow; by the first codicil of 1756 he had married her; in the second codicil of 1763 he was described as of Barton and Wolverton and she was his dear wife; in the final codicil of 1765 he was described as of Wolverton and Barton. The will with codicils was proved 13 October 1767 by Elizabeth Raymond formerly Craven executrix. TNA, PROB 11/933.
76   TNA, PROB 11/573.

After his death in 1767, Elizabeth was active in fulfilling Jemmett Raymond's wishes, signing off the charity's account in October 1767, which was balanced at £2,196 6s 1½d.[77] As Elizabeth Raymond, widow, she continued various acts of charity and commemoration. She had put thirteen children to school at Kintbury and in her will bequeathed a guinea to each of them, while she also made provision for the poor in the parishes where the family held lands.[78] She left a further £200, this time to erect a monument with two busts commemorating her husband and herself. She died in 1771 and was duly buried at Kintbury.

In addition to the family charity and almshouses, the family were commemorated in lavish monuments in the parish church of Kintbury. Pevsner describes that commemorating Philip Jemmett in the chancel as 'cartouche with beefy cherubs and cornucopias'.[79] That to Jonathan Raymond may contain work by Grinling Gibbons.[80] However, it is the monuments by the Flemish sculptors Peter and Thomas Scheemakers that dominate the parish church. They consist of life-size classical portrait busts in white marble of all five figures following the instructions contained in the wills of Jemmett and Elizabeth Raymond,[81] and originally stood on either side of the east window, acting as a focal point for worship. It is unusual to find monuments of such scale and artistic achievement in a rural parish church. The Raymonds' need for commemoration was strong, and they chose to identify themselves where they were buried rather than elsewhere where they had interests. They had ensured the perpetuity of their name in the charity and its almshouses and their presence in the parish church.

**

We have identified a number of features whose significance lies beyond the confines of the county of Berkshire. First, the Raymond almshouses reflect a tradition of charitable giving in general, and almshouse foundation in particular, that appears to have captured the imagination of some of the leading figures in Berkshire society. The county was relatively well endowed with almshouses in the seventeenth century, and by the mid-Victorian

---

77 BRO, N/QR2/1.
78 TNA, PROB 11/967.
79 G. Tyack, S. Bradley and N. Pevsner, *The buildings of England. Berkshire* (New Haven and London, 2010), p. 347.
80 Ibid.
81 I. Roscoe, 'Peter Scheemakers', *The Walpole Society* 61 (1999), 163–304 (pp. 163–77 and 245–6).

period they could be found in one in five Berkshire localities, their annual income accounting for over one-third of the return on all endowed charities. A great deal more research will be needed before the historical geography of philanthropy and almshouse foundation can be explained, but our case study shows how connexions between those born in the 'home counties' and London helped both to create the wealth and provide the inspiration for acts of charity of this kind. Clearly, commemoration of the donor family was part of the concern of those who established almshouses, and in the case of the Raymond family was reflected too in the church monuments they established. In this sense the Raymond almshouses formed part of a much longer tradition: in the period 1350–1539, McIntosh found that while 65 per cent of those institutions described as 'hospital' bore a religious name, this was true of only 9 per cent of almshouses. Of the almshouses, 40 per cent bore the name of their founder, while 13 per cent more were labelled by location.[82] That said, our Berkshire case study shows how those making such endowments were often actively involved in the day-to-day administration of the charities that bore their name. The deep involvement of successive Raymond family members is most impressive, suggesting that commemoration was only part of their concern, for their various legacies reveal a strong association with place, as well as a real concern to ensure the maintenance of the deserving poor in the parishes with which they were associated. Our case study also shows how difficult it is to strictly demarcate private philanthropy from public provision, as from 1763 the almshouse and related endowments were entrusted to the Corporation of Newbury, a move no doubt designed to ensure its longevity, and a strategy also adopted in the eighteenth century by Doughty's Hospital in Norwich. And, again like Doughty's, the present case study demonstrates the ability of such charities to persist through time, and to reinvent themselves as and when it became necessary.[83] Flexibility, and responsiveness to changing demands and expectations, has defined the almshouse movement through from the middle ages to the twenty-first century. And although the provision of these institutions has always been geographically erratic, and their contribution to the overall welfare of the elderly poor has been relatively small, their persistence across 700 years or more testifies to both the powerful need for commemoration, and to the continuing power of the voluntary impulse in English society.

---

82 McIntosh, *Poor relief in England*, pp. 63–4.
83 N. Goose and L. Moden, *A history of Doughty's hospital, Norwich 1687–2009* (Hatfield, 2010).

9

The Institutional Context of Serfdom in England and Russia

TRACY K. DENNISON

The role of institutions in economic growth and development has attracted considerable attention from social scientists in recent years. Law, in particular, and its importance in the assignment of property rights and contract enforcement, has been emphasised in the development economics and legal history literatures. Research on modern-day developing societies has revealed a robust link between the existence of formal legal institutions and the potential for economic growth and development.[1]

But not everyone is convinced. A more sceptical view of the role of institutions has emerged in recent years, particularly among economic historians. According to the sceptics, property rights and contract enforcement existed in many parts of early modern Europe, but not all of these experienced economic growth and development. One of the most extreme articulations of this view is in Gregory Clark's recent book, *A farewell to alms*, where he argues that 'there were preindustrial societies that had most, if not all, of the institutional prerequisites for growth hundreds, and probably thousands, of years before the Industrial Revolution'.[2] Clark points to medieval England as a place with 'extraordinary institutional stability' where '[m]ost individuals enjoyed great security both of their persons and of their property'. In this view, inhabitants of medieval England enjoyed

---

1 For an overview, see R. Pande and C. Udry, 'Institutions and development: a view from below', in *Advances in economics and econometrics: theory and applications, Ninth World Congress*, ed. R. Blundell, W. K. Newey and T. Persson, 3 vols (Cambridge, 2006), vol. 2, pp. 349–412.
2 G. Clark, *A farewell to alms: a brief economic history of the world* (Princeton, NJ, 2007), p. 145.

'low tax rates', security of property, and 'free markets' in land, labour, and goods – all the institutional features development economists point to as favourable for economic growth. Yet despite this favourable environment, the industrial revolution did not occur in medieval England. According to Clark, we can only conclude that institutions are of little relevance to questions of growth.[3]

A slightly different version of this debate has taken place among historians, especially with respect to one particular institution: serfdom. In this context, too, the sceptics view institutions as irrelevant to the local economy. Not because markets were free and property secure under serfdom, but because they were *not* free and property was *not* secure, yet we know that serfs nonetheless engaged in market transactions, made complex investment decisions, and even, in some cases, achieved a degree of social mobility. The overwhelming evidence for lively rural markets in land, labour, and credit in serf societies from medieval England to eighteenth-century Russia has brought some historians to the conclusion that serfdom could not have been all that constraining.[4] Some have even argued that serfdom was itself superstructure, something merely 'draped over' an underlying peasant culture which remained largely unchanged over time.[5]

One problem with these arguments is that they treat institutions as dummy variables, which are either present or absent, on or off, in any given society, with no degrees in between. Thus Clark has his checklist of desirable institutions: property rights, land markets, credit markets, social mobility, etc. If a feature is observed in the society under investigation, its box gets ticked with the result that, at the end of the exercise, medieval England is indistinguishable from modern England, and one is forced to conclude that institutions cannot matter very much. But is this the way we should be thinking about institutions and their effects? Why should we assume that it was all or nothing rather than a range of intermediate

3   For a critique of Clark on precisely this point, see R. C. Allen, 'A review of Gregory Clark's *A farewell to alms: a brief economic history of the world*', *Journal of Economic Literature* 46 (2008), 946–73 (esp. pp. 955–8).

4   This view is discussed in greater detail in T. Dennison, *The institutional framework of Russian serfdom* (Cambridge, 2011), pp. 15–17; T. K. Dennison and S. Ogilvie, 'Serfdom and social capital in Bohemia and Russia', *Economic History Review* 60 (2007), 513–44; S. Ogilvie, 'Communities and the "second serfdom" in early modern Bohemia', *Past and Present* 187 (2005), 69–119. See also the discussion in M. Cerman, *Villagers and lords in eastern Europe, 1300–1800* (Basingstoke and New York, 2012), pp. 1–39.

5   S. Hoch, 'The serf economy and the social order in Russia', in *Serfdom and slavery: studies in legal bondage*, ed. M. L. Bush (Harlow, 1996), pp. 311–22.

values? Does it really make sense to view property rights as uniform from place to place or over time?[6] Or land markets as uniformly 'free' where they exist?

A further, related problem with arguments like Clark's is that they assume we can identify corresponding institutions in different institutional contexts. In any given society, all the institutions present in that society are adapted to each other; they all function together as components of an overall institutional system, and it is only by a kind of provisional abstraction that we can talk about any one of them in isolation from the whole system of which it is a part.[7] But one of the dangers of such abstraction is that it can mislead us into comparing, or even identifying, apparently similar components of two such comprehensive systems in different times and places. For some purposes, such comparisons are harmless. But when they lead us to equate certain institutional components in twelfth-century England and certain apparently corresponding components in modern societies, without pausing to notice their different contexts and ramifications within the respective institutional systems of which they are components, then we can be fairly certain something has gone badly wrong.

The debate over 'serfdom' is a good example of such over-abstraction. Serfdom is said to have been relevant when we observe immiserated, powerless peasants, cowering under the landlord's knout, but insignificant when we find rural land and labour markets and significant socioeconomic stratification among enserfed peasants. But no criteria are offered for determining when the institutions of serfdom are genuine, or efficacious, and when they are merely superstructure. There are many different societies where peasant mobility is restricted and landlords have some form of property right in peasants' labour, in which the other institutional components vary widely. Most historians of serfdom would agree that it was not a uniform set of practices. So why should we assume uniformity in its effects?

The institutions of serfdom were much more complicated than these black-or-white, overly abstract approaches allow. There were significant qualitative differences in the way they functioned across space and over

---

6 S. Banner, *American property: a history of how, why, and what we own* (Cambridge, MA, 2011) argues convincingly for a negative answer to this question.

7 A more detailed discussion of this point can be found in S. Ogilvie, '"Whatever is, is right"? Economic institutions in pre-industrial Europe', *Economic History Review* 60 (2007), 649–84, esp. pp. 670–7.

time. In order to determine whether an institution, or, more plausibly, a set of institutions had an effect on the local economy, it is important to understand how exactly the institutions functioned at the local level. We cannot assume, for instance, that 'serfdom' implied the same overall institutional system from place to place, or even from manor to manor. To highlight these qualitative differences, this chapter compares two serf societies: medieval England and eighteenth-century Russia. Despite geographical and temporal disparities, there are remarkable similarities in the two forms of 'serfdom'. But, as we shall see, it is the differences that are most illuminating.

This is not the first time these two disparate societies have been considered together. Although few historians would argue now that the history of England can provide us with a guide to Russia's future development,[8] or that the nineteenth-century Russian peasantry was representative of all peasantries,[9] the comparative exercise is still instructive. First, it highlights the extent of variation in institutional arrangements such as 'serfdom' over time and space. There are broad similarities which make it possible to talk about something like 'serfdom' in both of these cases, while, at the same time, the significant differences make clear that there was no single system of 'serfdom' across Europe or across the centuries. Second, this comparison can indicate the extent to which 'institutions' – including formal rules which govern the society – influence behaviour. Do, for instance, different legal environments result in different economic and social outcomes?

This chapter focuses on several aspects of what we might call the 'institutional context' of serfdom. In the following section, the practice of serfdom in Russia is compared to serfdom in medieval England. The comparison focuses on three key components of rural society in these two societies: the community, the manor, and the state (or, more specifically, the law). The final section of the chapter looks at the implications of the similarities and differences. It is concluded that, despite certain general similarities, these two forms of 'serfdom' differed significantly, because they were embedded in fundamentally different institutional systems.

---

8 For a comprehensive account, see P. Gatrell, 'Historians and peasants: studies of medieval English society in a Russian context', *Past and Present* 96 (1982), 22–50; also, E. A. Kosminsky, 'Russian work on English economic history', *Economic History Review* 1 (1928), 208–33.

9 As in A. Macfarlane, *The origins of English individualism. The family, property, and social transition* (Oxford, 1978).

A preliminary warning is in order, for those readers who may be unaware of the very different literatures and archival sources being compared here: such an undertaking is necessarily somewhat removed from local detail. Much is abstracted from what a discussion of any particular society would need to take into account. Variation within each of the two societies, as well as change over time, are neglected in the interests of focusing attention on the broader qualitative differences between two institutional contexts. It is hoped that the resulting perspective will nonetheless cast new light on the question of serfdom, which historians of both societies will find interesting.

Communities, landlords, and states

The community

The similarities in the literatures on the nature and role of village communities in medieval England and pre-emancipation Russia are remarkable, considering how far apart in space and time these two serf societies were.[10] In both cases, the historiography has been characterised by lively debates between those who adhere to a 'communal autonomy' view of cohesive, independent communities, united against (and to some extent impervious to) 'outside' forces, especially the landlord or the state, and proponents of the 'manorial dominance' view of peasant communities as mere appendages of the feudal estate system.[11] And in both literatures, a more nuanced view of the village community has emerged in more recent years, based on detailed, empirical research for specific localities.[12]

---

10 This may be, to some extent, because the peasant community was the focus of many Russian historians of medieval England, including Vinogradov and others of his generation.
11 These views are outlined in greater detail in Dennison and Ogilvie, 'Serfdom and social capital'; and Ogilvie, 'Communities and the "second serfdom"'. They were given their most explicit articulation in the nineteenth-century Russian debates between the 'statists' (represented by Chicherin) and the 'slavophiles' (represented by Aksakov). The communal autonomy view for medieval England is perhaps most closely associated with the work of the 'Toronto School'. See, for instance, J. A. Raftis, *Tenure and mobility: studies in the social history of the medieval English village* (Toronto, 1964); E. Britton, *The community of the vill: a study of the history of the family and village life in fourteenth-century England* (Toronto, 1977).
12 An accessible overview for medieval England can be found in C. Dyer, 'Were late medieval English villages "self-contained"?', in *The self-contained village? The social history of rural communities, 1250–1900*, ed. C. Dyer (Hatfield, 2007), pp. 6–27. On

Villagers in both societies were more mobile than assumed by conventional views of serfdom. Rural communities were neither isolated nor autarkic; serfs in Russia and medieval England engaged in labour, credit, and land transactions beyond the boundaries of their local manors or estates. The existence of rural factor markets and the frequency of contact with 'outsiders' meant that serfs were less dependent on kin than older theories, especially those of Alexander Chayanov, have maintained. Both societies were characterised by a significant degree of socio-economic stratification and intra-communal conflict. Communities did have some degree of independence, as adherents of the 'communal autonomy' view have argued, but they were also integrated into larger feudal structures – though they were not, as the 'manorial dominance' view maintains, simply extensions of the manorial apparatus.

But looking beyond these superficial similarities, striking differences can be observed. The community – or commune – in Russian serf society was a formal corporate entity, which raised its own funds and assumed collective responsibility for a set of clearly defined obligations. Nearly all feudal burdens were levied collectively. Quitrents were assigned as a lump sum for communal officials to allocate among households. Labour obligations and recruitment levies were assigned in the same way, as was the state poll tax, for which all male serfs were assessed. Access to woodland and pasture was granted to the commune as a whole; rights to these resources were assigned to households by communal officials. Communes were responsible for selecting members to fill posts ranging from reeve or steward to tax collectors and constables.[13] They were supposed to use their collective funds to pay these officials, and to provide relief to their poorer members.[14]

While similar examples exist for medieval England – state taxes, and some feudal obligations, such as *tallage*, were apparently levied collectively – the community, it seems, was not formally institutionalised to the same extent. Indeed, from the Russianist's perspective, it is remarkable how much space is devoted in the literature on medieval England to defining

Russian communities, the work of Steven Hoch and Edgar Melton has been especially illuminating.

13 Wealthy landlords frequently hired outsiders as managers and to oversee the elected officials.

14 An overview of the Russian peasant commune can be found in D. Moon, *The Russian peasantry 1600–1930: the world the peasants made* (London, 1999). See also Dennison, *Institutional framework*, chap. 4.

what the community *was* in any given context. In some cases, the emphasis is on the village community; in others it is the parish community or the manorial community. It is clear that there were certain things medieval communities did: they coordinated agrarian production, they managed village resources, and they even monitored their neighbours' activities. But membership in medieval communities could be viewed as 'fluid and insecure'[15] in stark contrast to serf Russia, where membership was strictly and clearly defined. It is particularly relevant that feudal obligations and customary rights were not collectivised in medieval England; it was an individual's own legal status or the holding itself that determined rights and obligations.

Tenurial arrangements offer the clearest manifestation of these differences. The most distinguishing characteristic of the Russian peasant commune was communal land tenure. In Russia, the land allocated to serfs for their own use was given to the commune as a whole, rather than to individual households.[16] On quitrent estates, feudal dues were usually attached (and proportional) to this land, such that, in taking on an allotment, a serf household also accepted the obligation to pay a corresponding proportion of the total quitrent levy. In most cases, it was up to communal officials to allocate the land – and thus the tax burden – among member households. A serf's right to an allotment was therefore determined – but not guaranteed – by his (and sometimes her) membership in a commune. This was in contrast to medieval England, where it has been observed that

> property tenure was not vested in groups other than through various forms of joint-possession by which 'groups' had contracted to hold land or had inherited land as a set of individuals. In some circumstances, individuals might have certain common rights such as on the village waste for pasture, or within woods for pannage or fuel collecting. Access to those rights, however, was not acquired through membership of a group or residence within a village. Those rights were acquired through prior possession of land as an individual.[17]

---

15 P. R. Schofield, *Peasant and community in medieval England 1200–1500* (Basingstoke and London, 2003), p. 5.

16 This does not mean Russian peasants did not hold land privately in individual tenure – they did. But this was not estate land. The estate land allocated by lords for serfs' use was always held in communal tenure.

17 R. M. Smith, 'The English peasantry 1250–1650', in *The peasantries of Europe from*

Communal land tenure and 'collective responsibility' for feudal and
state obligations (including state taxes and conscription levies) had implications for the quality of village life in serf Russia. Because *all* obligations
were levied on the community as a whole, households that could not afford
to pay had to be subsidised by their neighbours. This gave rise in many
cases to forms of social control designed to ensure that households would
not default on their quitrent payments or their obligations to the state.
Neighbours scrutinised one another's behaviour carefully, and reported
indications of deviance to authorities.[18] Those deemed 'inadequate'
householders, including those who drank too much or engaged in other
behaviour detrimental to the household economy, were sent to the army or
even exiled to Siberia. Poorer serfs, especially widows with young children,
who were viewed as less likely to meet their obligations, were often deprived
of land, while larger shares were given to the more prosperous serfs, who
could be relied on to pay the attached fees.[19] Landlords (and state officials)
were largely uninterested in the way obligations were shared out, as long as
the work got done and rents and taxes were paid.

Collectively levied obligations came with the power to enforce them
– power usually vested by landlords in communal officials. Absentee
landlords were especially likely to grant communal officials the authority
to make decisions about their fellow serfs' requests to marry, to migrate,
to hire labourers, to practise a craft, or to buy or sell land. Most landlords
demanded communal approval for all such requests, since any of these
could potentially affect a household's economic viability. (Landlords
also retained the right to override any decision made by communal
authorities.) Serfs were generally required to live in complex, extended-
family households containing several able-bodied adults (fines and

---

the fourteenth to the eighteenth centuries, ed. T. Scott (London and New York, 1998),
pp. 339–71 (p. 340).

18   Estate archives contain a wealth of information on these forms of social control.
Some examples from the Sheremetyev family's Voshchazhnikovo estate include the case of
Ivan Sal'nikov, who was reported by his neighbours in 1825 for 'dissolute and disorderly
behaviour' and sent to Siberia (RGADA, f. 1287, op. 3, ed. khr. 941) and the cases of Yakov
Sheshunov, Andrei Plotnikov and Yegor Kalinin, who were all reported in 1807 for drunk-
enness and dissolution and subjected to corporal punishment by the authorities (RGADA,
f. 1287, op. 3, ed. khr. 661). Similar examples are reported by Steven Hoch for the Gagarin
family's Petrovskoe estate: S. L. Hoch, *Serfdom and social control in Russia: Petrovskoe, a
village in Tambov* (Chicago, 1986) esp. pp. 160–86.

19   Specific examples can be found in Dennison and Ogilvie, 'Serfdom and social capital',
esp. pp. 529–34.

other punishments were administered for non-compliance), since small households were viewed by authorities as economically precarious.[20]

The system of collective responsibility was convenient for the landlord, who could minimise administrative costs by forcing communal officials to allocate, collect, and deliver cash rents, allocate and organise labour obligations, and monitor the activities of their neighbours. It was less convenient for ordinary members of the community who found their behaviour closely scrutinised and their demographic and economic choices thwarted by fellow serfs, who were trying to ensure that their own households would not be required to subsidise others. Unfortunately for those who felt most constrained – such as unmarried women, the socially deviant, and the more entrepreneurial peasants – voluntary withdrawal from the commune was impossible, except in those rare cases when prosperous serfs were granted permission to purchase membership in another corporate entity (such as an urban guild).[21]

This is not to imply that communal coercion and social control were unknown to serfs in medieval England, nor that medieval village elites refrained from using their power to the disadvantage of their fellow serfs. But the kind of institutionalised, incentivised coercion we see in Russian serf communities was surely more constraining than the kind of social control we observe, more generally, in the average pre-industrial 'face-to-face' society without the extra communal reinforcement. The formal powers of village elites in medieval England, while indeed significant, were, it seems, considerably more limited than those of Russian communal officials, whose fiscal responsibilities and control over communally held resources gave them the authority to take important decisions about the distribution of taxes – state and feudal, as well as land and other resources within the community. While village elites in medieval England may have enjoyed considerable discretion in the allocation of lay subsidies,[22] they could not dictate how much land a serf household was entitled to nor

20 As shown by Hoch for the Petrovskoe estate, in *Serfdom and social control*; and Dennison for the Voshchazhnikovo estate in 'Serfdom and household structure in central Russia: Voshchazhnikovo, 1816–1858', *Continuity and Change* 18 (2003), 395–429.
21 Changes in status by serfs were usually noted in the soul revisions. Examples for the Sheremetyevs' Voshchazhnikovo estate can be found in RGADA, f. 1287, op. 3, ed. khr. 1941, 2553 (1834 and 1850).
22 C. Dyer, 'Taxation and communities in late medieval England', in *Progress and problems in medieval England: essays in honour of Edward Miller*, ed. R. Britnell and J. Hatcher (Cambridge, 1996), pp. 168–90.

the level of rents to be extracted from members. These arrangements were determined by custom (about which more will be said below) at the tenancy level rather than the community, or village, level.[23] Furthermore, there was considerable heterogeneity in tenants' legal statuses and the types of holdings on medieval English manors – free persons and villeins, for instance, could be (and were) tenants of the same lord, and reside in the same community, whereas one would not find free peasants as members of communes on Russian serf estates.[24] Similarly, it was not unusual for serfs in medieval England to reside in the same village community but owe obligations to different landlords.[25]

In order to better understand these differences, we must consider the larger institutional context within which serf communities were embedded.[26] Of particular importance is the manor or estate – the jurisdictional domain of the landlord. Indeed, what concrete knowledge we do have about serf communities in these two societies has been gleaned primarily from manorial records or, in the Russian case, archives of the wealthiest landlords. In both cases, the archival record makes clear that lordship could have significant effects on the nature and role of communities under serfdom.

The manor or estate

At first glance, there are, again, clear similarities at the manorial level in these two societies, especially in the juridical monopolies and rent-seeking

23   M. Müller, 'A divided class? Peasants and peasant communities in later medieval England', in *Rodney Hilton's middle ages: an exploration of historical themes*, ed. C. Dyer, P. Coss and C. Wickham (Oxford, 2007), pp. 115–31 (p. 125).
24   None of the local studies of Russian serf society undertaken so far has revealed the presence of free tenants in communes on landlords' estates.
25   While this may have had implications for community strength in England, one should probably refrain from making assertions of this sort in the comparative context, since multi-manor vills also existed under Russian serfdom. We still do not know enough, however, about the way these divided settlements functioned to draw even tentative conclusions about the relationship between residence patterns and communal strength in the Russian context and how this relationship compared with other serf societies. Still, it is worth emphasizing again that, in Russia, even in divided serf villages, feudal and state obligations would have been levied (and resources distributed) communally, creating the same incentives for coercion among those villagers obligated to the same feudal lord.
26   This point is made convincingly by Richard M. Smith in '"Modernization" and the corporate medieval village community in England: some sceptical reflections', in *Explorations in historical geography: interpretative essays*, ed. A. R. H. Baker and D. Gregory (Cambridge, 1984), pp. 140–79.

powers of landlords. Landlords in both societies were entitled to labour services or rents in cash and kind from serf tenants. Under both forms of serfdom, landlords were capable of interfering in the demographic decisions of their tenants, particularly marriage and migration, as well as inheritance practices. Landlords in both societies extracted additional fees for – to name just a few activities – marriage, mobility, and property transfers, as well as for manorial services (which serfs were often forced to use), from milling and distilling to contract enforcement and dispute resolution. Furthermore, in both societies, there was considerable variation in the way landlords managed their estates and made use of the powers at their disposal.

Once more, however, the similarities on the surface mask profound underlying differences. Medieval English manors, from the Russianist's point of view, were characterised by a remarkable degree of uniformity. Particularly striking was the widespread existence of manorial courts, which, while mostly concerned with upholding the rule of the lord of the manor and regulating the agrarian economy, also offered a broad (and varying) range of additional services to tenants – both free and unfree – including contract enforcement for a variety of land and credit transactions. Medieval historians have pointed out that there was significant variation in the customary laws upheld by these courts; much depended on the rule of the manor in question.[27] Just the notion that there *was* some form of customary law that manorial courts were there to enforce and uphold distinguishes medieval English serfdom from the later, Russian version.

On Russian serf estates there was no institutional equivalent to the manor court. Unlike medieval English lords, few Russian landlords offered judicial services to their serfs, and, as far as we can tell, none operated anything like a formal court. At the more institutionally precocious end of the spectrum, there were landlords like the wealthy Sheremetyev family, who offered their serfs contract enforcement services and a form of extra-local dispute resolution. But the system was administered from distant St Petersburg (their estates were scattered across seventeen provinces) and judgments relied on petitions and written reports from chosen 'jurors' and officials.[28] At the other end of the spectrum, were those landlords who left

27   As discussed in L. Bonfield, 'What did English villagers mean by "customary law"?', in *Medieval society and the manor court*, ed. Z. Razi and R. M. Smith (Oxford, 1996), pp. 103–16.
28   This is evident from documents in the Sheremetyev family archive: RGADA, f. 1287 and RGIA, f. 1088. A detailed description of this system is in T. Dennison, 'Contract

the day-to-day management of their estates, including dispute resolution, to communal authorities.[29] In between was a range of possibilities, including noble families like the Gagarins, who hired outside officials to reside on and run their estates. These employees were charged with direct intervention in all local affairs; decisions related to disputes and other issues related to estate management were made by the steward himself, in consultation with the landlord.[30] The degree of variation in the governance of estates appears to have been far higher in Russia than in medieval England.

This brings us back to the nature and role of local communities. In both serf societies an inverse relationship existed between community strength and the strength of lordship. Yet the relationship seems to have been much stronger in the Russian context. This may be because, in medieval England, the system of manorial courts (along with the absence of collective responsibility) constrained the powers of the village elite through the enforcement of customary law (about which more will be said shortly) and by making legal recourse accessible (or at least relatively accessible) to all tenants of the manor. Indeed there was no fee for initiating a case about debt, trespass, or breach of contract in the manor court. Thus poorer tenants, including widows, appear as plaintiffs in medieval court rolls, in contrast to the records for Russian estates where such people appear infrequently.[31] Such tenants could also apparently make use of the court's contract enforcement services, appearing as parties to credit and land transactions. This is not to claim that poorer tenants in medieval England were always everywhere on equal legal footing with their better-off neighbours. The village elite clearly had significant powers: as manorial officials they could influence which cases got to court; as jurors, they could influence outcomes. Village elites usually had considerable informal authority as well, thanks to wealth and extensive familial and social networks.[32]

enforcement in Russian serf society, 1750–1860', *Economic History Review* 66 (2013), 715–32.

29   As on the estate described by Edgar Melton in 'The magnate and her trading peasants in serf Russia: the Countess Lieven and the Baki estate, 1800–20', *Jahrbücher für Geschichte Osteuropas* 47 (1999), 40–55.

30   As discussed in Hoch, *Serfdom and social control*.

31   Concrete examples for medieval England can be found in L. R. Poos and L. Bonfield (eds), *Select cases in manorial courts 1250–1550: property and family law* (London, 1998). For Russia, see T. K. Dennison, 'Did serfdom matter? Russian rural society 1750–1860', *Historical Research* 79 (2006), 74–89.

32   S. Olson, 'Jurors of the village court: local leadership before and after the plague

Russian serf elites had all these powers, and no system of manorial courts – no customary law – to constrain them. Even where lordship was strong, and where the landlord provided extra-local conflict resolution services, there were large numbers of petitions from middling and poorer serfs against communal officials for corrupt practices, including embezzlement, illegal confiscation of land, taking bribes, double taxation, false imprisonment, and other such offences. Sheremetyev officials in St Petersburg demonstrated a willingness to rule against these powerful serfs if accusations could be justified, but the number of complaints in the archive indicates that communal elites continued to abuse their powers despite the threat of landlord intervention. Moreover, despite the Sheremetyevs' quasi-formal administrative framework, the poor had very few protections. They were denied communal land because they could not pay the attached feudal dues, they could not afford to pay bribes to communal officials, and they were excluded from formal channels of credit and other 'legal' market transactions since they could not afford the fees the Sheremetyevs demanded for their contract enforcement services. Poor serfs were even denied relief from communal funds; requests for assistance from poor young widows were regularly turned down by officials. All these serfs could do in such instances was petition the landlord to take pity on them.[33]

Most Russian estates lacked even a quasi-formal legal-administrative apparatus.[34] On these estates, poorer and other marginalised serfs were left entirely to the mercy of communal officials, whose main interests were allocating resources to themselves and their associates, and pushing rents and obligations onto others and away from themselves. On the Baki estate in Kostroma province, the communal oligarchs were so powerful they managed

in Ellington, Huntingdonshire', *Journal of British Studies* 30 (1991), 237–56; Schofield, *Peasant and community*, esp. pp. 120–4.

33   As in the cases of poor serf widows Vera Petrova in 1822 (RGADA, f. 1287, op. 3, ed. khr. 844) and Avdotia Stulova in 1849 (RGADA, f. 1287, op. 3, ed. khr. 850). Other examples are discussed in Dennison, *Institutional framework*, pp. 113–17.

34   This would have been especially true of so-called 'state peasants' (serfs of the crown), who are often assumed to have enjoyed greater freedom than proprietary serfs, since they were not ruled by landlords, but by state officials who demanded annual rents and taxes from them without the day-to-day oversight of local landlords. It is unlikely, however, that a lack of access to extra-local legal recourse (as unfree peasants they were still largely excluded from civil institutions) implied greater freedom. In fact, numerous constraints on their freedom are detailed in N. M. Druzhinin, *Gosudarstvennye Krest'iane i Reforma P. D. Kiseleva* (Moscow, 1946), esp. pp. 25–30.

to persuade the (absentee) landlord to dismiss the estate steward and allow them to manage local affairs, despite protests from the other villagers who claimed that the oligarchs routinely abused their authority, using positions of power to benefit themselves at the expense of their neighbours.[35]

The absence of a customary law to which Russian serfs could appeal had other important implications. On medieval English manors, there appears to have been a familiar set of servile obligations, such as *tallage, chevage, merchet*. The precise levies and the extent of enforcement may have varied from place to place, but the same kinds of obligations regularly appear in accounts of manorial economies. While this is broadly true of Russian serfdom, there was, again, much greater variability. All Russian serf estates demanded basic obligations in either labour or cash. Most of the largest serf-owning families demanded fees for marriage beyond estate boundaries, for migration, for approval of land transactions. Beyond these broad similarities, we observe significant variation in rents and taxes across estates. The Sheremetyev family levied taxes on all forms of economic activity (land transactions, hiring of labour, practising a craft), on undesirable demographic behaviour (such as remaining unmarried), demanded fees for legal services (drawing up a contract, filing it, hearing a dispute), and levied fines for breaking any of the more than a hundred rules and regulations set out in the estate 'instructions'.[36] The Gagarin family, on the other hand, did not bother with fees, fines, and taxes; they prohibited certain activities (migration, hiring labour, wage-earning, remaining unmarried) and relied mainly on corporal punishment and physical coercion to achieve compliance with their policies.[37]

Moreover, where medieval English serfs could protest against violations of their customary rights,[38] Russian landlords had the legal authority to raise their rent demands, levy new fees and taxes, and even expropriate serfs of their land and goods. This does not, of course, mean that all landlords did these things; it was in the interests of most to ensure

---

35 Melton, 'The magnate'.

36 As in RGADA, f. 1287, op. 3, ed. khr. 555 ('Instructions for years 1796/1800').

37 The Gagarins' enforcement policies are discussed in detail in Hoch, *Serfdom and social control*.

38 J. Hatcher, 'English serfdom and villeinage: towards a reassessment', *Past and Present* 90 (1981), 3–39; D. Crook, 'Freedom, villeinage and legal process: the dispute between the Abbot of Burton and his tenants of Mickleover, 1280', *Nottingham Medieval Studies* 44 (2000), 123–40; C. Dyer, 'Memories of freedom: attitudes toward serfdom in England 1200–1350', in *Serfdom and slavery*, ed. Bush, pp. 277–95.

that their serfs could continue to provide the rents and labour services they relied on. But the inherent uncertainty and the enormous scope for confiscation of surpluses must have had considerable implications for the Russian rural economy.

The state and the law

The contrasts outlined above almost certainly derived from larger institutional differences related to the role of the state and the legal framework within which serfdom existed in these two societies. One particularly striking feature of serfdom in medieval England is the extent to which there really was something like a coherent system of state law, within which manors and communities were embedded. This might strike some as ironic, since Russian serfdom was a phenomenon of the early modern – and by some conventions even modern – period, by which time the state in western Europe was much stronger and more centralised than in the medieval period. But England and Russia seem to have been at opposite extremes within Europe, with the central state in England emerging much earlier than on the Continent and the Russian state remaining (internally) weak for much longer.

In both Russia and medieval England, villages and manors were part of a larger institutional framework. In England, at least by the end of the twelfth century, this meant a system of law, extending outward from the Crown, into which local institutions, such as manorial courts, were integrated.[39] The existence of a unifying legal framework, grounded in a common law, seems to have had important implications for the practice of serfdom in England. The growing influence of the royal courts and the common law placed certain checks on landlords' powers over their tenants. Landlords 'were aware of the looming presence of the state, which inhibited [their] powers of justice through enquiries into franchises, and offered the peasants at least a hope of protection'.[40] While it is unlikely that tenants commonly brought suit against landlords in the royal courts – the risk involved must have been very high[41] – it is still plausible that

39   P. Brand, 'The formation of the English legal system, 1150–1400', in *Legislation and justice*, ed. A. Padoa-Schioppa (Oxford, 1997), pp. 103–22; A. L. Brown, *The governance of late medieval England 1272–1461* (London, 1989).

40   C. Dyer, 'The ineffectiveness of lordship in England, 1200–1400', in *Rodney Hilton's middle ages*, ed. Dyer, Coss and Wickham, pp. 69–86 (p. 75).

41   Some serfs, however, were undeterred. See the accounts in Crook, 'Freedom, villeinage and legal process'; Dyer, 'Memories of freedom'.

the mere existence of legal recourse beyond the manor had a significant impact on the landlord–tenant relationship. Furthermore, the royal courts were not the only option for extra-local legal recourse. Recent research on debt litigation in the thirteenth and fourteenth centuries provides compelling evidence of attempts by some manorial courts to compete for revenues by offering their services to a larger pool of plaintiffs.[42] The efforts certain lords took to stop their tenants from making use of alternative legal channels suggests that this competition was having some effect.[43] The result for tenants – free tenants, mainly – was greater choice in the court to which they brought their suits.

These legal developments had implications for serfs, too. Serfs' options were more constrained, as they were legally obliged to use their landlords' courts, but the changes introduced in some localities (and at least partly in their efforts to attract litigants) are thought to have benefited serfs as well as free tenants. There is evidence, for instance, that manorial courts in some regions began to adopt the language and procedures of the royal courts, including the use of written records as evidence for a wide variety of transactions.[44] Written records of court transactions enabled landlords to defend their rights to customary obligations from tenants in the case of challenges in the royal courts. It has been noted, however, that this practice also protected tenants, free and unfree, from arbitrary attempts – by their landlords and others – to deprive them of their lands or make other arbitrary demands of them. It is remarkable (at least to a historian of the 'second' serfdom) the extent to which serfs and free persons in medieval England had regular contact with the central state[45] and were integrated into the same increasingly universal system of law.[46]

The institutional context for Russian serfs was very different. In Russia, 'public law effectively stopped at the gates to the estate'.[47] Serfs were not only the legal subjects of their lords, they were considered their personal

---

42   C. Briggs, 'Manor court procedures, debt litigation levels, and rural credit provision in England, c.1290–c.1380', *Law and History Review* 24 (2006), 519–58.

43   C. Briggs, 'Seigniorial control of villagers' litigation beyond the manor in later medieval England', *Historical Research* 81 (2008), 399–422.

44   Smith, 'English peasantry'; Smith, '"Modernization" and the corporate medieval village'.

45   As discussed in Schofield, *Peasant and community*, pp. 169–85.

46   This is made strikingly clear in P. R. Hyams, 'What did Edwardian villagers understand by "law"?', in *Medieval society*, ed. Razi and Smith, pp. 69–102.

47   R. Bartlett, 'Serfdom and state power in imperial Russia', *European History Quarterly* 33 (2003), 29–64 (p. 48).

property. (It is perhaps worth pointing out here that a Russian serf would never have been referred to as a *tenant*, a term which implies some kind of contractual relationship.) Russian serfs could be sold, expropriated, physically abused, forced to marry or migrate, subjected to new and more onerous obligations, and they had no legal recourse beyond their own estates. The absence of formal checks on landlord power gave ample scope for abuses of this sort. But the lack of a larger legal framework – even a recognised form of local customary law – had more mundane and much more far-reaching implications. Serfs were not legally permitted to own land before 1848, and they were denied access to civil institutions (they could not bring cases to civil courts) before emancipation in 1861. These restrictions pushed much of their economic activity into the informal sector, where transactions involved a greater amount of risk. Serfs could purchase land in the names of their landlords, for instance, but they had no recourse should their landlords later decide to confiscate this land. They could engage in credit transactions but they had no legal recourse should a borrower fail to repay or relinquish collateral. They could establish rural manufactories, but they had little recourse against the confiscation of their capital. Their ambiguous legal status meant serfs were often forced to pay bribes for access to goods and services they could not obtain through formal channels.[48]

Even on estates like those of the Sheremetyev family, where there was a quasi-formal rule of law (the Sheremetyevs, as we have seen, offered contract enforcement services and were quite conscientious about upholding property rights), recourse did not extend beyond the estate. This not only meant that serfs could not stop the Sheremetyevs themselves from interfering in their economic affairs, but that they could only engage in transactions that were enforceable through the Sheremetyevs' administrative framework. These constraints become especially apparent in credit transactions, where Sheremetyev serfs borrowed extensively from outsiders and free persons (who could rely on the Sheremetyevs to force their serfs to repay) but lent only to other Sheremetyev serfs (since the Sheremetyev family had no authority over other lords' serfs or free persons).[49] Furthermore, as noted earlier, the fees charged for these services put them out of reach of the poorer serfs.

48 In some instances, bribes are even openly recorded in serfs' communal account books. The Sheremetyev family archive contains examples: RGADA, f. 1287, op. 3, ed. khr. 141 (for the year 1750), 189 (for the year 1754) and 530 (for the year 1787).
49 Dennison, *Institutional framework*, esp. pp. 186–93.

On estates without any legal-administrative system, serfs were at the mercy of their neighbours as well as their landlords. Communal land tenure and communal liability for obligations gave communal officials extensive powers over fellow villagers. Communal elites could expropriate their neighbours of land, extract additional rents from them, deny them relief from communal funds, force them to pay bribes, and prohibit land transactions, and there was very little the victims could do, especially if village elites were able, as on the Baki estate, to convince the landlord that this was in everyone's best interest. Not only was there no legal recourse for exploited villagers, it was virtually impossible for serfs to opt out of communal membership.

Outcomes and implications

There are many ways in which English and Russian serf societies were alike. They had similar institutional components: village communities, manors, central states. They shared many shortcomings of the institutional system we refer to generally as 'serfdom'. In both societies, economic growth and development were undermined by legal constraints on mobility and access to extra-local justice. Even in medieval England, where the law put greater checks on lordship, the balance of power strongly favoured landlords, whose rights to extract obligations from tenants must have created some disincentive among peasants for the generation of surpluses. Similarly, and perhaps ironically, serfdom in both forms created strong disincentives for innovation by the landowning classes – those with the wealth to undertake major investments – by guaranteeing them rents from enserfed tenants. It is not so surprising, given these constraints, that there was no industrial revolution in medieval England or in eighteenth-century Russia.

Still, a closer look reveals some very significant differences. In the medieval English case, the terms of tenancy were anchored in customary law, which was integrated, increasingly it seems, into a larger body of common law. This legal context seems to have placed at least some limits on the exploitative powers of landlords and village elites, creating, as a result, a greater degree of security of property than one would find in rural Russia under serfdom. If the scope for arbitrariness were reduced, there would have been less risk involved in economic transactions, making even unfree tenants more willing to engage in them. Indeed we do observe lively markets in land, labour, credit, and goods in medieval England in which serfs were regular participants. The extensive credit markets observed in medieval Cambridgeshire, with participants from a wide range of socio-economic strata, have no equivalent in eighteenth-century Russia.[50] There is much more abundant evidence for land market transactions in East Anglian manor court rolls than what we find in the archives of Russian seigniorial estates.[51] Access to these markets may have given serf households in medieval England more possibilities for economic diversification than were available to Russian serfs. This, in turn, may have reduced the extent to which the medieval English serf household was forced to rely on kin and neighbours for assistance.[52]

In Russia, where estates were not integrated into any larger legal framework, and serfs were explicitly excluded from any kind of civil law, serfdom was significantly more oppressive. It is no coincidence that Russian serfdom has so often been compared to American slavery.[53] Landlords could do what they wanted with their serfs, short of killing them (and even that prohibition was not always enforced). Archival records indicate that they could – and in certain cases did – expropriate the property of serfs,[54] buy and sell individual serfs without land,[55] levy new taxes and obligations,[56] and force serfs to work for others while confiscating their wages.[57] Even on those estates with a system in place for the enforcement of contracts and the upholding of property rights, and where participation in markets was merely taxed but not prohibited, serfs faced considerable risks. Because these local systems were not integrated into any larger body of law, serfs' rights were not acknowledged beyond

50   C. Briggs, *Credit and village society in fourteenth-century England* (Oxford, 2009).

51   Smith, 'English peasantry'; R. M. Smith, 'A periodic market and its impact upon a manorial community: Botesdale, Suffolk and the manor of Redgrave, 1280–1300', in *Medieval society*, ed. Razi and Smith, pp. 450–81; Dennison, *Institutional framework*, chap. 5.

52   As indicated in R. M. Smith, 'Kin and neighbors in a thirteenth-century Suffolk community', *Journal of Family History* 4 (1979), 219–56.

53   P. Kolchin, *Unfree labor: American slavery and Russian serfdom* (Cambridge, MA, 1987).

54   Some examples are given in J. Blum, *Lord and peasant in Russia from the ninth to the nineteenth century* (Princeton, 1961), pp. 434–5.

55   This practice was permitted until the late eighteenth century.

56   Landlords periodically revised the rules and regulations by which their estates were governed with updates to the inventory of obligations.

57   As on the Gagarin family's Manuilovskoe estate described by R. D. Bohac in 'Family, property, and socioeconomic mobility: Russian peasants on Manuilovskoe estate, 1810–1861' (unpublished Ph.D. thesis, University of Illinois at Urbana-Champaign, 1982).

the boundaries of the estate. Their ambiguous legal status made them easy targets for provincial and ecclesiastical officials who could extract bribes for access to services that could not be procured legally. Furthermore, while families like the Sheremetyevs allowed their serfs to purchase land and hold it in individual tenure, there was no extra-local recourse in the case of expropriation. The informal nature of this legal framework would almost certainly have raised concerns about continuity in the commitment of a new generation of landlords to the system devised by their predecessors. After all, there was nothing to stop a landlord's heir from putting an entirely different administrative framework in place. These constraints would surely have had some effect on the willingness of serfs to undertake risks associated with innovation in agriculture or rural industry. The disadvantages to poorer serfs – who could not afford to pay bribes, had restricted access to communal land, and could not afford to register their land and credit transactions – cannot be emphasised enough.

The property rights, the factor markets, the approximation to a rule of law shared by these two serf societies, while superficially similar, were embedded in two quite different institutional systems. In the English case, they were increasingly situated within a framework of interlocking legal institutions extending from the crown to the manor; in Russia, they were situated within a kind of 'composite state' of territorial mini-sovereignties ruled by grandees whose subjects were denied any sort of integration into a larger legal framework. The analogous institutional components apparently shared by these two societies had very different consequences and a very different significance within these two contexts (differences that would not be captured by a 'box-ticking' approach). The institutional components constituting 'serfdom' had significant effects in both places; they constrained growth and opportunities, especially to the poorest. But they led to (relatively) more benign outcomes in one context than the other because the overall institutional framework prevented the worst abuses and, over time, appears to have evolved in a way that undermined the system of serfdom itself. In the other case, the institutional paralysis spilled over even into the post-emancipation era, with the codification of communal land tenure and collective responsibility for taxes, as well as the establishment of a separate body of law to govern the 'former serfs'. In the second case, the economic and social effects of a weakly developed system of law, incorporating institutions at the local level, can still be observed in the present day.

Choices and Constraints in the
Pre-Industrial Countryside

SHEILAGH OGILVIE

This chapter addresses a central tension between two sides of rural history – one stressing peasant choices, the other the constraints on those choices. For the one side, key concepts are 'individualism', 'autonomy', 'rationality', 'voluntarism', and 'agency'. For the other, they are 'class struggle', 'exploitation', 'extra-economic coercion', 'social structure', and 'institutions'. This chapter argues that both strands of analysis can deepen our understanding of the pre-industrial countryside – not just in England but in many other societies. But pursuing the one and ignoring the other can lead us astray. Only by attentiveness both to people's choices and to the constraints on those choices can we arrive at a just understanding of the particular rural society we are studying and of rural development more widely.

Choices

Let us begin by considering whether rural people in pre-industrial societies really did have choices, in the sense of deciding, as individuals, between two or more possibilities. It is surprising how often one still encounters views to the contrary, sometimes explicit, sometimes implicit and hardly recognised by the scholars who enunciate them. These views take four main forms.

First is the view put forward by Alexander Chayanov and his modern followers, that peasants were governed by a mentality that did not view certain aspects of life as choice variables. So in the Chayanovian view, peasants do not make individual choices about labour, capital, farm size, technology, market participation, or consumption style. Instead, their cultural norms cause them to engage in self-exploitation (i.e., to go on putting labour into the farm past the point at which an individual agent making rational choices would stop), avoid debt and credit (i.e., to accept the ups and downs of consumption and production and not try to smooth them by borrowing or lending), retain the family farm at all costs (i.e., not buy or sell land to adjust to changes in prices or technology), avoid markets (i.e., not choose between self-consumption or market sales), and consume only traditional goods (i.e., not choose new consumer objects even when they are available).

According to this view, a deeply rooted peasant mentality so strongly guided rural people's behaviour that they could not – or at least did not – make individual choices about labour, capital, land, technology, markets or consumption. These assumptions are still often applied to rural societies, both historical and modern.[1] Werner Rösener, for instance, portrays medieval German peasants as avoiding markets, ignoring profits, pursuing limited aims, valuing land for its own sake (even when unprofitable), working for below-market wages, preferring leisure to income, seeking culturally defined consumption targets, and undertaking activities that were 'economically speaking, unprofitable'.[2] Peter Kriedte, Hans Medick and Jürgen Schlumbohm describe early modern European peasants and rural artisans as not making individual choices about costs, profits, or accumulation, but rather being guided by a Chayanovian mentality of 'limited goals'.[3] Many historians of Russia ascribe the country's centuries

---

1   See, for instance, E. R. Wolf, *Peasants* (Englewood Cliffs, NJ, 1966), pp. 12–17 and 37–50; T. Shanin, 'Introduction: peasantry as a concept', in *Peasants and peasant societies*, ed. T. Shanin (London, 1971), pp. 11–19; D. Thorner, 'Peasant economy as a category in history', in *Peasants and peasant societies*, ed. Shanin, pp. 202–18; F. Ellis, *Peasant economics: farm households and agrarian development* (Cambridge, 1988), pp. 5–6; P. C. Huang, *The peasant economy and social change in north China* (Stanford, CA, 1985), pp. 3–6. For a historiographical overview, see C. Dipper, 'Bauern als Gegenstand der Sozialgeschichte', in *Sozialgeschichte in Deutschland. Entwicklungen und Perspektiven im internationalen Zusammenhang, vol. 4: Soziale Gruppen in der Geschichte*, ed. W. Schieder and V. Sellin (Göttingen, 1987), pp. 9–33.
2   W. Rösener, *Peasants in the middle ages* (Urbana and Chicago, 1992), pp. 122–5 and 142.
3   P. Kriedte, H. Medick and J. Schlumbohm, *Industrialization before industrialization: rural industry in the genesis of capitalism* (Cambridge, 1981), pp. 41, 43–6, 52–3, 99–100, 106–8 and 114–15.

of economic stagnation, its divergence from western Europe, and the difficulties of its twentieth-century history, to a distinctive peasant culture.[4] According to all these scholars, rural people did not make individual choices but followed the dictates of peasant mentalities.

The second variant of this view recognises the existence of choice-making behaviour by rural individuals in *some* pre-modern societies but regards these as exceptional enclaves within the prevailing regime of peasant culture. That is, rural people were willing and able to make individual choices in some parts of Europe but not in others. Alan Macfarlane, for instance, argues that medieval and early modern England had a uniquely 'individualistic' culture that led its rural people to regard as choice variables many things – land transactions, labour market participation, credit, market participation, marriage – which peasants on the European continent regarded as beyond the realm of choice.[5] David Landes extends this view to the eighteenth century, arguing that England had a culture which regarded most aspects of life as subject to individual, rational decision-making; this, he argues, led to England's economic primacy compared with other parts of Europe where such individual choice was culturally unacceptable.[6] Tine De Moor and Jan Luiten van Zanden pursue the same argument, but include the Low Countries, arguing that together with England it formed a distinctive North Sea region, characterised by a culture in which individuals made their own choices about marriage, women's work, inheritance, and marital property rights; in other parts of Europe, and places such as China, they contend, individual choice in such matters was culturally inadmissible.[7] Many scholars who observe peasants making individual choices ascribe it to cultural influences

4   O. Figes, *Peasant Russia, civil war: the Volga countryside in revolution (1917–1921)* (Oxford, 1989), pp. 8–13; B. Mironov, 'The Russian peasant commune: after the reforms of the 1860s', in *The world of the Russian peasant: post-Emancipation culture and society*, ed. B. Eklof and S. Frank (Boston and London, 1990), pp. 7–44; B. Mironov, 'When and why was the Russian peasantry emancipated?', in *Serfdom and slavery: studies in legal bondage*, ed. M. L. Bush (Harlow, 1996), pp. 323–47 (p. 333); J. Pallot, *Land reform in Russia, 1906–1917: peasant responses to Stolypin's project of rural transformation* (Oxford, 1999), pp. 15–17 and 242–9; O. Figes, *Natasha's dance: a cultural history of Russia* (London, 2002), p. 258.
5   A. Macfarlane, *The origins of English individualism. The family, property and social transition* (Oxford, 1978).
6   D. S. Landes, *The wealth and poverty of nations: why some are so rich and some so poor* (London, 1999), *passim*.
7   T. De Moor and J. L. van Zanden, 'Girl power: the European marriage pattern and

from England or western Europe. In 1809, when the Wupper Valley in the Ruhr became one of the first German regions to set up cotton factories, a traveller described it as 'an England in miniature'.[8] More recently, Renate Blickle has argued that early modern Bavarian peasants shifted from a subsistence-oriented 'principle of needs' to individual, profit-maximizing choices only because of English 'liberal ideas, especially liberal conceptions of property'.[9] Winfried Schulze suggests that the individual choice-making economic behaviour observed among early modern peasants in Germany *east* of the Elbe resulted from the 'individualistic legal system' in their western German culture of origin, and could not have been found among Polish or Hungarian peasants at the same period.[10] All these scholars see peasant choice-making before c.1750 as restricted to certain cultures, particularly those of western Europe.

A third version of this idea ascribes the putative absence of peasant choice to serfdom, under which landlords are supposed to have suppressed all individual agency among serfs.[11] When Lieslott Enders pointed out widespread evidence of individual choices made by serfs in the Uckermark of Brandenburg, for instance, other scholars dismissed it on the grounds that the Uckermark had an atypical and fragmented form of serfdom compared with 'true' serf societies such as Schleswig-Holstein where 'probably this individualised form of behaviour did not exist'.[12] Others

labour markets in the North Sea region in the late medieval and early modern period', *Economic History Review* 63 (2010), 1–33 (pp. 6–9 and 11–12).

8   Quoted according to J. Engelbrecht, *Das Herzogtum Bern im Zeitalter der Französischen Revolution. Modernisierungsprozesse zwischen bayerischem und französischem Modell* (Paderborn, 1996), p. 10.

9   R. Blickle, 'From subsistence to property: traces of a fundamental change in early modern Bavaria', *Central European History* 25 (1992), 377–85; R. Blickle, 'Hausnotdurft. Ein Fundamentalrecht in der altständischen Ordnung Bayerns', in *Grund- und Freiheitsrechte von der ständischen zur spätbürgerlichen Gesellschaft*, ed. G. Birtsch (Göttingen, 1987), pp. 42–62.

10   As quoted in H. Kaak, 'Diskussionsbericht', in *Gutsherrschaft als soziales Modell. Vergleichende Betrachtungen zur Funktionsweise frühneuzeitlicher Agrargesellschaften*, ed. J. Peters (Munich, 1995), 439–502 (pp. 458–9).

11   This view of serfdom is described and criticised for medieval England in J. Hatcher, 'English serfdom and villeinage: towards a reassessment', *Past and Present* 90 (1981), 3–39 (pp. 3–8); for early modern Bohemia in S. Ogilvie, 'Communities and the "second serfdom" in early modern Bohemia', *Past and Present* 187 (2005), 69–119 (pp. 72–3); and for both Bohemia and Russia in T. K. Dennison and S. Ogilvie, 'Serfdom and social capital in Bohemia and Russia', *Economic History Review* 60 (2007), 513–44.

12   As quoted in Kaak, 'Diskussionsbericht', p. 457.

argued that Uckermark peasants manifested individual economic choices only because of their proximity to Berlin, and that German serfs uninfluenced by such large urban centres pursued the limited aims of the traditional 'family economy', avoided markets, and did not make individual choices oriented around costs and profits before 1750 at the earliest.[13] True serfdom, it is assumed, stifled all peasant choice.

The fourth variant of this approach contends that peasants were too poor to make choices: they merely responded to necessity. If we observe peasants borrowing money, for instance, it is because they were forced to do so by the threat of starvation, not because they wanted to smooth their production and consumption choices over time.[14] If we see peasants participating in market transactions, it was because they were being forced to pay feudal dues in cash, not because they were choosing between market and non-market options.[15] If we detect peasants working more hours, it is because they were compelled to do so by rising food prices and falling real wages, not because they were making individual choices about allocating time between labour and other activities.[16] If we observe peasants introducing innovations to increase the productivity of their farms, it was because they were being forced to pay higher taxes, not because they were making choices among alternative techniques.[17]

These four images of the choiceless peasant are widely held. But they sit uneasily with findings from microstudies. In medieval and early modern England, it has been recognised for decades that peasants engaged in individual choices in many major aspects of life.[18] By now, the debate is

---

13 Kaak, 'Diskussionsbericht', pp. 442–3.

14 For a survey of these ideas about early modern rural credit, see S. Ogilvie, M. Küpker and J. Maegraith, 'Household debt in early modern Germany: evidence from personal inventories', *Journal of Economic History* 72 (2012), 134–67, esp. pp. 134–5.

15 Wolf, *Peasants*, pp. 12–17, 37–50; Shanin, 'Introduction'; Thorner, 'Peasant economy', pp. 62–7; Ellis, *Peasant economics*, pp. 5–6; Huang, *Peasant economy*, pp. 3–6.

16 J. L. van Zanden, 'Wages and the standard of living in Europe, 1500–1800', *European Review of Economic History* 3 (1999), 175–97 (p. 192).

17 J. Bieleman, 'Rural change in the Dutch province of Drenthe in the seventeenth and eighteenth centuries', *Agricultural History Review* 33 (1985), 105–17 (pp. 114–15).

18 R. H. Hilton, *Bond men made free: medieval peasant movements and the English Rising of 1381* (London, 1973), p. 41; R. M. Smith, 'English peasant life-cycles and socio-economic networks: a quantitative geographical case study' (unpublished Ph.D. thesis, University of Cambridge, 1974); B. M. S. Campbell, 'Population pressure, inheritance and the land market in a fourteenth-century peasant community', in *Land, kinship and life-cycle*, ed. R. M. Smith (Cambridge, 1984), pp. 87–134 (p. 91); Macfarlane, *Origins*; J. Whittle, 'Individualism and the family–land bond: a reassessment of land transfer

not so much about *whether* peasants took individual choices, but about the restrictions on these choices in different periods (e.g., before and after the decline of serfdom) and different regions (e.g. East Anglia compared to the midlands).[19] Historians of the Low Countries, too, have pointed out that a great deal of individual peasant choice-making can be observed in the late medieval and early modern Dutch countryside.[20] In Holland, small farmers as far back as the thirteenth century can be observed making individual choices about using land, transferring its ownership, and flexibly participating in market transactions.[21] Even in less advanced Dutch regions, such as the eastern province of Drenthe, recent studies have found that as early as the fifteenth century, peasants were making individual choices in response to prices and market opportunities.[22]

It might be argued that societies outside the North Sea region had a more typical 'peasant' culture which did not accommodate such individual choices on everyday economic matters.[23] But microstudies of many other parts of Europe have also observed peasants making similarly individual choices. In Italy as early as the eighth century, ordinary rural people were buying and selling land individually, a development that accelerated in the

patterns among the English peasantry', *Past and Present* 160 (1998), 25–63 (pp. 27–8); C. Dyer, 'The ineffectiveness of lordship in England, 1200–1400', in *Rodney Hilton's middle ages: an exploration of historical themes*, ed. C. Dyer, P. Coss and C. Wickham (Oxford, 2007), pp. 69–86 (pp. 70, 75 and 85); B. M. S. Campbell, 'The agrarian problem in the early fourteenth century', *Past and Present* 188 (2005), 3–70 (p. 8).

19   Whittle, 'Individualism', pp. 49ff.

20   J. de Vries, *The Dutch rural economy in the golden age, 1500–1700* (New Haven, CT, 1974); J. de Vries, 'Peasant demand patterns and economic development: Friesland 1550–1750', in *European peasants and their markets*, ed. W. N. Parker and E. L. Jones (Princeton, NJ, 1975), pp. 205–38; B. J. P. van Bavel, 'The organization and rise of land and lease markets in northwestern Europe and Italy, c.1000–1800', *Continuity and Change* 23 (2008), 13–53 (p. 37–8); B. J. P. van Bavel and J. L. van Zanden, 'The jump-start of the Holland economy during the late-medieval crisis, c.1350–c.1500', *Economic History Review* 57 (2004), 503–32 (p. 509).

21   Van Bavel, 'Organization', 20–1.

22   J. Bieleman, *Boeren op het Drentse zand 1600–1910: een nieuwe visie op de 'oude' landbouw* (Utrecht, 1987); J. Bieleman, 'Boeren en Rekenmeesters', *Tijdschrift voor geschiedenis* (1988), 201–21; J. Bieleman, 'De verscheidenheid van de landbouw op de Nederlanse zandgronden tijdens "de lange zestiende eeuw"', *Beijdragen en Mededelingen betreffende de geschiedenis der Nederlanden* 105 (1990), 537–52.

23   As argued for England, for instance, in Macfarlane, *Origins*; A. Macfarlane, 'The myth of the peasantry: family and economy in a northern parish', in *Land, kinship and life-cycle*, ed. Smith, pp. 333–49; A. Macfarlane, *The culture of capitalism* (Oxford, 1987), esp. pp. 191–222; and for the North Sea area in De Moor and van Zanden, 'Girl power'.

eleventh century and has led historians to characterise farming in these regions as 'highly individualistic'.[24] In the German region of Paderborn, fourteenth-century peasants made individual choices in agricultural matters, leasing land and buildings for short periods to adapt to fluctuations in agricultural markets and labour supply, and buying and selling landholdings with no sign of attachment to the family farm.[25] In Upper Austria, too, poor peasants manifested individual economic calculation and maximizing behaviour throughout the early modern period.[26] In early modern southern France, rural proto-industrial producers have been observed making individualistic, entrepreneurial, and profit-maximizing choices.[27] In the south-west German village of Neckarhausen, David Sabean describes rural people making individual decisions in ways far removed from the Chayanovian concept of the peasant 'family economy'.[28] My own studies of the Württemberg Black Forest found widespread evidence of individual choices in demographic matters as well as markets in land, labour, credit, and output.[29] In northern Switzerland, Schnyder-Burghartz describes early modern peasants making individual choices in land and credit markets.[30]

This still leaves open the possibility that peasants made individual

---

24   For a number of examples, see L. Feller, 'Quelques problèmes liés à l'étude du marché de la terre durant le Moyen Âge', in *Il mercato della terra: secc. XIII–XVIII: atti della trentacinquesima settimana di studi, 5–9 maggio 2003*, ed. S. Cavaciocchi (Florence, 2004), pp. 21–47; C. Wickham, *Land and power: studies in Italian and European social history, 400–1200* (London, 1994); C. Wickham, *The mountains and the city: the Tuscan Apennines in the early middle ages* (Oxford, 1988), pp. 242–5; van Bavel, 'Organization', pp. 26–7 (quotation).

25   B. H. Lienen, 'Aspekte des Wandels bäuerlicher Betriebe zwischen dem 14. und dem 17. Jahrhundert an Beispielen aus Tudorf (Kreis Paderborn)', *Westfälische Forschungen* 41 (1991), 288–315.

26   H. Rebel, *Peasant classes: the bureaucratization of property and family relations under early Habsburg absolutism, 1511–1636* (Princeton, 1983), pp. 118–19.

27   J. K. J. Thomson, 'Variations in industrial structure in pre-industrial Languedoc', in *Manufacture in town and country before the factory*, ed. M. Berg, P. Hudson and M. Sonenscher (Cambridge, 1983), pp. 61–91 (pp. 66–7).

28   D. W. Sabean, *Property, production and family in Neckarhausen, 1700–1870* (Cambridge, 1990), pp. 94–7.

29   S. Ogilvie, *State corporatism and proto-industry: the Württemberg Black Forest, 1580–1797* (Cambridge, 1997), esp. pp. 7–11, 181–6, 225–30, 301–7 and 455–63.

30   A. Schnyder-Burghartz, *Alltag und Lebensformen auf der Basler Landschaft um 1700: vorindustrielle, ländliche Kultur und Gesellschaft aus mikrohistorischer Perspektive. Bretzwil und das das obere Waldenburger Amt von 1690 bis 1750* (Liestal, 1992), pp. 203–9.

choices in commercialised European regions but not in zones subject
to strong manorialism. This would rule out peasant choice both during
medieval serfdom in western Europe and during the early modern 'second
serfdom' further east. Doubt is cast on this view, however, by empirical
observations of individual decision-making by enserfed peasants in
medieval England,[31] thirteenth-century Silesia,[32] fourteenth- and fifteenth-
century Bohemia and Moravia,[33] seventeenth-century northern Bohemia,[34]
eighteenth-century Brandenburg,[35] and nineteenth-century Russia.[36]

Perhaps, though, individual choices were possible for elites but not
for lower strata who were too poor to do anything other than what they
were forced to do? Deeper research on marginal groups in the pre-modern
countryside have dispelled this assumption as well. The individuals choosing
to buy and sell land in ninth-century Italy included peasants and even
slaves.[37] In medieval England, not just men but also women made individual
choices about marriage, work, and property.[38] In rural Upper Austria, the

31 Whittle, 'Individualism', pp. 47–9.
32 J. J. Menzel, *Die schlesischen Lokationsurkunden des 13. Jahrhunderts. Studien zum
Urkundenwesen, zur Siedlungs-, Rechts- und Wirtschaftsgeschichte einer ostdeutschen
Landschaft im Mittelalter* (Würzburg, 1977), p. 458; quoted in M. Cerman, 'Social
structure and land markets in late medieval central and east-central Europe', *Continuity
and Change* 23 (2008), 55–100 (p. 62).
33 F. Graus, *Dějiny venkovského lidu v Čechách v době předhusitské, vol. 2: Dějiny
venkovského lidu od poloviny 13. stol. do roku 1419* (Prague, 1957), p. 230; as quoted in
Cerman, 'Social structure', p. 62.
34 S. Ogilvie, 'The economic world of the Bohemian serf: economic concepts, preferences and constraints on the estate of Friedland, 1583–1692', *Economic History Review*
54 (2001), 430–53.
35 L. Enders, *Die Uckermark: Geschichte einer kurmärkischen Landschaft vom 12. bis
zum 18. Jahrhundert* (Berlin, 1992), p. 148; L. Enders, 'Das bäuerliche Besitzrecht in der
Mark Brandenburg, untersucht am Beispiel der Prignitz vom 13. bis 18. Jahrhundert',
in *Gutsherrschaftsgesellschaften im europäischen Vergleich*, ed. J. Peters (Berlin, 1997),
pp. 399–427 (p. 404); L. Enders, *Die Prignitz: Geschichte einer kurmärkischen Landschaft
vom 12. bis zum 18. Jahrhundert* (Berlin, 2000), pp. 191–2; H. Harnisch, 'Bäuerliche
Ökonomie und Mentalität unter den Bedingungen der ostelbischen Gutsherrschaft in den
letzten Jahrzehnten vor Beginn der Agrarreformen', *Jahrbuch für Wirtschaftsgeschichte*
1989 (1989), 87–108, esp. pp. 88–9, 92, 99 and 106–8; J. Peters, 'Eigensinn und Widerstand
im Alltag. Abwehrverhalten ostelbischer Bauern unter Refeudalisierungsdruck', *Jahrbuch
für Wirtschaftsgeschichte* 1991 (1991), 85–103 (pp. 90, 92–3, 95–6 and 100–2).
36 T. Dennison, *The institutional framework of Russian serfdom* (Cambridge, 2011).
37 Feller, 'Quelques problèmes'; van Bavel, 'Organization', p. 26.
38 P. J. P. Goldberg, *Women, work, and life-cycle in a medieval economy: women in York
and Yorkshire, c.1300–1520* (Oxford, 1992).

poorest groups showed careful individual economic calculation, while it was the better off who supported the 'notions and practices of moral economy'.[39] In early modern Brandenburg, all strata manifested individual choice in economic and social matters.[40] Court records and land transfer registers in early modern Bohemia show the poorest serfs – women, labourers, the landless, those at the edge of starvation – making individual choices about time allocation, property, and consumption.[41]

These empirical findings suggest that individual choice was ubiquitous among rural people in pre-industrial Europe. Choice was not restricted to non-peasants, western Europeans, freemen, or the well off, but extended deep into peasant society, to southern and eastern Europeans, to enserfed rural people, and to women, the poor, and the marginal. In every pre-modern society that has been studied, it is quite clear that people in the countryside made choices.

But can we leave it at this? Is it enough to have discovered peasant agency, and can we now just focus on how peasants decided to exercise it? The recognition that peasants made choices about many aspects of life has led some studies to veer to the opposite extreme and assume that the constraints on peasant choices did not actually matter – that rural people just got around any obstacles.

Both theory and empirical findings cast doubt on this optimistic assumption. Just as it would be laughable to claim that 'peasant agency' was strong enough to remain unaffected by the natural environment, so too we should question the idea that it was unconstrained by the human environment – by the institutional rules and customs governing behaviour in rural societies.[42] As we shall see, rural societies were full of social

39 Rebel, *Peasant classes*, pp. 118–19.
40 L. Enders, 'Individuum und Gesellschaft. Bäuerliche Aktionsräume in der frühneuzeitlichen Mark Brandenburg', in *Gutsherrschaft als soziales Modell*, ed. Peters, pp. 155–78, esp. pp. 159–62, 170 and 176.
41 Ogilvie, 'Economic world', here esp. pp. 437–9 and 444–6; J. Grulich, 'Besitztransfer und regionale Mobilität der untertänigen Bevölkerung (Südböhmen, vom 16. bis 18. Jahrhundert)', in *Untertanen, Herrschaft und Staat in Böhmen und im 'Alten Reich'. Sozialgeschichtliche Studien zur Frühen Neuzeit*, ed. M. Cerman and R. Luft (Munich, 2005), pp. 127–51; D. Štefanová, *Erbschaftspraxis und Handlungsspielräume der Untertanen in einer gutsherrschaftlichen Gesellschaft. Die Herrschaft Frýdlant in Nordböhmen, 1558–1750* (Munich, 1999); H. Zeitlhofer, *Besitzwechsel und sozialer Wandel. Lebensläufe und sozioökonomische Entwicklungen in südlichen Böhmerwald, 1640–1840* (Vienna, 2014).
42 The well-known characterisation of institutions as 'the rules of the game in a society or, more formally … the humanly devised constraints that shape human interaction' was

and institutional constraints on peasant choice. So pervasive were these constraints, in fact, that this chapter has the space to focus on just three of them: manorial systems, peasant communities, and legal regimes.

Manorial constraints

Let us start with manorial institutions. The traditional view of the manorial system – whether medieval serfdom in western Europe or the early modern 'second serfdom' in eastern Europe – was that it imposed such severe restrictions that rural people were unable to make their own choices. According to this 'manorial dominance' view, under serfdom landlords used their institutional powers to prevent migration, dictate marriage, control landholding, and restrict most other choices a peasant might make. But recent decades have given rise to a revisionist view, according to which manorial institutions did not constrain peasant choices because people simply got around the constraints. Landlords did not have the quality or quantity of local-level personnel necessary to monitor individual behaviour or impose effective sanctions, it is claimed, so rural people easily circumvented manorial controls – they migrated, married, structured their households, hired and offered labour, borrowed and loaned money, bequeathed their farms, and bought and sold land, regardless of any manorial restrictions that might formally prevail.[43] The

---

first made by D. C. North, *Institutions, institutional change and economic performance* (Cambridge, 1990), p. 3. For a discussion of alternative approaches to the rise and survival of economic institutions in European history, see S. Ogilvie, '"Whatever is, is right"? Economic institutions in pre-industrial Europe', *Economic History Review* 60 (2007), 649–84.

43   For representative arguments to this effect, see E. Melton, 'Gutsherrschaft in East Elbian Germany and Livonia, 1500–1800: a critique of the model', *Central European History* 21 (1988), 315–49, here esp. pp. 315–16, 320–2, 333 and 340–1; J. Bushnell, 'Did serf owners control serf marriage? Orlov serfs and their neighbors, 1773–1861', *Slavic Review* 52 (1993), 419–45; J. Kochanowicz, 'The peasant family as an economic unit in the Polish feudal economy of the eighteenth century', in *Family forms in historic Europe*, ed. R. Wall, J. Robin and P. Laslett (Cambridge, 1983), pp. 153–66, esp. pp. 163–4; D. Štefanová, 'Herrschaft und Untertanen. Ein Beitrag zur Existenz der rechtlichen Dorfautonomie in der Herrschaft Frýdlant in Nordböhmen (1650–1700)', in *Gutsherrschaftsgesellschaften*, ed. Peters, pp. 199–210 (pp. 205–9); A. Plakans and C. Wetherell, 'The kinship domain in an east European peasant community: Pinkenhof, 1833–1850', *American Historical Review* 93 (1988), 359–86; L. Enders, 'Die Landgemeinde in Brandenburg. Grundzüge ihrer Funktion und Wirkungsweise vom 13. bis zum 18. Jahrhundert', *Blätter für deutsche Landesgeschichte* 129 (1993), 195–256 (p. 197); R. C. Hoffmann, *Land, liberties, and*

finding that under strong manorialism peasants were able to make *some* individual choices in which the manor did not intervene has thus led many scholars to conclude that there were *no* peasant decisions in which the manor was able or willing to intervene, and thus that manorial restrictions did not really matter. Peasant agency meant that serfdom was perfectly compatible with economic growth and rural development.[44]

But does this logically follow? The fact that people can be observed making choices does *not* in fact imply that the restrictions on those choices have no effect. People make choices subject to the constraints they face: their own budgets, the prices of goods, the available technology, the natural environment, and the rules and customs of their society – which, in many medieval and early modern societies, included the manorial system. If people make a choice that violates socially defined rules, they face the risk of being penalised, i.e. of incurring costs. This risk does not have to be 100 per cent in order to have a non-zero expected value. Thus, for instance, if in seventeenth-century Bohemia selling one's landholding without obtaining manorial consent carried a ten-*Schock* fine, even if there was only a 50 per cent chance of being caught, the expected cost of illegally selling that landholding was five *Schock* – which in some cases would exceed the expected benefit of violating manorial restrictions. On the margin, some farmers would refrain from illegally selling their holdings, even while others would go ahead. The same theoretical reasoning applied to migrating without manorial permission, refusing to marry when ordered by the manorial officials, setting up as a proto-industrial linen-weaver without paying manorial loom-dues, or buying beer from a private brewer rather than from the manorial brewery. All carried penalties of fines, imprisonment, or burdens on one's family; and for all, as manorial court records from at least some regions and time periods show, there was some risk of detection. As a result, the expected

---

lordship in a late medieval countryside: agrarian structures and change in the Duchy of Wroclaw (Philadelphia, 1989), pp. 358–62; W. W. Hagen, Ordinary Prussians. Brandenburg Junkers and villagers 1500–1840 (Cambridge, 2002); M. Cerman, Villagers and lords in eastern Europe, 1300–1800 (Basingstoke and New York, 2012).

44 As argued, for instance, by Hagen, Ordinary Prussians, pp. 597–601; Cerman, Villagers, pp. 6–9, 95–123; M. Cerman, 'Seigniorial systems in east-central and eastern Europe, 1300–1800: regional realities', in Schiavitu e servaggio nell'economia europea. Secc. XI–XVIII/Slavery and serfdom in the European economy from the 11th to the 18th Centuries. XLV settimana di studi della Fondazione istituto internazionale di storia economica F. Datini, Prato 14–18 April 2013, ed. S. Cavaciocchi (Florence, 2014), pp. 187–214.

cost of taking that action was non-zero, and there would therefore be some marginal migraters, marriers, linen-weavers, and beer-drinkers who would refrain from making that choice (which they would otherwise have made), even while others would go ahead. Only if the penalty or the detection risk for violating manorial restrictions were zero would no-one's choices be affected. The fact that some people can be observed making choices does not logically imply, therefore, that the institutional rules governing those choices had no effect.

Empirical studies, too, reveal few manorial systems in which landlords imposed absolutely no constraints on peasant choices. This is not to deny that peasants engaged in many individual actions without manorial interference. In most European rural societies, many marriages, land transfers, and even acts of migration occurred with little sign of manorial intervention. But just because we do not observe landlords intervening in *all* marriages or land transfers does not mean they lacked the power or interest to intervene in *any*. Quite the contrary. Even where manorial intervention took place, there are two reasons we should not expect to observe it being exercised very frequently. First, regulation was costly in terms of time and personnel, and landlords were only interested in forms of intervention that yielded benefits for themselves; this reduced the frequency of intervention. Second, awareness of manorial disapproval and the desire to avoid attracting it deterred many peasants from even trying to take certain actions. The very existence of manorial power to intervene in peasants' economic and demographic decisions meant that it did not actually have to be exercised very frequently.[45]

If manorial institutions truly exercised no significant effect on peasant choices, one would expect there to have been important arenas of decision-making that were off-limits to manorial intervention. Migration, marriage, and landholding are three of the most important choices rural people could make and are frequently adduced as spheres of peasant autonomy. But each of them illustrates the importance of manorial constraints on peasant choice.

The ability to migrate is often portrayed as a touchstone of peasant freedom.[46] Most studies show that under strong manorialism, peasants did indeed desire to migrate in order to work, trade, marry, get access to

---

45 For further reflections, see S. Ogilvie, 'Serfdom and the institutional system in early modern Germany', in *Schiavitu e servaggio*, ed. Cavaciocchi, pp. 33–58 (pp. 34–47).
46 Hatcher, 'English serfdom', pp. 29–30.

land, learn a craft, visit kin, practise their religion, and for many other reasons. But although enserfed peasants were not always prevented from migrating by their landlords, they did have to take manorial constraints into account. In many serf societies, permanent emigration required an emancipation certificate from one's landlord showing 'that one was released in goodwill'.[47] Lacking this, not only was the serf legally obliged to stay on the estate of his landlord, but if he migrated illicitly other landlords were legally obliged to send him back.[48] Illegal emigration was sufficiently costly that serfs were willing to pay substantial fees for migration permits.[49] Even temporary migration, for instance by a labourer who could not get employment on his native estate or a journeyman who wanted to travel for work, required manorial permission, payment of fees, providing pledges, or finding a replacement tenant or demesne worker.[50] Those who migrated without permission were often penalised – by fining, whipping, gaoling, forced service, or retribution against family members.[51] Even *threatening* to emigrate could attract penalties such as being pilloried or bonded with pledges.[52] Manorial courts also penalised other serfs who issued illegal emigrants with inheritance shares, made them gifts, provided them with information, or gave them shelter.[53] Landlords cooperated with

47 Státní Oblastní Archiv Litoměřice, Pobočka Děčín, Fond Rodinný archiv Clam-Gallasů, Historická sbírka, Kart. č. 315, Schriftstück 11, Jahrdings Artickeln 1636, fol. 4v, #27: 'dz er guttlich erlaßen worden'.

48 On eleventh- and twelfth-century England, see Hatcher, 'English serfdom', p. 30; on sixteenth- and seventeenth-century Bohemia, see Ogilvie, 'Communities and the "second serfdom"', p. 94.

49 Ogilvie, 'Communities and the "second serfdom"', p. 94.

50 On medieval England, see Whittle, 'Individualism', p. 46; C. Dyer, *Lords and peasants in a changing society: the estates of the Bishopric of Worcester, 680–1540* (Cambridge, 1980), pp. 105–6; Hatcher, 'English serfdom', pp. 10–14. On early modern Bohemia, see Ogilvie, 'Communities and the "second serfdom"', p. 94. On early modern Germany, see Ogilvie, 'Serfdom', p. 39; Cerman, *Villagers*, pp. 22–7. On early modern Denmark and Schleswig-Holstein, see C. P. Rasmussen, 'Forms of serfdom and bondage in the Danish Monarchy', in *Schiavitu e servaggio*, ed. Cavaciocchi, pp. 281–90 (pp. 285–8).

51 On early modern Bohemia, see Ogilvie, 'Communities and the "second serfdom"', p. 95. On early modern Germany, see J. Peters, 'Die Herrschaft Plattenburg-Wilsnack im Dreißigjährigen Krieg – eine märkische Gemeinschaft des Durchkommens', in *Brandenburgische Landesgeschichte und Archivwissenschaft: Festschrift für Lieselott Enders zum 70. Geburtstag*, ed. F. Beck and K. Neitmann (Weimar, 1997), pp. 157–70 (p. 160). On early modern Denmark and Schleswig-Holstein, see Rasmussen, 'Forms', pp. 286–8.

52 Ogilvie, 'Communities and the "second serfdom"', p. 95.

53 Ogilvie, 'Communities and the "second serfdom"', pp. 95–6.

one another and the princely state in penalizing illegally migrating serfs.[54] On larger estates under the same landlord, movement *within* the estate from one village to another was in principle unconstrained, but in practice the manorial authorities could also forbid this when it threatened manorial interests, for instance by leaving a farm vacant in a thinly settled village, thereby threatening communal capacities to deliver manorial dues.[55]

Conversely, migration decisions were sometimes *compelled* by the manorial authorities. In early modern Bohemia, for instance, landlords can be observed ejecting an offending farmer from his or her holding or from the entire estate, banishing an illegitimately pregnant woman, or moving a man to a completely different estate so that he could not continue consummating a marriage he had entered into, counter to manorial prohibition.[56] In eighteenth-century Poland, landlords sometimes forcibly moved a family to another farm to serve manorial interests.[57]

This does not mean that all enserfed peasants who wanted to migrate (or *not* to migrate) were deprived by their landlords of any choice in the matter. But it did mean that before making migration choices, peasants had to take into account whether they would be allowed to move, how much they would have to pay for permission, what the penalty would be if they migrated without a permit, and what was the risk of being caught migrating illegally. As Jane Whittle points out, not every medieval English villein who migrated paid the manorial fine for a permit, 'but this does not

---

54 On medieval England, see Hatcher, 'English serfdom', pp. 30–1; on early modern Bohemia, see Ogilvie, 'Communities and the "second serfdom"', p. 96; on early modern Poland, see P. Guzowski, 'The role of enforced labour in the economic development of church and royal estates in 15th and 16th-century Poland', in *Schiavitu e servaggio*, ed. Cavaciocchi, pp. 215–34 (p. 217); on early modern Denmark and Schleswig-Holstein, see Rasmussen, 'Forms', pp. 286–8.

55 Ogilvie, 'Communities and the "second serfdom"', p. 96.

56 Ogilvie, 'Communities and the "second serfdom"', p. 96.

57 A. Plakans, 'Peasant families east and west: a comment on Lutz K. Berkner's "Rural family organization in Europe: a problem in comparative history"', *Peasant Studies Newsletter* 2 (1973), 11–16; A. Plakans, 'Peasant farmsteads and households in the Baltic Littoral, 1797', *Comparative Studies in Society and History* 17 (1975), 2–35; A. Plakans, 'Seigneurial authority and peasant family life: the Baltic area in the eighteenth century', *Journal of Interdisciplinary History* 5 (1975), 629–54; W. Kula, 'La seigneurie et la famille paysanne dans la Pologne du XVIIIe siècle', *Annales. Histoire, Sciences Sociales* 27 (1972), 949–58; P. Czap, 'Marriage and the peasant joint family in Russia', in *The family in imperial Russia: new lines of historical research*, ed. D. L. Ransel (Urbana, IL, 1978), pp. 103–23; G. L. Freeze, 'The disintegration of traditional communities: the parish in eighteenth-century Russia', *Journal of Modern History* 48 (1976), 32–60 (p. 46).

undermine the point that they were liable to be charged because of their father's tenure and status'.[58] As soon as the decision to migrate was made more costly, even in monetary terms, this constrained every serf's choice set and deterred the marginal migrater.

The same applies to marriage choices. Many studies of societies under strong manorialism find that landlords did not interfere in many peasant marriages, and that marriage choices were influenced by many other factors, including individual preferences, family strategies, economic trends, and community pressures. But the fact that other factors influenced marriage choices and that the landlord did not frequently intervene does not mean that serfs' marriage choices were completely unconstrained by the manor. In many societies under strong manorialism, anyone wishing to marry outside the estate was expected to apply for permission, and was punished if he or she failed to do so.[59] In early modern Bohemia, for instance, marriage controls could be quite far-reaching.[60] Even when bride and groom were from the same village, they were expected to obtain landlord permission and pay a fee before getting betrothed. Subjection of either party to a different landlord was a major concern, since it created incentives to abscond and uncertainty about the servile status of offspring. A male serf's marriage to an outside woman was often only permitted on condition that the couple settle on the local estate. Even a female serf's marriage to an outside male usually required a substantial fee, promise of future reciprocity from the other landlord, or relinquishment of property, debts, and inheritance entitlements. Orphanhood of one or both partners was also a manorial concern since landlords were entitled to several years of forced service from orphaned youths before marriage, plus special marriage fines.[61] A widow's remarriage was conditional on her finding a 'capable holder' for her existing farm – or proving that her prospective husband satisfied that test. Whether the couple would be able to earn a livelihood could be another reason for landlords to refuse permission, to ensure that landholdings were occupied by those who would reliably

58   Whittle, 'Individualism', p. 46.
59   On early modern Bohemia, see Ogilvie, 'Communities and the "second serfdom"'; Dennison and Ogilvie, 'Serfdom and social capital'. On early modern Denmark and Schleswig-Holstein, see Rasmussen, 'Forms', p. 287.
60   On what follows, see Ogilvie, 'Communities and the "second serfdom"', pp. 98–101.
61   Several years of forced service on the demesne were required even of non-orphaned adolescent serfs in many early modern German societies under demesne lordship; see Ogilvie, 'Serfdom', pp. 36, 57.

render manorial burdens. Denial of manorial permits led to betrothals being dissolved, illegitimate pregnancies not being legitimised, and serfs eloping. Those who married without manorial consent were fined, gaoled, or even forcibly separated. It is hard to believe that even infrequent cases of this sort did not deter peasants from attempting to undertake marriages likely to attract manorial opposition.

Conversely, landlords also ordered serfs – particularly widows, but also orphaned daughters of deceased tenants – to marry, in order to ensure that each holding was occupied by a married couple that could reliably provide rents, taxes and labour dues.[62] There are examples of English manors in the thirteenth and fourteenth centuries in which the landlord put pressure on his tenants to marry and fined those who refused.[63] Even those who view medieval English serfdom as having been milder than traditionally portrayed describe marriage constraints on female villein heirs and widows as being imposed quite frequently.[64] At least in some parts of medieval England, 'it is clear that lords and members of certain village communities preferred to oust widows or force them into remarriage'.[65] In early modern Bohemia, likewise, landlords regarded female household heads as poor risks and put pressure on them to remarry or vacate their farms, often collaborating with village communities or male relatives in order to exert this pressure. In consequence, Bohemian female headship was low by western European standards and declined significantly between the sixteenth and the eighteenth century, as the 'second serfdom' intensified.[66]

Manorial systems in which landlords merely charged fees for marriage permits probably constrained peasant choices less than those in which landlords prohibited certain marriages and enforced others.[67] But even when landlords only occasionally forced serf women to marry against their will, or only demanded a licence fee, this increased the costs to the individual of making his or her own marriage choices. The marriage

---

62 On the existence of such rights in pre-Black Death England, see Hatcher, 'English serfdom', p. 13. On early modern Bohemia, see Ogilvie, 'Communities and the "second serfdom"', pp. 101–2.

63 P. R. Schofield, *Peasant and community in medieval England 1200–1500* (Basingstoke and London, 2003), p. 108.

64 Hatcher, 'English serfdom', p. 13. See also Schofield, *Peasant and community*, pp. 108–9.

65 Schofield, *Peasant and community*, p. 109.

66 S. Ogilvie and J. Edwards, 'Women and the "second serfdom": evidence from early modern Bohemia', *Journal of Economic History* 60 (2000), 961–94.

67 As argued in Hatcher, 'English serfdom', p. 10.

fines demanded by some medieval English landlords are acknowledged as constraining peasant choices: 'these sums were a burden, and peasants had to adjust their budgets to afford them, and in bad years they would cause real hardship'.[68] Likewise, manorial regimes in which landlords were unsystematic in requiring marriage permits were less restrictive than those in which all marriages were subject to manorial consent. But as Jane Whittle points out, even though not every medieval English villein's daughter who married paid the merchet, this does not take away from the fact that they were liable to do so, and thus that the constraint mattered.[69] Similarly, although John Hatcher warns us not to overestimate the burdens of serfdom in England before 1350 by focusing solely on the letter of the law, he is concerned not to deny 'that the weight of monetary exactions could in itself constitute a grave restriction of freedom'.[70]

Similar findings emerge for manorial regulation of land transactions. Most studies show serfs choosing to buy, sell, and bequeath real property – so much so that it is sometimes claimed that although landlords enjoyed the legal right of consent they seldom enforced it.[71] A major empirical bulwark of this view is the fact that manorial registers rarely record cases in which a farm transfer was prohibited by the landlord. However, one would not expect to observe frequent evidence of manorial intervention in such documentary sources, since recording a transfer in the register was unlikely to take place before manorial approval had been granted. Problematic transfers were blocked at an earlier stage or even deterred altogether by the awareness, on the part of individuals, communal officials, and manorial administrators, that certain types of transfer were inadmissible.[72]

This is borne out by findings from a number of serf societies showing that where a particular land transaction threatened the landlord's interests, the manorial administration was both able and willing to intervene. Under strong manorialism, a peasant had to obtain permission from the landlord before selling (or even bequeathing) his land, and this restriction can be observed being implemented in societies as diverse as pre-1350

68   Dyer, 'Ineffectiveness', p. 74 (quotation); see also Schofield, *Peasant and community*, p. 110.
69   Whittle, 'Individualism', p. 46.
70   Hatcher, 'English serfdom', p. 14.
71   See, for instance, Melton, 'Gutsherrschaft', pp. 340–1; Cerman, *Villagers*; Štefanová, 'Herrschaft', pp. 205–8.
72   Ogilvie, 'Communities and the "second serfdom"', pp. 103–4.

England, late medieval Flanders, early modern Bohemia, and early modern Brandenburg.[73] In early modern Bohemia and Germany under the 'second serfdom', manorial consent could be refused if the buyer was subject to a different landlord or was not regarded as a 'capable holder' who would reliably render manorial dues.[74] In parts of late medieval England and Flanders, in sixteenth-century Austria, and in seventeenth- and eighteenth-century Bohemia, landlords placed obstacles in the way of any sale that threatened the impartibility of standard holdings, which they regarded as a guarantee that labour services and other manorial dues would continue to be rendered reliably.[75] Even where manorial authorities usually granted permission for land transfers, they collected fees from both seller and buyer.[76] According to Christopher Dyer, in medieval England such entry fines were low compared with the purchase prices for the land, but still constituted 'the largest sums that were paid into most manorial courts', would have sent many incoming tenants to moneylenders to obtain funds, and 'must sometimes have discouraged them from buying a piece of land'.[77]

Manorial restrictions such as these affected not just peasants' choices about how to allocate land, as a key economic input, but also credit access, inheritance strategies, social stratification, wage labour, servanthood, family-land bonds, and even – according to some accounts – kinship and household structure.[78] Even manorial rules that were violated affected

73   On pre-Black Death England, see Hatcher, 'English serfdom', p. 9. On fourteenth-century England, see Campbell, 'Population pressure', pp. 107–8; Whittle, 'Individualism', p. 48. On medieval Flanders, see van Bavel, 'Organization', pp. 17–18. On early modern Bohemia, see Ogilvie, 'Communities and the "second serfdom"', pp. 105–6. On early modern Brandenburg, see H. Harnisch, 'Klassenkämpfe der Bauern in der Mark Brandenburg zwischen frühbürgerlicher Revolution und Dreißigjährigem Krieg', *Jahrbuch für Regionalgeschichte* 5 (1975), 142–72 (pp. 146–7); Harnisch, 'Bäuerliche Ökonomie', pp. 95 and 97–9.

74   On early modern Bohemia, see Ogilvie, 'Communities and the "second serfdom"', pp. 105–6. On early modern Germany, see Ogilvie, 'Serfdom', p. 42; Harnisch, 'Bäuerliche Ökonomie', pp. 95 and 97–9. On eastern-central Europe as a whole, see Cerman, 'Social structure', pp. 61 and 66.

75   On this behaviour by some late-medieval English landlords who continued to rely on labour services from their tenants, see Schofield, *Peasant and community*, pp. 65–9. On late medieval Flanders, see van Bavel, 'Organization', p. 18. On early modern Bohemia, see Ogilvie, 'Communities and the "second serfdom"', pp. 105–6. On early modern Austria, see Cerman, 'Social structure', p. 66.

76   Van Bavel, 'Organization', pp. 17–18 and 22–3.

77   Dyer, 'Ineffectiveness', pp. 80–1.

78   On medieval England, see Whittle, 'Individualism', pp. 51–3; Z. Razi, *Life, marriage and death in a medieval parish: economy, society and demography in Halesowen*

peasant choices by shifting land transfers into the informal sector where risks were high, contract enforcement poor, and exploitation rife.[79] As Bruce Campbell emphasises for medieval England, the manorial system created rigidities and rent-seeking throughout the whole rural sector, circumscribed peasant choices in factor and product markets, and exercised harmful knock-on consequences for growth and development in the wider economy.[80]

Perhaps the most vivid illustration of the impact of manorial restrictions on peasants' choices is that people voted with their feet. In 1142, for instance, the earl of Lincoln offered thirty-eight *rustici* the choice between taking servile land and leaving his domain: thirty-one of them chose to depart, landless but lordless.[81] Five centuries later, in mid-seventeenth-century Bohemia, the lord of Friedland suffered a continual haemorrhage of serfs who chose to leave behind property and family to set up as labourers over the border in Saxony rather than retain their landholdings which, although inheritable, subjected their holders to hereditary servility and an array of manorial burdens and restrictions.[82] The Worcestershire tenant who drowned himself in the Severn in 1293 rather than be forced by the earl of Gloucester's bailiffs to accept servile land evidently ascribed a very high expected cost to the constraints of serfdom.[83] Likewise, the landless north-Bohemian serf, Christof Herbig, who in 1651 resisted manorial pressure to take on a farm and instead chose to live as 'only a lodger, and earn a living from all sorts of dealing, even though he could take on a servile holding' bears witness to the fact that, at least for some

1270–1400 (Cambridge, 1980), pp. 94–8; Campbell, 'Agrarian problem', p. 49; Z. Razi, 'The myth of the immutable English family', *Past and Present* 140 (1993), 3–44 (pp. 16–18); J. A. Raftis, *Peasant economic development within the English manorial system* (Stroud, 1996), pp. 28–33. On early modern Bohemia, see A. Klein, 'The institutions of the "second serfdom" and economic efficiency: review of the existing evidence for Bohemia', in *Schiavitù e servaggio*, ed. Cavaciocchi, pp. 59–82. On early modern Germany, see Ogilvie, 'Serfdom', pp. 42–3, 57; Harnisch, 'Bäuerliche Ökonomie', p. 107.

79   On how manorial regulation of land markets created illicit subletting in medieval England, see Campbell, 'Agrarian problem', pp. 48–9 with n. 134. On the costs, risks, and development problems created by forcing rural people to operate in the informal sector, see Ogilvie, 'Whatever is, is right', pp. 671–4 and 681.

80   Campbell, 'Agrarian problem', pp. 8 and 50.

81   Hatcher, 'English serfdom', p. 31.

82   Ogilvie, 'Communities and the "second serfdom"'.

83   For this case, see R. H. Hilton, 'Peasant movements in England before 1381', *Economic History Review* 2 (1949), 117–36 (p. 135).

members of early modern Bohemian society, the constraints of hereditary servility mattered.[84] These two individuals may have been unusual, given that many other men in thirteenth-century England and seventeenth-century Bohemia did accept serf holdings and the numerous constraints that went with them, and most of these men did not choose suicide or life as a houseless lodger instead. However, this merely meant that for many members of these rural societies accepting servile land was the best of the available alternatives, not that the constraints of serfdom did not matter.[85]

Even in societies that were not subject to serfdom, manorial restrictions were capable of constraining peasant choices. In early modern Hohenlohe and Hessen-Kassel, for instance, there were lively markets in pure peasant land but very inactive markets in land subject to manorial law where landlord consent was needed for all transfers and farms could not be divided.[86] Even when manorial regulations were not fully complied with, they exerted an observable effect on peasant choices by compelling people who wanted to do things the manor prohibited to operate illegally in the informal sector. In the German county of Ravensberg, according to Stefan Brakensiek, manorial restrictions on peasant borrowing and land transactions stifled credit and land markets and 'promoted the adoption of illegal forms of arrangements among neighbours with respect to land use as well as unsecured and usurious methods of borrowing'.[87]

Individual choices by peasants thus do not imply, either in theory or in practice, that manorial constraints on those choices were irrelevant.[88]

---

84   For further detail on this case, see S. Ogilvie and M. Cerman, 'The Bohemian census of 1651 and the position of inmates', *Histoire Sociale/Social History* 28 (1995), 333–46 (pp. 344–5).

85   See Hatcher, 'English serfdom', p. 26.

86   On Hohenlohe, see E. Schremmer, *Die Bauernbefreiung in Hohenlohe* (Stuttgart, 1963), pp. 14–25; T. Robisheaux, *Rural society and the search for order in early modern Germany* (Cambridge, 1989), pp. 79–83. On Hessen-Kassel, see E. Sakai, *Der kurhessische Bauer im 19. Jahrhundert und die Grundlastenablösung* (Melsungen, 1967); F. Lütge, *Geschichte der deutschen Agrarverfassung vom frühen Mittelalter bis zum 19. Jahrhundert* (Stuttgart, 1967), pp. 198–9; T. Fox, 'Land tenure, feudalism, and the state in eighteenth-century Hesse', in *Themes in rural history of the western world*, ed. R. Herr (Ames, IA, 1993), pp. 99–139 (pp. 100–14).

87   S. Brakensiek, 'Farms and land – a commodity? Land markets, family strategies and manorial control in Germany', in *Landholding and land transfer in the North Sea area (late middle ages–19th century)*, ed. B. J. P. van Bavel and P. Hoppenbrouwers (Turnhout, 2004), pp. 218–34 (p. 228).

88   As emphasised for medieval England in Dyer, 'Ineffectiveness', pp. 85–6, and C. Briggs, 'English serfdom, c.1200–c.1350: towards an institutionalist analysis', in *Schiavitu e*

To differing degrees in different societies, peasants could make individual choices in which the manorial authorities did not intervene; but this does not mean that the manor *could* not intervene in those choices if it perceived its interests to be threatened. Peasants could also sometimes circumvent manorial regulations; but this does not mean that the existence of those regulations did not constrain peasants' choices. Unless the penalty for violation or the probability of detection was nil, there was a non-zero expected cost associated with making that choice, deterring the marginal person from doing so. Even when a peasant did successfully make a choice that was prohibited by the manorial authorities, the actions he or she took to avoid detection and punishment themselves consumed resources, imposed costs, and circumscribed the individual's other choices. Most manorial systems, moreover, imposed some constraints – especially those concerning payment of manorial burdens – that peasants could circumvent only with very considerable costs. To understand the impact of manorial institutions on rural societies, we have to recognise both that serfs made choices and that manorial restrictions constrained those choices – albeit in different ways in different times and places.

Community constraints

A second component of the institutional constraints on peasant choice was the village community. Here, too, the discovery of peasant agency has sometimes been taken to imply that such agency was totally unconstrained – even by community institutions. One widely held version of this view is that the rural community was merely a geographical entity and not an institution with rules or customs that affected individual choices, as suggested by Alan Macfarlane in his portrayal of medieval and early modern 'English individualism'.[89] A second widespread variant is to regard the rural community not so much as a *constraint* on peasant choice as an *expression* of it. A whole 'communal autonomy' school of thought has grown up around the assumption that the village community was an institution primarily directed at enabling peasants to implement their *own*

servaggio, ed. Cavaciocchi, pp. 13–32; for early modern Bohemia in Klein, 'Institutions'; for early modern Russia in Dennison, *Institutional framework*; and for early modern Germany in Ogilvie, 'Serfdom'.

89   Macfarlane, *Origins*.

choices against outside threats from landlords, princes, priests, or the natural environment.[90] While differing from the 'English individualism' school in other ways, the 'communal autonomy' school shares the view that community institutions did not constrain peasant choice.

But what do the facts show? Village communities varied widely. At one end of the spectrum, village communities in medieval and early modern England typically did not strictly regulate factor markets, output markets, settlement decisions, or demographic choices and thus left many peasant choices relatively unconstrained.[91] Membership in medieval England communities was 'fluid and insecure';[92] property tenure and access to common resources came from individual land ownership, not community membership.[93] In much of the western and central Netherlands, too, villages privatised and parcelled out common lands in the thirteenth and fourteenth centuries, removing a major source of communal regulation of individual choice.[94] Almost no early modern Dutch villages defined membership via communal 'citizenship' rights, and the few who tried had their claims rejected by the state.[95] In Tuscany and the Po Valley, the period after the Black Death saw the dissolution of many communal lands and rights, taking with them the associated restrictions on individual decision-making

90   G. C. Homans, *English villagers of the thirteenth century* (New York, 1941); J. A. Raftis, *Tenure and mobility. Studies in the social history of the medieval English village* (Toronto, 1964); P. Blickle, 'Kommunalismus, Parlamentarismus, Republikanismus', *Historische Zeitschrift* 242 (1986), 529–56; P. Blickle, 'Kommunalismus: Begriffsbildung in heuristischer Absicht', in *Landgemeinde und Stadtgemeinde in Mitteleuropa. Ein struktureller Vergleich*, ed. P. Blickle (Munich, 1991), pp. 5–38; P. Blickle, 'Einführung. Mit den Gemeinden Staat machen', in *Gemeinde und Staat im Alten Europa*, ed. P. Blickle (Munich, 1998), pp. 1–20; P. Blickle, *Von der Leibeigenschaft zu den Menschenrechten. Eine Geschichte der Freiheit in Deutschland* (Munich, 2003); Hatcher, 'English serfdom', pp. 23 and 33–4; Dyer, 'Ineffectiveness', pp. 79 and 85–6; R. M. Netting, *Balancing on an Alp: ecological change and continuity in a Swiss mountain community* (Cambridge, 1981); J. L. van Zanden, 'Chaloner Memorial Lecture: the paradox of the Marks. The exploitation of commons in the eastern Netherlands, 1250–1850', *Agricultural History Review* 47 (1999), 125–44 (pp. 129–30).

91   Schofield, *Peasant and community*, p. 5; R. M. Smith, 'The English peasantry 1250–1650', in *The peasantries of Europe from the fourteenth to the eighteenth centuries*, ed. T. Scott (London and New York, 1998), pp. 339–71 (p. 340).

92   Schofield, *Peasant and community*, p. 3.

93   Smith, 'English peasantry', p. 340.

94   Van Zanden, 'Chaloner Memorial Lecture', p. 128; van Bavel, 'Organization', p. 20.

95   J. L. van Zanden and M. Prak, 'Towards an economic interpretation of citizenship: the Dutch Republic between medieval communes and modern nation-states', *European Review of Economic History* 10 (2006), 111–145 (p. 122).

with regard to land use.[96] Not just in England, therefore, were there peasant villages that hardly constrained individual choices.

However, this minimalist type of peasant community was not universal. Even in England and the Low Countries, community institutions did constrain individual choices in some times and places. In the period before the Black Death, some English female villeins were pressed to marry because village communities 'were anxious to ensure that family holdings were efficiently run and able to meet their obligations'.[97] In fifteenth-century Dutch Drenthe, most villages were entitled to prohibit private land sales to non-locals and some compelled residents to sell food preferentially to locals over outsiders.[98] In early modern Drenthe, open-field villages prohibited enclosing arable land, mandated common grazing on stubble, and prevented farmers from controlling weeds by ploughing and harrowing immediately after harvest, resulting in low rye yield ratios of 1:3.[99] Only in the later eighteenth century were communal constraints on individual agricultural choices weakened, enabling yield ratios to rise to 1:5 or 1:6.[100] The Belgian provinces of Luxembourg and Namur retained communal property rights well into the eighteenth century, contributing to their low cereal productivity relative to East and West Flanders.[101]

Elsewhere, communities constrained peasant choices even more. In many early modern German societies, for instance, almost all the rights of adult life depended on formal community 'citizenship'. Villages strictly controlled admission of new citizens and 'sojourners', and imposed barriers to entry including admission fees, documentary requirements, freedom from serfdom, confessional affiliation, legitimate birth, number of offspring, wealth, property ownership, occupation, and reputation. These communal constraints were enforced: in 1740, one Württemberg

96   P. J. Jones, 'From manor to mezzadria: a Tuscan case-study in the medieval origins of modern agrarian society', in *Florentine Studies*, ed. N. Rubinstein (London, 1968), pp. 193–241 (pp. 206–14); S. R. Epstein, 'The peasantries of Italy, 1350–1750', in *The peasantries of Europe*, ed. Scott, pp. 75–110 (pp. 88–9); van Bavel, 'Organization', p. 27.

97   Hatcher, 'English serfdom', p. 13 (quotation); Schofield, *Peasant and community*, p. 109.

98   Van Zanden, 'Chaloner Memorial Lecture', pp. 131–2; van Bavel, 'Organization', p. 17.

99   Bieleman, 'Rural change', p. 111; van Zanden, 'Chaloner Memorial Lecture', p. 126.

100   Bieleman, 'Rural change', pp. 111 and 114; B. H. Slicher van Bath, *Een Samenleving onder spanning. Geschiedenis van het platteland in Overijssel* (Assen, 1957), p. 580; van Zanden, 'Chaloner Memorial Lecture', p. 136.

101   G. Dejongh, 'New estimates of land productivity in Belgium, 1750–1850', *Agricultural History Review* 47 (1999), 7–28 (p. 18).

community refused a widow even temporary 'sojourner' rights because 'the village is over-filled';[102] in 1765, another refused citizenship to a woman who wanted to marry one of its members 'because the community is already filled up with too many people, and poor ones';[103] and in 1785, a third refused admission to a man desiring to marry the daughter of a local citizen 'because he has the worst possible reputation and has revealed himself to be a poor householder'.[104] In Württemberg and many other central European societies, rural communities also constrained the choices of their existing members, including marriage, household structure, work, leisure, inheritance, land sales, borrowing, and consumption. Of course, even the strongest communities did not perfectly enforce their rules. But microstudies find that many central European villages carefully monitored and successfully controlled many of their members' choices. Yet the same microstudies richly document the existence of individual choice in these communities.[105] Peasant choice and communal constraints existed side by side, and rural societies cannot be understood by focusing on the one while ignoring the other.

Nor do the facts support the view that 'communal autonomy' invariably enhanced the realm of choice for rural individuals. It could certainly be argued that managing challenging ecosystems and organizing political resistance were ways in which community institutions facilitated peasant choices. Yet it must also be recognised that the choices which communities facilitated differed fundamentally from those discussed at the beginning

---

102 Hauptstaatsarchiv Stuttgart, A573 Bü 7133, petition of 7 May 1740, fol. 1r.
103 Hauptstaatsarchiv Stuttgart, A573 Bü 43, 13 Sep. 1765, fol. 60r.
104 Hauptstaatsarchiv Stuttgart, A573 Bü 6948, petition of 17 May 1785.
105 For examples, see A. Holzem, 'Religiöse Prägungen des Konsumverhaltens in frühneuzeitlichen Dorfgesellschaften: das Beispiel des Fürstbistums Münster', in *Der lange Weg in den Überfluss. Anfänge und Entwicklung der Konsumgesellschaft seit der Vormoderne*, ed. M. Prinz (Paderborn, 2003), pp. 79–103; R. Prass, *Reformprogramm und bäuerliche Interessen. Die Auflösung der traditionellen Gemeindeökonomie im südlichen Niedersachsen, 1750–1883* (Göttingen, 1997); C. Ulbrich, *Shulamit und Margarete: Macht, Geschlecht und Religion in einer ländlichen Gesellschaft des 18. Jahrhunderts* (Vienna, Cologne and Weimar, 1999); O. Volckart, 'Die Dorfgemeinde als Kartell: Kooperationsprobleme und ihre Lösungen im Mittelalter und in der Frühen Neuzeit', *Jahrbuch für Wirtschaftsgeschichte* 2004 (2004), 189–202; Ogilvie, *State corporatism*, chap. 3; Sabean, *Property*; Robisheaux, *Rural society*; P. Bierbrauer, 'Die ländliche Gemeinde im oberdeutsch-schweizerischen Raum', in *Landgemeinde und Stadtgemeinde in Mitteleuropa*, ed. Blickle, pp. 169–90; and many of the essays in A. Holenstein and S. Ullmann (eds), *Nachbarn, Gemeindegenossen und die anderen. Minderheiten und Sondergruppen im Südwesten des Reiches während der Frühen Neuzeit* (Epfendorf, 2004).

of this chapter. For one thing, these were the choices not of individuals but of groups – either the whole village or, more often, the village oligarchy. Furthermore, even where community institutions did facilitate the choices of the whole village to manage resources or organise resistance, they usually had to constrain the choices of individuals.

To manage common resources, communities typically imposed ceilings on grazing, limited wood-collection, forbade commercial as opposed to domestic use of resources, and refused resource access – or even settlement rights – to particular individuals and groups.[106] Nor did communities always do this in an egalitarian spirit, in which they distributed common costs and common benefits equally to all inhabitants. More usually, communities regulated common resources in the interests of a powerful oligarchy at the expense of less powerful inhabitants such as cottagers, female household-heads, or new settlers.[107] So we cannot view communities as merely enabling peasants to express their choices: typically, they expressed some peasants' choices more than others.[108]

Likewise, even though villages did organise resistance against landlords, the state, or the church, this does not justify a rosy view that this expressed the choices of all villagers. Greater powers for communities did not necessarily mean greater choices for all their members. Peasant communes were not egalitarian and harmonious spheres within which each villager had an equal chance of securing a fair hearing from well-meaning neighbours. Rather, villages were highly stratified and riven by conflict.[109] Community officials were recruited disproportionately from the top stratum of well-off farmers.[110] This oligarchy ran the commune in its own interests,

106   On these constraints in the eastern provinces of the Netherlands in the medieval and early modern period, see van Zanden, 'Chaloner Memorial Lecture', pp. 130–1 and 134–5.
107   On the differing access rights of full peasants and cottagers in the eastern provinces of the Netherlands in the medieval and early modern periods, see van Zanden, 'Chaloner Memorial Lecture', pp. 130–1 and 135; Bieleman, *Boeren*.
108   This point is made for medieval English communities by R. M. Smith, 'Families and their land in an area of partible inheritance: Redgrave, Suffolk 1260–1320', in *Land, kinship and life-cycle*, ed. Smith, pp. 135–95 (p. 174).
109   On stratification inside village communities in medieval England, see Campbell, 'Agrarian problem', pp. 54–6 and 62. On the eastern Dutch provinces of Drenthe, Overijssel, and Gelderland in the medieval and early modern periods, see van Zanden, 'Chaloner Memorial Lecture', p. 129. On early modern Bohemia, see Ogilvie, 'Communities and the "second serfdom"', p. 113. On eighteenth- and nineteenth-century Russia, see Dennison and Ogilvie, 'Serfdom and social capital', pp. 526–7.
110   On medieval England, see Smith, 'Families', pp. 159 and 173–5; Campbell, 'Agrarian

and its members and their relatives undoubtedly often benefited from powerful community institutions. But many communities implemented the choices of their most powerful members by limiting those of the least powerful – big farmers over labourers, men over women, middle-aged over young, married over unmarried, insiders over migrants.[111] For weaker villagers, manorial and princely courts, however biased their judgements, could provide a welcome alternative to village courts whose judgements favoured the village oligarchy and their cronies.[112] As such findings illustrate, the autonomy of strong rural communities must be analysed critically. It did not always – or even typically – express the choices of women, youths, landless labourers, land-poor strata, or non-members of the village oligarchy. It cannot be automatically equated with the choices or well-being of all members of the village, let alone all members of rural society more widely.

Empirical microstudies of a range of European societies, therefore, suggest that community institutions can be regarded neither as uniformly facilitating peasant choices nor as being irrelevant to them. Although peasants made many individual choices in which their communities did not intervene, this did not mean that peasant communities *could* not intervene, especially when the interests of powerful community members were at stake. To differing degrees in different societies, rural people circumvented community controls, but in doing so they faced costs and risks that deterred the marginal individual from violating those restrictions, and they consumed resources in evasive action. Even where communities enabled rural people to express or defend their choices against external challenges, they often did so only for a subset of village members. Communal institutions meant different things to different villagers, and control over village offices and a voice in communal decision-making was

problem', p. 46. On early modern Bohemia, see Ogilvie, 'Communities and the "second serfdom"', pp. 97 and 113. On eighteenth- and nineteenth-century Russia, see Dennison and Ogilvie, 'Serfdom and social capital', pp. 527–8.

111   Ogilvie, 'Communities and the "second serfdom"', p. 113; Dennison and Ogilvie, 'Serfdom and social capital'. On the implications of social stratification for East-Elbian communes, see Melton, 'Gutsherrschaft', pp. 345–7; K. Blaschke, 'Dorfgemeinde und Stadtgemeinde in Sachsen zwischen 1300 und 1800', in *Landgemeinde und Stadtgemeinde in Mitteleuropa*, ed. Blickle, pp. 119–44 (pp. 134–6 and 141); and T. Rudert, 'Gutsherrschaft und ländliche Gemeinde. Beobachtungen zum Zusammenhang von gemeindlicher Autonomie und Agrarverfassung in der Oberlausitz im 18. Jahrhundert', in *Gutsherrschaft als soziales Modell*, ed. Peters, pp. 197–218 (pp. 197, 200–3 and 212).

112   Smith, 'Families', pp. 175–7.

not enjoyed by all. We must therefore recognise both that peasants made choices, and that these choices could be blocked, rendered more risky, or channelled in alternative directions by the institutional practices of the communities in which they lived. Neither dismissing the community as irrelevant nor viewing it uncritically as a vehicle of peasant choice does justice to its complex influences. Only by analysing its empirical operation in the local context can we understand precisely how the peasant community affected peasant choice.

Legal constraints

The discovery of peasant agency has also sometimes been taken to imply that legal systems did not constrain peasant choices. This view takes two main forms. In its first form, the claim is that legal institutions were irrelevant to peasant action in *all* pre-modern societies, without distinction. Thus, Gregory Clark argues that the effectiveness with which property rights and contract enforcement were guaranteed did not change in England between 1300 and 1800, even while agricultural growth and factory industrialisation occurred; in his view, this demonstrates that legal institutions were irrelevant to medieval and early modern economic growth.[113] In a different manifestation of this view, Jürgen Schlumbohm argues that rural societies were unaffected by legal institutions because the pre-modern legal system consisted primarily of 'laws that were not enforced'. Instead, Schlumbohm argues, we should adopt Michel Foucault's view that medieval and early modern legal systems served a purely symbolic purpose – the assertion of sovereignty by a 'theatre state'.[114]

The second form this argument takes is different: it holds that legal institutions were irrelevant to peasant choices in *some* European societies, but significantly constrained them in others. Alan Macfarlane, for instance, regards the English legal system as a non-obstructive and facilitative instrument for rural individuals to implement their decisions, in contrast to the more restrictive legal systems prevalent in continental European

---

113   G. Clark, *A farewell to alms: a brief economic history of the world* (Princeton, NJ, 2007), pp. 147, 173 and 212–23.
114   J. Schlumbohm, 'Gesetze, die nicht durchgesetzt werden – ein Strukturmerkmal des frühneuzeitlichen Staates?', *Geschichte und Gesellschaft* 23 (1997), 647–63 (pp. 649–50 and 660–1); referring to M. Foucault, *Surveiller et punir: naissance de la prison* (Paris, 1975).

societies, where legal restrictions did constrain peasant choices.[115] Bas van Bavel makes similar claims for the medieval Low Countries, where he sees the legal system providing greater protection for peasant choices even than in England.[116] Similar ideas have been taken up by economists who explain differential economic development over the past eight centuries in terms of 'legal origins', according to which the 'common law' of the English-speaking world facilitated individual choices, whereas the 'civil law' tradition of continental Europe and its colonies significantly constrained them.[117]

The empirical findings, however, support a more differentiated view concerning both sets of claims – that legal systems did not constrain peasant choice anywhere, and that they constrained it only in certain societies. Even in England, the legal system was not fully facilitative of peasant choices. In some regions of medieval England, the public legal system did provide reasonably good property rights and contract enforcement to rural people, who were not restricted to their own landlords' manorial courts but could use courts operated by other lords, the church, and the crown.[118] These findings cast doubt on van Bavel's claim that legal protection of peasant property rights was weaker in England than the Low Countries because of 'the stronger power of lords and the weaker position of public authorities'.[119] However, counter to Clark's portrayal, the medieval English legal system did constrain the economic choices of rural people. To give just one example among many, customary law on some English manors permitted joint tenure and out-of-court land transfers from the fourteenth century onwards; on other manors these practices, which facilitated individual peasant choices, became legally permissible only in the fifteenth or sixteenth centuries.[120] Further changes,

115   Macfarlane, *Origins*; A. Macfarlane, 'The origins of English individualism: some surprises', *Theory and Society* 6 (1978), 255–77 (pp. 257–8, 261–2, 265 and 273); Macfarlane, 'Myth'; Macfarlane, *Culture*, esp. pp. 191–222.

116   Van Bavel, 'Organization', esp. p. 20.

117   E. L. Glaeser and A. Shleifer, 'Legal origins', *Quarterly Journal of Economics* 117 (2002), 1193–1230; R. La Porta, F. Lopez de Silanes and A. Shleifer, 'The economic consequences of legal origins', *Journal of Economic Literature* 46 (2008), 285–332, esp. pp. 305–6 and 312.

118   As emphasised for instance in Campbell, 'Agrarian problem', pp. 6–7; C. Briggs, 'Manor court procedures, debt litigation levels, and rural credit provision in England, c.1290–c.1380', *Law and History Review* 24 (2006), 519–58; Dyer, 'Ineffectiveness', pp. 75 and 78.

119   Van Bavel, 'Organization', p. 20.

120   Whittle, 'Individualism', p. 34; L. Bonfield and L. R. Poos, 'The development of the

for instance to legal forms of leasing, only occurred during the sixteenth or seventeenth century.[121]

For the Low Countries, too, the legal system was not altogether facilitative of peasant choices. For one thing, there was considerable regional variation, with much weaker legal protection for peasant property rights in inland provinces such as Drenthe than in western provinces such as Holland.[122] Furthermore, between the fifteenth and seventeenth centuries, the Dutch state introduced compulsory registration of land transactions in public law-courts, prohibiting use of private charters as in England or notarial recording as in France.[123] Public legal registration contributed to market transparency, according to van Bavel; but it also limited peasants' choices by exposing rural people more fully to state regulations and fiscal exactions. The Dutch legal system thus facilitated some peasant choices and constrained others, in different times and places.

Outside England and the Low Countries, differential availability of 'facilitative' components of the legal system – those that enabled individuals to guarantee their property rights and enforce their contracts – certainly affected peasant choices. Where the countryside was subject to a city-state, as in many parts of northern Italy, such legal facilitation was rationed by urban courts. In the countryside around fourteenth-century Florence and Siena, for instance, peasant choices were increasingly constrained by urban courts which extended their jurisdiction over the countryside, decided legal cases in favour of urban elites, and reduced security of peasant property rights.[124] Where the countryside was subject to a territorial state, the princely legal system constrained peasants' choices. The principality of Hohenlohe, for instance, became a rare island of impartible property rights in otherwise predominantly partible south-west Germany in the 1560s because its rulers incorporated impartibility into the national

deathbed transfer in medieval English manor courts', *Cambridge Law Journal* 47 (1988), 403–27.

121   M. Overton, *Agricultural revolution in England: the transformation of the agrarian economy 1500–1850* (Cambridge, 1996); R. C. Allen, 'Tracking the agricultural revolution in England', *Economic History Review* 52 (1999), 209–35; van Bavel, 'Organization', pp. 31–3; P. J. Bowden, 'Agricultural prices, farm profits, and rents', in *The agrarian history of England and Wales, IV: 1500–1640,* ed. J. Thirsk (Cambridge, 1967), pp. 593–695 (pp. 685–6).

122   Van Bavel, 'Organization', p. 23.

123   Van Bavel, 'Organization', pp. 23–4.

124   D. J. Osheim, 'Countrymen and the law in late-medieval Tuscany', *Speculum* 64 (1989), 317–37.

law-code for fiscal reasons, thereby restricting peasants' choices to divide farms among heirs, sell individual fields to manage economic shocks, or alienate them to finance micro-investments.[125] Similar examples of how even the 'facilitative' aspects of legal systems circumscribed peasants' choices can be replicated for most European rural societies.

What about Schlumbohm's idea that the *prescriptive* components of pre-modern European legal systems did not constrain peasant choice because they consisted of laws that were not enforced? Schlumbohm's evidentiary support for this argument is that states often promulgated the same law repeatedly and that people sometimes violated such laws. Early modern European states certainly could not always enforce all laws perfectly. But did this mean states never enforced *any* laws even partially?

In theory, does the fact that we observe pre-modern people violating laws mean that the legal system did not constrain their choices? Not in the least. So long as the probability of being detected breaking a law was non-zero, this imposed a non-zero expected cost on someone who was trying to decide whether to make that choice. A good way of thinking about this is to take one of the 'prescriptive' laws on which Schlumbohm focuses – a sumptuary ordinance, for instance. Sumptuary ordinances forbade ordinary people from wearing costly clothing, holding lavish weddings, or consuming other luxuries prohibited to their station in life, and laid down penalties for violations. Unless the probability of being detected was nil, an individual thinking about choosing to buy a silk neckerchief, for instance, faced a non-zero expected cost of making that choice, over and above the cost of the neckerchief itself. This did not necessarily always prevent him – or her, usually – from making that consumption choice, but by increasing the cost of the choice, it deterred the marginal consumer. Also, the actions she took to avoid detection and punishment themselves consumed resources and exercised an additional effect on the set of choices open to her.

Empirically, too, it is overoptimistic to assume that prescriptive laws never limited peasant choices. Schlumbohm dismisses the idea that sumptuary regulations, for instance, were ever enforced. It is certainly true that there were European societies that either ceased to enforce sumptuary regulations early on (like England after 1604) or never promulgated any (like the Dutch Republic after its formation in the 1560s).[126]

125   Brakensiek, 'Farms', pp. 224–5.
126   W. Hooper, 'The Tudor sumptuary laws', *English Historical Review* 30 (1915),

But in Germany, Austria, Switzerland, Scandinavia, Spain, Italy, and even France, sumptuary regulations survived long past 1600, were supported by many non-state institutions, and were enforced in practice, albeit selectively according to the interests of the social groups that endorsed them.[127] Indeed, it was precisely their frequent support by local elites that ensured that sumptuary regulations were sometimes enforced: the better sort wanted to demarcate their social status *vis-à-vis* the lower strata, men wanted to control women's behaviour, employers wanted to discipline servants and labourers, local guild masters wanted to protect their own markets against competition from exotic imports, and governments wanted to make ordinary people spend less on themselves so they could pay more in taxes.[128]

Microstudies show sumptuary laws sometimes being enforced quite systematically. For one rural Württemberg locality of only about 300 households, for instance, an early-eighteenth-century register lists 110 individuals (91 per cent of them female) fined during a period of twelve months for wearing 218 forbidden garments, most of them small items of silk or calico. Fines varied from the equivalent of a day's earnings for an adult male weaver to two weeks' wages for a local maidservant. A fine of this magnitude for wearing a forbidden garment did not make it *impossible* to make that choice, but it made it more costly and cannot fail to have deterred the marginal consumer, especially among women and the less well off. The enforcement of sumptuary controls in this community also

433–49 (pp. 448–9); A. Hunt, *Governance of the consuming passions: a history of sumptuary law* (Basingstoke, 1996), pp. 34, 40; R. Ross, 'Sumptuary laws in Europe, the Netherlands and the Dutch Colonies', in *Contingent lives: social identity and material culture in the VOC World*, ed. N. Worden (Cape Town, 2006), pp. 382–91 (pp. 385–6).

127   C. M. Belfanti and F. Giusberti, 'Clothing and social inequality in early modern Europe: introductory remarks', *Continuity and Change* 15 (2000), 359–65 (pp. 359–61); N. Bulst, 'Kleidung als sozialer Konfliktstoff. Probleme kleidergesetzlicher Normierung im sozialen Gefüge', *Saeculum* 44 (1993), 32–46, esp. pp. 32–8; C. Fairchilds, 'Fashion and freedom in the French Revolution', *Continuity and Change* 15 (2000), 419–33, esp. pp. 420–1; H. Freudenberger, 'Fashion, sumptuary laws, and business', *Business History Review* 37 (1963), 37–48 (pp. 37, 40, 43, 46 and 48); Hunt, *Governance*, pp. 17–41; J. B. Moyer, 'Sumptuary law in ancien régime France, 1229–1806' (unpublished Ph.D. thesis, Syracuse University, 1996), esp. pp. 231–6 and 244–336; D. Roche, *A history of everyday things: the birth of consumption in France, 1600–1800* (Cambridge, 2000), pp. 203–4 and 279.

128   For a detailed discussion, see Hunt, *Governance*, pp. 17–41; S. Ogilvie, 'Consumption, social capital, and the "industrious revolution" in early modern Germany', *Journal of Economic History* 70 (2010), 287–325 (pp. 304–6).

evoked enormous resentment and enduring conflicts – in one case, a nine-year-long feud between two rural families – providing additional evidence that even those who could afford to violate them perceived such laws as a real constraint.[129] Inventory studies of rural Württemberg find that clothing regulations were largely complied with until the abandonment of sumptuary legislation in the final decades of the eighteenth century; in turn, this may have contributed to the late onset of the Consumer Revolution in the rural societies of central Europe.[130]

Another aspect of the early modern legal system that Schlumbohm dismisses consisted of laws regulating geographical mobility. Certainly not all the brutal vagrancy laws of pre-modern rural societies were always enforced, but the fact that they *could* be enforced and the severity of the penalties that were sometimes imposed set a high expected cost on violations, which inevitably entered into the calculations of rural people in making their choices.[131] The seventeen female gypsies hanged after a summary trial in eighteenth-century Franconia for no crime other than their itinerant way of life would have been surprised to learn, had they been able to read Schlumbohm or Foucault, that the migration ordinances of the early modern Franconian legal system were 'laws that were not enforced' and merely served symbolic purposes in the assertion of sovereignty by a 'theatre state'.[132]

A final aspect of the legal system that constrained peasant choices consisted of marriage laws. As Josef Ehmer has shown, throughout the early modern period many parts of Germany, Austria and Switzerland imposed stringent legal restrictions on permission to marry, culminating in the notorious nineteenth-century regime of 'politische Ehekonsens' (political consent to marriage).[133] Microstudies in a variety of central European

---

129   So widespread is the evidence that consumption laws were sometimes enforced in practice that even Schlumbohm is compelled to acknowledge (in a footnote) that 'admittedly there absolutely is evidence of cases in which violations of clothes ordinances were punished'; see Schlumbohm, 'Gesetze', p. 653 n. 23.

130   H. Medick, *Weben und Überleben in Laichingen 1650–1900. Untersuchungen zur Sozial-, Kultur- und Wirtschaftsgeschichte aus der Perspektive einer lokalen Gesellschaft im frühneuzeitlichen Württemberg* (Göttingen, 1996), pp. 384–7, 398–406, 414 and 427; Holzem, 'Religiöse Prägungen'.

131   E. Schubert, *Arme Leute, Bettler und Gauner im Franken des 18. Jahrhunderts* (Neustadt a.d. Aisch, 1983), pp. 249–50, 295 and 323.

132   Schlumbohm, 'Gesetze', pp. 660–1.

133   J. Ehmer, *Heiratsverhalten, Sozialstruktur und ökonomischer Wandel. England und Mitteleuropa in der Formationsperiode des Kapitalismus* (Göttingen, 1991).

territories show these laws being enforced – not perfectly, but enough to affect the choices not just of the 6 per cent of individuals observed being denied permits in one well-known study, but of a wider penumbra of people who knew they would be refused a permit and hence did not even apply.[134] Jerg Rauschenberger from an isolated hamlet in the Württemberg Black Forest, who was refused permission to marry a young woman from the nearest village in 1743 on the grounds that 'the latest instructions from the district authorities relating to the many princely decrees and to the princely marriage ordinance totally prohibit recognition of such marriages any longer, and on both sides [groom and bride] there is nothing but pure poverty present', is unlikely to have agreed that early modern German marriage legislation consisted of 'laws that were not enforced'.[135]

A major reason central European marriage laws were enforced, as Ehmer shows, is that they served the interests of local elites concerned to prevent the proliferation of poor householders, keep welfare payments low, and maintain a cheap workforce of unmarried servants and labourers.[136] Between c.1700 and c.1870, marriage ages and celibacy rates increased across large swathes of German-speaking central Europe, rising more in those territories where the marriage laws were stricter.[137] These restrictions on access to marriage by 'economically and morally weak persons' not only limited the choices of ordinary people such as Jerg Rauschenberger, but had wider socio-economic consequences: epidemic male emigration, plummeting sex ratios, rocketing illegitimacy, and sky-high infant mortality.[138] The central European marriage regulations

134 On this, see, e.g., K.-J. Matz, *Pauperismus und Bevölkerung. Die gesetzlichen Ehebeschränkungen in den süddeutschen Staaten während des 19. Jahrhunderts* (Stuttgart, 1980), p. 233; E. Mantl, *Heirat als Privileg. Obrigkeitliche Heiratsbeschränkungen in Tirol und Vorarlberg 1820 bis 1920* (Vienna and Munich, 1997); E. Mantl, 'Legal restrictions on marriage: marriage and inequality in the Austrian Tyrol during the nineteenth century', *The History of the Family* 4 (1999), 185–207; S. Ogilvie, *A bitter living: women, markets, and social capital in early modern Germany* (Oxford, 2003), pp. 51–3, 74, 135, 177, 252, 311, 313 and 332–9; S. Ogilvie, 'Population growth and state policy in central Europe before industrialization', Centre for History and Economics Working Paper (1995), http://www.econ.cam.ac.uk/people/faculty/sco2/pdfs/Population-and-State-in-Central-Europe-1995.pdf.
135 Landeskirchliches Archiv Stuttgart, Pfarrarchiv Ebhausen, Kirchenkonventsprotokolle, Vol. IV, fol. 10v, 26.4.1743.
136 Ehmer, *Heiratsverhalten*.
137 Ogilvie, 'Population Growth'; Ehmer, *Heiratsverhalten*.
138 For consideration of the demographic implications of the marriage controls, see J. E. Knodel, 'Law, marriage and illegitimacy in nineteenth-century Germany', *Population*

illustrate vividly how even laws that are not perfectly enforced can affect individual choices and have far-reaching consequences for entire societies.

Empirical studies thus show clearly that legal systems facilitated some peasant choices and constrained others. Even legal institutions such as those of England or the Low Countries, which are described as most facilitative, affected the choices peasants could make. In other European societies, the legal system reached prescriptively into deeper aspects of individual choice, regulating consumption, migration, marriage, and other spheres of action. Although laws were never enforced perfectly, they did not need to be. Legal prescriptions equipped conflicting parties – fellow peasants, communal oligarchies, landlords, princes – with legitimacy in seeking to constrain others' choices. Even when peasants circumvented the law, the law nonetheless affected their behaviour through the actions they took to avoid detection and the risks they faced in acting illicitly. Even partial enforcement of laws on marriage, migration, property or consumption could have long-term effects on peasant choices and, through them, on wider demographic and economic developments.

Conclusion

Where does this leave us in thinking about choices and constraints in rural societies? In recent decades, as we have seen, one important strand of research has revealed the broad scope for individual choice exercised by pre-modern rural people while another has illuminated the strength, variety and complexity of the structural constraints on those choices. Yet these two strands of scholarship have often been pursued in apparent mutual obliviousness. If we bring these two strands together, what are the implications for how we think about rural societies more widely?

First, combining these perspectives casts doubt on the usefulness of 'peasant culture' or 'the choiceless peasant' as an explanation for rural economic stagnation. Many social scientists ascribe development failures in rural economies, both in modern poor societies and in pre-industrial Europe, to distinctive concepts and preferences among peasants, which prevent them from making individual choices in any meaningful sense

Studies 20 (1967), 279–94; T. W. Guinnane and S. Ogilvie, 'A two-tiered demographic system: "insiders" and "outsiders" in three Swabian communities, 1558–1914', *The History of the Family* 19 (2014), 77–119.

of the term. Among economists, the assumption that peasants did not make choices – that they would not respond positively to development assistance or negatively to deprivation – underpinned the disastrous post-1945 policies of 'squeezing agriculture' to support industry.[139] Among historians, the idea that peasants did not make individual choices underlay accounts of how agricultural change, proto-industrialisation, and 'forced commercialisation' were imposed on inert rural populations over the past 800 years.[140] Among historians of eastern Europe, the notion that peasant culture defined many demographic and economic activities as lying outside the realm of choice has been used to explain centuries of economic stagnation, divergence between eastern and western Europe, and the difficulties of twentieth-century history.[141] The idea that peasants do not make individual choices implies that it is the peasant mentality, not the organisation of peasant society, which generates exploitation, poverty and stagnation. This leads to the conclusion that peasant societies cannot change from within, but only through coercion or eradication of peasant culture by modernizing landlords, capitalists, or bureaucrats. A complete understanding of why rural economies are poor and undeveloped must await a more thorough analysis of their functioning, but the evidence on the broad scope of individual peasant choice suggests strongly that the obstacles to economic success in rural societies are external and institutional, not inward and cultural.

The second set of implications relates precisely to these external obstacles. The evidence discussed in this chapter casts doubt on the view that 'peasant agency' is so powerful that institutional constraints do not matter. The powers of landlords over peasants under the manorial system varied across Europe, but empirical studies leave little doubt that they constrained peasant choice. In some manifestations, such as medieval England, manorial systems were fairly loosely organised, leaving interstices within which peasants could make their own choices; but even here people incurred costs in circumventing manorial regulations. In other societies, landlords' powers were much greater and the penalties

139 I. M. D. Little, *Economic development: theory, policy, and international relations* (New York, 1982), pp. 149–60.
140 Kriedte, Medick and Schlumbohm, *Industrialization*, pp. 41–53 and 99–115; H. Wunder, 'Agriculture and agrarian society', in *Germany: a new social and economic history, vol. 2: 1630–1800*, ed. S. Ogilvie (London, 1996), pp. 63–99 (pp. 63–6 and 87–91).
141 Mironov, 'Russian peasant commune'; Mironov, 'When and why', p. 333; Figes, *Peasant Russia*, pp. 8–12; Pallot, *Land reform*, pp. 15–17 and 242–9.

for violating manorial constraints more severe. Even where landlords exercised their rights of intervention rarely, their entitlement to do so still affected people's decisions. Violations of manorial regulations simply created black-market 'informal sectors' in which the fact that transactions were illegitimate rendered them risky, costly, open to exploitation, and incapable of contributing to long-term development. The evidence suggests that manorial constraints affected peasant choice, but in ways that can only be teased out by local-level investigation into the everyday lives of rural women and men.

Communities constituted a second constraint on peasant choice. They sometimes enabled peasants to engage in collective action, magnifying the effectiveness of peasant choice, but in many cases, community institutions enhanced the power of choice only for a privileged oligarchy, while limiting choice for less powerful villagers. The strong communities of central Europe regulated nearly every realm of human action – which did not prevent individual rural people from making choices within that the framework of communal constraints. In nearly every rural society, part of the social structure within which individuals made choices consisted of the communities in which they lived. Without taking community constraints into account, we cannot understand peasant behaviour or rural development more widely.

Finally, legal institutions influenced peasant choices. In many rural societies, the legal system guaranteed property rights and enforced contracts in ways that facilitated individual peasant choices. This was the case not just in England and the Netherlands, but in most parts of medieval and early modern Europe. This does not mean, however, that there was no scope for change between 1300 and 1800 in the facilitative services offered by the English (or any other) legal system. Rather, variations over time, among regions, and across societies mean that contract enforcement and property rights differed in interesting ways which need to be taken into account in explaining divergent paths of rural development.[142]

Moreover, in many early modern European societies, legal systems not only facilitated peasants' own choices but sought to alter those choices prescriptively. Although some have argued that these prescriptive laws were of a primarily symbolic and theatrical nature and cannot be

142   For further exploration of this argument, see S. Ogilvie and A. W. Carus, 'Institutions and economic growth in historical perspective', in *Handbook of economic growth*, ed. S. Durlauf and P. Aghion, 2 vols (Amsterdam, 2014), vol. 2A, pp. 405–513 , esp. pp. 453–7 and 460–2.

regarded as a constraint on peasant choices, local studies suggest that this view is Panglossian. Where prescriptive laws promised benefits to local elites or powerful interest groups, they could be enforced to a surprising degree, sufficiently to impose significant constraints on the choices of rural individuals. Even laws that were not thoroughly enforced – those governing migration, consumption, or marriage – imposed an expected cost on certain actions, altering the calculus of peasant choice in ways that can be observed on the level both of the individual person and of entire rural societies. Imperfectly enforced laws shaped human action, if only in the forms of behaviour people undertook to evade the law. Individual choice alone was not sufficient: decisions made by individuals always took place in the context of legal frameworks.

Why does this matter? The functioning of rural economies is now widely recognised as central to long-term improvements in economic growth and human well-being. Policies based on the idea that rural people are unable or unwilling to make choices will fail. But policies based on the idea that peasant agency is sufficient and that rural people will just get around any constraining institutions will also fail. We need to recognise both that rural people make choices and that their choices are constrained in particular ways by specific institutions. Only then will we understand why different rural economies follow different paths of development. The past generation of path-breaking historical scholarship on choices and constraints in rural economies has shown us the way to a better understanding of these issues, both for the past eight centuries and for the challenges of the future.

Some Commercial Implications
of *English Individualism*

R. W. HOYLE

Some thirty years ago and more, Alan Macfarlane dropped a sizeable bombshell.[1] He told us, with some vigour, what we always knew to be true but had been inclined to overlook: that in England, property was owned by individuals and not by kin groups, and that the individual owners of property had the right of sale without reference to kin, even their children. Macfarlane saw this mostly in terms of the ownership of land and, as will be recalled, held that the sale of land was frequent and the continuity of ownership within families limited. This prompted much debate and even some empirical research, and having contributed to both, especially with Henry French, I hope that it might now be agreed both that Macfarlane's insight is correct, but that people disposed of their land, or disinherited their heirs, much less often than Macfarlane supposed on the basis of a fairly cursory analysis of the evidence from

---

1   A. Macfarlane, *The origins of English individualism. The family, property, and social transition* (Oxford, 1978). I make no apology for returning to *English individualism*. I suspect that many of our historical interests are shaped by the books current in our formative years as undergraduates. For Richard Smith, I imagine that it is *The world we have lost*. For me it is both Macfarlane and Brenner. Macfarlane I finally managed to get hold of in Leeds City Library during my first (winter) vacation as an undergraduate: its interest was all the greater for the way in which Chris Dyer and Rodney Hilton both felt that it misrepresented them. Richard, was, of course, in at the beginning of *English individualism*. The generation following mine have always been enthralled by Thompson's *Customs in common* which, when it finally appeared (after Thompson had disengaged from CND), my generation thought rather a damp squib. Some, of course, undergo a mid-life crisis and follow Pomeranz to the ends of the world. We might all to have to go there yet.

Earls Colne.[2] Moreover, it might also be agreed that the individualistic possession of land is by no means solely an English phenomenon, but a north European one at the least, and perhaps the necessary consequence of both the demographic conditions common to northern Europe but also the capitalistic (or at least market-orientated) behaviour of peasants – or do we mean farmers?

Other forms of property barely featured in Macfarlane's analysis. Neither he nor anyone else has really thought about the consequences of English Individualism for economic endeavour in general. Yet there might be something worth saying here, even if there is a danger of any discussion of these questions becoming a statement of the obvious or familiar. In this chapter we concentrate on trade with some sideways glances towards agriculture. From time to time we will give some illustrations from a relatively late source, the autobiography of the bachelor Lancaster grocer William Stout (1665–1752).[3]

I

Trade in late medieval and early modern England was conducted by individuals trading on their own behalf for their own profit.[4] This is not to say that partnerships were unknown, but they were not common. The sixteenth century saw the emergence of trading on joint-stock lines, but this too was normally to meet specific purposes, notably the need to raise capital beyond the ability of single individuals or where the risk of trade was so great that it needed to be shared.[5] (Joint-stock principles also allowed for sleeping

2   H. R. French and R. W. Hoyle, '*English individualism* refuted and reasserted: the land market of Earls Colne, Essex, 1550–1750', *Economic History Review* 56 (2003), 595–622; H. R. French and R. W. Hoyle, *The character of English rural society: Earls Colne, 1550–1750* (Manchester, 2007).

3   *The autobiography of William Stout of Lancaster, 1665–1752*, ed. J. D. Marshall (Manchester, 1967), hereafter *Stout*.

4   These individuals were normally men although they might less often be spinsters or widows: they were rarely married women for, by English law, they owned no property while they were married.

5   For a popular discussion of 'the company', J. Micklethwait and A. Wooldridge, *The company. A short history of a revolutionary idea* (London, 2003) (which is actually a study of the limited-liability joint-stock company as is admitted on p. 4); see also C. G. A. Clay, *Economic expansion and social change: England, 1500–1700*, 2 vols (Cambridge, 1984), vol. 2, pp. 191–202.

investors.) Joint-stock companies were exceptional forms of business organisation – from 1719 their creation was impeded by the so called 'Bubble Act'
– and the attention that has been paid to them – as the precursors of more
modern forms – has often disguised the fact that the normal form of business
organisation well into the twentieth century was the single individual trading
on his own or less often in partnership. As Mokyr says, surely correctly,

> In the type of business typical in Britain around 1760, the bulk of economic
> activity was still carried out by businesses run by their owner, whose living
> standards were regulated more by cash flow than by profits per se.[6]

These are the 'family firms' or family businesses discussed by business
historians but strangely misnamed by them as these were largely one-man,
or one-woman, affairs, that might have employed family but did often not
endure across the generations.[7]

In the same way as the owner of land held that land without reference
to kin, so the individual entrepreneur traded on his own behalf without
reference to kin. Should he die intestate, then kin had a claim over his assets;
but the businessman had no requirement to make provision for them in his
will. Conversely, should an individual engaged in trade fail and be declared
bankrupt, then there was no suggestion that kin had any obligation to
contribute to the pool of assets which could be secured from the bankrupt's
business. They might do, but this reflects a desire for kin to protect their own
reputation rather than any requirement placed on them.[8] But in the event of
bankruptcy, kin had no claim over the bankrupt's assets nor the bankrupt's
creditors over theirs.[9] It is true that sureties could be demanded when money
was being lent, and some quite elaborate networks of mutual responsibility

6   J. Mokyr, *The enlightened economy. An economic history of Britain, 1700–1850*
(London, 2009), p. 351.

7   For instance A. Owens, 'Inheritance and the life-cycle of family firms in the
early industrial revolution', *Business History* 44 (2002), 21–46; H. Barker and
M. Ishizu, 'Inheritance and continuity in small family businesses during the early industrial
Revolution', *Business History* 54 (2012), 227–44.

8   Stout gives an account of John Hull, a former apprentice, whom Stout thought was
unsuited to trade. But his father, a clergyman, set him up in grocery. After a few years
Stout was proved right and Hull 'broke', 'to the great grief of his father, who made out
with the creditors honourably'. Stout himself spent his own money after his nephew failed
in trade, as I explain below. *Stout*, pp. 150 and 208–10.

9   There is an unexplored paradox here: that kin had a claim in one direction, but had no
responsibility in the other.

could emerge. Sureties were especially used when men were handling taxation or other 'public' money.[10] The records of Chancery and the other equity courts show just often these relationships went sour and how people suffered great financial difficulties through the failure of men for whom they had stood surety, or were even further removed from someone who in some way failed and whose sureties were called upon to make up a shortfall. This may usefully be seen as a system of insurance and reinsurance. Nonetheless, the point remains that, for the most part, individuals traded on their own behalf.[11] Contemporaries recognised this in the language of credit and the informal processes that went on in judging whether an individual was credit-worthy: was dealing with someone, either by formally lending him money or selling him goods on credit, a good risk or not? The question was not whether he was backed by a good family, but whether as an *individual* he looked likely to be able to honour an agreement.

The individual trading enterprise lasted as long as the lifetime of the trader and no longer. It could be brought to an end earlier by bankruptcy or retirement, but it was almost certainly ended by death unless there had been some form of managed handover. On death, the chattels of the deceased, including any leases he possessed, passed to his executor for the settlement of his debts, the collection of any debts owing him and the distribution of what remained after his debts and legacies had been satisfied.[12]

II

This implies that businesses had a life cycle of their own. New entrants started with two assets: a knowledge of the practice of trade acquired

---

10   From 1553, all crown treasurers and receivers were supposed to be bonded. W. C. Richardson, *History of the court of Augmentations, 1536–1554* (Baton Rouge, 1961), p. 248, citing 7 Edward VI, c. 1. For this process at a much later date, and litigation against sureties to recover crown debts, E. Parkinson, *The establishment of the Hearth Tax, 1662–66* (London, 2008), pp. 44, 81–2.

11   C. W. Brooks, *Law, politics and society in early modern England* (Cambridge, 2008), p. 314. For examples, see H. Horwitz and C. Moreton, *Samples of Chancery pleadings and suits, 1627, 1685, 1735 and 1785* (List and Index Soc., 257, 1995), nos. 14, 24, 25, 43, 46, 59, 100, 117, 136, etc.

12   H. Swinburne, *A brief treatise of testaments and last wills* (1590; repr. London, 1978), pp. 209–10. The executor did not have responsibilities for the testator's lands. If he had an instruction to sell them to repay debts, he was to account for them separately (p. 218). The situation was unaltered by the time of the sixth edition (1743).

through practice or observation as an apprentice; and an endowment from either inheritance, savings or loans. The son of a small farmer near Lancaster, William Stout was apprenticed in the last year of his father's life to a Lancaster ironmonger when aged sixteen (1679). In 1687, as his apprenticeship was drawing to a close, he had the chance of a shop in Lancaster, and the young Stout launched forth into trade. Stout's working capital was money and some small parcels of land left him by his father. He was able to draw on a bond for £50 plus accrued interest, and sell the land that he had inherited for £66, making in all £119 10s. He borrowed £12, which he repaid out of his first year's profits, and a further £10 of his sister (he seems to have had no savings of his own to draw on). He then had the shop fitted out with 'chests and draw boxes'. Finally, he sought to be released a few weeks early from his apprenticeship to allow him to travel to London with a party of Lancaster shopkeepers, and there bought goods to the value of £200, putting half their value down in ready money. While his purchases came back by sea, Stout returned by way of Sheffield and spent his last £20 on Sheffield and Birmingham manufactures. By the time he opened for business, Stout reckoned that he had about £300 worth of stock in the shop.[13]

After nine years' trading, Stout took stock. He thought that his 'goods and effects together' were worth £1,320. He had outstanding debts of £203 giving him a 'clear estate of £1,100 or upwards, all supposed good' (i.e. all realisable and so excluding bad debts). 'So that my improvement in nine years was above £100 a year, one year with another, the above losses excluded'.[14] Thereafter Stout seems to have computed his worth in most years as a closing financial statement made in or around April. This sort of practice seems not to have been uncommon. Ralph Josselin did the same, as his diary shows,[15] but happily Stout recorded most of his annual statements in his autobiography and this allows us to track his capital formation to his retirement when he was worth 'near £5,000, omitting what I thought to be dubious'.[16] The implication of the figures taken from

13 *Stout*, pp. 88–90.
14 Ibid., pp. 119–20. He was carrying £220 in bad debts from insolvent debtors and reflected that in his early years he had been too slow in calling in debts.
15 For instance, *The diary of Ralph Josselin, 1616–83*, ed. A. Macfarlane (London, 1976), pp. 365 (1656), 394 (1657) and 421–2 (1658). For another example, W. K. Jordan, *The charities of rural England, 1480–1660* (London, 1961), pp. 332–3, citing a funeral sermon of 1633. This annual totalling of goods is, in itself, a phenomenon which needs investigating.
16 *Stout*, p. 202.

the *Autobiography* is that Stout's working capital, in the sense of shop
stock, was not terribly large. If he normally carried about £350–400 of
stock (having started with about £300 and ending with £370), the figures
also show that he normally owed about £200 which we may suppose to
be goods supplied on credit.[17] The majority of his wealth was not in his
immediate business but saved and accumulated profits. His 'improvement'
in the early 1720s was normally in excess of £200 per year. There were
perhaps real limits on the size of a retail or wholesale grocery business in
Lancaster. Stout dabbled in shipping and transatlantic voyages but did not
make a great deal this way and grew disillusioned with the high risks and
poor returns. For this reason he may have looked for investment opportunities outside his core business. Some at least of his investments may have
been in house and shop property and warehousing in Lancaster, although
he seems not to have bought agricultural land. One must assume that at
least some of it took the form of money out at loan.

Stout started with £120 and ended with close to £5,000. As a bachelor,
he never had to accommodate the costs of a wife (he employed his sisters
and nieces as housekeepers) nor children, although he seems to have been
generous to his nephews and nieces. He noted in his autobiography for
1719 (when he was aged fifty-five) that his purpose in continuing in trade
was to make provision for his brother Leonard's children. In this respect,
his acceptance of responsibility for his nephew and nieces' advancement
perhaps makes him more akin to a married man than might at first sight
appear. In particular, he set his nephew William Stout up in trade, when he
was aged twenty-two, at the request of Leonard, the younger Stout having
been his uncle's apprentice. This marked the elder Stout's retirement from
trade, although he had to return to sort out his nephew's business affairs,
and also appears to have been relied upon by others to manage their
concerns. From the time of his retirement, Stout no longer gives details of
his wealth and we do not have an inventory for him: whether he was able
to protect his nest egg of £5,000 is therefore undiscoverable but doubtful
given the scale on which he had to bail out his feckless nephew.

Stout therefore conforms to a familiar pattern of the self-made man,
growing his capital year on year (although not without reverses), and then
retiring from active trade in his fifties to live off his accumulated wealth.
At the same time he also started to pass sums to the next generation,

---

17   Stout's nephew illustrates how not to do it: on his first failure he had shop goods to
the value of about £400, money owed to him of about £240, and himself owed about £930.

especially at the time of their marriage. This was the pattern described by Edward Waterhouse in 1665, of twenty years' accumulation between age thirty and fifty followed by a period of distribution.[18] A rather earlier commentator likened a man who reached the age of fifty before making provision for his children as akin to a man 'who sought corn in the fields at the end of September'.[19]

As a shopkeeper with a limited retail range, Stout seems to have been able to manage on a fairly small shop (or warehouse) inventory so his working capital was relatively small. Other trades seem to have worked on a rule of thumb that the larger the business the greater the credit that the individual businessman carried, both as debts owned and credit extended. As Zell has said on the basis of his study of Kentish clothiers,

> the more capital invested in raw material and in cottage labour to process it, the larger were the clothier's profits. Success in manufacturing was a function of the amount of capital that could be deployed.[20]

In a sense, the successful clothier was a man who had mastered a succession of conjuring tricks: of maintaining confidence in his ability to pay while making deferred payments to his suppliers of wool and artisans, while at the same time waiting on his London contacts to pay him for cloth supplied, which might not in its turn have been sold, but which was sold to them on three to six months' credit. The suppliers of wool and the labourers employed in spinning and weaving extended credit to the clothier; the clothier in turn extended credit to the merchant. There may actually have been very little money in the system and the considerable wealth of clothiers, seen in the balance at the end of their inventories, could be outweighed by the debts they owed. There may even be a rule of thumb that the more successful the clothier, the greater the proportion of his estate in debts receivable.[21]

We are talking here of sums of money owed by private individuals. Profit attached to them personally; equally default was a personal issue. The

18   Cited by R. Grassby, *Kinship and capitalism: marriage, family, and business in the English speaking world, 1580–1720* (Cambridge, 2001), p. 397. Grassby is quite right to say that inventories do not measure business fortunes at their height.
19   Cited by R. Houlbrooke, *The English family 1450–1700* (London, 1984), p. 246.
20   M. Zell, 'Credit in the pre-industrial English woollen industry', *Economic History Review* 49 (1996), 667–91 (p. 676).
21   Ibid., tab. 2., p. 684.

problem faced by a clothier was to tap enough of his circulating capital to allow him to establish himself as rich, whether in terms of housing and furnishings, and other forms of consumption, or the possession of land. It was widely appreciated that clothiers who took their capital out of trade diminished the trade: i.e., that they were able to employ fewer people. Of the Newbury clothier Thomas Dolman, a local doggerel poet wrote

> Lord have mercy upon us, miserable sinners.
> Thomas Dolman has built a new house and turned away all
>   his spinners.[22]

This, as much as social conservatism, explains why there were complaints of clothiers buying land and occasional proposals that they should be prevented from doing so.[23] The purchase of land was entirely rational from the clothier's point of view and might be seen as a diversion of capital from a volatile form of activity into one of enduring security, but at the same time it reduced their capacity to employ. Of course, when a clothier's house of cards tumbled, perhaps because depressed or disrupted markets ceased to allow him to satisfy debts lower downstream, unemployment was bound to result until other clothiers could raise the capital to fill the space left by the bankrupt and offer new employment to the weavers and other textile workers. Clothiers may also have taken their money (such as they could obtain) out of the clothing trade when business was flat and looked for better opportunities. The complaints about a clothier who switched his money into malting in the depressed year of 1622–23 are suggestive.[24]

Death had the same effect. It needs to be emphasised that death brought a trading business to an end. In the case of a clothier it must have brought at least temporary unemployment to his workforce until a new clothier appeared who could offer them work. It might be thought that widows or apprentices could keep a business turning over, but this is unlikely for several reasons.

First, when a businessman – whether shopkeeper or clothier – died, his assets became his executor's (or administrator's), and their duty was to

---

22   Cited in D. M. Palliser, *The age of Elizabeth*, 2nd edn (London, 1992), p. 107.
23   For instance, R. H. Tawney and E. Power (eds), *Tudor economic documents*, 3 vols (London, 1924), vol. 1, p. 326. A proposal to prevent West Country clothiers from buying land actually made it into law in 18 Eliz., c. 16, sect. iii.
24   J. V. Lyle (ed.), *Acts of the Privy Council of England, 1621–23* (London, 1932), pp. 394–5.

gather the assets together for the settlement of debts and a distribution of the remainder according to the terms of the deceased's will, or, should he have died intestate, according to the rules of intestacy. Normally, keeping a business running was not an option. It may have been more so when a testator appointed his wife executor, thereby giving her the option to continue the trade. For the most part, however, the role of executors was to realise value from essentially volatile assets rather than enhance their value by further trading. They might well be under pressure to realise value for creditors and legatees as well.[25]

Second, it might be impossible for a widow simply to take the business forward. When Stout's friend Augustine Greenwood dropped dead in the street in Lancaster early one evening in 1701, there was no question of the business carrying on. His wife knew little of her husband's affairs, there was 'no apprentice that knew anything of the management of his business' (although because Greenwood was a wholesale grocer there was no shop, merely a warehouse). Greenwood's widow brought Stout the keys of the warehouse 'and desired me to make use of them as I thought necessary for the safety of the goods and disposing of them, and to inspect his books to know how his accounts were kept'. She preferred to sell the business, stock and all, perhaps feeling that she had no great choice in the matter. After one purchaser failed to bring forward the necessary sureties, Stout reluctantly found himself buying his friend's business and relaunching it after a space of some weeks.[26] Stout was certainly not against women in trade. After Ralph Baynes, a soap- and candle-maker, was bankrupted and abandoned his family, Stout lent Elizabeth Baynes some £30 to restart her husband's business, which she did with the aid of his apprentice and with such success that she repaid Stout – and less happily, attracted her errant husband back to Lancaster.[27]

Third, businesses were underpinned by credit in the Muldrewian sense

---

25   There is a fundamental distinction from farming which needs to be considered. Farming testators were normally careful to bequeath their stock. The reason may well be that this protected the farm as a working enterprise. But, my feeling is that farmers' legacies were often to be paid out of future profits while clothiers' and tradesmen's were paid out of current assets. In this sense the farm is a continuing enterprise where the shop is not.

26   *Stout*, pp. 132–3.

27   Her husband, hearing of her success, returned to Lancaster and claimed the business from her 'till he wasted what she had'. He then abandoned her a second time for London and she was reduced to keeping a 'pot house'. *Stout*, pp. 125–6.

of reputation.[28] This was not a transferable asset. The deceased may have
been well respected, even solid, but there was no reason for creditors to
feel that this would simply rub off either on his wife, especially if she
was inexperienced in trade, or on an apprentice. A new proprietor of a
business could not expect to have the same credit extended to him or her
as the previous owner had received until they became a known quantity. In
any case, the normal rule of thumb in intestacy was for a widow to receive
only a third of her husband's goods if there were children or a half if there
were none:[29] it would rarely be possible for a business to keep going on the
same scale under a widow because of the abstraction of capital. Hence,
a widow was almost certainly faced with pressures to wind down, if not
wind up, her husband's business from creditors *including her husband's
administrators or executors* who might want their money out of her
husband's estate, or be reluctant to extend credit on the terms to which
her husband had been accustomed.

III

Although the phrase is rarely employed in this context, we are used to
thinking of farming as being essentially dynastic in that farming families
stayed on the same land for generations, son succeeding father. Land, or
in some circumstances a tenancy, was a much more tangible asset than
business capital, goodwill and skill.[30]

The death of a farmer brought his enterprise to an end in exactly the
same way as it did for a clothier or merchant. We would expect an inventory
to be taken, but the final record showing how the estate was wound up
is the probate account made after the debts and legacies of the deceased
had been paid.[31] What probably happened in many cases is outlined by the
Lancastrian diarist and nonconformist minister Peter Walkden in his diary

28   C. Muldrew, *The economy of obligation. The culture of credit and social relations in
early modern England* (Basingstoke and London, 1998).
29   See here the summary of inheritance rights in A. L. Erickson, *Women and property in
early modern England* (London, 1993), pp. 26–8.
30   There is much that is relevant to this discussion in D. Stead, 'The mobility of English
tenant farmers, c.1700–1850', *Agricultural History Review* 51 (2003), 173–89.
31   Probate accounts remain Cinderella documents: see A. Erickson, 'Using probate
accounts', in *When death do us part. Understanding and interpreting the probate records
of early modern England*, ed. T. Arkell, N. Evans and N. Goose (Oxford, 2000), pp. 103–19.

entries relating to the post-mortem affairs of a farmer in his congregation called Richard Parker. He visited Parker on 20 February 1733 and found him close to death; returning the following day he found that he had died during the night. His widow Ellen asked Walkden to read her his will (actually a deed of gift). Parker had given all his goods to one Brian Parker to see his debts settled and funeral expenses paid. Parker was then to pay interest on the balance to Parker's widow for life, for her support. On 24 February, Walkden went to help make the inventory, starting with the debts that Parker owed and then the money he had out at loan. He and his colleagues then viewed the animals on the farm, the goods in the shippon, the barn and lastly the house, omitting a bed and its bedclothes which they adjudged to belong to Parker's widow. She also claimed the sheep, her right to which Walkden and the others making the inventory queried, but chose not to value in the inventory. Nor did they include Parker's clothes, which Brian Parker thought should be given to some of his relations. They ended by agreeing to sell off Parker's goods on the following Wednesday and Walkden, among others, went off with handwritten bills announcing the sale. However, this was delayed as Brian Parker was advised that he needed to take the administration of the estate first. He also seems to have received advice about how Parker's widow should be treated. The deferred sale took place on 6 March, Walkden acting as clerk. Beforehand, Parker sent word that Ellen Parker would have to buy the household goods she wanted (including the bed) at the valuations in the inventory, which she did, and then the sale proceeded.[32]

Now this example, detailed as it is, contains some odd features. There were evidently no children to consider. Richard Parker thought that his widow's best interest was served by placing his goods in the hands of Brian Parker (one assumes a relation). We are not told what provision was made for the farm itself although the implication seems to be that Ellen Parker did not inherit it and it is possible that it was held on a life tenancy without any widow's right. On the other hand, the key features were surely of general applicability. The widow's rights were very limited and except for the customary minima, essentially at the discretion of her husband. She had no control over his goods, or, in this case, it seems, knowledge of his intentions towards her. The executors or administrators were responsible for a general cashing up of the estate, for the repayment of debts, the securing of any credits and the payment of any legacies.

32   P. Walkden, *A diary from January 1733 to March 1734 written by the Reverend Peter Walkden* (Otley, 2000), pp. 33, 34–5, 38–9, 46 and 52.

Let us consider a slightly different scenario in which the deceased had an adult inheriting son. The son might have received the farming stock together with implements and other fixed assets from his father as a legacy, but one assumes that debts and credits would still have to be reconciled and settled. This might entail the executors releasing cash by the sale of assets, for instance stock or implements, which the farm needed to function efficiently. The payment of legacies might be deferred especially where the legatees were children; or only interest paid on them until the legatee wished to receive payment.[33] Now even if the son took over on the day his father died, he was a different personality in legal terms. He would probably start with the handicap of a farm denuded of stock as realizable assets were paid to close his father's accounts with his creditors and laden with debt in the forms of legacies due to family members. There is a further obvious scenario which we can consider. Suppose that the deceased left a widow and small children: again his estate would have to be wound up – debts paid, credits perhaps called in – but here there was the additional complication of whether the widow could keep the farm turning over until one of her sons came of age to take it over. If the widow was a freeholder or had a lease, then there were obvious strategies available to her: letting the farm for a period, employing a farm bailiff to manage the farm on her behalf or even remarrying if the will permitted her to do so. If, however, her husband had just been a tenant at will, then the widow's options were really at the discretion of the estate. There is some evidence that nineteenth-century estate stewards were sceptical of the ability of women to farm on their own account and 'make the rent', and for that reason they were prone to discharge widows from their husband's farms.[34] The preference of nineteenth-century farmers to be tenants at will could therefore rebound on their widows.[35]

33   See here the very detailed analysis of the account book of Richard Latham by Andrew Gritt. He notes that Latham paid legacies (with interest) due under his sister's will of 1725 in 1740–41. A. J. Gritt, 'The farming and domestic economy of a Lancashire smallholder: Richard Latham and the agricultural revolution, 1724–67', in *The farmer in England, 1650–1980*, ed. R. W. Hoyle (Farnham, 2013), pp. 101–34 (p. 130).
34   N. Verdon, 'The "Lady Farmer": gender, widowhood and farming in Victorian England', in *The farmer in England*, ed. Hoyle, pp. 241–62 (pp. 247–8); also R.W. Hoyle, 'Introduction: recovering the farmer', in the same volume, pp. 1–42 (pp. 17–18).
35   The development of tenant right could give a widow a capital sum on which to draw if, for whatever reason, she gave the farm up: G. E. Mingay, 'The farmer', in *The agrarian history of England and Wales, VII: 1850–1914*, ed. E. J. T. Collins, 2 vols (Cambridge, 2000), vol. 1, pp. 759–809 (pp. 793–7).

The ideal scenario at which farmers perhaps aimed, even if few achieved it, was to establish an inheriting son on the farm; to convey to him, formally or informally, its working assets; and then retire. In this way, and perhaps in no other, could the continuity of farming be protected. Of course it required a combination of circumstances to make this possible: the farmer living long enough for him to have a son of the right age. Even in this scenario, what we see is the creation in every generation of a new legal entity that was distinct from what went before. Where this ideal scenario was not achieved, inheriting sons did not simply pick up where their fathers left off, but had to negotiate the settlement of the father's estates and the multiple costs and disadvantages this brought them. An incoming son could therefore be capital-poor but still had to meet his rent out of a farm operating at a less than optimal level.

IV

Maintaining a business over two or more generations was therefore not easy. One simple question had to be whether the two generations were equally placed: the one ready to give up the business and the other old enough to take it on. Ideally the younger generation would be of an age that the older generation could establish it in business by transferring capital (and perhaps workforce and clients) to it while allowing the older generation to take money out of the business. In a managed devolution of property, sons could receive capital, perhaps (as in Stout's case) the shop, workshop and warehouses, while daughters might have money assigned them for portions. But what also matters is the aptitude of the younger man for trade. A man still in trade in his fifties or sixties had surely displayed some skill in managing his affairs for, as Stout tells us many times, this skill was far from universal. Many of those who started out ended up in difficulties (including some of Stout's own apprentices), and some who were successful lost their touch and saw their businesses decline (including Stout's old master and mentor, Henry Coward).[36]

Stout's own business was passed to his nephew, another William, who had served the older Stout as his apprentice. In 1728, Stout assigned William junior the contents of the shop, its cellars and warehouse (worth

---

36 *Stout*, p. 121. Drawing on *Stout*, Ralph Houlbrooke itemises some of the reasons for the failure of Lancaster merchants: *English family*, p. 244.

£370) and gave him £32 in ready money with which to buy Sheffield goods. Stout junior also had the shop and its fittings (valued at £20), its cellars and warehouse, rent free. Stout quickly found that his nephew did not welcome his advice and his suspicion that he was not suited to trade turned out to be correct. In 1731–32, Stout had to take control of his nephew's affairs and sort out his debts. In 1732, when the younger Stout started out in trade a second time (but apparently no wiser), his uncle the autobiographer reflected that he had cost him £800 and more in four years.[37] Recapitalised by his uncle and with some money from his father-in-law, William Stout continued in trade for a few years thereafter but was made bankrupt in 1737. We last hear of him and his family living off a pension of £40 per annum given them by his uncle.[38] However, the point is that although the younger Stout was trading from his uncle's shop and using his stock initially, there was no legal connection between uncle and nephew in the sense that both were trading on their own account, and while Uncle William was concerned to sort out his nephew's affairs (and embarrassed by his failure), there was never any suggestion that he was liable for the shortfall.

Superficially, this looks like a trading dynasty, but there is no suggestion then that the two were trading in partnership. Did father/son partnerships nonetheless exist, or did sons set up independently in the same or a similar branch of trade as their fathers? Talk of merchant dynasties has obfuscated this matter and yet it has to be doubted whether it was really possible for them to exist in anything other than a sort of coincidental manner. Take here the Springs of Lavenham, four successive generations of prominent clothiers, and one of whom, Thomas Spring III (d.1523), is known to have been extremely wealthy. In the assessments made for the forced loan of 1522, he is reported to have had lands worth £20 (almost certainly an underestimate), movables in his own possession worth £1,800, 'sperate' debts (i.e. realisable debts) of £1,400 and desperate debts of £800. His loan was therefore calculated on the basis of goods worth £3,200, which was largely his working capital rather than realisable wealth (which was in his land).[39]

We have wills for all three Thomas Springs, and for family members of

37   *Stout*, p. 210.
38   Ibid., pp. 208–9, 210, 221–2, 232 and 238.
39   R. W. Hoyle, 'Taxation and the mid-Tudor crisis', *Economic History Review* 51 (1998), 649–75 (pp. 654–5); *The military survey of 1522 for Babergh hundred*, ed. J. Pound (Suffolk Record Soc., 28, 1986), p. 75.

the next generation, and none of them contain any suggestion that father and son were engaged in any sort of joint venture.[40]

In the case of Thomas Spring III, we do not have an inventory, but we do have a probate account which shows that the total value of his estate was a little over £8,000.[41] The only business-related expenses in the account are the payment of ulnage on 411 cloths, a necessary step before they could be sold. The whole value of the inventory was distributed in accordance with Spring's will: £3,400 went in legacies, and the greater part of £900 in charitable donations. About £1,300 is unaccounted for (because the account is damaged),[42] but the executors disposed of £5,500. Their purchase of land to establish a chantry took another £200. This left a balance of £2,389. The executors then agreed a further distribution to other family members, and gave an additional £100 to the tower and south aisle of Lavenham church and further £100 to the repair of roads. Having expended a further £2,303, the account was closed with a balance of £85 15s 9d. It is possible that this may not have been quite as the account suggests and that some of this money could have been left as working capital in a family business, but taken at face value, everything was realised and paid out as ready cash.

There is no suggestion here that the account deals with a half share of a family 'firm' or that any of it was left in the 'firm' to be paid at a later date when a legatee called for it. On the contrary, one would suppose that much of it was transformed into gold in the chest at the bottom of the legatees' beds. John Spring, his father's eldest son, had a legacy of £200 and household goods. The impression is that that the Spring family must have had to set about recreating their fortune, which they seem not to have done on anything like the same scale as they achieved in the previous generation. Spring's assets were dispersed among his family with no

40   The genealogy of the later Spring family can be found in J. Corder (ed.), *The visitation of Suffolk, 1561* (Harleian Soc., new ser. 11, 1981), pp. 32–3, including references to wills: their wills themselves mostly printed in J. J. Howard (ed.), *The visitation of Suffolke, 1561*, 2 vols (London, 1866), vol. 2, pp. 170–89. For the three Thomas Springs, the texts in D. Dymond and A. Betterton, *Lavenham. 700 years of textile making* (Woodbridge, 1982), pp. 68–70 are to be preferred. The Springs cry out for a new study to replace B. McClenaghan, *The Springs of Lavenham and the Suffolk cloth trade in the XV and XVI centuries* (Ipswich, n.d., ?1924), a pioneering study by a student of Eileen Power, but now terribly dated.

41   Printed in Dymond and Betterton, *Lavenham*, pp. 71–3. Of course, the probate account makes no comment on the disposition of land.

42   The missing £1,300 was probably mostly accounted for by the 1,600 marks left by the testator to his widow, and the household goods divided between her and John Spring.

protection for 'partners'. Indeed, it is very hard to see how a partnership could have worked when the death and distribution of goods seems to have been so total – and immediate. Any business, even if formally constituted as a partnership, must have been wrecked by the sudden abstraction of capital on the death of a partner.

Now this does lead to the suggestion that what we call merchant dynasties in the middle ages are merely successions of related individuals plying the same trade. The younger generation may well have been supplied by the older with capital (in both senses of the word), and as the older generation withdrew from trade, they may well have directed business to the younger. The accumulated profits of the business were probably transferred from working capital into land, endowments for younger children and memorial foundations such as chantries, schools and almshouses, leaving the younger generation to start the process of capital accumulation a second time. Yet the businesses of the two generations were – legally if not practically – separate entities.

Perhaps what is unusual about the Springs is that three successive generations remained in trade. Stout's vignettes of Lancaster life tells us something rather different: that sons often lacked the aptitude of their fathers for trade even if brought up to it. Now we know that the merchants often shifted their capital into land in the final phase of their trading lives and tended to establish their sons as landed gentry. Take here the example of the Bristol merchant John Smyth (d.1556) who remained a merchant, living in the town, but who established his elder son as a country gentleman while the younger son followed a career as a London lawyer until he inherited from his elder brother late in life.[43] Behaviour of this sort is often taken as evidence that merchants aspired to be leisured gentlemen, yet it is also an acknowledgement that entrepreneurial skills and judgment in trade were not hereditary and unlikely to be replicated in two successive generations. The safest way to perpetuate a fortune was in land.

V

Shopkeepers like Stout were not significant employers. They had apprentices and shop assistants, but no more. Employment was associated with

---

43 It might be noted that Smyth was a second-generation merchant. See J. H. Bettey, *The rise of a gentry family. The Smyths of Ashton Court, c.1500–1642* (Bristol, 1978).

manufacturing rather than with retailing. For Robert Reyce, describing the Suffolk clothier of the early seventeenth century,

> he which maketh ordinarily 20 broad clothes every week, cannot set so few a-work as 500 persons, for by that time his wool is come home, and is sorted, *saymed*, what with breakers, dyers, woodsetters, wringers, spinners, weavers, burlers, sheerman and carriers, besides his own large family, the number will soon be accomplished. [S]ome there be that weekly set more a work, but of this number there are not many.[44]

Clothiers could cease business in one of three ways. They could depart in a managed sense by retirement or in an unmanaged way by bankruptcy or death. The last two are remarkably similar. Third parties, whether commissioners in bankruptcy or executors, sought to seize whatever assets were available (and the making of an inventory was perhaps integral to both processes). Assets were realised and sold and then distributed, in bankruptcy to the creditors, in executorship to legatees or family. Where trading stopped abruptly, one must imagine that economic activity ceased: nothing more was put out; that which was available was gathered in.[45] The result must have been unemployment until another clothier stepped in to take on some of the pool of labour left by the bankrupt or deceased. In the event of bankruptcy because of adverse trading conditions, it might perhaps be some time before that gap was filled as men may well have lacked capital to invest, and those who did have capital available might well be cautious about investing it in flat market conditions. Indeed, one might suggest that bankruptcy left capital tied up in the wreck of the bankrupt's estate and produced both a discouragement to invest but also a shortage of capital with which to invest. It is therefore easy to see how merchants' and clothiers' bankruptcies could be an issue of concern even to the Privy Council because of their impact on employment.[46] Death, however, may well have resulted in capital leaking out of trade into

---

44 *Suffolk in the XVIIth century. The Breviary of Suffolk by Robert Reyce, 1618* (London, 1902), p. 22.

45 One might also notice that as friends of the bankrupt/deceased, they might be the same people. Where executors declined to act, creditors might be appointed to administer the estate making the similarity with a commission of bankruptcy very close indeed.

46 See here J. V. Lyle (ed.), *Acts of the Privy Council of England, 1619–21* (London, 1930), pp. 79–80, a petition from eighty clothiers of Suffolk and Essex, clients of Gerard Read, a bankrupt London merchant, and 'many thousand of poor men', or Lyle (ed.), *Acts of the Privy Council of England, 1621–23*, pp. 278 and 381, the Council intervening in the

non-mercantile forms of investment. Some, of course, may have been lent within the trading community – we do not and cannot know – but money which was assigned to marriage dowries or kept in reserve for the education of children may well have been held as cash under the bed until the development of mortgaging as a long-term form of investment in the seventeenth century and government annuities and other similar investments later in that century.

VI

Having shown the way in which death brought an end to a business enterprise, *de jure* if not *de facto*, let us now consider an example where it did not. This is the Crowley enterprise discussed many years ago by Professor Flinn and not much considered since.[47] At first sight this looks like a multigenerational firm, but in law, it too was merely the private possession of a succession of related individuals.

Three generations of the family need to be considered. Ambrose Crowley II (d.1721) was in essence a Stourbridge ironmonger who acquired a range of investments in iron goods and nail manufacturing. His son, Sir Ambrose Crowley III (1658–1713), was apprenticed in London and played little or no role in the west midland industry nor, with the possible exception of any pump-priming capital he received, did he share in his father's estate. This was largely dispersed pre-mortem among his children by a second marriage on the elder Crowley's retirement from trade in 1710–11. Ambrose II did retain some business interests (in the form of his share of partnerships) and made a will in 1713 primarily in favour of the daughter who acted as his housekeeper. When he died in 1721 it was found that the estate would not cover the bequests contained in the will.[48] There was no trading connection between him and his son, Sir Ambrose, who may well have been the richest entrepreneur of his age, with ironworks and forges in County Durham, a warehouse in London and substantial interests in both the export trade and naval contracting. His business continued through into the nineteenth century, but for most of the eighteenth it was never more than the singular possession of a private individual.

affairs of Samuel Salmon of Creeting in Suffolk, clothier, and his creditors: the council expresses anxiety about getting his workmen (said to number 200) back to work.
47   M. W. Flinn, *Men of iron. The Crowleys in the early iron industry* (Edinburgh, 1962).
48   Ibid., pp. 18–23.

In the absence of the business's own records, we need to fall back on what remains in other archives. The Crowley business passed from Sir Ambrose to his son John, who in turn died in 1728 before he had reached the age of forty. As John's eldest son was only aged nine or ten at his father's death, there is a period in which we have slightly more extant documentation arising from the administration of the firm by Crowley's executors. In the period 1728–31, an account shows that the firm was making an annual average gross profit of £13,000 before any allowance is made for depreciation. In a little over four years between 1728 and 1732, the 'stock' of the business rose by £28,623. At the end of the decade, the annual increase in stock value was over £10,000 per annum.[49]

This was not though the value of the company as such: it was the personal wealth of the owner. Just as the Springs' wealth was largely in the form of unsold cloth, so the wealth of John Crowley on his death in 1728 was largely stock held in his warehouses, whether in the form of bar iron awaiting forging, or finished goods awaiting sale, or debts owed by the purchasers of his goods. An inventory made of his goods and assets in 1728 shows that the factory and warehouse stocks were then worth £92,886 and debts owed to Crowley £87,112.[50] So while Flinn can say that 'the capital assets of the firm, [were] valued in 1728 at £153,000',[51] these were actually the capital assets of the late John Crowley held by his executors. For this reason, the inventory includes what we would regard as personal possessions: the furnishings of Crowley's houses in London and Greenwich, and the wine in his cellars. As there was no distinction to be made between the firm's money and its owner's money, it was entirely Crowley's choice how much he took out of the firm for personal and family expenditure, for savings and for investment in land. Where Crowley perhaps differed from others in the same position was the sheer scale of the surplus that the company generated. At £8,000 per annum, the estimated expenditure of £50,000 on the dowries of his daughters by Sir Ambrose or £36,000 on land in Suffolk by John Crowley was not a great pressure on the business but it was, of course, money that could have been reinvested in it.[52] In all of these respects, the make up and legal standing of

49   Ibid., pp. 176–7.
50   Ibid., pp. 174–5. I am grateful to Professor Chris Evans (who unintentionally set me thinking about the Crowleys) for sending me his notes on the inventory.
51   Flinn, *Men of iron*, p. 171.
52   Ibid., pp. 43, 86 (Sir Ambrose's expenditure on dowries) and p. 178 (investment in land).

the company was no different from that of any other family firm or corner shop or farm. The ownership was vested in a single individual. After all, it was Sir Ambrose Crowley and not his business that was rumoured to have gone bankrupt in 1713.[53]

John Crowley died in 1728 leaving an injunction that the business was to be continued. That it was possible for this to be done reflects the family's reliance on a managerial cadre who offered the corporate continuity that individual owners could not. It was when the company's manager died in 1730 that the executors despaired of finding someone who could adequately manage the business and thought of winding it up. In the event, a managerial succession was readily achieved, but what is uncertain is just how closely the general managers were supervised by the adult family members during the minority of Ambrose Crowley IV.[54]

Of course, the scale of the Crowley business exceeded virtually everything else in its own times, but it is not its scale but the introduction of managers that marks the breach between the medieval and the modern, for they allowed the company to continue through minorities. Moreover, they allowed the company to be carried forward when the owner lacked interest or aptitude, or chose to retire and withdraw from the everyday management of the company. Nonetheless, they made no difference to the company's standing at law.

VII

In one of the discontinuities with which history abounds, there is an entirely separate body of writing on the family firm, written largely by business historians, and starting largely in the later eighteenth century. Much of what we have suggested here applies directly to this literature.[55]

---

53   D. Cranstone, 'From slitting mill to alloy steel: the development of Swalwell Ironworks', *Industrial Archaeology Review* 33 (2011), 40–57 (p. 42). I owe my knowledge of this to Professor Chris Evans.

54   Flinn, *Men of iron*, pp. 77–8.

55   I have found useful – besides the papers noted subsequently – M. B. Rose, 'The family firm in British business, 1780–1914', in *Business enterprise in modern Britain, from the eighteenth to the twentieth century*, ed. M. W. Kirby and M. B. Rose (Manchester, 1994), pp. 61–87; P. Hudson, 'Financing firms, 1700–1850', in *Business enterprise in modern Britain*, ed. Kirby and Rose, pp. 88–112; and A. Colli and M. B. Rose, 'Family firms in comparative perspective', in *Business history around the world*, ed. F. Amatori and G. Jones (Cambridge, 2003), pp. 339–52.

The family firm is rather sneered at and held to be inferior to the managerial firm.[56] It is seen as being largely anomalous in the twentieth century and later, and this colours perceptions of its eighteenth- and nineteenth-century forms. Individual family firms are largely transient, from which the implication is drawn that they were unsuccessful. Few early firms went into a second generation and it has been suggested that second generation proprietors were less successful than the founders of businesses.[57] Other writing has suggested that one of the chief problems faced by family businesses was the succession to the management of the firm and the intergenerational conflict between family members that succession provoked.[58] Now one might suggest that this all slightly misses the point. It would be conceded that the family firm as a term includes a wide range of enterprises with very different levels of family involvement, but the essential cleavage in its character surely falls between those that were perceived by their owners as being essentially one-generational and those that were intended to endure into a second or third generation. This is surely a question of *mentalité*, although many who saw themselves as dynasts may have had their ambitions thwarted by cruel and capricious demographic events. Where a family firm was seen as the work of a single generation, then we have Stout's life cycle of first, accumulation, followed second, by a shifting of assets out of the firm into investments, be they in property or loans or bonds, and third, retirement. The aim of the firm might be to generate assets for the support of the entrepreneur and his wife in retirement and the establishment of his children in trade or marriage. Assets are largely dispersed in the third phase of life, the next generation starts at perhaps the same low level as the old generation and the cycle of accumulation, investment and retirement is repeated again. Where the firm is seen as spanning generations and the younger generation are expected to take over its management (as with the Crowley enterprise), then there is no break on investment and accumulation. Retiring family members, rather than running down their business, had every incentive to keep it going as best they could, so that in retirement they continue to take a profit from the enterprise while keeping the firm plump to be handed over to an heir.

This interpretation places us firmly in the company of those business

56   See the summary of the literature in Colli and Rose, 'Family firms', pp. 341–3.

57   See here the useful survey of the literature in Barker and Ishizu, 'Inheritance and continuity', pp. 227–8.

58   Colli and Rose, 'Family firms', pp. 346–51.

historians who have stressed the *family* in family firm and seen the firm as being an instrument to serve the needs *of the family*.[59] These historians have noted that some businessmen wanted their businesses liquidated and the assets distributed among their heirs after their deaths, whereas others wanted family members to take their business forward. Of course, the choice that businessmen made cannot be separated from their individual family circumstances: whether there were family members old enough to take a business on, or with an aptitude to take it forward. Some capitalists consciously made it less likely that this would be possible by selecting a grammar school education – for a career in the church or the law – for their children. The option of retiring and then distributing assets, or asking for the firm to be sold up post mortem, were both legitimate means of meeting the parental instinct of assisting the next generation. But then, so too was keeping the firm turning over, but this probably depended on fathers being able to hand their businesses over to sons of the right age and experience, which we might suggest was around 55–60 years of age for the father and 25–30 years for the son. This was almost certainly easier to achieve in the eighteenth century with a falling age at marriage and a rising expectation of life. One may speculate that the nearer one gets to the nineteenth century, the greater the possibility of a managed handover of a businesses from the older to the younger generation. If that could be achieved, then all to the good: otherwise there was a danger of the firm going through a testamentary process with the calling in of debts and credits.

On the other hand, farming might offer an alternative to those many areas of commerce where businesses were essentially volatile. Where the prime asset was the land, or most likely a lease of the land, a farming enterprise had to be kept turning over if only to pay the rent to the landlord. We noted earlier that there was probably a reluctance on the part of farming families to lose the tenancy or run down their capital as without both, re-entry into farming would be difficult. So it is probably in agriculture that we should expect to find dynastic behaviour, with multi-generational businesses, perhaps though of short duration. We know that these existed, although little has ever been done to describe their numbers or dynamics.[60]

59   Owens, 'Inheritance and the life-cycle of family firms'; Barker and Ishizu, 'Inheritance and continuity', pp. 228–9.
60   There is some interesting material here in J. Broad, 'Farmers and improvement, 1780–1840', in *The farmer in England*, ed. Hoyle, pp. 165 –92 (pp. 176–9).

VIII

Property in England was vested in individuals; but they were largely male individuals. Women who owned property in their own right had their interest subsumed in their husband's property. Even if an enterprise was a joint effort, with the active contribution of both partners, on the husband's death it came to an end. There was a cashing up, a settlement of the (husband's) debts, probably a distribution of money to the next generation. There was no concept, akin to normal will-making practice today, that the husband's estate should be transferred to his widow lock, stock and barrel, for her support and for her to undertake the eventual distribution. Why were there so many poor widows in England? Why was it so hard for them to carry on their husband's businesses? Why did so many widows look to remarry to maintain their standard of living? The answer lies in fundamental structures within English law.

Now these have important implications for the capital growth in trade. As we have already suggested, men may have remained in trade for a fairly short period of their lives – perhaps a quarter century or thirty years – before scaling down their activities or, rather, starting to run their activities in order to display their success and to make provision for their children by transferring money into landed assets. Both imply the abstraction of capital from trade. None of this made any difference so long as men falling out of trade were matched by men coming into trade. But let us envisage two circumstances in which this might not be the case.

The first is simply regional. If by death or bankruptcy a district is no longer served by clothiers, then by implication, it ceases to be active in textiles. The absence of clothiers implies the absence of employment. The regional decline of a textile industry, whether in East Anglia or the West Country, is plainly a matter that has several aspects, but one of them is the lack of capital, and that, in turn, implies a lack of individuals with capital who are willing to hazard it.[61] In these circumstances we find attempts to create faux-capitalists to offer employment: through village stocks for instance, or through municipal work schemes.

Second, let us envisage a situation in which there are random moments of high mortality. Death, we have established, brings a trading venture

---

61   See here the interesting paper by L. Flisher and M. Zell, 'The demise of the Kent broadcloth industry in the seventeenth century', *Archaeologia Cantiana* 129 (2009), 239–56.

to an end. The capital invested in it (and there may not be a great deal after all claims have been settled) probably leached out of trade into non-productive forms of investment. If a widow carried on her husband's venture with, say, an apprentice, then it had to be at a lower level of economic activity than her husband's business because so much of the capital would have been dispersed. Sudden death must have reduced the capital available to industry as money was transferred into widows' endowments and legacies for the next generation. Some too went into the changing forms of religious observance aimed at memorialisation and the saving of the deceased's soul. Furthermore, death must have reduced the human capital (in the form of knowledge and understanding of the business) but also social capital (in the disruption of the networks that made trade possible). Seen in this light, it becomes possible to see how waves of disease must have had a serious impact on economic activity and so created unemployment and a lower level of production.

Random mortality must have truncated many business careers before they achieved their apogee: it must have disrupted capital accumulation. Was the stabilisation of mortality therefore necessary to allow capital accumulation to proceed apace? Did it allow the emergence of multi-generational enterprises? Or did it simply result in more men living to enjoy their gains in the form of ostentation and a life in the country in their third (spending) phase of life?

The individualistic ownership of property, as seen in trade, certainly produced disadvantages. The life cycle restricted the scale of the enterprise by limiting the process of capital accumulation to twenty-five or thirty years. And yet what we do not see in the middle ages or the early modern period is the emergence of 'firms' as partnerships or joint-stock lines as corporate entities which could endure beyond the lifetimes of their founders. Those that we do see after the mid sixteenth century serve a different purpose, of allowing investors to pool their money to engage in expensive (and high risk) forms of trade. And so there are questions to be asked about why something – an evolution of economic structures – did not happen, about whether anybody thought that it was desirable that it did happen, or whether there was a total acceptance with the way things were.

These are fundamental questions: I do not know that they have been much thought about. The company has recently been exalted as one of the great inventions of western society.[62] If this institutional development

---

62   Micklethwait and Wooldridge, *Company*.

did so much to advance economic development, how far did the individual ownership of economic property retard it? In turn, how far was the individual ownership of property coloured by the underlying demographic conditions of the age, of mortality, life expectation, and the rising and falling chances of handing a business over to a successor? I do not know the answers, but the questions seem worth asking.

Select Bibliography

Boulton, J., and L. Schwarz, '"The comforts of a private fireside"? The workhouse, the elderly and the poor law in Georgian Westminster: St Martin-in-the-Fields, 1725–1824', in *Accommodating poverty: the housing and living arrangements of the English poor, c.1600–1850*, ed. J. McEwan and P. Sharpe (Basingstoke, 2011), pp. 221–45.

Briggs, C., *Credit and village society in fourteenth-century England* (Oxford, 2009).

Briggs, C., 'English serfdom, c.1200–c.1350: towards an institutionalist analysis', in *Schiavitu e servaggio nell'economia europea. Secc. XI–XVIII/Slavery and serfdom in the European economy from the 11th to the 18th centuries. XLV settimana di studi della Fondazione istituto internazionale di storia economica F. Datini, Prato 14–18 April 2013*, ed. S. Cavaciocchi (Florence, 2014), pp. 13–32.

Briggs, C., 'Manor court procedures, debt litigation levels, and rural credit provision in England, c.1290–c.1380', *Law and History Review* 24 (2006), 519–58.

Broad, J., 'Parish economies of welfare, 1650–1834', *Historical Journal* 42 (1999), 985–1006.

Campbell, B. M. S., 'The agrarian problem in the early fourteenth century', *Past and Present* 188 (2005), 3–70.

Campbell, B. M. S., 'Population pressure, inheritance, and the land market in a fourteenth-century peasant community', in *Land, kinship and life-cycle*, ed. R. M. Smith (Cambridge, 1984), pp. 87–134.

Cavaciocchi, S. (ed.), *Schiavitu e servaggio nell'economia europea. Secc. XI–XVIII/Slavery and serfdom in the European economy from the 11th to the 18th centuries. XLV settimana di studi della Fondazione istituto internazionale di storia economica F. Datini, Prato 14–18 April 2013* (Florence, 2014).

Cerman, M., *Villagers and lords in eastern Europe, 1300–1800* (Basingstoke and New York, 2012).

Clark, G., *A farewell to alms: a brief economic history of the world* (Princeton, NJ, 2007).

De Moor, T., and J. L. van Zanden, 'Girl power: the European marriage pattern and labour markets in the North Sea region in the late medieval and early modern period', *Economic History Review* 63 (2010), 1–33.

Dennison, T., *The institutional framework of Russian serfdom* (Cambridge, 2011).

Dennison, T. K., and S. Ogilvie, 'Serfdom and social capital in Bohemia and Russia', *Economic History Review* 60 (2007), 513–44.

Dyer, C., 'The ineffectiveness of lordship in England, 1200–1400', in *Rodney Hilton's middle ages: an exploration of historical themes*, ed. C. Dyer, P. Coss and C. Wickham (Oxford, 2007), pp. 69–86.

Dyer, C., 'Poverty and its relief in late medieval England', *Past and Present* 216 (2012), 41–78.

Green, D. R., *Pauper capital: London and the poor law, 1790–1870* (Farnham, 2010).

Hajnal, J., 'European marriage patterns in perspective', in *Population in history. Essays in historical demography*, ed. D. V. Glass and D. E. C. Eversley (London, 1965), pp. 101–43.

Hindle, S., *On the parish? The micro-politics of poor relief in rural England c.1550–1750* (Oxford, 2004).

Innes, J., 'The "mixed economy of welfare" in early modern England: assessments of the options from Hale to Malthus (c.1683–1803)', in *Charity, self-interest and welfare in the English past*, ed. M. Daunton (London, 1996), pp. 139–80.

Kelly, M., and C. Ó Gráda, 'The poor law of old England: institutional innovation and demographic regimes', *Journal of Interdisciplinary History* 41 (2011), 339–66.

King, S., *Poverty and welfare in England 1700–1850: a regional perspective* (Manchester, 2000).

Landers, J., *Death and the metropolis: studies in the demographic history of London, 1670–1830* (Cambridge, 1993).

Laslett, P., 'Family, kinship and collectivity as systems of support in pre-industrial Europe: a consideration of the "nuclear-hardship" hypothesis', *Continuity and Change* 3 (1988), 153–75.

Macfarlane, A., *The origins of English individualism. The family, property and social transition* (Oxford, 1978).

North, D. C., *Institutions, institutional change and economic performance* (Cambridge, 1990).

Ogilvie, S., 'Communities and the "second serfdom" in early modern Bohemia', *Past and Present* 187 (2005), 69–119.

Ogilvie. S., '"Whatever is, is right"? Economic institutions in pre-industrial Europe', *Economic History Review* 60 (2007), 649–84.

Pelling, M., and R. M. Smith, 'Introduction', in *Life, death and the elderly: historical perspectives*, ed. M. Pelling and R. M. Smith (London, 1991), pp. 1–38.

Poos, L. R., Z. Razi and R. M. Smith, 'The population history of medieval English villages: a debate on the use of manor court records', in *Medieval society and the manor court*, ed. Z. Razi and R. M. Smith (Oxford, 1996), pp. 298–368.

Raftis, J. A., *Tenure and mobility: studies in the social history of the medieval English village* (Toronto, 1964).

Razi, Z., *Life, marriage and death in a medieval parish: economy, society and demography in Halesowen, 1270–1400* (Cambridge, 1980).

Schofield, P. R., *Peasant and community in medieval England 1200–1500* (Basingstoke and London, 2003).

Schwarz, L. D., *London in the age of industrialisation: entrepreneurs, labour force and living conditions, 1700–1850* (Cambridge, 1992).

Slack, P., *Poverty and policy in Tudor and Stuart England* (London, 1988).

Smith, R. M., 'Ageing and well-being in early modern England: pension trends and gender preferences under the English old poor law c.1650–1800', in *Old age from antiquity to post-modernity*, ed. P. Johnson and P. Thane (London, 1998), pp. 64–95.

Smith, R. M., 'Charity, self-interest and welfare: reflections from demographic and family history', in *Charity, self-interest and welfare in the English past*, ed. M. Daunton (London, 1996), pp. 23–49.

Smith, R. M., 'The English peasantry 1250–1650', in *The peasantries of Europe from the fourteenth to the eighteenth centuries*, ed. T. Scott (London and New York, 1998), pp. 339–71.

Smith, R. M., 'Families and their land in an area of partible inheritance: Redgrave, Suffolk 1260–1320', in *Land, kinship and life-cycle*, ed. R. M. Smith (Cambridge, 1984), pp. 135–95.

Smith, R. M. (ed.), *Land, kinship and life-cycle* (Cambridge, 1984).

Smith, R. M., 'Measuring adult mortality in an age of plague: England, 1349–1540', in *Town and countryside in the age of the Black Death: essays in honour of John Hatcher*, ed. M. Bailey and S. Rigby (Turnhout, 2012), pp. 43–85.

Smith, R. M., 'Plagues and peoples: the long demographic cycle,

1250–1670', in *The peopling of Britain: the shaping of a human landscape*, ed. P. Slack and R. Ward (Oxford, 2002), pp. 177–210.

Smith, R. M., 'Social security as a developmental institution? The relative efficacy of poor relief provisions under the English old poor law', in *History, historians and development policy: a necessary dialogue*, ed. C. A. Bayly, V. Rao, S. Szreter and M. Woolcock (Manchester, 2011), pp. 75–102.

Solar, P. M., 'Poor relief and English economic development before the Industrial Revolution', *Economic History Review* 48 (1995), 1–22.

Tomkins, A., *The experience of urban poverty, 1723–82: parish, charity and credit* (Manchester, 2006).

van Zanden, J. L., *The long road to the industrial revolution: the European economy in a global perspective, 1000–1800* (Leiden, 2009).

Webb, S., and B. Webb, *English local government: English poor law history: part I. The old poor law* (London, 1927).

Williams, S., 'Malthus, marriage and poor law allowances revisited: a Bedfordshire case study, 1770–1834', *Agricultural History Review* 52 (2004), 56–82.

Wrigley, E. A., 'British population during the "long" eighteenth century, 1680–1840', in *The Cambridge economic history of modern Britain, 1: Industrialisation, 1700–1860*, ed. R. Floud and P. Johnson (Cambridge, 2004), pp. 57–95.

Wrigley, E. A., 'Coping with rapid population growth: how England fared in the century preceding the Great Exhibition of 1851', in *Structures and transformations in modern British history*, ed. D. Feldman and J. Lawrence (Cambridge, 2011), pp. 24–53.

Wrigley, E. A., 'English county populations in the later eighteenth century', *Economic History Review* 60 (2007), 35–69.

Wrigley, E. A., 'Rickman revisited: the population growth rates of English counties in the early modern period', *Economic History Review* 62 (2009), 711–35.

Wrigley, E. A., 'The transition to an advanced organic economy: half a millennium of English agriculture', *Economic History Review* 59 (2006), 435–80.

Wrigley, E. A., and R. S. Schofield, *The population history of England, 1541–1871: a reconstruction* (London, 1981).

Wrigley, E. A., R. S. Davies, J. E. Oeppen and R. S. Schofield, *English population history from family reconstitution, 1580–1837* (Cambridge, 1997).

Index

PEOPLE, MARKETS, GOODS:
ECONOMIES AND SOCIETIES IN HISTORY

ISSN: 2051–7467

PREVIOUS TITLES

Printed and bound by CPI Group (UK) Ltd, Croydon, CR0 4YY

11/09/2024

14554899-0001